WARTIME ECONOMIC CO-OPERATION

A STUDY OF RELATIONS BETWEEN CANADA AND THE UNITED STATES

WARTIME ECONOMIC CO-OPERATION

A STUDY OF RELATIONS BETWEEN
CANADA AND THE UNITED STATES

BY

R. WARREN JAMES

*Issued under the auspices of the
Canadian Institute of International Affairs*

THE RYERSON PRESS ~ TORONTO

The Canadian Institute of International Affairs is
an unofficial and non-political organization founded in
1928. The Institute has as its objects to promote and
encourage in Canada research and discussion in international affairs and to give attention to Canada's position
both as a member of the international community of
nations and as a member of the Commonwealth of
Nations.

The Institute, as such, is precluded by its Constitu-
tion from expressing an opinion on any aspect of public
affairs. The views expressed, therefore, are those of
the writer.

PRINTED AND BOUND IN CANADA
BY THE RYERSON PRESS, TORONTO

To

MY MOTHER AND FATHER

PREFACE

THE CANADIAN INSTITUTE OF INTERNATIONAL AFFAIRS asked me to write this book in November, 1946. It was hoped that an account of the economic relations between Canada and the United States during the war might throw some useful light on the problems of adjustment in the immediate post-war period. It has taken much longer to finish the book than I had originally expected. Despite the delay, some of the matters which are dealt with may be found to have some relevance for issues in the field of economic relations between Canada and the United States which exist at the present time and which may arise in the future.

Although I was employed as a civil servant during part of the period covered by this book as well as when it was being written, it is in no sense an official history. I have consulted many government officials and others on specific points and several members of the Research Committee of the Canadian Institute of International Affairs read the manuscript and made valuable suggestions. I am indebted to those who helped and encouraged me and I am sure they will not consider me ungrateful if I do not enumerate them individually.

I should, nevertheless, acknowledge my great obligation to Mr. Jules Charron who typed the manuscript in various stages with remarkable care and precision. I am also grateful to Miss Grace S. Lewis and Mr. Bernard Ower of the Library of the Dominion Bureau of Statistics as well as to the staff of the Library of Parliament, who helped me on innumerable occasions.

R. W. J.

Ottawa,
May, 1949.

FOREWORD

THIS FOURTH VOLUME in a series of studies on international relations sponsored by the Canadian Institute of International Affairs deals with the intimate economic co-operation between Canada and the United States during the second world war. Such co-operation was founded on the principles enunciated in the Hyde Park Declaration of 1941, and developed to the point where priority assistance was conceded by the United States to Canadian industry on substantially the same basis as to the domestic industry. Similar procedures were adopted by the two countries to co-ordinate production and limit consumption, and daily consultation took place upon the varied issues of common policy. Thus was established an elaborate régime of co-ordinated economies. That a country of the British Commonwealth should achieve with its neighbour such intimate action without impairing either its Commonwealth ties or its national status is in itself significant in the life of the whole English-speaking community; it illustrates the remarkable liaison possible between the members of this community and the flexible character of their democratic techniques. Such co-operation between Canada and the United States was never merely bilateral since it was linked with the close economic relations of both countries with Great Britain and the other Britannic nations. It was a crucial section in the vast co-operative effort of the United States and the British Commonwealth.

The author, Mr. R. Warren James, is a graduate of the universities of Toronto and Chicago. A former official of the Wartime Prices and Trade Board and of the Combined Production and Resources Board in Washington (1942-1945), he was able at first hand to scrutinize the policies and administrative arrangements in the co-operation which he now assesses. But he writes primarily, not as a civil servant, but as a scholar anxious to present an objective examination of a significant phase in international action. Not the least valuable portion of his study, is the candid and acute evaluation of what was attempted and why the attempt occasionally failed.

ALEXANDER BRADY,
Chairman of the Research Committee,
Canadian Institute of International Affairs.

CONTENTS

For what greater glory and advantage can any powerful Nation have, than to be thus richly and naturally possessed of all things needful for Food, Rayment, War and Peace, not onely for its own plentiful use, but also to supply the wants of other Nations, in such a measure, that much money may be thereby gotten yearly, to make the happiness compleat.

THOMAS MUN,
England's Treasure by Forraign Trade.

Wartime Economic Co-operation

CHAPTER I

THE BACKGROUND OF ECONOMIC CO-OPERATION BETWEEN CANADA AND THE UNITED STATES

CANADA, as a member of both a hemispheric and an imperial economic system, has historically been drawn in two directions. The dual influences of the United States and the United Kingdom have shaped not only the economic development but the political and cultural outlook of Canada as well. Like the White Knight, Canada has had plenty of practice in keeping a proper balance.

Internal economic developments in Canada tended to supplement one or the other of these external pulls at different periods. The early years of the twentieth century in Canada were characterized by the rapid development of the wheat-growing areas of western Canada and a phenomenal increase in population. Canadian wheat could be sold to the United Kingdom in return for the textiles, chinaware, hardware, and iron and steel products needed by the Canadian economy. During that period, the prospects of closer economic relations with the United States in the form of a reciprocal abandonment of tariffs did not seem attractive enough to Canada to outweigh the undoubted advantages of economic integration with the United Kingdom. Then, as a result of the first world war, there was a remarkable change in Canada's industrial potential and status in international affairs. The rapid growth of industrial capacity tended to diminish Canada's dependence on agriculture. Moreover, emphasis was shifting to other primary products. The Underwood Tariff of 1913 permitted newsprint to enter the United States duty-free, a factor which, together with the high wartime demand in the United States, had fostered the rapid expansion of Canadian output of newsprint and other forest products. The mining industry in Canada also grew with great rapidity during and after the first world war. The fact that the major market for Canadian metals and forest products lay in the United States was a powerful influence in bringing about increasingly close economic relations between Canada and the United States.

In the early 1930's, the Hawley-Smoot Tariff and the Ottawa Agreements reversed this trend and also gave rise to a certain lack of cordiality between Canada and the United States. The revision of the official attitude

1

in the United States to tariffs, exemplified by the Trade Agreements Act of 1934, permitted some modification of the restrictionist policies which had been adopted by both countries. The Trade Agreement between Canada and the United States concluded at the end of 1935 was an important forward step in reducing tariff obstacles to trade between Canada and the United States. In addition, Canada undertook to modify certain administrative practices, particularly those relating to methods of valuing imports for duty purposes, which had become a protective device in the early 1930's. A supplementary trade agreement which became effective at the beginning of 1939 provided for an extended range of mutual tariff concessions. Thus, immediately before and during the early years of the war, there had been a consistent trend to lower tariff barriers. This removal of some of the hindrances to trade between Canada and the United States contributed to the economic integration of the two countries, prior to the wartime period of economic mobilization.

With the outbreak of the second world war, the economic influence of the United Kingdom again became dominant. As the war developed, the Canadian economy concentrated on producing the raw materials, manufactured goods, and food needed by the United Kingdom. In turn, this increased Canadian dependence on the United States and in this way the historical pattern of Canadian relationships with the United States and the United Kingdom tended to be reinforced by the pressure of wartime developments.

One of the most striking developments was this increased dependence of Canada on the United States. For a long time, Canada had been importing technical knowledge from the United States as well as machinery and components, which is probably a normal relationship between two countries at different stages of economic development. Quite generally, Canadian industry expects to import components or sub-assemblies or repair parts from the United States on short notice. Any interference with this state of affairs is certain to impair Canadian production. For example, Canadian production of most heavy electrically-operated consumers' durable goods would be crippled if fractional horsepower motors could not be obtained from the United States. Time and again, the question of Canadian supplies of components, as well as machinery and machine tools, from the United States arose during the war, and it will be seen that it was absolutely vital from the Canadian point of view to be able to procure this essential equipment with a minimum of delay or difficulty. The growing closeness of economic relations between Canada and the United States during the war occurred at a time when the normal triangular pattern of the relations between the United Kingdom, the United States, and Canada was being superseded by something new. A process of economic fusion occurred which eliminated old problems and created new ones.

The main aim of this book is to examine the new problems which developed during the war in the economic relations between Canada and the United States. It must be borne in mind that this is merely one aspect of the complex inter-relations of the three countries. To attempt to deal with the three countries at once is a formidable task and one which would require a careful analysis of domestic developments in each country. In view of the difficulties of integrating such material, it has seemed preferable to concentrate attention on relations between Canada and the United States. In particular, the purpose is to describe and assess various measures taken by the two countries to promote economic co-operation. Attention is restricted in almost all cases to bilateral problems but it must be borne in mind that Canada and the United States were often associated in negotiations and planning leading to the creation of, and in the subsequent activities of a number of international organizations concerned with economic problems. Except for rather incidental mention, no attempt has been made to describe the place of the two countries in such temporary agencies as the United Nations Relief and Rehabilitation Administration, the United Nations Interim Commission on Food and Agriculture, and the Provisional International Civil Aviation Organization; nor in such permanent bodies as the International Bank for Reconstruction and Development, the International Monetary Fund, the Food and Agriculture Organization of the United Nations, the International Civil Aviation Organization, the International Labour Organization, or the Economic and Social Council of the United Nations. Generally speaking, the work of these organizations is regarded as outside the scope of this book.

In one sense, the issues which arose between Canada and the United States during the war were old ones. Ever since the emergence of national states, the existence of large and small nations side by side has necessitated some definition of the terms on which they shall co-operate, for co-operation in some degree is unavoidable. Often, in the past, the larger country had been able to impose its wishes on the smaller because of its superior economic or military power. So far as Canada and the United States are concerned, it was clearly recognized that any undue pressure by the United States on Canada would be fiercely resisted. There was an enormous increase in the formal and informal negotiations between the two countries during the war, and it became doubly important for Canada to insist, at least tacitly, on the right to pursue an independent course of action. This is not to suggest that there was any consistent divergence in the policies of the two countries; on the contrary, the degree of co-ordination was remarkable. Crises or apprehended crises continually arose during the war, many of which required joint action or consultation. As a result, new policies and new channels of communication between the two governments were needed. There were issues to be settled in nearly every aspect of the relations between the two countries: political, military, and economic. The main emphasis here is on economic co-operation, which is meant to refer to arrangements relating directly or indirectly to trade between the two countries, and only passing mention is made of the other fields. The first problems arose in connection with the shipment of munitions from the United States to Canada after the outbreak of war.

1. NEUTRALITY AND DEFENCE

The fact that Canada declared war on Germany on September 10, 1939, while the United States remained neutral at once required a reconsideration of the relations between the two countries. In the years immediately before the outbreak of war, the official relations between the two countries were marked by complete amity. Moreover, popular sentiment was either tolerant or beneficent except perhaps in a few imperialist strongholds in Canada. One major factor in promoting goodwill was the personal and almost universal popularity of President Roosevelt in Canada. Amid the menacing developments in Europe in 1938, it was comforting for Canadians to reflect on President Roosevelt's speech at Queen's University on August 18, 1938, in which he said, after referring to the fact that Canada was a member of the British Empire, "I give to you assurance that the people of the United States will not stand idly by if domination of Canadian soil is threatened by any other Empire."[1] Shortly after, on August 20, the Prime Minister in acknowledging this undertaking in a speech at Woodbridge, Ontario, stated:

We, too, have our obligations as a good friendly neighbour, and one of them is to see that, at our own instance, our country is made as immune from attack or possible invasion as we can reasonably be expected to make it, and that, should the occasion ever arise, enemy forces should not be able to pursue their way, either by land, sea, or air to the United States, across Canadian territory.[2]

It was of some importance also that there were frequent and evidently friendly meetings between the President and the Prime Minister. The problems of joint defence would have provided a natural, if somewhat speculative, topic of conversation between the Prime Minister of Canada and the President of the United States at almost any time between the two wars. By the late 1930's, the conversations had started to lose their academic quality and serious consideration was reportedly given to ways and means of repelling any threat to North American security. Any doubts that there was an effective, if tacit, military alliance between Canada and the United States were completely dispelled by the bold assurances of the two political leaders. This, of course, did not involve any reversal of the traditional and deep-rooted attitude of the United States to the undesirability of foreign, especially European, entanglements.

The ingrained pacifist attitude of the United States, supplemented by the belief widely current in the 1930's that international commerce in munitions contained the seeds of war, led to legislative attempts to isolate the country from the contagious influence of belligerents. The Neutrality Act of 1935 was intended to accomplish this by prohibiting the export of arms, ammunition, or implements of war to any belligerent countries once the President had proclaimed that a state of war existed.[3] This law also prohibited the transportation of munitions to any warring country by vessels of the United States, and contained a number of other provisions intended to prevent the United States from becoming involved. The original legislation did not specifically refer to civil war, but, in January, 1937, a Congressional joint resolution broadened the scope of the law[4] and a formal embargo on munitions exports to Spain was imposed by Congress[5] on May 1. The neutrality legislation was modified at the same time to permit the prohibition of the export of any goods, not merely munitions, to belligerents in vessels of the United States. Also, goods shipped in the vessels of other countries had to be paid for in advance. In response to the Congressional action, a presidential proclamation was issued listing the munitions covered by the embargo.[6] In the early part of 1939, disturbed conditions in Europe and in the Far East led to urgent demands by the executive branch of the government for a repeal of the Neutrality Act, but Congress was unwilling to risk the dangers which repeal was believed to involve. The basic weakness of the neutrality law was that it was not likely to hinder or deter an aggressor country seriously and yet it robbed a country which was attacked of any hope of material assistance from the United States.

On September 5, 1939, a few days after the Nazi armies invaded Poland, the President issued a proclamation pursuant to the Neutrality Act prohibiting the export of munitions to Germany, Poland, France, the United Kingdom, Australia, India, and New Zealand.[7] Canada, not yet having declared war, was not named in the original proclamation. However, the provisions of the Neutrality Act were extended to Canada on September 10, immediately following the Canadian declaration of war.[8] A simultaneous proclamation cut off shipments of munitions from the United States to Canada.[9]

The weaknesses of the neutrality legislation in the face of the armed conflict in Europe were apparent and the President again appealed to Congress for a modification of the law. As a result, the Neutrality Act was amended on November 4, 1939, and the outright prohibition of exports of arms to belligerents was eliminated.[10] The revised Act required that no munitions exports could be made to belligerents until the purchaser had paid for them and taken title to them. This principle of "cash-and-carry" applied fully to Canada as well as to other belligerent countries.

A day or two after war broke out, the neutrality proclamations and embargoes were clarified by the issuance of supplementary regulations by the President making it clear that loans to belligerent countries were also prohibited.[11] Short-term commercial credits were treated separately in the presidential statement, which read, in part:

I hereby find that it will serve to protect the commercial and other interests of the United States and its citizens to except from the operations of Section 3 of the joint resolution of Congress approved May 1, 1937, as made applicable to Germany and France, Poland and the United Kingdom, India, Australia and New Zealand by the Proclamation of the President of September 5, 1939, issued under the authority of Section 1 of such joint resolution, ordinary commercial credits and short-time obligations in aid of legal transactions and of a character customarily used in normal peacetime commercial transactions; and they are hereby excepted.[12]

From the point of view of Canada, this meant that the neutrality legislation did not significantly influence ordinary commercial transactions. Short-term credit could continue to be extended by United States exporters on shipments of goods (other than arms, ammunition, or implements of war) consigned to private buyers in Canada. The condition that the Canadian government had to pay cash for purchases in the United States was not a hardship at that time. The Neutrality Act of 1939 was obviously of great importance to both Canada and the United Kingdom and removed a serious obstacle to the wartime co-operation between these two countries and the United States.

The fall of France and the Battle of Britain led to a rapid shift in public sentiment in the United States on the question of entry into the war and the risks involved in foreign aid. Apart from this, military leaders in the United States saw that if the threatened invasion of the British Isles was successful, the security of the United States would be irreparably damaged. Action was taken by the Administration to give some material assistance to the United Kingdom but the aid which the United States was able to offer was limited. Surplus stocks of Army and Navy equipment including rifles, machine guns, field artillery, aircraft, and ammunition were transferred to the United Kingdom and arrived during the critical period after Dunkirk. Further action of the same sort was taken at the beginning of September, 1940, when the United States agreed to transfer to the United Kingdom fifty over-age destroyers, originally constructed for convoy duty in the first world war, in return for the right to use or construct air and naval bases in some of the British possessions in the Western Hemisphere. Six of these destroyers were immediately turned over to Canada to become a part of the growing Royal Canadian Navy.

During the critical period of May and June, 1940, close but informal understandings were arrived at between Prime Minister Churchill and President Roosevelt concerning the disposition of the British fleet in the event of the Nazi conquest of the British Isles. It is said that the President expressed the hope that the British fleet would be dispersed to various overseas bases and stated that the United States fleet would take over responsibility for defending the Western Hemisphere, including Canada.[13] In the light of these commitments, it is not surprising that a more formal agreement on mutual defence was reached between Canada and the United States in the summer of 1940. On August 18, 1940, the President and the Canadian Prime Minister, after meeting for a day, issued a brief statement providing for the creation of a Permanent Joint Board on Defence which would study the problems of defending North America. The conversations between the Prime Minister and the President took place at Ogdensburg, New York, and the result is generally referred to as the Ogdensburg Agreement. The text of the statement released after the meeting was:

The Prime Minister and the President have discussed the mutual problems of defence in relation to Canada and the United States.

It has been agreed that a Permanent Joint Board on Defence shall be set up at once by the two countries.

This Permanent Joint Board on Defence shall commence immediate studies relating to sea, land, and air problems including personnel and material.

It will consider in the broad sense the defence of the north half of the Western Hemisphere.

The Permanent Joint Board on Defence will consist of four or five members from each country, most of them from the services. It will meet shortly.[14]

The Permanent Joint Board on Defence was purely an advisory body and there was no undertaking on the part of either government to accept its recommendations. The Board was concerned almost exclusively with quasi-military planning and was of great importance in facilitating military co-operation between the two countries during the war. For example, it may be surmised that the Board was intimately concerned with the problems involved in construction of air bases and other facilities in northeastern and northwestern Canada. While the Board was the first of a wartime galaxy of joint committees and influenced the pattern of future organizations, it had no significant influence on the pattern of economic co-operation. For this reason, as well as for reasons of security, any detailed account of its activities would be out of place here.

The establishment of the Permanent Joint Board on Defence was indicative of the rather unusual relations between the two countries in the period when Canada was a belligerent and the United States was, technically at least, a neutral. Because of this, there was a certain etiquette to be observed in Canadian intercourse with the United States. Despite Canada's traditional position, an executive order had been issued by the President after the outbreak of war specifically warning the executive arm of the government to observe the conventions of neutrality in dealing with Canada. The preamble to this order, which read as follows, was clear enough:

Under the treaties of the United States and the law of nations, it is the duty of the United States, in any war in which the United States is a neutral not to permit the commission of unneutral acts within the jurisdiction of the United States.[15]

By the summer of 1940, the neutrality of the United States was rapidly becoming a legal fiction. The attitude of the Administration in the United States was definitely hostile to the Axis. Despite this, it was clear that any Canadian attempts to influence public opinion in the United States by propaganda or other means would be very dangerous. Isolationist sentiment was both powerful and widespread and any ill-considered actions by Canada or Canadians might merely crystallize opposition to intervention. The reticence of Canadian officialdom was not always matched by officials of the United States. For example, James H. R. Cromwell, the United States Minister to Canada, in a speech in Toronto in March, 1940, emphatically condemned the Nazi government as a serious threat to democracy in the world and criticized the "cynical minded groups" who opposed intervention by the United States.[16] Naturally enough, these hostile comments by a diplomatic officer of the United States were embarrassing to the Department of State, which issued a public reprimand shortly afterwards. Such remarks by an official of the United States were out of place but they reflected accurately the views of many of his countrymen, and certainly struck a responsive chord in Canada. The gradual development of a belligerent state of mind and the recognition by the United States of its interest in the defence of the United Kingdom were particularly heartening to Canada. The material assistance of the United States to Canada was also acknowledged gratefully by the Prime Minister in November, 1940, when he said:

I should like to say a word about how much our own Canadian war effort owes to the cooperation of the United States. Aircraft and tanks for training purposes, and destroyers for active service, are outstanding among the many essentials of warfare which the United States has so generously made available to Canada.[17]

Apart from some private querulousness in Canada concerning the continued neutrality of the United States, the atmosphere was dominated by understanding and tolerance. In mid-February, 1941, the Prime Minister of Canada gave the House of Commons a brief review of Canadian relations with the United States, in which he said:

It is a matter of special satisfaction that, in spite of the stresses and strains of war, our relations with our great neighbour, the United States, have, if anything, grown more cordial, friendly, helpful, and constructive. It is particularly gratifying also to see that there exists not only between our two governments but between our two nations, so perfect an understanding.[18]

Events moved quickly in the spring of 1941 and the official attitude of the United States became blunter than ever. With the declaration by the President in May, 1941, that there existed a state of unlimited national emergency, the United States was clearly mobilizing for war. Part of the presidential proclamation issued at this time read as follows:

A succession of events makes plain that the objectives of the Axis belligerents in such war are not confined to those avowed at its commencement, but include overthrow throughout the world of existing democratic order, and a worldwide domination of peoples and economies through the destruction of all resistance on land and sea and in the air, . . .

Indifference on the part of the United States to the increasing menace would be perilous, and common prudence requires that for the security of this nation and of this hemisphere we should pass from peacetime authorizations of military strength to such a basis as will enable us to cope instantly and decisively with any attempt at hostile encirclement of this hemisphere, or the establishment of any base for aggression against it, as well as to repel the threat of predatory incursion by foreign agents into our territory and society.[19]

This was a clear demonstration, if one were needed, that the United States would sooner or later become involved as an active belligerent.

From the Canadian point of view, as the Prime Minister pointed out, it was particularly satisfactory that the gradual conversion of the United States had occurred without causing any disharmony between the two countries. From the summer of 1940 on, the political and military aspirations of the governments of the two countries seemed to match.

The same spirit dominated the approach to the common economic problems of the two countries. Since the analysis of this particular aspect of relations between Canada and the United States absorbs most of the rest of this book, it is essential to have a clear understanding of the meaning and significance of economic co-operation.

2. THE DEFINITION OF ECONOMIC CO-OPERATION

Although it is usually not defined very precisely, economic co-operation seems to refer to two aspects of international trade. First, it implies the existence of special international agreements to facilitate trade and second, it must also refer to a relatively large volume of trade. Both of these are necessary conditions if two countries are to co-operate in an economic sense.

Since Canada and the United States were pursuing the same political and military aims, it was natural that agreement should be reached on certain general principles of economic co-operation designed to stimulate trade between the two countries. The fact that these principles were formally enunciated did not mean that they involved anything inherently new. In fact, they underlie the normal peacetime relations of Canada and the United States. Briefly, the basic idea is that if there is a flow of goods back and forth across the border, some people at least in the United States and Canada benefit from this interchange. It is also true that, at different times, the benefits of this exchange of goods have been questioned, and involved devices have been developed by the governments of the two countries to impede the flow. The historical role of the governments has been to impose barriers to trade between the two countries, barriers which have been growing higher and more complex for a long period. There was initially a multiplication of the obstacles to the exchange of goods with the gradual mobilization of the economies of Canada and the United States, as a natural concomitant of the wider extension of domestic controls. As a result of the inherent tendency for wartime planners to think in national rather than in international terms, there was a definite risk that a serious decline in economic co-operation between Canada and the United States would occur. The most important single problem in this field was the tendency to impose embargoes on exports or to erect special barriers to exports on the grounds that scarce or critical commodities might be dissipated in this way or that the military and economic strength of the exporting country might be weakened.

The effects of the new barriers made it evident that the total output of the two countries could be increased by their removal. Continual efforts were made by the two countries either to eliminate or standardize special barriers and discriminatory regulations. Consultation between officials was continuous throughout the wartime period, and an intricate network of committees and sub-committees was created to deal with general or specific problems. While many of the committees were specialized and temporary, and operated outside the sphere of normal diplomatic inter- course, the basic rules of economic co-operation were established by agree- ments of the political leaders of the two countries. These agreements had a certain vagueness and flexibility and were subject to interpretative modifi- cation to fit special cases as they arose. Usually, the agreements also had a familiar ring. Their general tenor was that there should be international specialization of production and the freer exchange of goods. There is some presumption that this leads to gains under normal circumstances. In war- time, the gains are at once more certain and more concrete. Unfortunately, a country at war, particularly if it is endowed with a wide range of productive capacity and raw materials, is usually under heavy pressure to pursue a policy of autarchy. This certainly facilitates the planning of war production and may have certain short-run strategic advantages. In the United States and Canada there was a welter of controls whose aim was to prevent the dissipation of scarce goods in export markets or in non- essential domestic uses. The reduction of these special obstacles, which are natural in a war economy, was of primary importance in the case of Canada and the United States. The adoption of increasingly restrictive controls over commerce would be certain to counteract the gains visualized by a policy of economic co-operation.

The second condition, the existence of a large volume of trade, was fulfilled in a most striking fashion. The following summary table shows clearly the rapid wartime increase in Canadian exports to and imports from the United States:

	Monthly Average Exports	Monthly Average Imports
1938	$ 22,500,000	$ 35,390,000
1939	31,700,000	41,410,000
1940	36,900,000	62,020,000
1941	50,000,000	83,710,000
1942	73,800,000	108,720,000
1943	95,800,000	118,640,000
1944	108,400,000	120,600,000
1945	99,700,000	100,200,000[20]

The three-fold or four-fold increase in imports and exports within a period of a very few years shows clearly that, from the point of view of the volume of trade, the policy of economic co-operation was a resounding success.

3. THE IMPORTANCE OF PERSONAL RELATIONSHIPS

Apart from the substantive problems involved, the opening of new channels of communication between government officials and agencies gave rise to problems of international organization which had not existed before in the case of Canada and the United States. The creation of new channels of communication became possible as a result of the singularly cordial relations between the two countries. This was not only true of the two governments but it extended to the officials themselves. The informality of many of the wartime arrangements between Canada and the United States was possible only because of the intimate contact maintained by operating officials of both countries. Apart from this, there was evidently a warm friendship between the wartime Prime Minister and President. The Canadian Minister (later Ambassador) to the United States in the period from March, 1941, to July, 1944, was also a personal friend of the President. The tone of the relations between the two countries was influenced by these somewhat accidental factors. There was also a great deal of visiting back and forth between Ottawa and Washington by administrative officials of the two countries. These men often had very similar cultural or business backgrounds with the result that it was usually easy for them to reach a sympathetic understanding very quickly. One senior Canadian official who was intimately concerned with relations between the two countries during the war has this to say on the importance of friendliness and understanding:

The official pronouncements, the committees, and the practical achievements do not adequately represent the degree of co-operation achieved. The intangibles have been equally important but more difficult to set out. There has been the open exchange of confidences between the Americans and the Canadians, the warm welcome, the freedom from formality, the plain speaking, and the all-pervading friendship. Neither is it easy to enumerate the conditions which made the high degree of co-operation possible. Co-operation was, of course, a sensible course to follow. It stood on its own merits. However, common sense is not always able to prevail over sovereignty, and self-interest, and special national interests. That the course was followed, or at least adopted so readily and successfully, is due in part to the friendly disposition that existed, attributable no doubt to our common background of language and culture and to the close trade and industrial relationship; in part it is due to the fact that our approach to problems is similar. We both attach much importance to facts and figures, the Americans perhaps more than we. They are fond of brass tacks, of talking turkey, and of claiming they are from Missouri. We do not take it amiss when the United

States asks us to present facts and figures in support of a requirement, we do not feel that our prestige is lowered, or that it is beneath our dignity to corroborate our request.[21]

As this quotation emphasizes, the influence of the geniality, which marked the personal relationships of officials in the two countries is intangible but vital.

From another point of view, the personal characteristics of those responsible for relations between Canada and the United States were of dominant importance in determining the channels through which negotiations would be carried on. As an example, the liaison arrangements made by the Department of Munitions and Supply may be cited. The Minister of Munitions and Supply, being both a vigorous and an independent administrator, was averse to entrusting negotiations with the United States on supply problems to other government departments. In particular, the leisurely pace of operations which characterized some of the old-line departments such as the Department of External Affairs contrasted sharply with the seething activity of the Department of Munitions and Supply. Apart from this, the older departments were not usually staffed by persons familiar with wartime industrial problems. But it was the desire of the Minister of Munitions and Supply to retain control of activities affecting his department which led to the establishment of independent channels of communications with wartime agencies in the United States. This fact created a precedent and at a later period, the Wartime Prices and Trade Board also established representation in Washington which was largely independent of existing diplomatic machinery. There were doubtless great advantages in these arrangements since negotiations and agreements could usually be concluded informally and quickly at a time when speed was essential.

The virtues of informal understandings can be exaggerated. Casual agreements are not very satisfactory when a crisis develops and the national interest becomes involved. As it was, the path of economic co-operation between the two countries was smoothed because, in general, consumption was increasing in both countries. If it had been necessary to reduce consumption in both countries to austerity levels over a wide range of essential commodities, it is certain that domestic political pressures would have strained even the formal agreements between the two countries. This would almost certainly have meant that almost all intercourse between the two governments would have had to be conducted at the highest levels, i.e., there would have been much heavier reliance on diplomatic negotiations.

The techniques which were employed involved an element of risk although this comment should not be interpreted as implying that inter-governmental negotiations should be dealt with through diplomatic channels in all or most cases. It might nevertheless have been useful to have some of the informal policies clarified and confirmed in this way. In some cases agreements were excessively informal and were liable to misunderstanding or re-interpretation although usually there would have been no great difficulty in having these agreements written down and properly authorized.

Initially, however, a good deal of reliance was placed on formal intergovernmental agreements although they were preceded by extensive informal discussion by both diplomatic and non-diplomatic officials. The nature of these agreements and the reasons for them will throw some light on both the organizational and economic aspects of co-operation between the two countries.

REFERENCES FOR CHAPTER I

1. *New York Times,* August 19, 1938, p. 1.
2. *Ibid.,* August 21, 1938, p. 29.
3. *49 U.S. Statutes* 1081; c. 837, Joint Resolution of August 31, 1935.
4. *50 U.S. Statutes* 3; c. 1, Joint Resolution of January 8, 1937.
5. *50 U.S. Statutes* 121; c. 146, Joint Resolution of May 1, 1937.
6. Proclamation 2237, May 1, 1937, 2 *Federal Register* 776.
7. Proclamation 2349, September 5, 1939, 4 *Federal Register* 3819.
8. Proclamation 2359, September 10, 1939, 4 *Federal Register* 3857. The time lag of a week in the Canadian declaration of war raised what was at the time a nice constitutional issue. Some constitutional experts felt that a British declaration of war would automatically involve Canada as a result of the so-called indivisibility of the Crown. It has been said that President Roosevelt, rather than risk offending the national sensibilities of Canadians, telephoned the Canadian Prime Minister for advice. Joseph Alsop and Robert Kintner, *American White Paper* (New York: Simon & Schuster, 1940), p. 71.
9. Proclamation 2360, September 10, 1939, 4 *Federal Register* 3857.
10. *54 U.S. Statutes* 4; c. 2, Joint Resolution of November 4, 1939.
11. Regulations concerning credits to belligerents, September 6, 1939, 4 *Federal Register* 3852.
12. *Ibid.*
13. Robert E. Sherwood, *Roosevelt and Hopkins: An Intimate History* (New York: Harper & Brothers, 1948), p. 146.
14. Canada, Treaty Series, 1940, No. 14, *Declaration by the Prime Minister of Canada and the President of the United States of America Regarding the Establishing of a Permanent Joint Board on Defence Made on August 18, 1940* (Ottawa: King's Printer, 1941).
15. Executive Order 8249, September 10, 1939, 4 *Federal Register* 3889.
16. *New York Times,* March 20, 1940, p. 1.
17. *Canada, House of Commons Debates,* November 12, 1940, p. 53. The quotation should not be interpreted to mean that "essentials of warfare" were given to Canada by the United States.
18. *Ibid.,* February 17, 1941, p. 815.
19. Proclamation 2487, May 27, 1941, 6 *Federal Register* 2617.
20. Dominion Bureau of Statistics, *Canadian Statistical Review,* January, 1948, pp. 97 and 102. The figures refer to merchandise exports and imports.
21. S. D. Pierce and A. F. W. Plumptre, "Canada's Relations with War-time Agencies in Washington," *Canadian Journal of Economics and Political Science,* August, 1945, pp. 410-11. The comment is by S. D. Pierce.

CHAPTER II

THE BEGINNINGS OF FINANCIAL AND ECONOMIC COLLABORATON[1]

THE Ogdensburg Agreement symbolized the new phase of relations between Canada and the United States which began with the disastrous Allied military reverses in the spring of 1940, culminating in the fall of France. Before June, 1940, the impact of the war on the Canadian economy had been slight, a situation which changed rapidly with the sudden acceleration of the demands of the United Kingdom for Canadian *matériel.* Canada was faced with the urgent necessity of mobilizing all available production facilities to meet these new demands. This involved the rapid expansion of plant and equipment specifically designed to produce raw materials and munitions. It was both necessary and natural that Canada should turn to the United States for a large part of the capital equipment required to meet the new production goals. The case of machine tools was typical; Canadian output was inadequate and the demands for imported metal-working machinery from the United States increased apace. It was fortunate that this rich source of capital goods existed, but there was also a cloud on the horizon.

During 1940 and 1941, there was a spectacular growth in output in Canada and the United States and it became apparent that the outcome of the war would depend heavily on the extent to which the North American surplus could be made available to the beleaguered victims of Axis aggression. The existence of enormous physical production capacity was not all, however. In addition, traditional methods of international finance were discarded when new and revolutionary methods of foreign aid, exemplified by lend-lease, were introduced. Overshadowing all other developments in this early period was the genesis of mutual aid schemes for supplying other Allied nations with the products of North America. In a sense, Canada and the United States provided each other with mutual aid but the rationale was quite different. The aim of these two countries was to maximize the economic power of the North American continent, the major arsenal of the United Nations.

1. CANADA'S FOREIGN EXCHANGE PROBLEM

The relative ease of procurement in the United States and the inflated demands for imports of all kinds immediately gave rise to the problem of a high and growing adverse balance of payments with the United States. The sharp rise in imports of capital equipment, raw materials and components needed for war production was accompanied by an increased demand for consumption goods from the United States resulting from expanded incomes in Canada. These developments early in the war accentuated a trend which had been apparent in the period 1935-39. The summary table shown below gives the average net Canadian current account balances in millions of dollars with the United States, Continental Europe, and the United Kingdom.[2]

	United States	Continental Europe	United Kingdom
1935-1937..............	− 35	+35	+105
1938-1939..............	−130	+20	+130

Thus, the Canadian balance of international payments in the five years before the war was marked by a large current account deficit with the United States and an even larger surplus with Europe and the United Kingdom. So long as Canada's deficit with the United States could be offset by sterling or other surpluses, the high level of imports from the United States could be maintained without difficulty. The outbreak of war disrupted the adjustment process almost completely since the convertibility of sterling was suspended by the United Kingdom.

Nevertheless, there was a good deal of stability in Canada's exchange position during the first nine months of the war. It was not until after the calamitous military reverses of the spring of 1940 and the subsequent rapid expansion of United Kingdom orders in Canada, accompanied by greatly increased domestic orders, that Canadian reserves of United States dollars began to dwindle. The avalanche of orders from the United Kingdom in 1940 signified a complete reversal of British policy in the initial stages of the war when it was believed that large-scale war production in Canada would be unnecessary, indeed that Canadian military requirements could be supplied largely from production in the United Kingdom. Since the United States content of Canadian munitions output was roughly 30 per cent, it is clear that the Canadian shortage of United States dollars was to a major extent a result of United Kingdom orders. A summary picture of the wartime requirements of the United Kingdom in Canada in the period 1940-44 and the changing methods of paying for them can be obtained from the following table, in which the figures represent millions of Canadian dollars at current prices :[3]

	1940	1941	1942	1943	1944	Total
United Kingdom requirements:						
Munitions and military supplies	50	353	643	916	978	2,940
Food	239	320	325	384	470	1,738
Raw materials (wood and metals)	185	191	176	229	209	990
Other exports	68	50	90	65	55	328
Freight	60	110	114	128	124	536
Air training and other war services	32	145	196	202	208	783
Miscellaneous current requirements	27	24	23	23	29	126
Total	661	1,193	1,567	1,947	2,073	7,441
Sources of finance:						
Mutual Aid and 1942 contribution from Canada	..	..	1,000	501	775	2,276
Provision of supplies and services in exchange by the United Kingdom to Canadian forces abroad	20	40	85	430	1,005	1,580
Net accrual to the United Kingdom of normal commercial credits from exports and other current transactions	154	244	304	207	195	1,104
Loans, book credits, security purchases, gold payments, and other capital transactions (net)	487	909	178	809	98	2,481
Total	661	1,193	1,567	1,947	2,073	7,441

The special steps which were taken to finance expenditures of the sterling area, mainly the United Kingdom, in Canada in the period 1939-42 can also be summarized conveniently in tabular form. The following table shows the relative magnitudes, expressed in millions of Canadian dollars, of the extraordinary methods of financing that were adopted :[4]

	1939	1940	1941	1942
Canadian official repatriation of securities	75	137	188	296
Canadian private repatriation of securities	50	41	46	38
Sale of gold and United States dollars to Canada	2	248	..	23
Canadian accumulation of sterling balances	..	82	728	−818
Interest-free loan by Canada to the United Kingdom	..	..	..	700
Billion-dollar contribution by Canada	..	..	..	1,000

The most serious development from the Canadian point of view was the fact that by the end of 1940, the United Kingdom was unable to make available to Canada additional amounts of either gold or United States dollars. This meant that the measures of exchange conservation which had been imposed in Canada early in the war had to be successively tightened.

Foreign exchange control and its attendant administrative machinery had been introduced in Canada in September, 1939, shortly after the outbreak of war, in order to reserve Canadian supplies of United States dollars for necessary purposes and to prevent unrestricted capital exports.[5] In addition, fixed buying and selling rates were announced by the Foreign Exchange Control Board to eliminate the wide fluctuations in the Canadian exchange rate which might otherwise be expected. By the spring and summer of 1940, it was necessary to supplement existing measures of foreign exchange control. The first major step was the Foreign Exchange Acquisition Order of April 30, 1940, requiring Canadian residents to sell their foreign exchange holdings to the Foreign Exchange Control Board.[6] This was followed in June, 1940, by the imposition of the War Exchange Tax, a 10 per cent excise tax on most imports from non-sterling countries, and sharply increased excise taxes on automobiles.[7] On July 5, 1940, it was announced that the Foreign Exchange Control Board would no longer provide United States dollars for pleasure travel, a measure which was designed to eliminate annual expenditures of from $60,000,000 to $75,000,-000 in United States funds.[8] By the end of the year, more drastic measures were introduced with the passage of the War Exchange Conservation Act, which prohibited a long list of non-essential and luxury imports from non-sterling areas and imposed import controls on other articles of a more essential character.[9] Despite this series of conservation measures, Canada ended the year 1940 with a current deficit of $292,000,000 on the year's transactions with the United States and a small surplus of $22,000,000 on trading with other non-sterling countries.[10] By the end of 1940, there were clear indications that Canada's dollar position would deteriorate in the future, particularly since the United Kingdom could no longer be counted on to make up any of the Canadian deficit.

The United Kingdom was experiencing a much more critical shortage of United States dollars in the latter part of 1940. The liquidation of dollar securities held in the United Kingdom had been carried out on a large scale but, despite such emergency measures, the United Kingdom missions had practically stopped the issuance of contracts in the United States by mid-December, 1940. It was shortly before the end of 1940 that President Roosevelt publicly discussed a new and revolutionary proposal to extend aid to the United Kingdom. The novel plan, said to have originated in the Treasury Department in the summer of 1940,[11] was to lease munitions to the United Kingdom. Legislation to authorize this was introduced in both the Senate and the House of Representatives on January 10, 1941. Specifically, the aim of the bill was to authorize the President to manufacture or procure "defense articles" on behalf of the governments of any countries whose defence was regarded as vital to the defence of the United States and to "sell, transfer title to, exchange, lease, lend, or otherwise dispose of" these "defense articles." The "lend-lease" plan was the subject of intense debate both in Congress and in the press and was finally approved by Congress on March 11, 1941. Formally, the legislation was known as "An Act to Promote the Defense of the United States" and was familiarly known as the Lend-Lease Act.[12] A large-scale procurement programme was instituted in the United States immediately to provide munitions, food, and equipment for the United Kingdom, the cost to be met out of lend-lease appropriations. The substitution of the lend-lease procedure for "cash-and-carry" marked the beginning of a new and important phase of Anglo-American relations. These developments also had important repercussions on relations between Canada and the United States.

2. THE FORMAL MACHINERY OF CONSULTATION

In the early period of the war, munitions orders placed in the United States by foreign governments and by the United States Army and Navy were relatively small, by later standards. The orders of foreign governments amounted to only $600,000,000 in the period January 1 to June 1, 1940.[13] Then, with the military setbacks in Europe, both foreign and domestic orders increased with great rapidity. Foreign contracts placed in the last half of 1940 amounted to nearly two and one-half billion dollars.[14] Late in June, the United States Congress authorized the expenditure of about one and three-quarter billion dollars for the expansion of production capacity and the procurement of munitions.[15] A few weeks afterwards, the President asked Congress for a supplemental appropriation of about five billion dollars.[16] Events in the United States in the last half of 1940 demonstrated beyond doubt that the economy of the United States was rapidly being placed on a war footing. In the first few months of 1941, following the President's "arsenal of democracy" speech, war orders were being placed on a fantastic scale. Bottlenecks were developing and mandatory priorities were being introduced piecemeal by new agencies created to stimulate war production. It was also clear, early in 1941, that if Congress approved the Lend-Lease Act, lend-lease orders would give a tremendous fillip to munitions production. These developments were naturally applauded in Canada.

War industry in Canada in the latter part of 1940 and early in 1941 was also expanding very quickly in response to the accelerated demands of the United Kingdom and increased domestic requirements for munitions. As a result of the mushroom growth of munitions production in North America and the new relationship between the United States and the United Kingdom, Canada was faced with a number of problems of adjustment.

The increasing volume of exports of munitions to the United Kingdom in 1940 and early 1941, created a double-edged difficulty for Canada. Canada's reserves of United States dollars were being drained by the heavy volume of United States imports needed to fill war contracts of the United Kingdom and for other purposes. At the same time, the United

Kingdom was faced with a serious deficiency of Canadian dollars which was being met in a number of ways already described. The Canadian government undertook to repatriate government or government-guaranteed securities prior to maturity and there was a good deal of unofficial repatriation of securities as well. Sterling balances were also accumulated by the Foreign Exchange Control Board. The United Kingdom had been able to make available to Canada $250,000,000 in gold and United States dollars in 1939 and 1940 but the maintenance of large-scale transfers of this sort seemed unlikely at the end of 1940.[17] The fact that the United Kingdom could not provide United States dollars to Canada meant that Canadian imports from the United States and, consequently, the Canadian war production programme, might have to be limited unless a solution to the difficulty were found.

These matters were the subject of detailed and frequent examination beginning shortly after the outbreak of war among financial and diplomatic officials of the United Kingdom, the United States, and Canada. Representatives of the Department of Finance, the United States Treasury Department and Department of State, and the British Treasury held a series of discussions in Washington concerning the problems arising out of purchases by the United Kingdom in the United States and Canada and the related problem of Canadian purchases in the United States, as well as general wartime financial relations between the three countries. One of the consequences of these meetings was the appointment of a Financial Attaché to the Canadian Legation in March, 1941, who was to represent the Department of Finance and to act as a liaison officer in Washington in the financial field.

The really significant outcome of these discussions, and related consultations with representatives of the three countries concerned with supply problems, was an agreement to adopt certain measures which would alleviate Canada's foreign exchange difficulties. The negotiations culminated in a meeting between President Roosevelt and Prime Minister King shortly after the middle of April, 1941, at Hyde Park, the President's home, and resulted in the public announcement of an important economic and financial agreement between the two countries dealing not only with long-run policy but with certain practical devices which were to be adopted immediately. The agreement was contained in a brief statement, later called the Hyde Park Declaration, which was issued on April 20, 1941. The full text of the announcement is as follows:

Among other important matters, the President and the Prime Minister discussed measures by which the most prompt and effective utilization might be made of the productive facilities of North America for the purposes both of local and hemisphere defence and of the assistance which in addition to their own programs both Canada and the United States are rendering to Great Britain and the other democracies.

It was agreed as a general principle that in mobilizing the resources of this continent each country should provide the other with the defence articles which it is best able to produce, and, above all, produce quickly, and that production programs should be co-ordinated to this end.

While Canada has expanded its productive capacity manifold since the beginning of the war, there are still numerous defence articles which it must obtain in the United States, and purchases of this character by Canada will be even greater in the coming year than in the past. On the other hand, there is existing and potential capacity in Canada for the speedy production of certain kinds of munitions, strategic materials, aluminum, and ships, which are urgently required by the United States for its own purposes.

While exact estimates cannot yet be made, it is hoped that during the next twelve months Canada can supply the United States with between $200,000,000 and $300,000,000 worth of such defence articles. This sum is a small fraction of the total defence program of the United States, but many of the articles to be provided are of vital importance. In addition, it is of great importance to the economic and financial relations between the two countries that payment by the United States for these supplies will materially assist Canada in meeting part of the cost of Canadian defence purchases in the United States.

In so far as Canada's defence purchases in the United States consist of component parts to be used in equipment and munitions which Canada is producing for Great Britain, it was also agreed that Great Britain will obtain these parts under the Lease-Lend Act and forward them to Canada for inclusion in the finished articles.

The technical and financial details will be worked out as soon as possible in accordance with the general principles which have been agreed upon between the President and the Prime Minister.[18]

The principal aim of the agreement embodied in the Hyde Park Declaration was obviously to solve Canada's critical foreign exchange problem. It was moreover essential that action be taken without delay since the drain on Canadian reserve of United States dollars was so heavy during the first few months of 1941 that the complete disappearance of the reserve was an immediate prospect. In view of the possibility of lend-lease assistance from the United States, it is perhaps unrealistic to suggest that the dollar shortage might have been allowed to develop to the point where the Canadian war effort was threatened. Nevertheless, the Canadian policy was to manage without lend-lease aid and the alternative solution, which visualized large-scale purchases by the United States, offered definite short- and long-run advantages. The specialization of munitions production in Canada and the United States would yield all the gains traditionally attributable to the division of labour and would stimulate Canadian exports of certain types of munitions and raw materials to the United States. Apart from the exchange difficulties arising out of the disruption of the normal course of Canadian trade, there were other and obvious reasons for seeking to promote closer economic co-operation between the two countries. Clearly, a more efficient North American production programme could be achieved by co-ordinating production plans in the two countries.

One important consideration was that Canada had at least the potential capacity to supply some of the needs of the United States. Gains would surely result if the construction of new facilities were undertaken in the two countries to make the best use of the raw materials, labour, and power available in North America. In addition, there was already some capacity available to meet the immediate requirements of the United States for specific items. The Hyde Park Declaration proposed a very satisfactory solution of the two-fold problem—the wasteful use of resources in the two countries and the maintenance of reasonable balances of United States dollars in Canada.

Steps were taken at once to create the administration machinery needed to handle the sale of "defence articles" to the United States. A Crown company, War Supplies Limited, was set up about the middle of May, 1941, under the Minister of Munitions and Supply, to handle orders for munitions to be manufactured in Canada for the United States government.[19]

The whole question of economic relations between Canada and the United States had also been under consideration by diplomatic officials of Canada and the United States. This should not be allowed to obscure the fact that the negotiations leading up to the Hyde Park Declaration were conducted through other channels, although the Department of State did play a relatively minor role in the discussions. After some study of mutual economic problems, the Canadian government outlined its tentative views in a communication to the Department of State about a week after the passage of the Lend-Lease Act. This document stated, in part:

The Canadian Government have been giving consideration to the military, economic and social problems which are likely to arise in Canada unless steps are taken to examine the possibility of arranging for co-operation between the war-expanded industries of Canada and the United States or for their co-ordination or integration. It is the belief of the Canadian Government that the promotion of economy and efficiency during the present period of crisis, the solution of the problems which will be posed during the period of transition from war to peace, and adequate and effective provision for the continuing requirements of hemispheric defense, all demand that early and detailed study be given to this question. Such a study might include an examination of the possibility and advisability of preventing duplication and mutually injurious competition by arranging for co-operation between the two countries in the further definition of all strategic, critical and essential war materials, and in the establishment of stock piles of certain of them.[20]

Accompanying the aide-mémoire was a memorandum on economic co-operation with the United States which had been prepared for submission to the War Committee of the Cabinet on the recommendation of the Wartime Requirements Board.[21] The memorandum, dated February 25, 1941, pointed out that the object of closer economic co-operation was to achieve a more economic, efficient and co-ordinated use of the combined resources of the two countries during the war and to minimize the dislocations which might occur after the war. It was proposed that a joint committee of inquiry, consisting of three members from each country, be appointed to study the following subjects:

(a) The making of an inventory of the available supplies of materials in each country, an analysis of the probable needs for them, and the allocation of these materials between the two countries, with due regard to the necessary priorities;

(b) The policy of building up inventories of strategic or critical materials, such as rubber, tin, and steel alloys, and the amounts to be accumulated in each country, with special regard to materials of which the supply might be cut off because of unfavourable developments;

(c) The possibility, in some degree, of each country specializing in the production of finished and semi-finished articles which it can produce more economically and to greater advantage;

(d) The possibility, in some degree, of each country specializing in the production of materials; e.g., chemicals, steel, aluminum, brass, zinc, etc., etc., which it can produce more economically and to greater advantage;

(e) The most economic and efficient use of the shipping and port facilities of the countries;

(f) The available power supply and the supply of coal and oil in each country;

(g) The exchange of technical knowledge relating to production, and the exchange of technicians between the two countries;

(h) Coordination of priority policies in each country;

(i) The exchange of information relating to the requirements of labour, materials and plant for production, and of current information relating to actual and anticipated production.[22]

In addition to these negotiations on particular or general financial and economic problems, other discussions were being carried out independently by representatives of the two countries with a view to co-ordinating the raw material resources of North America. The United States Chairman of the Permanent Joint Board on Defence, Mayor Fiorello

H. LaGuardia, recognized that the passage of the Lend-Lease Act might have important implications for his organization and requested the Office of Production Management around the middle of February, 1941, to appoint a liaison officer to co-operate with the Permanent Joint Board on Defence after the Lend-Lease Act was passed by Congress.[23]   There were some preliminary discussions of the proposal between the Minister of Munitions and Supply and the Director of Priorities of the Office of Production Management during which it was evidently agreed that the creation of an independent joint committee would be preferable to the appointment of a liaison officer as originally suggested.   At the end of March, the Minister of Munitions and Supply wrote to the Director of Priorities designating the Canadian members of the proposed committee.   The formal concurrence of the Office of Production Management was expressed in a letter from the Director-General to the Minister of Munitions and Supply on April 30, 1941,[24] following a discussion by the Council of the Office of Production Management a day earlier.[25]   In this letter, the committee was referred to as the "Matériel Co-ordinating Committee—United States and Canada," but since it came to be known usually as the Materials Co-ordinating Committee, this name will be used instead.   The approval of the United States was acknowledged by the Minister of Munitions and Supply who expressed briefly his hopes for the new Committee as follows:

I feel that an exchange of information on raw material and supplies through the agency of the Committee will be most helpful, and that misunderstandings having to do with the situation of both our countries may be avoided through its agency.[26]

The formation of the Committee was concurred in by President Roosevelt and by Mayor LaGuardia on behalf of the United States Section of the Permanent Joint Board on Defence and its establishment was publicly announced on May 14, 1941.[27]

The status of the Committee was unusual from the Canadian point of view since its authority rested on an exchange of letters between the Office of Production Management and the Minister of Munitions and Supply, unsupported by an order-in-council.   The Committee was set up at a time when the formation of committees to deal with the economic problems of the two countries was already under active discussion and provided a valuable means by which the Department of Munitions and Supply could approach the United States directly in connection with raw material problems.   The terms of reference of the Committee were never precisely outlined but a concise statement of its intended functions is contained in one of the letters of the Minister of Munitions and Supply to the Office of Production Management discussing the formation of the Committee. The letter stated, in part:

The purpose would be to enable the pooling of the resources of the two countries to avoid shortages of supplies of metals, alloys, chemicals, and other components of finished war products, in order that the best possible use could be made of the production of the two countries. Such an exchange of information might enable our two countries to take joint action when the curtailment of domestic consumption is necessary.[28]

The Canadian members of the Committee were the Metals Controller and the Power Controller of the Department of Munitions and Supply and the United States members were the Director of the Priorities Division and the Deputy Director of the Production Division of the Office of Production Management. The Committee did not function as an operating or executive agency but rather as a consultative body. Sometimes the recommendations of the Committee could be put into practice by the members directly while in other cases, the concurrence or co-operation of other officials or agencies was necessary.

The scope of the activities originally outlined for the Committee was very wide. It was understood at the time of its formation that the Committee would be concerned with joint supplies and productive capacity for the following formidable list of items: aluminum, antimony, copper, cobalt, lead, mercury, nickel, pulp, radium, titanium ore, zinc, phosphorus, ammonia, calcium carbide, dinitrotoluol, picrite, potassium perchlorate, gas-mask carbon, nitrocellulose rifle powder, pthalic anhydride, asbestos, arsenic, brass rods, fertilizers, hardwood, charcoal, mica, and selenium.[29] While many of these commodities received scant attention from the Committee, it did serve as a clearing-house for the exchange of information about the production and supply of important raw materials, and for the consideration of plans for the expansion of the North American output of metals and other basic materials. Four sub-committees were later established to deal with special problems relating to copper, zinc, ferroalloys, and forest products. The operations of the Materials Co-ordinating Committee and its sub-committees will be considered in greater detail later, principally in the section describing Canadian allocations to the United States.

Shortly after the announcement of the creation of the Materials Co-ordinating Committee, action was taken to implement the Canadian proposal to form a joint committee to study ways of promoting economic co-operation. During the first week of June, the Department of State acknowledged the fact that existing channels of communication between Washington and Ottawa were not suitable for dealing with most of the economic problems originally outlined by the Canadians, although with the creation of the Materials Co-ordinating Committee, contact had been established between officials dealing with priorities and with production of war material.[30] The Canadian government was also informed that a committee to represent the United States had been tentatively designated. On June 17, 1941, the Department of State was advised that a corresponding Canadian committee had been named.[31]

The committees created as a result of these negotiations were called the Joint Economic Committees and consisted of two national committees or sections. Both the United States Section and the Canadian Section met as separate committees, and somewhat less frequently as a joint committee. The substantial part of the terms of reference of the Committees was taken almost verbatim from the original Canadian memorandum on economic co-operation and stated that the Committees were:

To study and report to their respective governments on the possibility of

(1) effecting a more economic, more efficient and more co-ordinated utilization of the combined resources of the two countries in the production of defence requirements (to the extent that this is not now being done) and

(2) reducing the probable post-war economic dislocation consequent upon the changes which the economy in each country is presently undergoing.[32]

The responsibilities of the Joint Economic Committees were strictly advisory; they had no administrative authority. It was also agreed by the Committees that they would confine themselves to the broad features of economic collaboration and leave the detailed policies to be worked out by the appropriate administrative agencies in the two countries.

During the course of their existence, the Joint Economic Committees considered a wide range of topics. For some time, at least, they served as a clearing-house for the exchange of information on new problems which were not within the scope of existing administrative agencies. The Committees discussed the problems of economic co-ordination in the fields of export control, shipping, priorities, agriculture, foreign exchange, tariffs, the movement of labour, prices, and war production policy. Despite the rather wide range of topics dealt with, the effectiveness of the Committees was limited, and, in general, their deliberations were usually merely the prelude to the assignment of specific responsibility to existing or new agencies. The specific activities of the Joint Economic Committees will be dealt with in conjunction with the account of the new issues which arose as the war progressed, and a more detailed account of the weaknesses of the Committees will be given later.

Apart from their own work, the Joint Economic Committees sponsored the establishment of another committee which became more influential perhaps than the parent Committees. It was the belief of some of the members of the Joint Economic Committees, particularly among the representatives of the United States, that production facilities were being duplicated in the two countries and that this was leading to the misallocation of North American resources. It was suggested that a joint committee be formed to review the facilities available in each country for the production of munitions and that the procurement agencies of the two countries place their orders with a view to making the most efficient use of the joint capacity. The point was also made that both Canada and the United States appeared to be striving for self-sufficiency in munitions production and that Canada, in particular, was attempting to produce too wide a variety of military equipment and supplies. One of the main functions of the proposed new committee was to be to encourage procurement agencies in the United States to place contracts in Canada for the manufacture of a restricted range of munitions in order to encourage larger scale and presumably more efficient production.

The Joint Economic Committees recognized that military production problems were involved and that the participation of technical experts or production officials would be necessary. As a matter of diplomacy, it was decided that it would not be practicable to invite high-ranking military or other government officials to sit on a sub-committee of the Joint Economic Committees. For these reasons, the Committees recommended that separate formal machinery be set up to handle the co-ordination of specific war production programmes in Canada and the United States. The duties of the new committee, as outlined in the recommendation submitted by the Committees to the President and the Prime Minister, were:

To survey the capacity and potential capacity for the production of defence matériel in each country to the end that in mobilizing the resources of the two countries, each country should provide for the common defence effort the defence article which it is best able to produce, taking into consideration the desirability of so arranging production for defence purposes as to minimize, as far as possible, and, consistent with the maximum defence effort, maladjustments in the post-defence periods.[33]

The recommendation was approved by the President and the Canadian War Cabinet and, accordingly, the Joint Defence Production Committee was created at the end of October, 1941. The Committee was to report directly to the President and the Prime Minister and there were thus no formal ties with the Joint Economic Committees.[34] The establishment of the Committee was announced by the Prime Minister on November 5,

1941, and the first meeting of the Committee was held on December 15.[35] With the entry of the United States into the war, the name of the Committee became inappropriate and was changed to the Joint War Production Committee.[36] Originally, the Chairman of the Canadian Section was the Deputy Minister of Munitions and Supply and the Chairman of the United States Section was the Executive Director of the Economic Defense Board, later the Board of Economic Warfare. The members of the Committee were senior administrators concerned mainly with production and procurement in the two countries.[37]

The first meeting of the Committee was held about a week after Pearl Harbor in the super-charged atmosphere of Washington. The upshot of the meeting was a set of sweeping recommendations on war production policy which again emphasized the goal of an integrated war production programme in Canada and the United States. The text of the Committee's recommendation was:

Having regard to the fact that Canada and the United States are engaged in a war with common enemies, the Joint War Production Committee of Canada and the United States recommends to the President of the United States and the Prime Minister of Canada the following statement of policy for the war production of the two countries:

1. Victory will require the maximum war production in both countries in the shortest possible time; speed and volume of war output, rather than monetary cost, are the primary objectives.

2. An all-out war production effort in both countries requires the maximum use of the labor, raw materials and facilities in each country.

3. Achievement of maximum volume and speed of war output requires that the production and resources of both countries should be effectively integrated, and directed towards a common program of requirements for the total war effort.

4. Each country should produce these articles in an integrated program of requirements which will result in a maximum joint output of war goods in the minimum time.

5. Scarce raw materials and goods which one country requires from the other in order to carry out the joint program of war production should be so allocated between the two countries that such materials and goods will make the maximum contribution toward the output of the most necessary articles in the shortest period of time.

6. Legislative and administrative barriers, including tariffs, import duties, customs and other regulations or restrictions of any character which prohibit, prevent, delay or otherwise impede the free flow of necessary munitions and war supplies between the two countries should be suspended or otherwise eliminated for the duration of the war.

7. The two governments should take all measures necessary for the fullest implementation of the foregoing principles.[38]

Shortly after, on December 22, 1941, President Roosevelt issued a public statement strongly supporting the policies of the Joint War Production Committee in these words:

The Joint War Production Committee of Canada and the United States have unanimously adopted a declaration of policy calling for a combined all-out war production effort and the removal of any barriers standing in the way of such a combined effort.

This declaration has met the approval of the Canadian War Cabinet. It has my full approval.

To further its implementation, I have asked the affected departments and agencies in our government to abide by its letter and spirit, so far as lies within their power.

I have further requested Mr. Milo Perkins, the Chairman of the American committee, to investigate with the aid of the Tariff Commission and other interested agencies, the extent to which legislative changes will be necessary to give full effect to the declaration.

Through brute force and enslavement, Hitler has secured a measure of integration and coordination of the productive resources of a large part of the Continent of Europe.

We must demonstrate that integration and coordination of the productive resources of the Continent of America is possible through democratic processes and free consent.[39]

Except for the paragraph dealing with legislative and administrative barriers, all the essential principles in this statement of policy were contained in the Hyde Park Declaration. The emphatic reiteration of the principles of co-operation was reassuring to Canada in view of the murmurings which were heard in some quarters that the United States should reconsider its attitude to foreign aid. It is significant also that the statement of policy originated with administrators intimately concerned with war production. In itself, this was added assurance that the principles would be observed in the solution of the practical problems of co-ordination.

The main work of the Joint War Production Committee was carried on through a series of sub-committees consisting of senior production officials concerned with specific programmes in the two countries. Separate committees were created to deal with tanks and automotive vehicles, artillery, ammunition, small arms, chemicals and explosives, signals equipment, aircraft, naval and merchant shipbuilding, and conservation.

By the end of 1941, an imposing array of joint committees had been established as a result of special wartime agreements between Canada and the United States. The Permanent Joint Board on Defence had been given the responsibility for co-ordinating defence plans. The basic policy that economic resources should be pooled had been subsequently laid down in the Hyde Park Declaration. To achieve a co-ordinated North American production programme required not only agreement on basic policy, but extensive machinery for dealing with the complex of economic problems arising out of a joint programme. Part of the responsibility was given to the Materials Co-ordinating Committee which was to be concerned with the production and allocation of raw materials. The desirability of creating an agency with responsibility for reviewing the range of wartime economic problems was recognized by the two governments when the Joint Economic Committees were established. Once technical production problems became important, it was necessary to create the Joint War Production Committee. The Joint Economic Committees were free to investigate the general field of economic co-operation, but their effective scope was substantially reduced when the Joint War Production Committee was assigned the responsibility for the integration of munitions programmes in the two countries.

These committees all operated outside the sphere of normal diplomatic relations between the two countries. The establishment of these extra-diplomatic channels was recommended by Canada in the original memorandum on economic co-operation which stated that existing means of communication between Washington and Ottawa did not provide adequate facilities for the consideration of so complicated and technical a subject, a view which was concurred in by the United States. The mention of existing means of communication, presumably in reference to the use of diplomatic personnel, might justify the surmise that some consideration had been given to strengthening or broadening diplomatic channels, but that this alternative had been rejected. This implicit or explicit decision was an important one, since it set a precedent of some significance for later developments.

The policy declarations of 1941 left no doubt that the aim of the two countries was to integrate completely North American resources and facilities. Unfortunately, this goal conflicted to some extent with Canadian commitments and ties to the United Kingdom. Canadian war output was dominated by the production of so-called "British-type stores" which were in general use by the armed forces in both the United Kingdom and Canada. These were usually essentially different or involved different specifications from munitions required by the armed forces of the United States. For this reason, there was a limit to the extent to which the Canadian production of munitions could be adapted to United States production schedules. Apart from this, Canada's shortage of United States dollars had a good deal of influence on Canadian domestic policy and also on the operations of a number of the joint committees concerned with co-operation. It would have been an obvious, if not simple, solution to accept lend-lease assistance from the United States. The Canadian policy of avoiding reliance on direct lend-lease help throws a good deal of light on the relations between the United States and Canada and deserves to be examined in some detail.

3. Canada, Lend-Lease, and Related Matters

The passage of the Lend-Lease Act was greeted with enthusiasm in Canada. Mr. Mackenzie King stated in the House of Commons the day after the Act was passed by Congress:

The signature by the President of the United States of the lease-lend bill . . . will stand throughout time as one of the milestones of freedom. It points the way to ultimate and certain victory. . . . The people of Canada have never doubted what the great-hearted people of the United States would do. . . . We in Canada may feel more than a little pride in the share we have had in bringing about the closer relationship between the United States and the British Commonwealth.[40]

As noted earlier, the Lend-Lease Act authorized the President of the United States to arrange for the manufacture or procurement of defence articles and "to sell, transfer title to, exchange, lease, lend, or otherwise dispose of" such articles to the government of any country whose defence he considered to be important to the defence of the United States. A remarkable feature of the Act of March 11, 1941, was the fact that the question of repayment was left to the discretion of the President. The relevant clause of the Act read:

The terms and conditions upon which any such foreign government receives any aid . . . shall be those which the President deems satisfactory, and the benefit to the United States may be payment or repayment in kind or property, or any other direct or indirect benefit which the President deems satisfactory.[41]

There was no doubt of Canada's eligibility for lend-lease aid nor was there any indication that the United States was unwilling to provide such aid. Despite this, Canada did not request and did not receive direct lend-lease assistance from the United States during the war. Lend-lease aid would certainly have been very convenient for Canada and would have solved, temporarily at least, the Canadian balance-of-payments problem. The alternative solution, which was embodied in the Hyde Park Declaration, was beset with uncertainty and implied a somewhat more Spartan approach to the problem.

There was never any serious discussion of the possibility of Canadian participation in lend-lease between responsible Canadian and United States representatives. Of course, a number of possible solutions to the Canadian exchange problem were discussed at different times prior to the Hyde Park Declaration and after but, if lend-lease assistance was mentioned, it was only as an alternative to be adopted if other remedies should fail. The Minister of Finance, in referring to the Canadian attitude to lend-lease aid at a later date, said :

We never wished to ask the United States for lend-lease assistance— we always felt that, as a nation in a favoured position, free from the ravages of war, we were in duty bound to stand on our own feet and indeed to share with the United States in assisting other less fortunate of our allies in carrying on the war against the common enemy.[42]

It seems clear, even from this one statement, that the Canadian desire for independence was of dominant importance. The precise form which any loss of independence entailed in lend-lease assistance might have taken is far from obvious. There seems to be a deep-rooted Canadian tradition, amounting almost to a passion, for independence and freedom from moral obligation to the United States. This is a sociological phenomenon which probably develops whenever a small country and a large country are juxtaposed.

It must also be recalled that lend-lease was a very controversial issue in the United States early in 1941 and it could confidently be predicted at that time that there would be a great deal of public interest in lend-lease operations and that they would be scrutinized very carefully by Congress. There might well have been either public or Congressional pressure on Canada to modify internal policies to conform to criteria established in the United States. There was then some risk of either subtle or open pressure on Canada which might restrict the ability of Canada to manage the Canadian war programme without external interference. There was a natural national pride in the amount of Canada's resources which could be directed to the Allied war effort, and there was a corresponding reluctance to share the credit with any other country, albeit a friendly one.

Apart from this, the existence of a balance-of-payments problem in Canada was partially the result of Canadian efforts to supply munitions to the Allies. It was, therefore, not Canadian needs which would have been filled by the receipt of lend-lease aid from the United States. There would be little point in establishing a circuitous route for aid which would eventually go to the Allies in any case. The amount of aid forthcoming from the United States was extremely generous but there was an upper limit to it. Consequently, any lend-lease appropriations used for Canada would eventually be subtracted from those available for other countries whose needs were much more urgent.

From the financial point of view, the Hyde Park Declaration visualized two major expedients. The first clearly recognized that part of Canada's shortage of United States dollars was attributable to the heavy volume of imports for incorporation in munitions destined for the United Kingdom. It was therefore agreed that components needed to fill United Kingdom contracts in Canada would be lend-leased to the United Kingdom, transferred to Canada, and incorporated there into equipment or supplies being produced for the United Kingdom. The second was that Canada would undertake to produce military supplies and other goods for shipment to the United States in quantities which might amount to as much as $300,000,000 in the year following the Hyde Park Declaration.

In the first instance, the procedure was to have the United Kingdom file lend-lease requisitions to cover articles imported by Canada for incorporation in munitions destined for the United Kingdom. When the imports retained their identity throughout the production process and the quantities going to the United Kingdom were clearly specified, the requisitions were known as *Canship* requisitions. For example, certain components, such as tank transmissions, could be traced to their ultimate destination in the United Kingdom. A more complex procedure was required to deal with imports which lost their identity in the course of manufacture. Imports of coal or steel, for example, might be needed to fill contracts of the United Kingdom but it would be impossible to relate any particular shipment to a specific contract. To get around this obstacle, it was proposed to transfer certain goods to Canada from supplies in the hands of the United Kingdom, which was to submit *Canex* requisitions to the Office of Lend-Lease Administration to cover such transfers. Some such requisitions were, in fact, filed but they gave rise to administrative difficulties and the system soon fell into disuse. On the basis of the Hyde Park Declaration, it might have been appropriate to attempt to recompense Canada completely for all non-identifiable imports, but, for practical reasons, the volume of *Canex* requisitions never became significantly large. Canada also made use of the procurement machinery set up by the Office of Lend-Lease Administration to facilitate purchases from United States government agencies. The arrangement was that Canada submitted "cash reimbursement requisitions" known as *Canpay* requisitions, primarily as a matter of convenience. The use of such cash reimbursement requisitions was explained as follows in a Presidential report to Congress:

This system of purchasing provides for the procurement of an item in precisely the same way as that used for other lend-lease operations, with the exception that the foreign government deposits cash with the United States Treasury against the value of the goods to be purchased.

The use of the lend-lease mechanism for the making of such purchases is beneficial to the United States defense program because, under such a system, foreign orders, even though paid for in advance, become United States government contracts under the supervision and control of United States government agencies. This obviates the need for separate foreign priority ratings as well as limiting the chances for conflicting production, exorbitant prices, and the misuse of raw materials, labor and plant facilities.[43]

The requirement that cash deposits be made in advance was later relaxed in the case of requisitions of this class, although Canada always maintained cash balances well ahead of any *Canpay* requisitions submitted.

Two things should be noted about the use of *Canship* and *Canex* requisitions. First, the fact that Canada was relieved of the necessity of paying dollars for imports on United Kingdom account never became an important element in improving Canada's balance of payments with the United States. Mainly this was because of the administrative difficulties involved in segregating the United Kingdom's prospective share of Canadian imports and in clearing the requisitions through the complex channels of the lend-lease system. At the time of the Hyde Park Declaration, a good deal of importance was apparently attached to the device but the magnitude of the adjustments did not become large enough to be of major significance. Second, the transfers of goods to Canada through lend-lease channels arising out of purchases on behalf of the United Kingdom was apt to give the impression that Canada was a recipient of lend-lease aid. While this was certainly not the case, the explanation of the arrangements to the general public could not be made as simply as might be wished. The use of *Canship* requisitions was easily understood, but the *Canex* procedure was particularly liable to misunderstanding and misrepresentation despite the fact that the Canadian government was careful to restrict any *Canex* transfers to a small fraction of the total which Canada was spending on non-identifiable imports for the United Kingdom. Since the *Canex* procedure tended to give the superficial impression that Canada was receiving lend-lease aid in an indirect way, there was some uneasiness over the possibility of unfriendly criticism of the arrangements. In particular, the United States Congress was apt to be critical of any aspect of lend-lease which was not perfectly straightforward and easily explained. Finally, in the spring of 1943, *Canex* requisitions, which had come to be recognized as both ineffective and liable to misinterpretation, were abandoned altogether. Later on, in a general financial settlement between the two countries, Canada repaid the United States in cash for all *Canex* imports.

The sale of Canadian *matériel* to the United States government through

War Supplies Limited was by far the most important aspect of the financial agreement contained in the Hyde Park Declaration. Initial progress was slow but once the United States had entered the war, the volume of United States orders in Canada increased sharply. The volume of sales rose from $275,000,000 in 1942 to $301,000,000 in 1943. It increased still further to $314,000,000 in 1944 and declined to $189,000,000 in 1945.[44] Procurement in Canada by the United States through War Supplies Limited had a dual aspect. From one point of view, it enabled Canada to supply certain types of *matériel* urgently needed by the armed services in the United States. From another point of view, it was a device to provide Canada with United States dollars.

One feature of the financial arrangements between the two countries was that orders needed to fill direct or indirect requirements of the United States were diverted to Canada for procurement through War Supplies Limited to alleviate Canada's dollar shortage. The physical disposition of the goods, once they had been bought, was the responsibility of the United States authorities, and there was nothing to prevent them being lend-leased to other countries. It is probable that some off-shore purchases of the United States were transferred in this way. This procedure was both a sensible and convenient way of easing Canada's foreign exchange problem but it, like *Canex* requisitions, could not be explained readily and simply.

In any event, by early 1943, the Canadian foreign exchange position had improved remarkably. This was not only a result of sales through War Supplies Limited but was in part a result of large-scale expenditure by the United States government on military projects in Canada. After Pearl Harbor, the strategic importance of Alaska was more clearly recognized with the result that the United States undertook enormous construction operations, including the Alaska Highway, the Canol Project, communication lines, airfields, and naval bases. The resulting expenditures in Canada contributed in a substantial way to Canadian reserves of United States dollars. There had also been a marked rise in the purchase of Canadian securities by investors in the United States, the gross purchases rising from about $100,000,000 in 1942 to $200,000,000 in 1943.[45] The upshot of these developments was that Canada's dollar holdings were growing, despite the high level of imports throughout this period.

The accumulation of large dollar balances in Canada was apparently not foreseen at the time that the financial understanding between the two countries was reached, and it became clear by early 1943 that steps should be taken to regulate the system to prevent undue accumulation. Accordingly, negotiations were undertaken with the United States Treasury Department to reconsider the financial relations of the two countries in the light of the unanticipated growth in Canada's dollar balances. Agreement was reached during these discussions on what would be reasonable upper and lower limits for Canada's United States dollar reserves. The understanding was that when the Canadian balance approached the minimum, additional United States orders would be placed in Canada and when the maximum had been reached, orders placed with War Supplies Limited would be diverted to non-Canadian sources.

Despite the modifications of the financial aspects of the Hyde Park Declaration agreed to in early 1943, and the agreement on minimum and maximum balances, Canadian reserves of United States dollars continued to grow and by the end of 1943 were about $650,000,000. Although the maximum-minimum balances agreement was apparently designed to deal with a situation in which Canadian reserves of United States dollars were fluctuating, it became obsolete in view of the steady increase in Canadian reserves. It was therefore possible to dispense with the agreement in early 1944. At this point, Canada's exchange reserves were sufficiently large to make it unnecessary for the United States to take into account the Canadian dollar shortage by diverting orders for war material to Canada. From this point on, orders were placed by the United States solely with a view to meeting the needs of the United States. At the same time, a financial settlement was reached, partly designed to discharge the Canadian obligations relating to the maximum exchange reserve of United States dollars. Large payments were made by Canada to the United States primarily to reimburse the United States for costs which had been incurred in improving permanent Canadian airfields.[46]

The Canadian foreign exchange problem in the earlier years of the war was a symptom of the maladjustment of the normal triangular interchange of goods between Canada, the United Kingdom, and the United States. There was some risk that this maladjustment might impair the combined war effort. Once it was clearly recognized that financial considerations were of minor importance in the light of the possibility of an Axis victory, new and forthright steps were taken to solve the real issues involved. The brilliant device of lend-lease provided a means of supplying the United Kingdom with urgently needed goods, while a cognate but more complex scheme was adopted to obtain a better allocation of North American raw materials and other resources.

There was one particular aspect of the lend-lease arrangements which was of considerable interest to Canada, despite the fact that Canada was not directly concerned at first. This was the commitment with respect to post-war trade policy incorporated in the various lend-lease agreements between the United States and recipient countries. For example, Article

VII of the Master Lend-Lease Agreement with the United Kingdom concluded on February 23, 1942, contained an undertaking to remove "all
forms of discriminatory treatment in international commerce, and to the
reduction of tariffs and other trade barriers. . . ."[47] There was a good
deal of speculation about the precise significance of this commitment and
it has been suggested authoritatively that the original intention of the
United States was to press for the elimination of the British Preferential
Tariff. Mr. Cordell Hull, Secretary of State at the time the lend-lease
agreements were drawn up, has confirmed this view by referring to the
article in question as follows:

> Article VII of our basic Lend-Lease agreement with Britain, signed in
> 1942 . . . provided that Britain would adopt a non discriminatory com-
> mercial policy after the war, meaning that she would give up imperial
> tariff preferences.[48]

Whatever the original intent was, it is safe to say that the United States
did sponsor a series of wartime agreements on commercial policy intended
to inhibit the adoption of restrictive trade regulations in the post-war world.
In line with this, Canada was officially approached by the United States
around the end of November, 1942, and requested to concur in a statement
of post-war trade policy. One paragraph of the United States note pointed
out:

> Our two Governments are engaged in a cooperative undertaking,
> together with every other nation or people of like mind, to the end of laying
> the bases of a joint and enduring world peace securing order under law
> to themselves and all nations. They have agreed to provide mutual aid both
> in defence and in economic matters through the Ogdensburg and Hyde
> Park Agreements and subsequent arrangements. They are in agreement
> that post-war settlements must be such as to promote mutually advantageous
> economic relations between them and the betterment of worldwide economic
> relations.[49]

The object of the note is abundantly clear when its essential paragraph
is placed side by side with Article VII, as shown below:

United States Note	Article VII
The Governments of the United States of America and Canada are prepared to cooperate in formulating a program of agreed action, open to participation by all other countries of like mind, directed to the expansion, by appropriate international and domestic measures of	They [the terms of the lend-lease settlement] shall include provision for agreed action by the United States of America and the United Kingdom, open to participation by all other countries of like mind, directed to the expansion, by appropriate international and

United States Note	Article VII
production, employment, and the exchange and consumption of goods, which are the material foundations of the liberty and welfare of all peoples; to the elimination of all forms of discriminatory treatment in international commerce, and to the reduction of tariffs and other trade barriers. . . .[50]	domestic measures, of production, employment and the exchange and consumption of goods, which are the material foundations of the liberty and welfare of all peoples; to the elimination of all forms of discriminatory commerce, and to the reduction of tariffs and other trade barriers. . . .[51]

Apart from this particular point concerning post-war trade policy, it was also suggested in the United States note that the two countries should:

seek to furnish to the world concrete evidence of the ways in which two neighbouring countries that have a long experience of friendly relations and a high degree of economic interdependence, and that share the conviction that such reciprocally beneficial relations must form part of a general system, may promote by agreed action their mutual interests to the benefit of themselves and other countries.

Canadian concurrence in the proposals of the United States was immediately signified. The pressure of wartime events had thus brought about a *rapprochement* of the United States and Canada in the field of commercial policy, a state of affairs which seemed far distant in the early 1930's. While the exchange of notes did not refer to wartime trade except incidentally, the agreement on basic post-war policy might also be expected to apply to more immediate circumstances. At least one instance of a Canadian appeal to the principles laid down in the exchange of notes is cited later. It was not unusual that agreements on specific subjects were extended by interpretation to cover a broader field. This was certainly the case with civilian production, where the basic policies of co-operation were applied with perhaps even more success than to military production.

4. SOME SPECIAL ASPECTS OF ECONOMIC CO-OPERATION

The measure of economic co-operation achieved by Canada and the United States was partly a by-product of the attempt to solve Canada's balance-of-payments problem. There were, of course, other conditioning factors which influenced the economic relations between the two countries. One important issue was the extent to which the war production programmes of the two countries were inherently autonomous and independent. Another consideration was the interaction of civilian production and consumption in the two countries. These supplementary factors are of basic significance and should be examined in more detail.

It should be recognized at once that there were a number of significant obstacles in the way of complete economic co-operation between Canada and the United States. Some of these were created by deep-rooted historical factors or by rigidities in national policies. These limiting and conditioning factors must be borne in mind in any assessment of the policy of economic co-operation or the way in which it was put into effect.

By far the most important consideration was the basic fact that Canada and the United States were engaged in filling two different and, in many ways, independent sets of requirements. For this reason, the goal of integration enunciated in the Hyde Park Declaration had some unrealistic aspects. The Canadian production programme was specifically designed to meet specifications common to the armed forces of Canada and the United Kingdom. In the United States, on the other hand, the construction of new facilities and the production of munitions which were not suited to the prospective needs of the United States were discouraged, at least in the initial phases of rearmament. Foreign munitions orders placed in the United States after the end of 1939 had to be approved by the Interdepartmental Committee for the Coordination of Foreign and Domestic Military Purchases, familiarly known as the President's Liaison Committee,[52] and it was the policy of this Committee to approve the production of standard items only. This meant that, so far as North American purchases were concerned, the United Kingdom was under pressure to concentrate on standard items in the United States and on non-standard items in Canada.[53] As a result, there never was a completely co-ordinated set of requirements to which production in Canada and the United States could be adapted. This point was clearly brought out in the following statement contained in a radio speech by the Prime Minister concerning Canadian war production plans for 1941 :

As the United States is prepared to manufacture for Britain only such munitions as are in common use for United States' war purposes, Canadian armament production during 1941 will be concentrated on types of war equipment and weapons which are not obtainable in the United States, such as tanks, small arms, machine-guns, anti-aircraft and anti-tank guns. The production of a wide range of naval guns and field guns will be enlarged; Canada is the only source of supply outside Britain for these guns. Canada will also specialize in the production of ammunition for these weapons, and in the manufacture of explosives.[54]

This should not be interpreted as meaning that there was no room for co-ordination. On the contrary, it became evident once defence preparations were well under way in the United States, that care should be taken to avoid the inefficient allocation of North American resources. This was recognized in Canada and was noted in the Canadian memorandum of February, 1941, which foreshadowed the establishment of the Materials Co-ordinating Committee and the Joint Economic Committees. At first, then, Canada was urging co-ordination with the Canadian production programme. By the summer of 1941, Canada was being urged to modify production to fit the plans of the United States. The argument advanced at that time by senior United States officials was that both countries were bent on producing a complete catalogue of munitions. Canada was setting out to produce airplanes, tanks, and ordnance of types which could probably be produced more efficiently in the United States. Why, it was argued, did not Canada concentrate on standardized types of military equipment instead of branching into several types of combat aircraft and two types of tanks? It was suggested that Canada should specialize in producing such items as machine guns, trainer planes, Bren gun carriers, and other military vehicles. The United States, on the other hand, was better equipped to produce complex munitions which rapidly became obsolete and needed large numbers of technical personnel and specialized machine tools. There is little question that specialization of the type proposed would have led to a more efficient allocation of resources. Indeed, considerations of this sort led Canada to abandon plans to manufacture airplane engines in Canada and to import them from the United States instead. Nevertheless, the extent to which this policy of integrating war production could be carried was limited by a number of factors. First, the more specialization there was, the more dependent Canada was on the United States and vice versa. Complete interdependence under the circumstances was apt to be uncomfortable. The policy of the United States with respect to the export of critical munitions was far from clear in the fall of 1941. There was always some danger that an internal shift of administrative responsibility in the United States, such as a transfer of power from civilian to military agencies, might lead to the introduction of policies which did not favour the export of essential components needed in Canada. In both countries, there was a close but obscure relation between military strategy and war production and there was some risk that failures or delays in some production programme might hamper scheduled military operations. Dependence on domestic output would give military authorities closer control than if some essential requirements were being produced in another country. Second, there was initially some reluctance on the part of military procurement officials in the United States to place munitions orders in Canada. Shortly after the Hyde Park Declaration, there were newspaper reports that a mission of United States civilian and military officials had made a tour of Canadian war plants to investigate the possibility of buying such things as shells, rifle cartridges, trucks, and universal carriers.[55] As noted earlier, Canadian sales of munitions to the United States were not substantial in 1941, which may be taken as an indication that large-scale procurement was not started immediately. In part, the delay was attributable to certain legal barriers to foreign procurement by government agencies in the United States. Third, the international specialization of war production had certain complicated post-war implications. A tremendous expansion of a few lines of production would create a difficult reconversion problem after the war, whereas diversified and presumably smaller facilities might well be more easily converted to peacetime use.

It was not too difficult to reach agreement on certain general principles of economic co-operation between Canada and the United States in the field of war production since the gains of collaboration were obvious. The two major policy statements were contained in the Hyde Park Declaration which was an agreement between the two political heads of the two countries, and the statement of policy of the Joint War Production Committee which was specifically approved by the President and the Canadian War Cabinet. No agreement at a comparable level was ever reached concerning civilian production in the early stages of the war. Administrative officials in the two countries did at different times agree on certain basic concepts of parity but the formal status of these agreements was usually uncertain. The truth is that the precise terms of the Hyde Park Declaration were often a little vague in the minds of some United States officials, and it seemed reasonable to believe that the policy of pooling and integration applied to the whole field of production and consumption. Later in the war, the issue of comparable treatment of civilians arose with uncomfortable frequency, particularly in the case of textiles. On one occasion in May, 1944, the Under-Secretary of War expressed some wonder about the expansion of textile exports to Canada in a meeting of the War Production Board. The Director of the Textile, Clothing and Leather Bureau of the War Production Board, in commenting on the situation, stated, "The Joint War Production Committee is supposed to accord like treatment to the civilian economies of the United States and Canada, although this policy is not invariably followed."[56] Although the Under Secretary of War was a member of the Joint War Production Committee, he apparently did not challenge this somewhat vague interpretation of the policy of the two countries.

It seemed eminently reasonable that civilians in North America should be treated alike, with special allowance being made for climatic influences or customary differences in consumption patterns. Agreements in this field were many and varied and usually the product of informal negotiations between officials in the two countries. If disagreements arose, it was always possible to refer to the Hyde Park Declaration but this was seldom necessary. The officials or wartime administrators were generally people with similar problems and similar interests who were prepared to make reasonable concessions. In the field of civilian production and consumption, the co-operative agreements which were reached depended mainly on the goodwill and friendly attitudes of individual negotiators and not on the existence of any overriding policy agreement between Canada and the United States. Thus, informal agreements between individuals and between agencies played an important role in the wartime relations between the two countries. A detailed discussion of these agreements will perhaps be more meaningful after the administrative agencies concerned with wartime economic relations have been described.

REFERENCES FOR CHAPTER II

1. Although part of this chapter deals with the wartime financial negotiations between Canada and the United States, it should be emphasized that a detailed official version of these negotiations has never been publicly released. This account is based almost exclusively on published material and not on any inside information about the events which occurred.

2. Foreign Exchange Control Board, *Report to the Minister of Finance, March, 1946* (Ottawa, 1946), p. 6. The balances with the United States include gold exports.

3. This table is taken from the Report of a Special Combined Committee set up by the Combined Production and Resources Board, *The Impact of the War on Civilian Consumption in the United Kingdom, the United States and Canada, September, 1945* (Washington: U.S. Government Printing Office, 1945), p. 148. The original source is the Canadian Department of Finance.

4. Foreign Exchange Control Board, *Report to the Minister of Finance, March, 1946*, p. 33.

5. P.C. 2716, September 15, 1939.

6. P.C. 1735, April 30, 1940.

7. *Canada, House of Commons Debates,* June 24, 1940, pp. 1020-1.

8. *Ibid.,* July 30, 1940, p. 2128.

9. *Statutes of Canada,* 4-5 Geo. VI, c. 2 (1940-1). The War Exchange Conservation Act is discussed more fully in Chapter VIII which deals with trade barriers between Canada and the United States.

10. Foreign Exchange Control Board, *Report to the Minister of Finance, March, 1946*, p. 24.

11. E. R. Stettinius, *Lend-Lease: Weapon for Victory* (New York: Macmillan, 1944), p. 63.

12. *55 U.S. Statutes* 31; c. 11, Act of March 11, 1941.

13. E. R. Stettinius, *op. cit.,* p. 45.

14. Historical Reports on War Administration, Bureau of the Budget, No. 1. *The United States at War* (Washington: U.S. Government Printing Office, 1946), p. 19.

15. *Ibid.,* p. 21.

16. *Ibid.*

17. Foreign Exchange Control Board, *Report to the Minister of Finance, March, 1946,* p. 33.

18. Canada, Treaty Series, 1941, No. 14, *Declaration by the Prime Minister of Canada and the President of the United States of America Regarding Co-operation for War Production Made on April 20, 1941* (Ottawa: King's Printer, 1943).

19. War Supplies Limited was incorporated on May 13, 1941, under sec. 6(3) of the Department of Munitions and Supply Act (1939) as amended.

20. U.S., Department of State, *Executive Agreement Series 228* (Washington: U.S. Government Printing Office, 1942), p. 1.

21. The Wartime Requirements Board, consisting of a group of senior civil servants and administrators in wartime agencies, was appointed under the Department of Munitions and Supply on November 16, 1940, by P.C. 6601, and was assigned rather general planning and co-ordinating responsibilities relating to war production and exports.

22. U.S., Department of State, *Executive Agreement Series 228,* p. 3. It was also suggested that, if the Minister of Munitions and Supply agreed, the committee might consider the allocation of machine tools between the two countries and the extent to which machine tool production should be specialized.

23. Historical Reports on War Administration: War Production Board, Documentary Publication No. 2, *Minutes of the Council of the Office of Production Management December 21, 1940, to January 14, 1942,* February 18, 1941 (Washington: U.S. Government Printing Office, 1946), p. 5. This volume is cited hereinafter as *Minutes of the Council of the Office of Production Management.*

24. W. S. Knudsen to C. D. Howe, April 30, 1941. This letter is contained in an annex to the "History of the Material Coordinating Committee, 1941-1945," prepared by the War Production Board in November, 1945, but not published.

25. *Minutes of the Council of the Office of Production Management,* April 29, 1941, pp. 15-16.

26. C. D. Howe to W. S. Knudsen, May 1, 1941, "History of the Material Coordinating Committee, 1941-1945," Annex II.

27. *New York Times,* May 15, 1941, p. 11.

28. This letter is quoted in "History of the Material Coordinating Committee, 1941-1945," p. 1. No date is given and it is stated that it was to W. S. Knudsen. It is likely, however, that it was addressed to E. R. Stettinius, Jr.

29. *New York Times,* May 15, 1941, p. 11.

30. U.S., Department of State, *Executive Agreement Series 228,* pp. 4-5.

31. *Ibid.*

32. P.C. 4500, June 20, 1941.

33. *Canada, House of Commons Journals,* No. 97, November 5, 1941, pp. 617-18.

34. The Canadian Section of the Committee was appointed by P.C. 8441, October 31, 1941.

35. *Canada, House of Commons Debates,* November 5, 1941, p. 4098.

36. P.C. 22, January 2, 1942.

37. The United States members were the Under-Secretary of the Navy, the Director of the Production Division of the Office of Production Management, the Under-Secretary of War, the Administrator of the Office of Lend-Lease Administration and the Vice-Chairman of the United States Maritime Commission. The Canadian members were three Directors-General of the Department of Muni-

tions and Supply in charge of the Chemicals and Explosives Branch, the Munitions Production Branch, and the Aircraft Production Branch respectively, together with the President of Wartime Merchant Shipping Limited and a senior official of the Department of Finance. The composition of the Canadian Section was changed somewhat by P.C. 10792, November 26, 1942, following a reorganization of the United States membership.

38. *New York Times,* December 23, 1941, p. 5.

39. *Ibid.*

40. *Canada, House of Commons Debates,* March 12, 1941, pp. 1456-7.

41. Section 3(b), *55 U.S. Statutes* 31; c. 11, Act of March 11. 1941.

42. *Canada, House of Commons Debates,* April 21, 1944, p. 2227.

43. *Second Report under the Act of March 11, 1941 (Lend-Lease Act)* (Washington: U.S. Government Printing Office, 1941), p. 7.

44. Foreign Exchange Control Board, *Report to the Minister of Finance, March, 1946,* p. 26. This report does not show any sales by War Supplies Limited in 1941. As F. A. Knox points out, "the Hyde Park procedures made no significant contribution to the solution of our dollar problem in 1941." He goes on to say, "As the difficulties and delays of that summer have not been revealed, it is hardly possible to do more than speculate about them." "Canada's Balance of International Payments, 1940-5," *Canadian Journal of Economics and Political Science,* August, 1947, p. 350. Some of the problems related to purchases by the United States in Canada are discussed in Chapter VIII which deals with trade barriers.

45. Foreign Exchange Control Board, *Report to the Minister of Finance, March, 1946,* p. 26.

46. See *Ibid.,* p. 20, and *Canada, House of Commons Debates,* April 21, 1944, p. 2227.

47. U.S., Congress, *Report on the First Year of Lend-Lease Operations,* House Document No. 661, (77th Cong., 2d sess.), Appendix IV (Washington: U.S. Government Printing Office, 1941), pp. 51-2.

48. *The Memoirs of Cordell Hull* (New York: Macmillan, 1948), II, p. 1614.

49. Canada, Treaty Series, 1942, No. 17, *Exchange of Notes (November 30, 1942) Between Canada and the United States of America Constituting an Agreement Respecting Post-war Economic Settlements in Force November 30, 1942* (Ottawa: King's Printer, 1944).

50. *Ibid.*

51. U.S., Congress, *Report on the First Year of Lend-Lease Operations,* pp. 51-2.

52. This Committee was created by Presidential letter on December 6, 1939, to represent the United States government in all questions relating to foreign procurement of military and naval supplies, materials, and equipment. The Committee was disbanded in accordance with a letter from the President to the Secretary of the Treasury dated April 14, 1941, as a result of the new machinery being established to handle lend-lease transactions.

53. E. R. Stettinius, *Lend-Lease: Weapon for Victory,* p. 51.

54. The radio broadcast, which was given on February 2, 1941, is quoted in W. L. M. King, *Canada at Britain's side* (Toronto: Macmillan, 1941), p. 207.

55. *New York Times,* May 18, 1941, p. 11.

56. Historical Reports on War Administration: War Production Board, Documentary Publication No. 4, *Minutes of the War Production Board, January 20, 1942, to October 9, 1945,* May 2, 1944 (Washington: U.S. Government Printing Office, 1946), p. 335. This document will be referred to as *Minutes of the War Production Board.*

CHAPTER III

THE ADMINISTRATIVE SETTING OF WARTIME SUPPLY AND PRICE CONTROLS

ONE of the important stimuli in shaping the Canadian economy during the war was the pattern of needs of the United Kingdom. In agriculture, finance, and war production, this stimulus was of primary importance. The maintenance of the flow of supplies to the United Kingdom originally necessitated the adoption of a wide range of controls and restrictions in Canada. At the same time, the mutual interdependence of the economies of Canada and the United States exerted a strong influence over the control measures which were adopted by Canada. The structure of controls in the United States developed mainly in response to the difficulties of meeting the enormous production goals with which the unprepared economy was suddenly faced. Because of Canada's heavy dependence on the United States for capital equipment and materials for the Canadian war production programme, it is natural that Canada should have been intimately concerned with the various devices used in the United States to control the allocation of materials and critical equipment. It will be the aim of the following three chapters to explore the inter-relations of controls over materials and end products in the two countries and to examine the practical consequences of the broad policy agreements of the two countries.

The present chapter will be devoted to a brief account of the agencies responsible for the wartime controls over raw materials and finished products. In Canada, the Department of Munitions and Supply and the Wartime Prices and Trade Board were primarily concerned with production and distribution controls throughout the war. In the United States, a number of control agencies existed at one time or another, culminating in the War Production Board. If the detailed negotiations which took place between the agencies of Canada and the United States are to be properly understood, it is necessary to describe the relationships of the agencies to each other and to view them within the overall administrative structure.

1. THE STRUCTURE OF CANADIAN CONTROLS

(a) *The Department of Munitions and Supply*

In the summer of 1939, certain unsatisfactory features of the procurement operations of the Department of National Defence led to the transfer of responsibility for military procurement to the Defence Purchasing

Board, created by the Defence Purchases, Profits Control and Financing
Act.[1] With the outbreak of war, it became evident that the severe restrictions imposed on the Defence Purchasing Board would hinder efficient
procurement and, as a result, a new body known as the War Supply Board
was established to replace the Defence Purchasing Board effective November 1, 1939.[2] During the special session of Parliament in September, 1939,
the Munitions and Supply Act[3] was passed, providing for the creation
of a Department of Munitions and Supply, which was, however, not to
materialize until formally proclaimed. The proclamation was issued on
April 9, 1940,[4] following some revisions of the legislation.[5] At first, the
Department of Munitions and Supply was solely a procurement agency.
The new department took over responsibility for the purchasing of military
needs from the War Supply Board. Apart from its procurement functions,
the Department of Munitions and Supply was also authorized to direct the
use of materials and facilities, an aspect of its work which became increasingly important as the war progressed. This function was exercised
mainly through a number of Controllers who were given extensive powers
of control over individual materials or groups of materials and products.
Not long after the Department began operations, a Timber Controller,[6]
Steel Controller,[7] Oil Controller,[8] and Metals Controller[9] were appointed.
The Wartime Industries Control Board, whose membership consisted of
the individual Controllers, was also established about this time to co-
ordinate the growing volume of regulatory actions.[10] As the tempo of
war production increased and the critical list of materials grew, more and
more Controllers were appointed.

Largely for administrative reasons, the Department of Munitions and
Supply made extensive use of wholly owned Crown companies as agencies
of control. These companies were organized under Section 6 (3) (a) of
the Department of Munitions and Supply Act and operated under agreements with the Minister of Munitions and Supply. Although the agreements were approved by the Governor-in-Council, these Crown companies
were quite distinct from statutory corporations created by Act of Parliament. The Minister of Munitions and Supply had absolute discretionary
authority over the Crown companies under him, although it was the practice to delegate rather wide responsibilities to them. This constituted an
administrative arrangement of great flexibility and had the advantage that
industrialists or businessmen familiar with industrial problems could be
appointed to managerial positions in these companies where they were more
or less free from the restrictive controls normally applying to government
business. Most of the original Crown companies were primarily engaged
in buying and selling critical commodities such as rubber, silk, and machine

tools. Such companies were usually given the sole power to purchase critical materials outside of Canada. As the war progressed, it became increasingly common to form companies to supervise and co-ordinate all or some aspects of a war production programme or to construct plants and produce munitions of a specialized type.

During the fall of 1940 and on later occasions, some consideration was given to the use of formal priorities as an instrument of control. It was evident that the system of preferential deliveries in the process of developing in the United States in 1940 would be extremely important for Canada. For example, the order-in-council which established the Wartime Requirements Board in the Department of Munitions and Supply noted that "it may be necessary shortly to formulate and promulgate rules and regulations to ensure that war needs in the order of their importance shall have priority over all other needs."[11] It was to be one of the functions of the Wartime Requirements Board to weigh the relative importance of various wartime projects in Canada. Several months after its establishment, the Wartime Requirements Board did produce an inclusive Plan in respect of Priorities which proposed the appointment of a Priorities Officer "to determine, whenever necessary, priorities of production, transport and delivery, and the amount, number, quantity or proportions of any munitions and/or supplies or of any specified article or articles to be made immediately accessible to the various purchasing agencies of His Majesty and to industries . . . ."[12] Even before this recommendation was made, in September, 1940, a Priorities Section of the Munitions Production Branch of the Department of Munitions and Supply had been created. On the basis of the recommendations of the Wartime Requirements Board, provision was made in February, 1941, for the appointment of a Director-General of Priorities who was also to serve as Priorities Officer.[13] Extensive powers were granted to the Priorities Officer to establish mandatory priorities in Canada, but, while extensive plans were discussed on several occasions, a formal system of domestic priority ratings was never established in Canada. The example of the United States may not have been a very enticing one. However, the powers of the Priorities Officer were invoked informally on many occasions to break production bottlenecks and to establish delivery schedules. Since a large proportion of Canadian munitions output was destined for the United Kingdom, an independent Canadian priorities system was not very sensible. Essentially, it was the responsibility of the United Kingdom to determine the priorities to be attached to its orders. The introduction of formal priorities by the Priorities Officer would have meant that the continual modifications, which are an inherent part of the system, would have had to be dictated by the United Kingdom. Clearly any attempt to force British orders into an unfamiliar pattern would have contributed little but confusion and delay.

Because of their mutual interests in procurement for the United Kingdom, the Department of Munitions and Supply and the British Supply Council in North America[14] quickly established working arrangements in both New York and Washington. Liaison was also established in the Department of Munitions and Supply with a number of different Ministries of the United Kingdom government in London. In view of the importance of Canadian procurement in the United States, the Washington office of the Department of Munitions and Supply quickly developed into a large and vigorous organization. Furthermore, the Crown company, War Supplies Limited, which had been created to handle purchases by the United States armed services in Canada, was an agency of the Department of Munitions and Supply and was an important adjunct of its Washington office. Since it was responsible for government procurement in the United States, it was natural that the Department of Munitions and Supply should have been intimately concerned with the controls exercised by means of priorities and allocations by various war agencies in the United States. Later, these controls were also to be the concern of the Wartime Prices and Trade Board which had primary responsibility for civilian supply problems.

(b) *The Wartime Prices and Trade Board*

Upon the outbreak of war in Europe, the Wartime Prices and Trade Board was established by order-in-council "to provide safeguards under war conditions against any undue enhancement in the prices of food, fuel and other necessaries of life, and to ensure an adequate supply and equitable distribution of such commodities."[15] The Board, which consisted of a number of senior civil servants, was responsible to the Minister of Labour for the first two years of its life and was then transferred to the Minister of Finance.[16] By the spring and summer of 1941 retail prices had begun to increase rapidly, and it was evident that price controls would have to be extended widely. Prior to this time, the Board had fixed maximum prices in only a few emergency situations of a temporary nature. A number of Administrators had been appointed in the fall of 1939 to deal with the supply and price problems for such commodities as wool, sugar, hides and leather, and coal, but, with a few exceptions, serious shortages of civilian goods had been temporary. In anticipation of a general deterioration in civilian supply, and of inflationary price movements, steps were taken in August, 1941, to expand the powers and functions of the Wartime Prices and Trade

Board. At about the same time, the responsibilities of the Wartime Industries Control Board were extended and the respective jurisdictions of the two Boards clarified.[17] There had been some division of responsibility for price control between the two Boards, but the new orders-in-council assigned complete authority in this field to the Wartime Prices and Trade Board. At the same time, any restrictions on the powers of the Wartime Prices and Trade Board implied by the clause in the original order-in-council limiting its jurisdiction to "food, fuel and other necessaries of life" were eliminated by the substitution of "goods and services." While the Wartime Industries Control Board was to be responsible for the supply and distribution of any materials required for war production, jurisdiction over the residuum of goods not specifically the responsibility of the Controllers of the Department of Munitions and Supply was assigned to the Wartime Prices and Trade Board. To minimize the problem of jurisdictional dispute, a *modus vivendi* was reached early in 1942 providing for the co-ordination of the work of the two Boards by making the Controllers of the Department of Munitions and Supply Administrators of the Wartime Prices and Trade Board in respect of their price control functions, and by appointing the Chairman of each Board a member of the other.

On October 18, 1941, the Prime Minister announced in a radio broadcast the introduction of a sweeping anti-inflation programme, the main feature of which was to be a general ceiling on prices to be administered by the Wartime Prices and Trade Board. The price ceiling was established by the Maximum Prices Regulations and went into effect on December 1, 1941.[18] At the same time, the additional powers required for the administration of the new price control regulations were established by the "Wartime Prices and Trade Regulations."[19]

Soon after the introduction of the price ceiling there was a rapid multiplication of the supply problems facing the Wartime Prices and Trade Board. For one thing, the maintenance of rigid price ceilings for imported goods in the face of rising import costs made subsidies for imports necessary and thus directed attention to the quantities of goods on which subsidies could be paid. More important was the fact that, with the entry of the United States into the war, there was a sharp decline in the proportion of the United States output of civilian goods, especially those containing critical materials, available for consumption by civilians in either the United States or Canada. By early 1942, the Wartime Prices and Trade Board was faced with difficulties in maintaining imports of civilian goods from the United States. The problems were similar to those encountered earlier by the Department of Munitions and Supply in connection with imports of machine tools and other equipment needed for war production.

During the early period of the overall price ceiling in Canada there was continual consultation with price control authorities in the United States on techniques and experience, and it was a matter of some importance for the Wartime Prices and Trade Board to keep fully informed of developments in the United States. As a result, the Wartime Prices and Trade Board appointed a Washington representative, the appointee serving incidentally as Financial Attaché of the Canadian Legation. The representation of the Board in Washington grew rapidly in 1942 in response to the growing importance of civilian supply problems. Price problems receded into the background and the bulk of the work of the Washington Division of the Wartime Prices and Trade Board, as it was later known, concerned the needs of Canada for civilian commodities in short supply.

The Wartime Prices and Trade Board in Washington, in accordance with the precedent set by the Department of Munitions and Supply, operated independently and was not subject to direction or control by the Canadian Legation or Embassy. However, since the head of the Wartime Prices and Trade Board in Washington was also a diplomatic official, close, if informal, contact was always maintained. Such contacts were much less close in the case of the Department of Munitions and Supply.

Many of the detailed negotiations with authorities in the United States were carried out by officials of the Wartime Prices and Trade Board and the Department of Munitions and Supply. The Canadians in the United States in the early part of the war were faced with a bewildering number of agencies whose inter-relations were not always clear. The next section of this chapter will be devoted to the organization and responsibilities of the War Production Board and its predecessor agencies, with whom the main agreements relating to production and distribution controls were worked out.

2. WAR AGENCIES IN THE UNITED STATES

In the interval between the two world wars, a limited amount of preparatory planning for war had been carried out in the United States by the Planning Branch of the War Department and the Joint Army and Navy Munitions Board. A master plan for the mobilization of the economy in the event of war was drawn up and revised on a number of occasions. The first Industrial Mobilization Plan was produced in 1931 and after a number of modifications a revised plan was ready by the spring of 1939. A War Resources Board, consisting of a few prominent industrialists and educationalists was appointed on August 9, 1939, to review the Industrial Mobilization Plan and to assist in drawing up concrete defence plans. The Board submitted a report to the President in the fall of 1939, but its perpetuation did not fit in with other administrative plans and late in November it was disbanded.

Partly in response to the threatening international situation, steps had been taken in the United States in the late 1930's to overhaul the administrative machinery of the executive branch of the government. The Reorganization Act of 1939 had authorized the creation of the Executive Office of the President to assist the President in dealing with administrative matters. An executive order issued in September, 1939, transferred the Bureau of the Budget, the National Resources Planning Board, the Office of Government Reports, the Liaison Office for Personnel Management, and the offices and advisory staff of the President to the Executive Office of the President and also provided for the creation of "such office for emergency management as the President shall determine."[20] Accordingly, in May, 1940, the President set up the Office for Emergency Management to co-ordinate the activities of new executive agencies.[21] Most of the wartime agencies which were created later were set up within the administrative framework of the Office for Emergency Management.

(a) *The Advisory Commission to the Council of National Defense*

The first important wartime agency concerned with economic problems was an exception. This was the Advisory Commission to the Council of National Defense. The Council of National Defense had been created by Act of Congress in 1916 and was responsible, among other things, for the "co-ordination of industries and resources for the national security and welfare."[22] The 1916 legislation designated as members of the council the Secretary of War, the Secretary of the Navy, the Secretary of the Interior, the Secretary of Agriculture, the Secretary of Commerce, and the Secretary of Labor. The act also stated that, on the recommendation of the Council of National Defense, the President could appoint an advisory commission of persons with special knowledge of some industry, public utility, natural resource, or persons who were otherwise qualified to investigate and recommend to the executive authorities techniques of mobilizing the economy in wartime. Since it did not involve any new appeal to Congress for legislative authority, it was decided by the Administration to reconstitute the Advisory Commission to the Council of National Defense. The necessary recommendation of the Council of National Defense was submitted to the President proposing the appointment of an Advisory Commission to deal specifically with the problems of industrial production, industrial materials, employment, farm products, price stabilization, trans-

portation, and consumer protection.[23]   Members of the Advisory Commission to the Council of National Defense with responsibility for these
fields were appointed by the President in late May or early June, 1940.
The Council of National Defense itself dropped into the background and
the members of the Advisory Commission assumed the responsibility for
planning defence preparations in their own fields.

By the time the Advisory Commission was established the impact of
military demands on the productive capacity of certain industries and on
the available supplies of some raw materials had begun to be felt in the
United States.   To ensure that the urgent needs of the armed services
would be met, Congress provided that domestic military orders could take
priority over civilian or export orders at the discretion of the President by
legislation approved June 28, 1940.[24]   The issuance of relative urgency
ratings for military supplies was entrusted to the Priorities Committee of
the Joint Army and Navy Munitions Board.[25]   The underlying theory was
that the strategic plans of the Army and Navy would determine the relative
urgency of different classes of munitions.   A Priorities Directive, subject
to periodic modification, was drawn up placing military requirements in
order of urgency, and Priorities Critical Lists were compiled covering
materials to which priority ratings could be applied.   In view of the rapid
growth of the military procurement programme in the summer of 1940, the
Priorities Directive was subject to continuous modification, and more
materials were added to the Priorities Critical List as the supply situation
became tighter.

Meanwhile, efforts were being made to prevent the disruption of
markets by introducing orderly methods of placing military contracts.   The
post of Co-ordinator of National Defense Purchases had been created in
the Procurement Division of the Treasury Department although, in effect,
the appointee served as a member of the Advisory Commission.[26]   The
Co-ordinator was an active proponent of the wider extension of preference
or priority ratings who believed that economy and effectiveness in the procurement of defence materials could best be promoted by a system of preferences supported by the voluntary co-operation of industry, an opinion
which was shared by the Army and Navy Munitions Board.   The proposal
was outlined in more detail in a memorandum prepared for submission to
the President by the Advisory Commission to the Council of National
Defense.   In part, the proposed scheme was to work in the following way:

Whenever a contracting officer of the Army or Navy, in placing a
contract for an item, believes it necessary to expedite procurement of the
item by arranging for preferential attention to it on the part of the contractor, he may assign a preference rating to the contract. . . .

The delivery date will be controlling. The preference rating will require that the order be given the indicated degree of precedence over other orders only if and to the extent that this may be necessary to assure delivery on the date specified. Under the supervision of the contracting officer or his inspector, a contractor may extend the preference ratings on his contract to the necessary subcontracts. . . .[27]

The initial decision of the Advisory Commission was to rely on voluntary priorities and not to attempt to enforce them legally. To assist in the administration of priorities, the Council of National Defense created a Priorities Board on October 18, 1940, consisting of several Commissioners and an Administrator of Priorities. The creation of this Board was approved by the President who turned over to it the discretionary powers assigned to the President by the Act of June 28, 1940.[28] Once the power to assign priorities had been thus formally delegated, the way was clear for the expansion of the priorities system.

As its name implies, the Advisory Commission to the Council of National Defense was not an operating agency, although almost immediately after its creation some of the Commissioners were required to take some action to control or direct production and materials. Nevertheless, the main function of the Commissioners was to build up a staff of experts and to formulate plans for dealing with defence production problems. By the fall of 1940 practical problems of shortages and rising prices were multiplying rapidly, although the administrative machinery of the Advisory Commission was not adequate to deal with them. The Commission had originally been designed to be a more or less independent group of advisers and, while it had acted as a policy-making group, it was not a suitable agency to administer the kind of controls which seemed to be called for. The rather loose administrative arrangements which existed during the régime of the Advisory Commission to the Council of National Defense were unsatisfactory in the face of the difficult problems of economic mobilization. Some realignment of responsibilities was essential.

(b) *The Office of Production Management*

After careful consideration of the political and administrative problems involved, the President created the Office of Production Management early in 1941, and turned over to it those divisions of the Advisory Commission to the Council of National Defense responsible for industrial production, industrial materials, and labour.[29] The new agency was made responsible for assuring an adequate supply of raw materials required for the defence production programme, and for assigning priorities to deliveries of materials. The executive order establishing the Office of

Production Management assigned administrative responsibility for the operations of the agency to a Director-General and an Associate Director-General, and provided that policy matters should be handled by a Council, consisting of the Director-General, the Associate Director-General, the Secretary of War, and the Secretary of the Navy. Subsequent regulations provided for the creation of a Division of Production, a Division of Purchases, and a Division of Priorities in the Office of Production Management.[30]

To clarify a certain diffusion of responsibility for priorities which had occurred, all priority powers were centralized in the Office of Production Management. The Division of Priorities was to be the operating arm, while the Priorities Board which had been carried over into the new agency was to deal with matters of policy. The system of priorities had two main aspects: the determination of ratings, and the issuance of priority certificates. The Army and Navy Munitions Board was responsible for fixing the relative urgency of items required for military purposes, while the Office of Production Management was to determine other priorities. Foreign military purchases were treated slightly differently and were required to bear the recommendation of the Interdepartmental Committee for the Coordination of Foreign and Domestic Military Purchases, usually called the President's Liaison Committee. After being cleared through these channels foreign orders would be formally rated by the Army and Navy Munitions Board. At the time of its establishment, however, the Office of Production Management was to be responsible for the issuance of all priority certificates, with the general guidance of the Priorities Board.

In mid-March, 1941, formal instructions were issued by the Army and Navy Munitions Board outlining in detail the priority powers which had been delegated to the Army and Navy by the Office of Production Management.[31] The terms of these instructions made it abundantly clear that the Office of Production Management was to retain final authority on all questions relating to priorities, although the Army and Navy Munitions Board was to be responsible for the administrative work involved in issuing preference ratings on items contained in the Priorities Critical List. From time to time there had been pressure to give the Army and Navy control over the priorities system, but with the creation of the Office of Production Management and the issuance of these instructions, the retention of priority powers in civilian hands was temporarily settled.[32]

The legislative delegation of authority to the President to assign priorities was incomplete. The Act of June 28, 1940, provided for priorities only on Army or Navy orders. Such priorities were legally enforceable, but the same did not apply to other priorities issued by the Office of

Production Management covering foreign orders, essential civilian needs, and plant expansion, all of which remained on a voluntary basis. It was, nevertheless, assumed by the Administration that the issuance of these other priority ratings was not in conflict with the intent of Congress and, in fact, many such priority orders were issued. Some doubt about the legality of these priorities remained and eventually action was taken by Congress to clarify the powers of the President by authorizing the establishment of priorities not only for Army and Navy orders, but also for the delivery of materials required to fill orders of any country whose defence was deemed vital to the defence of the United States, or to other defence contracts and sub-contracts. The Act also went on to stipulate:

Whenever the President is satisfied that the fulfilment of requirements for the defense of the United States will result in a shortage in the supply of any material for defense or for private account or for export, the President may allocate such material in such manner and to such extent as he shall deem necessary or appropriate in the public interest and to promote the national defense.[33]

This new legislation paved the way for the rapid expansion of the priorities system which was to take place during the next few months, and also made it clear that the President could allocate materials when necessary.

When the Office of Production Management was established, its major concern was defence production, the question of its responsibility for civilian production and supply being left in abeyance. In April, 1941, two remnants of the Advisory Commission to the Council of National Defense, the Price Stabilization Division and the Consumer Protection Division, were merged to form the Office of Price Administration and Civilian Supply. Among other things this new agency was authorized to:

Take all lawful steps necessary or appropriate in order (1) to prevent price spiralling, rising costs of living, profiteering, and inflation resulting from market conditions caused by diversion of large segments of the Nation's resources to the defense program, by interruptions to normal sources of supply, or by other influences growing out of the emergency; (2) to prevent speculative accumulation, withholding and hoarding of materials and commodities; (3) to stimulate provision of the necessary supply of materials and commodities required for civilian use, in such manner as not to conflict with the requirements of the War, Navy and other departments and agencies of the Government, and of foreign governments, for materials, articles and equipment needed for defense . . . ; and (4) after the satisfaction of military defense needs to provide, through the determination of policies and the formulation of plans, and programs, for the equitable distribution of the residual supply of such materials and commodities among competing civilian demands.[34]

There was theoretically at least a close link between the new agency and the Office of Production Management. The implementation of the programmes of the Office of Price Administration and Civilian Supply for the distribution of civilian goods was dependent on the priority powers of the Office of Production Management. This was not a happy administrative arrangement and for this and other reasons there was some friction between the two agencies.

During the summer of 1941, when the military production programme was expanding and the entry of the United States into the war appeared more imminent, there were inter-agency conflicts and bickering between the military and civilian groups over specific or general questions of responsibility and authority. This prompted a correspondent of the London *Economist* to report from Washington, "The atmosphere here in late July is a curious combination of *Midsummer Night's Dream* and *Walpurgisnacht*."[35]

(c) *The Supply Priorities and Allocations Board*

In an effort to resolve inter-agency conflicts and to centralize the consideration of allocations, the Supply Priorities and Allocations Board was created in the summer of 1941 as a policy-making body to co-ordinate the activities of all agencies concerned with the production and allocation of materials and to guide the operations of the Office of Production Management.[36] The membership of the Board was to consist of the Director-General and Associate Director-General of the Office of Production Management, the Secretary of War, the Secretary of the Navy, the special presidential assistant responsible for lend-lease, the Administrator of the Office of Price Administration and the Chairman of the Economic Defense Board, as well as an Executive Director appointed by the President. The Supply Priorities and Allocations Board was specifically required to ascertain civilian, military, and other needs for materials and commodities and to "determine policies and make regulations governing allocations and priorities with respect to the procurement, production, transmission, or transportation of materials, articles, power, fuel, and other commodities among military, economic defense, defense aid, civilian, and other major demands of the total defense program."[37] Under the new arrangement, the Office of Production Management was formally assigned the widened priority powers given to the President by the Act of May 31, 1941, and was to formulate plans for controlling and stimulating production subject to the guidance of the Supply Priorities and Allocations Board on matters of policy. The functions of the Priorities Board of the Office of Production Management were absorbed by the new agency.

At the same time, there was a shift in the responsibility for the civilian sector of the economy. The executive order creating the Supply Priorities and Allocations Board split off the Civilian Allocation Division of the Office of Price Administration and Civilian Supply and re-established it within the Office of Production Management as the Division of Civilian Supply. Shorn of its responsibilities for civilian supply, the old price and supply agency was re-christened the Office of Price Administration. The new Division of Civilian Supply was charged with the responsibility for formulating "plans and programs providing for the equitable distribution among competing civilian demands of the materials, articles, power, fuel, and other commodities made available by the Supply Priorities and Allocations Board for civilian use."[38] It was of some significance that the transfer separated and assigned to independent agencies the responsibility for price control and the responsibility for supply problems.

(d) *The War Production Board*

The next major step in administrative reorganization occurred in January, 1942, with the creation of the War Production Board.[39] The War Production Board itself was an inter-agency committee with consultative and advisory functions. All the executive authority of the agency was vested in the Chairman who had been delegated sweeping presidential powers and was to be responsible for the general direction of the war procurement and production programme, the determination of plans, policies, and procedures of all federal agencies relating to war procurement and production, and the allocation of materials and resources to particular purposes. The War Production Board was the direct lineal descendant of the Supply Priorities and Allocations Board and with a few exceptions, the membership was the same.

The power of the Chairman of the War Production Board to direct procurement by the Army and Navy involved a number of complex and delicate issues. While the Chairman of the War Production Board was not concerned with the kind of munitions required by the military agencies, the Army and Navy were required to determine their requirements for supplies and facilities and to keep the War Production Board continually informed of them. Whether the raw materials, facilities or components could be allocated to the military agencies was a matter to be determined by the Chairman of the War Production Board in the light of all competing demands. The power to assign priorities remained firmly in the hands of the War Production Board. In practice, the detailed work of assigning priority ratings had been delegated to the Army and Navy Munitions

Board which was naturally better equipped to assess the relative urgency of military requirements than any civilian agency, but these ratings were still to be determined in the light of policies and procedures approved by the Chairman of the War Production Board. Furthermore, the Army and Navy Munitions Board was to report to the President through the Chairman of the War Production Board. Originally, priorities were assigned only to items specified on the Priorities Critical List of the Army and Navy Munitions Board, but about the middle of February, 1942, the War Production Board directed that the Priorities Critical List be abolished.[40]

Since it was responsible for assuring the maintenance of a virile civilian economy, the War Production Board reaffirmed the functions of the Division of Civilian Supply which it had inherited from the Office of Production Management.[41] The Division of Civilian Supply was to formulate statements of anticipated civilian requirements for raw materials, finished goods and services, and, in general, to represent essential industry not engaged in war production. The policy of the agency was based on the view that the preservation of minimum civilian needs was a necessary condition for the achievement of maximum war output. The name of the Division of Civilian Supply was changed to the Office of Civilian Supply on July 8, 1942. On May 1, 1943, the Office of Civilian Requirements succeeded the Office of Civilian Supply.

On October 3, 1942, the President issued an executive order creating the Office of Economic Stabilization, an agency which was designed to co-ordinate the stabilization programme and to adjudicate differences between various agencies over policies and methods.[42] The functions of the Director of Economic Stabilization gradually broadened, and late in May, 1943, he was appointed Director of the Office of War Mobilization, a new agency created by executive order to exercise general supervision over domestic war production and the economy in general.[43] The functions of this agency were later absorbed by the Office of War Mobilization and Reconversion which was provided for in the War Mobilization Act of 1944.[44] Despite the importance of these agencies, they were concerned with broad policy problems and internal issues and their activities had little direct influence on Canada.

So far as Canada was concerned, the main features of the administrative structure of controls over production in the United States were stabilized with the establishment of the War Production Board. It was not until after the defeat of Germany and Japan that further major reorganizations were to occur. There was, however, a rather kaleidoscopic quality about the war agencies and super-agencies in the United States. Canadian officials who engineered various agreements on production and distribution controls with the United States before Pearl Harbor were faced with a rapid succession of agencies and internal shifts of responsibility, and, in general, with an unstable situation. This was in sharp contrast to the situation in Canada. In particular, there were great differences in the power vested in the executive arm of the government in the two countries, a factor which was to have an indirect but significant influence on their wartime economic relations.

3. A COMPARISON OF EXECUTIVE POWER AND PRICE CONTROLS

The various mobilization plans developed by the Army and Navy Munitions Board in the United States before the war were based on the supposition that the executive branch of the government would have ample grants of legislative authority to control and mobilize the economy. As things turned out, executive power was often inadequate to take eminently desirable administrative steps. Continual appeals had to be made to Congress for permissive legislation, and when the Congressional temper was uncertain, these appeals were often postponed or other expedients were resorted to. Moreover, the divided attitude of the country towards entry into the war made it inadvisable to move too quickly. After Pearl Harbor, the First and Second War Powers Acts did strengthen the hand of the President, but by this time, much of the wartime administrative machinery was in existence, in a rudimentary form at least. Despite the great presidential powers, Congress played a very active role and was able to exert a strong influence over the plans of the executive.

In Canada, in contrast, when war broke out the executive automatically was vested with plenary powers about which there was no doubt. The War Measures Act assigned extraordinary powers to the Governor-in-Council in the case of real or apprehended war, invasion or insurrection. This meant that emergency regulations having the force of law could be issued by the government concerning, among other things, "trading, exportation, importation, production and manufacture . . . appropriation, control, forfeiture and disposition of property and the use thereof."[45] This covered a rather wide field.

One outstanding feature of the Canadian wartime administrative structure was the extent to which responsibility continued to rest with the Cabinet and its committees. Ultimate responsibility could not be delegated, in the nature of things, with the result that it was possible to achieve an internally consistent control programme. The fact that it was not necessary to appeal to Parliament for legislative authorization to impose controls was also of great importance in facilitating speedy action.

On the other hand, the United States Cabinet lacked both authority and unanimity. Executive powers delegated by the President tended to overlap in many cases and inter-agency and inter-departmental rivalry became acute at different times. Conflicts could be resolved by an appeal to the President, but the inherent complexity of the problems meant that new issues were bound to arise. There was also continual pressure for the tempering or modification of policies to conform to Congressional attitudes.

Government attempts to control prices throw an interesting sidelight on the differences in administrative powers in the two countries. For this and other reasons, the effectiveness of price control varied and commodity prices in general increased faster in the United States than in Canada. An indication of the divergent course of prices can be obtained from the following comparison of the official cost-of-living indexes in the two countries for both of which January, 1940=100 :[46]

		Canada	United States
1940	January	100.0	100.0
	April	100.8	100.4
	July	101.7	100.8
	October	103.1	100.7
1941	January	104.3	101.3
	April	104.6	102.7
	July	107.8	105.8
	October	111.3	109.8
1942	January	111.2	112.6
	April	111.6	115.7
	July	113.6	117.6
	October	113.5	119.6

The dangers of inflationary price movements became clear during 1941 and action was taken in both countries to develop methods of holding down prices. In Canada, the Wartime Prices and Trade Board had been in existence since September, 1939, and had been given ample power to control prices of commodities which affected the cost of living. In August, 1941, the Board was reconstituted and strengthened in order to deal with inflationary pressures which were becoming apparent. In contrast, the Office of Price Administration, which came into existence about two weeks later, had quite inadequate authority to control prices. A concerted effort was made to enlist the voluntary co-operation of industry in keeping prices down, but there were no real penalties for ignoring such requests. In the period prior to Pearl Harbor it was considered that selective price control would be adequate in the United States, and Congress was asked to enact legislation which would permit such price fixing. A bill was submitted on July 30, 1941, and the House of Representatives proceeded to consider the proposals over the next several months. From this preliminary consideration, it became clear that the major issues in such legislation revolved around the failure of the bill to provide for wage controls and the levels at which the prices of agricultural products could be fixed. The bill was passed by the House of Representatives shortly before the entry of the United States into the war and incorporated certain features designed to protect the level of agricultural prices. When the bill was under consideration by the Senate there was very strong pressure from farm groups for even more liberal safeguards for farm prices. When the bill, known as the Emergency Price Control Act of 1942, was passed in January, it confirmed and approved the existence of the Office of Price Administration and authorized the Price Administrator to fix ceiling prices which were fair and equitable and which took due account of prices existing in the period October 1 to October 15, 1941. The powers of the Price Administrator to fix the prices of agricultural commodities was restricted by the Act, which stated that such price ceilings were not to be less than the highest of the following prices: (a) 110 per cent of parity or a comparable price; (b) the market price on October 1, 1941; (c) the market price on December 15, 1941; (d) the average price in the period July 1, 1919 to June 30, 1929. These special restrictions were designed to make the price ceilings for many of the most important agricultural commodities higher than they would have been if a uniform base period had been used. At about the same time that this price control legislation was first submitted to Congress in the United States, consideration was being given in Canada to the adoption of more rigorous price controls. In particular, the device of an overall price ceiling, which was enthusiastically advocated by Mr. Bernard Baruch, was being planned by the summer of 1941. Following the transfer of the Wartime Prices and Trade Board from the jurisdiction of the Minister of Labour to that of the Minister of Finance and a widening of the powers of the Board, the principle of a general price ceiling was officially approved in mid-October and announced by the Prime Minister on October 18, 1941. Canadian price controls were embodied in the Maximum Prices Regulations, effective December 1, 1941, which stated that the highest price at which any goods or certain specified services could be sold was the maximum price in the base period, September 15 to October 11, 1941. The essential effect of these regulations was to freeze prices at their levels in the base period.

The Canadian experience in the administration of this programme was naturally of keen interest to the Office of Price Administration. Arrangements were made for the assignment of an observer from the Office of Price Administration to Ottawa and there were detailed exchanges of information on the subject of price controls. With the intensification of the war effort in the United States in early 1942 and the concurrent rapid increase in prices, it became clear that a more vigorous anti-inflation campaign was essential. This was emphasized by the President in a seven-point plan for the stabilization of the cost of living which was presented to Congress on April 27, 1942. On the following day, the Office of Price Administration issued the General Maximum Prices Regulation, which imposed an overall price ceiling similar to that in effect in Canada, although the base period in the United States was March, 1942. In addition, certain specific commodities were covered by separate regulations issued at the same time.

The maintenance of the price ceiling in the United States was handi-capped by the legislative exemption of a number of agricultural products from such price control. For example, the prices of eggs, poultry, milk, flour, lambs and sheep could not be limited in this way, which meant in effect that stabilization of the cost of living was very difficult. The problem of the so-called "squeeze," resulting from the tendency of replacement costs to approach or even exceed retail ceilings also proved to be difficult to deal with in view of Congressional opposition to subsidies, a price control device which was rather widely used in Canada. By September, food prices had risen substantially and threatened the whole stabilization programme. Early in October, after considerable pressure from the President, Congress enacted the Stabilization Act of 1942[47] which modified the previous exemptions on agricultural products. It was at this time that the President created the Office of Economic Stabilization, one of whose main responsibilities was to iron out differences relating to the control of agricultural prices.

It will be evident from this account that there were serious administrative and jurisdictional obstacles in the way of establishing effective price control in the United States until late in 1942. While some of the same issues existed in Canada, they were never so important and, as a result, prices rose much more slowly in Canada. Before considering the effects of this difference in an illustrative case, cattle exports from Canada to the United States, some attention should be devoted to the policies of the two countries with respect to export prices.

Historically, exporters have often sold in foreign markets at prices below prevailing domestic levels. Often, too, this practice has been actively encouraged by governments. However, with the development of acute shortages during the war, foreign demand for many commodities was inflated and offering prices correspondingly high. This was particularly true in Latin America during the war when importers were often willing to pay extremely high prices for goods from the United States or Canada. This whole issue was discussed at the Inter-American Conference of Foreign Ministers in Rio de Janeiro in January, 1942, and the United States agreed to a resolution which recommended, in part, "that the American nations take measures to prevent commercial speculation from increasing export prices of basic and strategic products above the limits fixed for the respective domestic markets."[48] Accordingly, the United States issued the Maximum Export Price Regulation on April 25, 1942,[49] which established ceiling prices for exports. Apart from contributing to international price stability, this regulation eliminated the inequities which arise when certain sellers are able to obtain premium prices on export sales.

There was some discussion of the issues involved in export price control between the Wartime Prices and Trade Board and the Office of Price Administration, and it was made clear that Canada did not intend to impose ceilings on export prices. Partly, this was because the volume of commercial exports from Canada to countries other than the United States was relatively small, and exports to the United States would be covered by domestic ceilings established by the Office of Price Administration. The fact that price ceilings in the United States were generally higher than in Canada, in conjunction with the Canadian decision to leave export prices uncontrolled, was to have a profound effect on the economic relations between the two countries during the war. The superior attractiveness of the United States markets tended to lead to excessive exports in the sense that commodities urgently needed in Canada were drained off to the United States. This general problem will be dealt with on numerous occasions in later chapters, but it may be worthwhile to cite the case of cattle exports as an illustration.

One of the tariff concessions granted to Canada by the United States as a result of the trade agreements made under the auspices of the Trade Agreements Act of 1934 permitted the entry of quarterly quotas of live cattle from Canada. This was of some importance early in the war when Canadian beef shipments to the United Kingdom were suspended temporarily. Surplus Canadian cattle were shipped to the United States and, since there was a differential increase in United States prices, this was a very attractive market. At the same time that exports to the United States were rising domestic demand was increasing in Canada. In part, this arose from the heavy requirements of the armed services and the expansion in civilian consumption resulting from higher family incomes. There was evidence of a meat shortage in the spring of 1942 when Canadian cattle exporters quickly filled the quota on exports to the United States for the second quarter of the year. There were also indications that cattle were being held off the domestic market in the hope that they could be shipped to the United States once the next quarterly quota became available. Not only was the orderly flow of cattle to the market being disrupted, but the maintenance of retail ceilings on beef was becoming difficult in the face of rising prices for cattle. At the end of May, 1942, the Wartime Prices and Trade Board announced that steps were to be taken to restrict cattle exports to the United States beginning July 1 when quota shipments were scheduled to start again.

The method of control was to have a Crown company, Wartime Food Corporation, purchase Canadian cattle at United States prices up to the amount of the quota. The Corporation could then divert any of these cattle to the domestic market if needed and the surplus, if any, would be available for shipment to the United States. The effect of this action was to suspend cattle exports to the United States almost completely. This fact is apparent from the following figures which show quarterly exports in 1942 and annual exports of cattle (excluding dairy cattle) for the other years in the period of 1940-46.[50]

1940		207,098
1941		221,450
1942	1st quarter	58,452
	2nd quarter	81,258
	3rd quarter	37,805
	4th quarter	797
1943		1,929
1944		1,168
1945		2,071
1946		1,346

At a later date in the war, beef shipments to the United Kingdom were resumed under contracts with the Ministry of Food. One part of the agreements was that the United Kingdom would purchase all surplus Canadian beef. The net result was that Canada effectively ceased to export cattle to the United States from the middle of 1942 on and even when the supply situation became much easier later in the war any available surplus was diverted to the United Kingdom. The case of cattle is merely an example of a situation which developed in connection with many Canadian exports to the United States. Usually the basic ingredients were a differentially high price in the United States, a formal or informal commitment to fill the needs of the United Kingdom or other Empire markets and domestic shortages of varying seriousness. Action to restrict exports to the United States was usually unavoidable under such circumstances although it sometimes appeared to commentators in the United States that such restrictions conflicted with the general policy of economic co-operation.

Part of these difficulties may be indirectly attributed to differences in the concentration of executive power in the two countries which resulted in less effective price control in the United States, particularly for agricultural products. There was one other point of difference that was of some importance. This was the existence of a high degree of fluidity in administrative agencies in the United States. From the Canadian point of view, the divided authority and the shifts in power which occurred meant that it was essential not to become too closely dependent on any one group or agency. It was also the case that over-generous concessions to Canada by government agencies in the United States, or Canadian domestic actions which attracted critical public attention in the United States might lead to a modification of the policy towards Canada and thus to some lessening of the benefits of mutual co-operation between the two countries. The handicaps which might have resulted will be more obvious after the specific co-operative agreements and concessions are examined in the following chapters.

REFERENCES FOR CHAPTER III

1. *Statutes of Canada*, 3 Geo. VI, c. 42 (1939).
2. P.C. 2696, September 15, 1939.
3. *Statutes of Canada*, 3 Geo. VI, c. 3 (1939, 2d sess.).
4. P.C. 1435, April 9, 1940.
5. *Statutes of Canada*, 4 Geo. VI, c. 31 (1940).
6. P.C. 2716, June 24, 1940.
7. P.C. 2742, June 24, 1940.
8. P.C. 2818, June 28, 1940.
9. P.C. 3187, July 15, 1940.
10. P.C. 2715, June 24, 1940.
11. P.C. 6601, November 16, 1940.
12. P.C. 1169, February 20, 1941.
13. P.C. 17/1327, February 22, 1941, effective February 12, 1941.
14. The British Supply Council in North America was a rather loose-jointed organization of purchasing and technical missions in the United States formed on December 12, 1940.
15. P.C. 2516, September 3, 1939.
16. P.C. 6332, August 14, 1941.
17. P.C. 6834 of August 28, 1941, dealt with the Wartime Prices and Trade Board and P.C. 6835 of August 29, 1941, with the Wartime Industries Control Board.
18. P.C. 8527, November 1, 1941.
19. P.C. 8528, November 1, 1941.
20. Executive Order 8428, September 8, 1939, 4 *Federal Register* 3864.
21. Administrative Order of the President, May 25, 1940, 3 CFR Cum. Supp., p. 1320.
22. *39 U.S. Statutes* 649; c. 418, Act of August 29, 1916.
23. Rules and Regulations of the Council of National Defense, May 29, 1940, 5 *Federal Register* 2114.
24. *54 U.S. Statutes* 676; c. 440, Act of June 28, 1940. The Presidential power to compel the acceptance of domestic military orders and to assign priority to them

was later strengthened by section 9 of the Selective Service and Training Act, *54 U.S. Statutes* 885; c. 720, Act of September 16, 1940.

25. The Joint Army and Navy Munitions Board was established in 1922 as a result of an agreement between the Secretary of War and the Secretary of the Navy to co-ordinate military procurement. Its membership consisted of the Assistant Secretary of War, the Assistant Secretary of the Navy and three officers from each arm of the services. In accordance with the usual practice, the Board will hereafter be referred to as the Army and Navy Munitions Board. The Priorities Committee of the Army and Navy Munitions Board was created on June 17, 1940.

26. The position was created by an order of the Council of National Defense, approved June 27, 1940, 5 *Federal Register* 2446.

27. Historical Reports on War Administration: War Production Board, Documentary Publication No. 1, *Minutes of the Advisory Commission to the Council of National Defense June 12, 1940 to October 22, 1941*, August 28, 1940 (Washington: U.S. Government Printing Office, 1946), p. 77. Hereinafter cited as *Minutes of the Advisory Commission to the Council of National Defense.*

28. Executive Order 8572, October 21, 1940, 5 *Federal Register* 4199.

29. Executive Order 8629, January 7, 1941, 6 *Federal Register* 191.

30. Office of Production Management, Regulation No. 1, March 7, 1941, 6 *Federal Register* 1595; Regulation No. 2, March 7, 1941, 6 *Federal Register* 1595; Regulation No. 3, March 8, 1941, 6 *Federal Register* 1596.

31. Memorandum, Priorities Instructions, to Supply Arms and Services of the Army and Bureaus and Offices of the Navy Department from the Under-Secretary of War and the Under-Secretary of the Navy, March 15, 1941.

32. For example, plans were made at the time the Selective Service Bill was before Congress to include an amendment giving the Army and Navy authority to fix their own priorities. *Minutes of the Advisory Commission to the Council of National Defense*, September 4, 1940, p. 80.

33. *55 U.S. Statutes* 236; c. 157, Act of May 31, 1941.

34. Executive Order 8734, April 11, 1941, 6 *Federal Register* 1917.

35. "America's War Economy," *The Economist*, August 16, 1941, p. 99.

36. Executive Order 8875, August 28, 1941, 6 *Federal Register* 4484.

37. *Ibid.*

38. *Ibid.*

39. Executive Order 9024, January 16, 1942, 7 *Federal Register* 329. There was a brief interval when the War Production Board was supposed to have supervisory powers over the Office of Production Management but the new agency absorbed the Office of Production Management by authority of Executive Order 9040, January 24, 1942, 7 *Federal Register* 527.

40. War Production Board, Priorities Regulation 6, 7 *Federal Register* 945.

41. War Production Board, General Administrative Order 17, March 3, 1942.

42. Executive Order 9250, October 3, 1942, 7 *Federal Register* 7871.

43. Executive Order 9347, May 27, 1943, 8 *Federal Register* 7207.

44. *58 U.S. Statutes* 785; c. 480, Act of October 3, 1944.

45. *Revised Statutes of Canada*, 1927, c. 206, Sec. 3.

46. Dominion Bureau of Statistics, *Prices and Price Indexes. 1913-43* (Ottawa: King's Printer, 1945), *Prices and Price Indexes, 1913-40* (Ottawa, 1942); Dominion Bureau of Statistics, *Cost-of-living Index Numbers for Canada, 1913-46* (Ottawa, 1947).

47. *56 U.S. Statutes* 765, c. 578, Act of October 2, 1942.

48. *New York Times*, January 17, 1942, p. 1.

49. Maximum Export Price Regulation, April 25, 1942, 7 *Federal Register* 3096.

50. The figures on cattle exports are taken from the annual and quarterly publications of the Dominion Bureau of Statistics *Trade of Canada*, and include "cattle n.o.p." of all weights, classes which exclude dairy cattle. In the period 1943-6, the vast majority of the shipments were cattle weighing less than 200 pounds.

CHAPTER IV

THE BEGINNINGS OF CANADIAN PARTICIPATION IN THE UNITED STATES SYSTEM OF PRIORITIES

THE gradual adoption of an almost universal system of priorities in the United States raised a number of serious and unprecedented problems for Canada. The main issue was the relative status of the military and industrial requirements of the two countries in the preferential system which was adopted. It became finally a general rule to accord Canada complete parity of treatment with the United States. The elimination of major and minor obstacles to parity is one of the most striking examples of the co-operative measures which were taken by the two countries during the war.

Essentially, a priorities system is a simple method of controlling the flow of materials and finished products. Certain priority ratings, presumably based on military necessity, are assigned to different munitions in such a way that those most urgently needed will be produced first. So long as the volume of production covered by priorities is relatively small, the mechanism will probably achieve its aim. However, once the issuance of priorities reaches a certain level, the value of a rating is apt to deteriorate in a kind of inflationary process. This is precisely what happened in the United States and the attempts to shore up the priorities system led to the introduction of increasingly complex administrative control devices which involved priorities, allocations, directives, and various combinations of these. Not the least of the Canadian difficulty with the whole priorities system was to understand it. Modifications were introduced rapidly as the simple priorities system began to break down and each change involved new elements of jargon often baffling to the Canadian industrialist. The following long quotation, taken from an official United States government publication, may help to clarify the kinds of controls over materials which were adopted. There were, according to this source, the following major elements in the system of materials control introduced by the Office of Production Management and supplemented by the War Production Board:

I. *Prohibitions*

(a) Materials orders prohibiting the use of scarce materials in the manufacture of given articles, such as chrome in auto trim or baby carriages. About 400 of these were issued during the war, the bulk of them in 1942.

(b) Limitation orders which limited or prohibited the manufacture or use of specified articles except on military contracts. About 350 limitation orders were issued during the war, most of them in 1942.

(c) Inventory limitation orders.

II. *Priorities*

Priorities were general instructions to producers and dealers requiring them to fill orders bearing a higher rating before they fill orders of a lower rating. In any industrial queue, those with priorities went directly to the head of the line, no matter how many others were there ahead of them.

The system started in the summer of 1940, when special military orders were given priorities, and the Army-Navy Munitions Board issued a "critical list." This was extended in March, 1941, by Priority Administrative Order No. 1 issued by OPM. The first priorities were simply A, B, and C, each letter with 10 sub-divisions, which took precedence in that order. As soon as the A's began to crowd each other in some factories, new systems of lettering came in with A-1-a, etc., and finally AA's and AAA's.

III. *Allocations*

Allocations were used as the basis of control where the entire supply of a commodity like copper or wood pulp was brought under accounting control by the War Production Board and was completely budgeted on a time and quantity basis, and withdrawals for any purpose were prohibited except in accordance with a WPB authorization.

IV. *Apportionment*

Apportionment was used as the basis of control where the WPB in effect took direct ownership of a specified commodity, like crude rubber, and issued the material to specific manufacturers as required.

V. *Order Board (Delivery) Control*

In some individual factories, WPB reviewed orders on hand, cancelled or rearranged deliveries; determined in what order things would be manufactured or delivered.

VI. *Scheduling*

In "scheduling," WPB worked directly with the management to get out required production on a timetable, arranging to have required material and components on hand to meet the timetable.

VII. *Overriding Directives*

Specific orders to deliver a specific article or quantity of commodities at or during a given time in spite of all other orders or controls were known as "overriding directives." (Used for components for escort vessels, landing craft, to deal with unforeseen emergencies.)

VIII. *Integrated Control*

Finally, the effort was made to limit procurements by manufacturers of a selected list of critical materials to a quantity in balance to complete articles required on a balanced program basis. (Production requirements plan and later controlled materials plan.)

These eight types of production controls were developed step by step starting with I and II and ending up with VI, VII, and VIII. In the end, all eight were being used side by side, or layer on layer, though the major emphasis shifted from priorities (II) to integrated control, scheduling, and, in emergencies, to overriding directives (VI, VII, and VIII).[1]

1. THE TREATMENT OF CANADIAN PURCHASES OF MACHINE TOOLS IN THE UNITED STATES

When the tremendous military power of the Nazis was fully recognized in the spring of 1940, the conversion of Canadian industry to war became a matter of the utmost urgency. The immediate problem was to expand Canadian capacity for the production of a wide range of munitions. This expansion of capacity was necessarily dependent on the availability of machine tools, a large part of which had to be imported from the United States. Concurrently the tempo of war production was increasing in the United States, with the result that machine tool needs in that country rapidly multiplied. Since the problem of Canadian procurement of critical articles in the United States first arose in the case of machine tools, it is instructive to examine in some detail the treatment of Canadian purchases in the United States. The developments in the case of machine tools were important for two reasons: the essentiality of machine tools to the Canadian war production programmes, and the invaluable precedents which were established in the agreements reached by officials of the two governments.

The control of machine tools in Canada was in the hands of the Machine Tools Controller of the Department of Munitions and Supply, an office which had been created in August, 1940.[2] Control was exercised partly through Citadel Merchandising Company Limited, a Crown company which had been assigned control over the purchase of machine tools needed to fill government war contracts in Canada.[3] In June, 1940, following the French collapse, immediate action was taken by Citadel Merchandising Company Limited to secure for Canada a share of the tools which had been destined for shipment to France. Negotiations were carried on for a period of months and resulted in the diversion of a substantial number of French machine tools to Canada, at a time when they were badly needed.

In July, 1940, the dominant rôle which machine tools would play in the rearmament programme was recognized and a full-time representative of Citadel Merchandising Company Limited was sent to Washington. By that time, the Advisory Commission to the Council of National Defense had been functioning for several months, and had seen the necessity for some sort of control over machine tools. It was, therefore, essential for Canada to be fully informed of any developments in this direction in the United States. This was the first appointment of a permanent representative of a Canadian wartime agency in Washington, and the success of this early mission was to have a significant influence on the expansion of similar non-diplomatic representation during the war.

One of the first problems arose because of the imposition of export control over shipments of machine tools to Canada. This control was basically different from the distribution controls later adopted and formed part of the underlying problem of trade barriers which is discussed in detail in Chapter VIII.

As early as January 1, 1940, the Secretary of the Treasury was conferring informally with the machine tool industry to arrange for priority for orders placed by United States manufacturers of airplane engines.[4] In September, 1940, the first step was taken by the Advisory Commission to the Council of National Defense to direct the distribution of machine tools. A circular letter was sent to the machine tool industry on September 9, requesting preferential status for orders for machine tools covered by priority ratings issued by the Army and Navy Munitions Board. Since, at this time, priorities, except for domestic military orders, had no legal force, this was essentially a request for the voluntary co-operation of the industry.

Competition of domestic and foreign requirements for machine tools was meanwhile becoming intense, and, in October, a committee was established by the Advisory Commission to the Council of National Defense to review applications for the export of machine tools to British Commonwealth countries and to deal with the diversion of tools ordered by the United Kingdom to other users. The question of diversion arose as a result of the fact that the British Purchasing Commission had placed enormous orders in the United States which absorbed much of the capacity for certain types of machine tools. For example, during 1940 British and French orders for machine tools for export were valued at more than $100,000,000, while an additional $138,000,000 had been furnished to manufacturers in the United States for the purchase of tools for use in domestic plants.[5] When specific needs of the production programmes of the United States and Canada became urgent, it sometimes became desirable to divert equipment covered by these contracts. The Committee which reviewed these matters was known as the "Clearance Committee on British Machine Tools," and on it were represented the United States Army and Navy, the Advisory Commission to the Council of National Defense, the British Purchasing Commission, and the Canadian Machine Tools Controller.

After the Office of Production Management was created, the Committee was continued under its auspices and renamed the "British-American Allocation Committee." Finally, in August, 1941, when the need for export clearance had disappeared, the committee was disbanded and questions of diversion were handled in an informal manner. Through the medium of this Committee, it was possible to achieve remarkable success in protecting Canadian orders from diversion or deferment.

The status of Canadian orders under the developing priorities system was also safeguarded by the official action of wartime agencies in the United States. The first important instance of this kind arose at the beginning of November, 1940, when the Machine Tools Division of the Advisory Commission to the Council of National Defense requested all manufacturers of metal-working machinery not to defer or divert machine tools ordered by either the United Kingdom or Canada without official instructions from the Commission.[6] In effect, this meant that the Canadian position on production schedules was frozen.

The next important development was the issuance of a request at the end of January, 1941, by the Office of Production Management to all machine tool manufacturers not to fill any orders after the end of February unless they had been assigned an official priority rating.[7] This was again an appeal for the voluntary co-operation of the industry. It was also specifically stated that this request did not countermand the instructions issued in November that the relative place of British and Canadian orders was to be preserved.

The issuance of these instructions, despite their shaky legal status, brought to the fore the question of the relative priority to be assigned United States defence orders and comparable orders placed by the governments of the United Kingdom, Canada or other foreign countries. This question had arisen originally in January, 1940, when the Secretary of the Treasury, acting as chairman of the President's Liaison Committee, had appealed to the machine tool industry to give priority to the orders of manufacturers of airplane engines. At that time, the Secretary of the Treasury was quoted as saying in connection with airplanes: "Naturally we'll see that our own demands are met first. We've got to strike a balance. We've got to take care of air transport and our own army and navy first."[8] He was also supposed to have said that all foreign orders now booked would be filled in due time, but that priority of production and delivery would always be reserved for any United States Army, Navy or commercial aviation orders. By the fall of 1940, this was a far cry from the official policy of the Administration. Early in November, a few days after his re-election, President Roosevelt announced that deliveries of airplanes and war materials needed by the armed forces of the United Kingdom and Canada, and the United States, were to be divided "on a 50-50 basis."[9] This followed the news released by the Priorities Board of the Advisory Commission to the Council of National Defense that the British Purchasing Commission would be permitted to place orders for 12,000 airplanes in the United States. The President said that this rule-of-thumb had been determined as a result of recent applications by the United Kingdom and Canada for the delivery of certain kinds of munitions. It was made clear that the ruling was flexible and did not mean that all United States munitions output would be divided precisely in two parts, one for domestic use and one for export. The obvious implications of the rule were that foreign military demands were to be given a priority status roughly equivalent to domestic need, except perhaps in unusual cases. The significance of the President's statement was not lost in Canada where the Prime Minister referred to it before the House of Commons in the following words:

> The president's announcement . . . of the priorities being given to Britain and ourselves is only the most recent example of United States assistance magnanimously given to the United Kingdom and to Canada. Every member of the house will, I am sure, join with me in an expression of our appreciation and gratitude.[10]

The Administration clearly did not regard the developing priorities system as a means of establishing some absolute preference for the military needs of the United States. In order to obtain a formal ruling on the priorities status of foreign orders, the question was referred by the Director of Priorities to the heads of the Office of Production Management for a ruling. It was decided by the Director-General and approved by the Council of the Office of Production Management that foreign contracts for the production of war material which had been approved by the President's Liaison Committee were to receive priority ratings comparable to those assigned to similar domestic defence contracts.[11] The establishment of this policy was obviously a matter of importance for the Canadian war production programme. It was not long in bearing fruit.

On February 24, 1941, the Director of Priorities of the Office of Production Management issued another letter to machine tool makers prohibiting any further delivery of machine tools except to fill defence orders with a priority rating.[12] This was regarded as a mandatory instruction authorized under the Act of June 28, 1940, and the executive order creating the Office of Production Management.

In accordance with the policy of assigning equivalent priority ratings to British defence orders, which included Canadian orders, a supplementary letter of instruction was distributed by the Office of Production Management stating that orders for machine tools "to be used directly or indirectly in filling British defense orders shall be given the same priority status as that granted for a similar material to be used in, or in the making of, corresponding products for the Army and Navy."[13] This publicly clarified the status of Canadian purchases in the United States and meant, for example, that Canadian plants manufacturing anti-aircraft guns for shipment to the United Kingdom were entitled to the same priority ratings in purchasing machine tools as a United States manufacturer making similar equipment on Army or Navy contracts.

The moral, if not the legal, status of preference ratings for other than Army and Navy orders was bolstered appreciably in March, 1941, by the issuance of Regulation No. 3 of the Office of Production Management which authorized the Director of Priorities:

To assign or provide for the assignment of preference ratings to all contracts and sub contracts and material directly or indirectly necessary to the defense program; . . .

To establish preferences with respect to indirect defense material, and domestic and foreign material, pursuant to such agreement and co-operation as may be necessary. . . .[14]

The regulation was countersigned by the President and provided a stimulus for the issuance of more formal priority orders by the Office of Production Management, although the basic enabling legislation was still lacking.

Toward the end of March, 1941, the Office of Production Management consolidated certain earlier directives concerning machine tools in a formal order, General Preference Order E-1, which provided that all metal-working equipment must be delivered in accordance with preference ratings, and assigned an automatic rating of A-10 to defence orders. The inclusion of Canadian orders was made quite clear in the following section of the regulation:

Contracts or orders . . . for delivery of machine tools which are to enter directly or indirectly into the manufacture of any materials for the defense purposes of Great Britain or the British Empire, including Canada (hereinafter called "British Defense Orders") are hereby assigned the same preference rating status as that assigned to contracts of orders for machine tools entering into the manufacture of similar or corresponding material for the

Army or Navy. All British Defense Orders, which are not thus assigned a higher preference rating . . . are hereby assigned a preference rating of A-10. . . .[15]

By the summer of 1941, the effectiveness of priority ratings in the machine tool industry had begun to diminish. Many manufacturers were booked to capacity with orders bearing the highest priority rating. As a result, a new device was necessary to determine precedence of deliveries within the top priority band. This was accomplished by the issuance of Supplementary Order No. 1 to General Preference Order E-1, which provided that deliveries be scheduled in accordance with preference lists based on the urgency of the various production programmes of the United States armed services.[16] No such preference lists existed for Canadian contractors, but fortunately a clause of the supplementary order, which read as follows, offered more than adequate protection for Canadian orders:

Notwithstanding any other provision of this order, production and delivery schedules under contracts or orders which have heretofore been placed by Great Britain or by any part of the British Empire, including Canada, shall not be changed, pending further order or direction of the Priorities Division.[17]

This provision afforded something more than parity to Canadian orders. Orders of United States contractors which were low on the preference lists were set back seriously, while the Canadian position remained unimpaired. Although this favourable position was enjoyed for several months, it was clear that it could not last indefinitely. Arrangements were therefore made to include Canadian contractors in the Numerical Master Preference List which had been established.

Accordingly, at the end of January, 1942, the War Production Board issued a supplement to the Numerical Master Preference List containing the names of Canadian contractors and assigning them individually an urgency standing established by the Canadian authorities.[18] This re-established the parity of treatment of contractors in Canada and the United States.

The critical position of machine tools shortly after Pearl Harbor is illustrated by the attempts to attain continuous operation of machine tools in the United States. Canadian representatives in Washington were somewhat shocked to receive advice from the Army and Navy Munitions Board that Canadian priority certificates for critical machine tools would not be countersigned unless they bore a certified statement that all similar tools in the purchaser's plant were in operation twenty-four hours a day, including Sunday.[19] Canadian authorities were opposed to continuous operation on the grounds that it was inefficient in most cases, but recognized the ruling as something of a menace in view of the fact that over a million dollars worth of Canadian priority applications were pending at the time. After an argument lasting several weeks, it was finally agreed that it would be satisfactory to add the following escape clause to Canadian certifications: "except in those instances where for good reasons of which we have knowledge, it is impracticable to do so."[20]

The enormous foreign demand for machine tools was a heavy burden on the capacity of the industry in the United States and gave rise to recurrent problems. In October, 1941, the Director-General of the Office of Production Management reported that the United Kingdom had submitted requirements for 2,100 tools a month and the Union of Soviet Socialist Republics also wanted 1,200 tools a month. In order to protect domestic needs the Office of Production Management adopted a policy of limiting exports to 25 per cent of aggregate output and 25 per cent of any specific type of tool.[21] Despite this, the military agencies were clamouring for more rigorous controls. In the spring of 1942, the Army and Navy Munitions Board pressed for a revision of existing methods of controlling the distribution of machine tools. A number of different plans were considered and, finally, at the end of April, a proposal of the Army and Navy Munitions Board to set aside 75 per cent of the monthly output of machine tools for "service purchasers" was accepted by the War Production Board, which issued a revised regulation outlining the new distribution controls.[22] Service purchasers included United States military and quasi-military agencies and their prime contractors and sub-contractors. The remaining 25 per cent of the output was to go to "foreign" and "other" purchasers, the latter group specifically including Canadian rated orders not classed as service purchases.

At the time the revised system was originally proposed, it was planned that the allocation of machine tools for foreign purchasers would be assigned *en bloc* by the Machine Tools Subcommittee of the Requirements Committee to the Office of Lend-Lease Administration. Then, individual country allocations would be established on the recommendation of the Office of Lend-Lease Administration which would also be responsible for directing procurement.[23] Canada at once asked to be excluded from the foreign purchasers category. The Canadian objection to the proposal was that procurement through lend-lease channels was slow and cumbersome, and that the imposition of the financial controls inherent in lend-lease purchasing would impede the Canadian war production programme. It was agreed, after some discussion, not to class Canada as a foreign purchaser, but to treat Canadian needs in the same way as United States domestic requirements. This meant that Canadian requirements could be filled either from

the United States domestic pool, or in the case of Canadian contractors producing for the United States services, from the pool set aside for service purchasers.

The Canadian position was still not completely satisfactory. The remaining drawback was that, while orders of foreign purchasers had been assigned an automatic A-1-a priority rating, the ratings assignable to orders placed by "other" purchasers, usually domestic non-war contractors, were lower in many cases. The Canadian representatives appealed for treatment equivalent to that accorded foreign orders procured through lend-lease channels and, as a result, a regulation was issued by the War Production Board assigning a preference rating of A-1-a to all Canadian purchases of machine tools.[24]

From this review of the treatment of Canadian requirements for machine tools under the priorities and allocations systems which were developed in the United States, it is abundantly clear that Canada received comparable and sometimes preferred treatment in comparison to the domestic requirements of the United States. The same general situation applied with respect to diversions of machine tools, which was such a common device for dealing with an emergency situation. Although Canada purchased about 40,000 machine tools in the United States during the critical period from July 1, 1940, to July 1, 1943, in only seventeen cases were tools diverted without the concurrence of Canadian officials. In many cases, of course, it was possible to divert Canadian orders without hampering Canadian production, and every effort was made to co-operate with United States officials in arriving at a schedule of deliveries which would contribute most to a common effort. As a result, arbitrary diversion or interference with Canadian orders was minimized. Even at the time of Pearl Harbor, when there was great pressure to divert Canadian orders to United States projects, the Tools Section of the Office of Production Management was scrupulous in its treatment of Canadian orders and directed that no diversions would be permitted unless approved by the Council of the Office of Production Management.[25]

It must be emphasized that the favourable treatment of Canada was not automatic. The Canadian Machine Tools Controller was aware of the necessity of keeping the authorities in the United States fully informed of the Canadian situation and of carefully substantiating Canadian requirements. The maintenance of continuous personal contact and the development of intelligent and aggressive liaison in Washington were of outstanding importance in preserving favourable treatment for Canada in the midst of rapid shifts of power and successive revisions of the control regulations. Eternal vigilance was the price of parity.

The problems encountered in buying machine tools had a special character and, of course, their solution did not always apply to other procurement problems. A case of particular importance arose in connection with the extension of priority ratings to Canadian contractors.

2. THE APPLICABILITY OF PRIORITY RATINGS TO CANADIAN WAR INDUSTRY

It was evident that the establishment of a formal system of priorities on deliveries of munitions and related articles would have a marked effect on purchases in the United States by both the United Kingdom and Canada. Although the problem first became acute in connection with machine tools, priorities rapidly covered a wide field of industry and raised a number of complex questions concerning the place of Canadian industry in the new structure of controls.

Fortunately, in the summer of 1940, a representative of the Machine Tools Controller was in Washington and in a good position to assess the significance of the new developments. At his suggestion, negotiations were begun by the Department of Munitions and Supply to enable Canadian firms to use priority ratings in making purchases in the United States.

By degrees, the details of Canadian participation in the rudimentary priorities system were worked out and an agreement was reached that the Priorities Officer of the Department of Munitions and Supply would be responsible for the submission of priority requests, together with any required explanations or documentation. The request would be embodied in a special form used for foreign priority requests labelled "Permission to Negotiate Release," and submitted for approval by the appropriate Canadian official in Washington to the President's Liaison Committee. Once approved, the "PNR" form could be turned over to a supplier in the United States to facilitate the delivery of equipment or material.

Early in 1941, the United States Section of the newly constituted Priorities Branch of the Department of Munitions and Supply established an office in Washington under the wing of the British Supply Council in North America. This intimate association was natural since a major part of Canadian requirements in the United States stemmed from war contracts of the United Kingdom in Canada. Moreover, the Minister of Munitions and Supply was a member of the British Supply Council in North America, a fact which facilitated the establishment of working arrangements.

It was agreed that the Canadians and the British would make common cause, and request the same treatment under the United States regulations governing priorities. As a general rule, therefore, any rulings referring to "British defense orders" were understood to include Canadian orders. At this time, the official attitude was very sympathetic to the United Kingdom and there is no question that Canada benefited by sharing in the concessions which were granted to the British.

On the basis of the initial priorities legislation, the Army and Navy Munitions Board had been authorized to determine the relative urgency or priority rating of different types of munitions and equipment. Apart from this, the administrative work involved in the issuance of priority ratings on prime contracts, i.e., contracts placed directly by the United States Army or Navy, was delegated to the Priorities Committee of the Army and Navy Munitions Board by the Office of Production Management in the spring of 1941.[26] At approximately the same time, a member of the British Supply Council in North America was appointed to the Army and Navy Munitions Board to represent British and Canadian interests. This immediately gave the Canadians an official channel to the Priorities Committee and a means of suggesting amendments to the Priorities Directive and the Priorities Critical List which would solve specific Canadian procurement problems.

During the early part of 1941, the Canadian production programme was being hampered by the fact that priority ratings were not applicable to Canadian sub-contracts. This meant that, although a Canadian firm manufacturing military vehicles under contract to the Department of Munitions and Supply could use specified priority ratings to cover requirements from the United States, a sub-contractor making parts for the firm on a sub-contract was not entitled to this privilege. This was a serious handicap and an appeal was made to President Roosevelt to authorize the more general use of priority ratings in Canada. In April, 1941, the White House approved the assignment of priority ratings to all Canadian prime contracts as well as directly related sub-contracts. These prime contracts referred to contracts between the Department of Munitions and Supply and suppliers *either* in Canada or the United States. A special directive concerning priorities to be assigned to the British and Canadian orders was issued by the Army and Navy Munitions Board on April 4, 1941, setting forth the detailed procedure.[27] So far as items on the Priorities Critical List were concerned, the Priorities Committee of the Army and Navy Munitions Board was authorized to assign ratings to orders placed directly by the Department of Munitions and Supply, while contracting officers of the United States Army and Navy could issue priority ratings on items being procured by the United States armed services on behalf of Canada. Preference ratings and certificates for any items not on the Priorities Critical List were to be issued by the Priorities Division of the Office of

Production Management. It was further specified that the ratings were to be issued on form PD-5, specially designed for foreign government orders, or on form PD-3, normally applicable to Army and Navy orders, when the Canadian orders were placed by the United States military agencies. The priority rating assigned to a prime contract for items on the Priorities Critical List could be extended, subject to certain specific rules, to any purchases in the United States of materials or equipment needed to fulfil related sub-contracts. The quite remarkable feature of the rating procedure was that these United States priorities were assigned to contracts of the Department of Munitions and Supply with Canadian firms.[28] This was to take advantage of the fact that the rating of the prime contract was extensible to the related sub-contracts. Under these new arrangements, a steadily increasing flow of PD-5 forms began to move from the Priorities Branch of the Department of Munitions and Supply to the Canadian representatives in Washington for submission to the Army and Navy Munitions Board through the British Supply Council in North America. In practice, authority to recommend preference ratings on Canadian orders was delegated by the Army and Navy Munitions Board to the British Supply Council in North America, who re-delegated the authority to the Priorities Officer of the Department of Munitions and Supply. As a result, priority certificates arrived in Washington ready for signature by the appropriate official of the Army and Navy Munitions Board. The beneficial effects of the new arrangements on Canadian production schedules were felt immediately.

In May, 1941, in recognition of the growing importance of the priorities problem and other aspects of the procurement work of the Department of Munitions and Supply, a separate office was established in Washington, independent of the British agencies located there. The British no longer had the same direct interest in priority problems following the passage of the Lend-Lease Act but were represented by the Division of Defense Aid Reports[29] in negotiations with other United States agencies. Consequently, the Canadians made their own approaches to the Priorities Committee of the Army and Navy Munitions Board and by-passed the British representative.

By the late spring of 1941, considerable progress had been made in acquainting Canadian industry with the mysteries of the priorities system. The Canadian representatives in Washington were rapidly perfecting the technique of expediting applications for preference ratings or negotiating for new ratings. At that particular time, however, Canadian procurement continued to be hampered by the lack of *automatic* extensibility of priority ratings on prime contracts. In the United States, a rating assigned to a prime contract could be extended to related sub-contracts without further approval. Canadian contractors, however, required a new preference rating certificate for every individual order placed in the United States. An application for the first extension of a priority rating had to be applied for through the Department of Munitions and Supply in the same manner as the initial request for priority assistance on the original prime contract. While provision was made for the re-extension of ratings, if approved by certain British officials, this was only a minor convenience. The inability to extend preference ratings automatically was cumbersome and inefficient and involved a very heavy volume of paper work. For example, during October and November, 1941, applications for the extension of priority ratings (excluding re-extensions) were being submitted to the Washington office of the Department of Munitions and Supply at the rate of 2,000 a week.

The assignment of priority ratings by the Army and Navy Munitions Board was limited to materials or equipment on the Priorities Critical List, which covered items of direct military significance. However, by mid-1941, the priorities system was gradually being extended over a wide range of civilian products, especially those containing scarce metals. Formal arrangements had been made to secure priority assistance from the Office of Production Management for Canadian war contracts even when the items were not under the jurisdiction of the Army and Navy Munitions Board. The arrangements concerning the issuance of preference ratings for Canadian orders which were not specifically to fill war contracts were more informal. Until late in the spring of 1941, Canadians had been submitting the so-called "PNR" forms, together with supporting information, to obtain priority aid from the Office of Production Management. At that time, the PD-1 form was adopted, which became one of the basic documents of the whole priority system. This application form was used for rating orders for a wide range of miscellaneous capital goods. While no formal agreement was announced, Canadian priority applications of this type were dealt with as though they had originated in the United States.

The convenient arrangements for handling applications for individual items of capital equipment did not apply to priorities for new construction. Until the early summer of 1941, it was difficult to assess the impact of the munitions production programme on the economy of the United States. Once the size of the military programme was known, it was clear that all available resources and facilities would be needed and that facilities used for manufacturing civilian goods would have to be converted to the production of munitions. Under these circumstances, the channelling of scarce materials into an indiscriminate large-scale programme of plant expansion would delay the production of urgently needed finished munitions, a course which was opposed by high military officials.[30] Preferential assistance had been given by the Army and Navy Munitions Board to new construction projects intended solely for the production of munitions by assigning priority ratings to the construction project which were the same as those applying to the finished output of the plant. This technique, however, did not deal adequately with new construction required to expand non-munitions output.

The Office of Production Management began to issue priority ratings for new Canadian construction projects in July, 1941. Applications for priority ratings on projects involving the expansion of Canadian plants were made by the Department of Munitions and Supply to the Office of Production Management. These ratings were also applicable to related Canadian purchases in the United States, but application had to be made separately for each piece of equipment. The processing of project applications in the Office of Production Management was a slow, heart-breaking operation. The application itself involved the preparation of an exhaustive brief concerning the project and its essentiality. Originally, it often required more than a month to dispose of Canadian project applications, despite constant intercession and pressure from the Department of Munitions and Supply. In October, 1941, to make matters worse, the Office of Production Management decided that all Canadian project applications must be reviewed by the Economic Defense Board before a priority certificate could be issued. This extra clearance contributed little except delay, and by the end of the year, reference to the Economic Defense Board was dropped at the request of Canadian officials in Washington.[31] There were inherent difficulties involved in allocating resources between new construction and current output, difficulties which tended to grow with a swelling army's need for finished munitions. However, the problems involved in assigning priority ratings to construction projects were not specifically Canadian, but arose in the United States as well.

3. CANADIAN PARTICIPATION IN BLANKET PREFERENCE RATINGS

A project rating was a blanket rating, in the sense that the priority originally assigned could be applied to all critical materials or equipment required for the project. The use of blanket ratings became general with the issuance of a series of general preference rating orders or P-orders by the Office of Production Management. These orders usually applied to a whole industry, and permitted the firms in the industry to use a specified priority rating either for repairs or maintenance or for supplies needed for manufacturing or other purposes. For example, once the Office of Production Management had approved the participation of a particular manufacturer of farm machinery in the P-order governing farm machinery, he would be entitled to endorse any of his orders with some authorized and uniform priority rating. By the late summer of 1941, any firm which could not participate in these blanket preference rating orders was seriously handicapped.

The status of Canadian industry with respect to blanket preference rating orders was, in general, both unclear and unsatisfactory, and it required the most strenuous efforts during the fall of 1941 to remedy the situation. The first blanket preference rating orders to be extended to Canada referred to: (a) the construction and maintenance of freight cars; (b) the construction of locomotives; and (c) the maintenance of locomotives. The Canadian companies manufacturing railway rolling stock were all granted an automatic priority rating of A-3 under General Preference Rating Orders P-8,[32] P-20,[33] and P-21,[34] respectively. However, the benefits of General Preference Rating Order P-18-a,[35] respecting manufacturers of cutting tools, were extended to only one Canadian company, and it was later stated by the Office of Production Management that this concession was an error.

One consequence of the exclusion of Canadian firms was that manufacturers in the United States were appealing to the Canadian government to release the critical materials necessary to fill Canadian orders. Such releases would merely deplete the supply available in Canada and weaken the effectiveness of the priorities control of the Office of Production Management. It was agreed by representatives of the Department of Munitions and Supply and the Office of Production Management that such special allocations to United States manufacturers should not be made by Canada.

The issue of Canadian participation in blanket preference orders assumed serious proportions as a result of the issuance of Preference Rating Order P-22, which allowed twenty essential industries and services to use automatic priority ratings for materials for repair or maintenance.[36] This order referred to common carriers, fire and police services, educational institutions, farm machinery and equipment, food processing, highway maintenance, railroads, hospitals, clinics and sanatoria, communications, and other vital sectors of the economy. The Office of Production Management decided that Canada would be specifically excluded from the coverage of this order, presumably on the grounds that the extension of the order would lead to an undesirable increase of Canadian orders in the United States. This policy was confirmed by a formal interpretation of Preference Rating Order P-22 which stated: "This order does not assign a preference rating to deliveries of material which is to be used for the repair of property or equipment located outside the limits of the United States of America, its territories and possessions."[37]

Shortly after the issuance of P-22, the provisions in this order relating to mines were replaced by a new order dealing only with mines. The new blanket order, P-56, provided for the issuance of serial numbers to approved mines authorizing them to use specified ratings, but was worded in such a way that it applied only to mines in the United States.[38] Within a few days, however, the order was amended to permit the Director of Priorities to issue ratings to foreign mines when he saw fit.[39] Subsequently, certain specific mines in Canada producing base metals, coal, iron, gypsum, and asbestos were authorized to use blanket ratings under P-56. In the fall of 1941, Canadian companies were extended the full benefits of orders assigning blanket priority ratings to materials required for ship repairs, and to the requirements of ship chandlers. This order allowed the use of an A-2 rating for repair materials for inventory and an A-1-a rating for emergency repair materials. Clearly, in view of the importance of several Canadian ports as repair bases for the United Nations, the extension of these orders could hardly be regarded as a concession to Canada. These particular orders were not issued by the Office of Production Management, but by the United States Maritime Commission, which was using priority powers delegated to it by the Office of Production Management. Moreover, the arrangements were concluded by the Controller of Ship Repairs and Salvage of the Department of Munitions and Supply who was not concerned with the more general problem. The procedure for handling ship repairs therefore could not be regarded as a precedent for the general extension of blanket ratings.

Despite isolated examples of Canadian participation, the benefits of blanket preference rating orders were not generally granted to Canadian industry, with the result that it was extremely difficult to obtain essential maintenance and repair supplies as well as production materials. For example, despite the urging of Canadian officials, the use of blanket preference ratings was not granted to Canadian firms producing medium and heavy trucks or to Canadian manufacturers of agricultural implements.[40] Sometimes, the Office of Production Management insisted that, since the blanket preference orders did not specifically mention Canada, they must be interpreted as applying to the United States only. Furthermore, the Office of Production Management specifically stated that the inclusion of one Canadian company did not constitute a precedent for the inclusion of the whole industry; individual applications had to be considered on their merits. Often it took several months after the issuance of a P-order to arrange for the inclusion of a Canadian company, a delay which was a grave matter in view of the resultant disadvantage of Canadian industry in competing for scarce supplies.

The exclusion of most of Canadian industry from blanket priority privileges was a matter of serious concern to Canadian officials. In view of the rapid depreciation of priority ratings, the piecemeal determination of ratings, and the consequent burden of paper work and negotiation, Canadian procurement was being hampered, with noticeably bad effects on Canadian production in some industries.

After a period of unsuccessful negotiation, it was decided by the Canadian officials in Washington to press the Office of Production Management for a policy decision in a test case. The guinea pig was General Preference Rating Order P-18-a which assigned blanket ratings to manufacturers of metal cutting tools. A formal request was submitted to the Office of Production Management for the inclusion of the Canadian machine tool industry under the terms of this order. The Canadian proposal was also considered in other influential quarters. The Materials Co-ordinating Committee considered the general question at a meeting in November and after noting the undesirability of Canada making special allotments to United States manufacturers to fill Canadian orders, recommended the extension of blanket ratings to Canada. The matter was also referred to the Policy Committee of the Economic Defense Board which, late in November, 1941, signified concurrence in the Canadian proposal in a memorandum to the Director of Priorities of the Office of Production Management.[41] Anyone who expected an epochal policy decision as a result was disappointed, for the Director of Priorities merely wrote to the Chief of the Tools Section, Production Division of the Office of Production Management saying, in effect, that he favoured the inclusion of Canadian concerns in the terms of General Preference Rating Order P-18-a and could see no reason why they should not be included.[42] While the memorandum was distributed by Canadian officials to the chiefs of various commodity branches in the Office of Production Management in the hope that it would create the impression that the wished-for policy had been adopted, it did little more than create a precedent. Nevertheless, the Canadian officials felt that the Office of Production Management would henceforth be obligated to furnish specific reasons if further Canadian applications were refused.

The Department of Munitions and Supply continued to press the matter and finally it was agreed by the Director of Priorities that no objection would be raised to the extension of general preference rating orders to specific Canadian companies provided that the necessary steps would be taken to prevent the misuse of scarce materials obtained under general preference rating orders and that penalties for infractions of the regulations, similar to those in force in the United States, would be provided. The implication of this was that parallel limitations and restrictions on the use of critical materials would be enforced in both countries. The arrangement was confirmed formally by an exchange of letters between the Director of Priorities of the Office of Production Management and the Priorities Officer of the Department of Munitions and Supply around the beginning of 1942.

The condition that substantially the same controls over the use of critical materials were to be imposed in Canada as in the United States was again emphasized in a formal directive issued by the Director of Industry Operations of the War Production Board early in February, 1942, outlining the rules governing the extension of preference rating orders to Canada.[43] This directive stated that preference rating orders were not to apply automatically to Canadian industry; each Canadian firm was required to submit a specific application for inclusion to the War Production Board. It was made clear that preference ratings were not to be used to obtain material available in Canada from the United States. Provision was also made for the appointment of a Priorities Specialist to represent the War Production Board in Ottawa, who was to be responsible for the preliminary examination of PD-1 or the successor PD-1A certificates, originating in Canada. The Priorities Specialist was authorized to reject priority applications if the prospective use was judged to be non-essential or if the material required could be obtained in Canada. All Canadian applications were to be considered invalid unless they bore a legend to the effect that any Canadian user was to be subject to penalties set out in the Wartime Industries Control Board Regulations if he failed to comply with the terms of the relevant preference rating order or certificate or if he made a false statement on his application. It was further noted that preference rating orders issued in the future were to be worded in such a way that they were applicable to Canada as well as to the United States. An important illustration was an amendment to Preference Rating Order P-100, the order replacing Preference Rating Order P-22 and dealing with repair materials for certain essential public utilities and services. This amendment, issued in February, 1942, stated that the order was to be applicable to "any person located in the Dominion of Canada, to whom and in whose name a copy of this order is specifically issued."[44] While the goal of automatic inclusion of Canadian industry had not yet been reached, this was a long step forward.

The agreement providing for the inclusion of Canadian companies in blanket preference rating orders was a major development in the gradual process of eliminating barriers to Canadian participation in the benefits of the priorities system of the United States. The applicability of blanket preference rating orders to Canada was not the only problem in this field. Other aspects of the priorities system were causing Canadian officials a good deal of concern throughout the fall of 1941.

4. THE ACHIEVEMENT OF COMPLETE PARITY BY CANADIAN INDUSTRY

The coverage of the priorities system grew rapidly with the issuance by the Office of Production Management of the Defense Supplies Rating Order in May, 1941.[45] This new order provided for the use of priority ratings in purchasing "off-the-shelf" items which could be classed as "defense supplies." The order defined "defense supplies" as any materials, parts or assemblies required to fill contracts for material to be used: (a) by the Army or Navy; (b) for the defense of Great Britain; (c) as lend-lease supplies. Also included were any materials rated A-10 or higher, or any material to be used in manufacturing any of the foregoing. Any producer of "defense supplies" was authorized, subject to certain filing requirements, to apply a preference rating of A-10 to scarce materials required from a supplier. Such a rating was extensible in the sense that it could be passed on by suppliers and sub-suppliers. Of course, if the output of the original producer had been assigned a preference rating higher than A-10, the higher rating could be extended. In effect, this meant that all suppliers could rate their orders on the basis of the rating pattern of their customers. There were serious difficulties involved in including Canadian suppliers within the Defense Supplies Rating Plan. The main difficulty was that Canadian suppliers did not in general supply customers who had a well-defined rating pattern, although, as explained earlier, prime contracts of the Department of Munitions and Supply with Canadian firms were often rated to facilitate procurement of related supplies from the United States. Since the scheme was not legally applicable to Canada, suppliers in the United States tended to get whatever competitive advantage there was in using an A-10 rating while similar Canadian firms were not entitled to such a rating. In some cases, it is believed that Canadian firms were not aware of the fine points of the regulation and did, in fact, affix their own ratings to orders in the United States, a convenient if unorthodox solution to the problem. During the last half of 1941, a good deal of effort was devoted by Canadian officials to securing Canadian participation in the Defense Supplies Rating Plan, but these attempts were abandoned in December, 1941, when, with the announcement of the Production Requirements Plan, major revisions in the priorities system were in prospect.

By the fall of 1941, certain inadequacies of the priorities system were becoming painfully apparent, the main difficulty arising out of the large volume of rated orders which had grown up. Throughout the early months of 1942, the fraction of total output covered by the priorities system continued to expand rapidly. For example, the number of applications for priority assistance of all types slightly more than trebled between January and May, 1942. The monthly volume of applications submitted to the War Production Board for this period was as follows:

January	96,906
February	105,651
March	168,412
April	203,405
May	304,201[46]

The rapid growth of the outstanding volume of approved priority applications led to a correspondingly sharp depreciation of ratings. An A-10 rating became quite valueless once a sufficient number of A-1 priorities had been issued.

There had been an overall revision of the pattern of military priorities in August, 1941, but by early 1942, it was becoming clearer what the impact of a full-scale war production programme would be. Accordingly, in mid-February, 1941, the Army and Navy Munitions Board proposed a basic revision of the priority ratings for military programmes. It was hoped that this would permit military requirements to be co-ordinated with the needs for the indirect war and non-war sector of the economy. The Army and Navy Munitions Board, in this period, exercised control over military priorities, under authority delegated by the War Production Board. The suggestion of the Army and Navy Munitions Board was concurred in by the War Production Board and military planning staffs at various levels carried out an intensive study of the relative urgency of munitions which appeared to be required by the current strategic plans. It should be added that considerable anxiety was being evinced at about this time concerning the possibility of meeting urgent production objectives. On May 1, 1942, President Roosevelt wrote to the Chairman of the War Production Board expressing his concern and stating, in addition:

I have instructed the Joint Chiefs of Staff to issue the necessary directive to the Army and Navy Munitions Board so that it may revise and submit for your immediate consideration the proposed priorities and allocations of critical materials which will be in accord with the strategical objectives which they have presented and on which this letter is based. I know that your office will assist the Army and Navy Munitions Board in this revision and in approving the necessary changes without delay.[47]

The revised priorities directive of the Army and Navy Munitions Board, the details of which were made known on May 20, involved some basic changes in the priorities system. The directive proposed a new series of super-ratings consisting of four general classes: AA-1, AA-2, AA-3, and AA-4 to which was added an emergency rating of AAA. The AA-1 and AA-2 ratings were to be limited to urgently needed munitions while the balance of military production and the construction of new facilities for munitions production were to be assigned the AA-3 and AA-4 priorities. This new rating band replaced items in the old A-1-a category but referred exclusively to the military programmes of the United States Army and Navy. The directive explicitly stated that no other items were to be assigned the AA-priorities, nor should the military production programme be otherwise disturbed without the concurrence of the Army and Navy Munitions Board. The remarkable feature of the new scheme was that it provided no place among the new super-priorities for civilian requirements, including indirect military needs, nor for exports. Thus, both lend-lease and Canadian requirements were omitted from the new directive.

While there were a number of serious objections to the new priorities directive, it must be recalled that it was drawn up by the Army and Navy Munitions Board at the specific request of the President and that the jurisdiction of this Board did not extend to the excluded programmes. The War Production Board was strongly opposed to certain features of the re-rating plan and before its final issuance on June 12 it had been modified in some particulars which would allow merchant shipping and some civilian needs to be included in the AA-band. The fact that the President had sponsored the drastic action of the Army and Navy Munitions Board complicated what might have appeared to be a contest between military and civilian authorities.

The complex internal issues in the United States probably did not arouse much sympathy on the part of the Canadian officials responsible for war production, who were primarily interested in the fact that the Canadian munitions programme had been completely omitted from the new AA-ratings. The details of the proposed new directive on priorities became known to Canadian representatives in Washington a few days before a scheduled meeting of the Joint War Production Committee in Washington. The senior officials of the Department of Munitions and Supply representing Canada at the Committee meeting protested that the proposed directive would upset the Canadian production programme and could hardly be reconciled with the basic policy of co-operation which it had drawn up some months earlier. One account of the meeting states that the Canadian request for reconsideration was initially resisted but that after a dramatic interruption of the deliberations by an air-raid alarm, the representatives of the War Department agreed that the decision should be reconsidered and that Canada would not be discriminated against. There were, naturally enough, some heated Canadian objections to the United States proposal before it was modified in the course of the meeting. At this time, it was decided that the major or the strategic items in the Canadian military production programme would be assigned ratings in the AA-band comparable to those assigned to the military requirements of the United States. A catalogue showing the anticipated size of the Canadian munitions programme was presented to the Army and Navy Munitions Board shortly after this time and, once the pattern of priority ratings had been approved, immediate action was taken to assign new priority ratings to all Canadian contractors involved. The exclusion of all essential civilian requirements from the new priority ratings was obviously unsatisfactory and by August, the Army and Navy Munitions Board had concurred in the action of the Requirements Committee which authorized the use of a new AA-2X priority rating for essential civilian needs.[48] This rating was between AA-2 and AA-3 and was to be applicable to essential civilian orders originating in both Canada and the United States. The threat to parity for Canadian requirements, after looming large for a short period, rapidly disappeared.

In July, 1942, the War Production Board issued a regulation making it quite clear that Canadian military requirements were to be accorded precisely the same status as the military requirements of the United States, so far as the priorities system was concerned. The essential part of this regulation, which merely confirmed the existing situation, was as follows:

Whenever any order or regulation heretofore or hereafter issued by the Director of Industry Operations of the War Production Board (or the Director of Priorities of the Office of Production Management) regulates in any manner the production, delivery, sale or use of any material and includes specific provisions with reference to transactions with or for the account of one of the United States Government agencies listed below, or transactions related thereto, the corresponding Canadian agency or agencies named below shall be deemed to be included in such reference, unless such order or regulation specifically excludes the Canadian agency or agencies:

U.S. Agencies	Corresponding Canadian Agencies
U.S. Army or War Department	Canadian Army and Air Force
U.S. Navy or Navy Department	Canadian Navy
U.S. Maritime Commission	Wartime Merchant Shipping, Ltd.
	Trafalgar Shipbuilding Co., Ltd.[49]

At about the same time, the precise status of Canadian civilian industry with respect to the priorities system was again considered by the Department of Munitions and Supply and the War Production Board. These discussions resulted in an agreement that, unless a preference rating order specifically excluded Canada, it was to be assumed that Canadian participation had been authorized, subject only to the concurrence of the Deputy Director-General for Priorities Control of the War Production Board. Subject again to this minor proviso, it was clearly stated as a matter of policy that Canada could participate immediately upon application in any general preference rating order issued by the War Production Board. The procedure to be followed was outlined in a formal administrative circular issued by the War Production Board, which set forth in detail the terms and conditions of the agreement. The instructions also named the Canadian Priorities Review Division as the sole channel through which problems relating to priorities should flow both in Ottawa and Washington. Considerable attention was devoted to the technique of processing individual priority applications from Canada, all of which were to bear the recommendation of the Priorities Officer of the Department of Munitions and Supply and the concurrence of the Canadian Priorities Review Division. One significant proviso of the agreement on the semi-automatic extension of blanket preference ratings to Canada was that the Canadian authorities would take steps to eliminate any substantial differences in the control of scarce materials, enforcement and compliance.

On September 7, 1942, action was taken by the Chairman of the War Production Board to centralize the issuance of priorities and to revoke the priority powers of the armed services.[50] At this time, the War Production Board assumed complete control over the issuance of priority ratings. Previously, contracting officers of the United States Army and Navy acting on behalf of the Army and Navy Munitions Board had been authorized to grant priority ratings on military contracts. This had been one of the factors leading to the over-issuance of priority ratings and the inflationary developments which had endangered the whole system. Once the authority of the field officers of the Army and Navy to issue priority ratings had been revoked and reassigned to the regional representatives of the War Production Board, the Board was solely responsible for the operation of the priorities system. From the Canadian point of view, this development was of some significance. Previously, the power of United States Army and Navy field officers to assign ratings meant that Canadian military orders were sometimes relegated to lower priorities than military requirements of the United States. The centralization of control in civilian hands meant that uniform priorities would be maintained for the military requirement of the two countries.

By the summer of 1942, the place of Canadian industry in the priorities system of the United States was well defined. The extension of priority assistance to Canadian industry on substantially the same terms as industry in the United States was of great benefit to the Canadian war production programme. In some specific cases, parity of treatment was granted almost automatically, but serious difficulties were involved in the acceptance of parity as a matter of general policy. For the most part, the actions of war agencies in the United States were open-handed and generous but there were other cases which involved continual intercession by Canadian officials over a long period. For example, reference might again be made to the extension of blanket preference ratings to Canadian manufacturers of metal cutting tools. The original preference rating order was issued in the United States in mid-August, 1941, and the way was not cleared for Canadian participation in the order until December. One should not therefore gain the impression that equivalent treatment was automatically extended to Canada in all cases. Even when over-riding policy agreements concerning Canadian participation in the priorities system were reached, they were hedged with conditions concerning the comparability of controls in Canada and the United States. This particular issue assumed a good deal of importance at various times and it is worthwhile to examine in greater detail the precise agreements which were reached and their consequences.

REFERENCES FOR CHAPTER IV

1. Historical Reports on War Administration, Bureau of the Budget No. 1, *The United States at War* (Washington: U.S. Government Printing Office, 1946), pp. 117-19.

2. P.C. 4101, August 22, 1940.

3. Citadel Merchandising Company Limited was incorporated on May 17, 1940.

4. *New York Times,* February 2, 1940, p. 6.

5. E. R. Stettinius, *Lend-Lease: Weapon for Victory,* p. 23.

6. Letter from Mason Britton, Machine Tool Division, Advisory Commission to the Council of National Defense, to Metal Working Machinery Manufacturers, November 2, 1940.

7. Letter from the Director of Priorities, Office of Production Management, to Machine Tool Manufacturers, January 31, 1941.

8. *New York Times,* January 26, 1940, p. 10.

9. *Ibid.,* November 9, 1940, p. 1.

10. *Canada, House of Commons Debates,* November 12, 1940, p. 53.

11. *Minutes of the Council of the Office of Production Management,* January 31, 1941, p. 4.

12. *New York Times,* February 25, 1941, p. 12. A similar directive establishing mandatory priorities for aluminum was issued at the same time.

13. Letter, E. R. Stettinius, Jr., to Machine Tool Builders, February 27, 1941.

14. Office of Production Management, Regulation No. 3, March 8, 1941, 6 *Federal Register* 1596.

15. General Preference Order E-1, March 26, 1941, 6 *Federal Register* 1676. With minor variations, the same provisions were included in an order directing the distribution of aluminum issued about the same time. See General Preference Order M-1, March 21, 1941, 6 *Federal Register* 1598.

16. Supplementary Order No. 1 to General Preference Order E-1, July 7, 1941.

17. *Ibid.,* para. V.

18. Supplement No. 1 to Exhibit A of General Preference Order E-1-a, January 28, 1942.

19. Memorandum, E. B. White, Army and Navy Munitions Board, to J. J. D. Brunke, Department of Munitions and Supply, January 12, 1942.

20. Letter, Geoffrey Smith, War Production Board, to W. H. Hutchison, Citadel Merchandising Company Limited, January 30, 1942.

21. *Minutes of the Office of Production Management,* October 21, 1941, p. 68.

22. General Preference Order E-1-b, April 30, 1942, 7 *Federal Register* 3231.

23. This arrangement was in fact made by War Production Board Directive No. 4, May 14, 1942, 7 *Federal Register* 3710.

24. General Preference Order E-1-c, June 19, 1942, 7 *Federal Register* 4615.

25. Staff Directive, Albert M. Stedfast, Tools Section, Office of Production Management, December 22, 1941.

26. Office of Production Management, Priorities Division Administrative Order No. 1, March 17, 1941.

27. Directive from the Army and Navy Munitions Board to the Supply Arms and Services of the Army and Bureaus and Offices of the Navy, April 4, 1941.

28. Priority certificates issued for Canadian prime contracts bore a notation to the effect that the priority ratings applied only to directly related sub-contracts or orders placed in the United States. Nevertheless, it seems likely that these ratings may have had a perceptible, if unofficial influence on Canadian suppliers.

29. The Division of Defense Aid Reports was created by executive order on May 2, 1941, and was responsible for co-ordinating, clearing and processing lend-lease requests. Executive Order 8875, May 2, 1941, 6 *Federal Register* 2301.

30. Letters from the Secretary of War and the Under Secretary of the Navy to the Director-General of the Office of Production Management dated May 28 and May 29, 1941, to this effect are cited in *Minutes of the Council of the Office of Production Management,* June 3, 1941, p. 28.

31. The licensing of special war projects was continued for some time by the Economic Defense Board and its successors. These War Project Licenses covered all requirements involved in the construction of special projects of direct military significance in foreign countries. See Board of Economic Warfare, Office of Exports, *Current Controls Bulletin* No. 19, April 30, 1942.

32. General Preference Rating Order P-8, June 18, 1941, 6 *Federal Register* 3009.

33. General Preference Rating Order P-20, July 21, 1941, 6 *Federal Register* 3646.

34. General Preference Rating Order P-21, July 21, 1941, 6 *Federal Register* 3647.

35. Preference Rating Order P-18-a, August 28, 1941, 6 *Federal Register* 4525. This order revoked and superseded a similar preference rating order P-18, issued on July 31, 1941, 6 *Federal Register* 3863.

36. Preference Rating Order P-22, September 9, 1941, 6 *Federal Register* 4665.

37. Interpretation No. 3 of Preference Rating Order P-22, September 26, 1941, 6 *Federal Register* 4920.

38. General Preference Order P-56, September 17, 1941, 6 *Federal Register* 4786.

39. Preference Rating Order P-56, Amendment 1, September 22, 1941, *Federal Register* 4866.

40. Blanket preference ratings were assigned to similar manufacturers in the United States by General Preference Order P-33, August 22, 1941 (farm machinery) and by General Preference Order P-54, September 12, 1941, 6 *Federal Register* 4731.

41. Memorandum from Policy Committee, Economic Defense Board re Canadian participation in blanket preference rating orders, November 24, 1941.

42. Memorandum from Donald Nelson to Mason Britton, December 5, 1941.

43. War Production Board, Division of Industry Operations Memorandum No. 1, February 3, 1942.

44. Preference Rating Order P-100, as amended, February 10, 1942, 7 *Federal Register* 925.

45. Preference Rating Order P-6, May 31, 1941, 6 *Federal Register* 2716.

46. U.S., Congress, House of Representatives, *Hearings before the Subcommittee of the Committee on Appropriations on the First Supplemental National Defense Appropriation Bill for 1943*, (77th Cong., 2d sess.), part 2 (Washington: U.S. Government Printing Office, 1942), p. 418.

47. This letter from the President to Donald Nelson of May 1, 1942, is quoted in *Industrial Mobilization for War: History of the War Production Board and Predecessor Agencies 1940-1945;* Vol. I, *Program and Administration* (Washington: U.S. Government Printing Office, 1947), p. 295, Hereinafter, this volume is cited as *Industrial Mobilization for War.*

48. *Ibid.*, p. 443.

49. War Production Board, Priorities Regulation No. 14, July 8, 1942, 7 *Federal Register* 5272. This regulation was amended on May 2, 1944, by the addition of the War Shipping Administration to United States agencies and the substitution of Wartime Shipbuilding Ltd. and the Controller of Ship Repairs and Salvage for Wartime Merchant Shipping, Ltd., and Trafalgar Shipbuilding Co., Ltd., 9 *Federal Register* 4641.

50. War Production Board, Press Release, WPB-1769, August 28, 1942.

Chapter V

THE CO-ORDINATION OF PRODUCTION CONTROLS

So FAR as priority regulations were concerned, Canadians were able to buy scarce goods in the United States in much the same way as residents of that country. This was a natural, if implicit, corollary of agreements reached by the political leaders of the two countries. At a somewhat different political level, the precise way in which resources were to be shared was a matter of immediate practical importance. For a number of reasons, there had to be safeguards so that scarce resources would not be used for non-essential purposes in one country and not in the other. The close personal contact between industrialists of the two countries meant that any real or fancied differences in the regulations governing the use of scarce metals would provoke complaints. Again, with the widespread adoption of consumer rationing, public interest in the relative stringency of restrictions on civilians in the two countries heightened and stimulated a critical examination of the whole field of controls. The first part of this chapter concerns principally the attempts to co-ordinate controls designed to limit the consumption of critical materials by formal agreements, and deals briefly with the less formal influences which were at work. The second part concerns the restrictions on gold mining in the two countries which for special reasons were different.

1. FORMAL AND INFORMAL ARRANGEMENTS

The main purpose in restricting the use of scarce raw materials was obviously to divert badly needed supplies to military production. While there was not much need for discussion of the principle, production officials of the two countries frequently compared notes on the techniques and results of restrictions. This was a subject which came within the scope of the Materials Co-ordinating Committee and agreement was reached there that it was desirable to impose similar restrictions on the use of scarce materials in the two countries. At the initial meeting of the Committee, this question was raised and, as a result, the Metals Controller agreed to introduce additional restrictions on the use of zinc and nickel for non-war purposes. On a later occasion, the Committee reviewed in detail civilian restrictions on the use of copper and considered the advisability of supplementary restrictions. With the development of the priority system, there was a heightened interest in such matters.

In the United States, the basic regulations of the priorities system stated that anyone purchasing materials or components under a preference rating order was required to use them in accordance with existing limitation and conservation orders. It was reasonable, therefore, that Canadian manufacturers should be subject to approximately the same prohibitions and limitations if they were to participate fully in the priorities system. As a result of the agreement reached early in 1942 concerning the extension of blanket preference rating orders to Canada, steps were taken to adjust Canadian enforcement and compliance controls to match those in effect in the United States. The legal position of Canadians obtaining priority assistance from United States agencies was, in fact, obscure. United States applicants who misused material in contravention of priorities regulations were subject to penalties fixed by a section of the Criminal Code which states that it is a criminal offence to make a false statement or representation to any United States government agency on any matter within its jurisdiction.[1] To comply with the condition of the priorities agreement that comparable penalties be provided for in Canada, the Wartime Industries Control Board issued an order in February, 1942, the text of which read in part:

> Any Canadian applicant for or user of a United States Preference Rating Order or Certificate shall comply with the terms of such United States Preference Rating Order or Certificate and shall be liable to the penalties provided by Order-in-Council P.C. 6835, as amended (being the Wartime Industries Control Board Regulations), for failing to comply with the terms of such Preference Rating Order or Certificate or for making a false statement or representation thereunder.[2]

This was a somewhat curious regulation since, in effect, it meant that Canadian applicants for priority assistance in the United States were required to comply with orders and regulations established by the War Production Board. In practice, of course, Canadians were governed by Canadian orders and Wartime Industries Control Board Order No. 1 was nothing more than an amicable gesture.

Approximately the same rules were contained in Priorities Regulation 22 issued by the War Production Board in October, 1943. This regulation, after stating that priority ratings or allotments to Canadians would only be made on the recommendation of the Department of Munitions and Supply, prescribed that the following certification had to be added to purchase orders originating in Canada:

> The undersigned purchaser certifies subject to the penalties of section 15 of the Canadian Wartime Industries Control Board Regulations, to the seller, to the Canadian Priorities Officer, and to the War Production Board,

that, to the best of his knowledge and belief the undersigned is authorized under applicable Canadian orders and under applicable War Production Board regulations or orders to place this delivery order, to receive the item(s) ordered for the purpose for which ordered, and to use any preference rating or allotment number or symbol which the undersigned has placed on this order.[3]

The regulation went on to say that purchase orders bearing this certification must be treated by United States suppliers in the same way as orders bearing priority ratings or allotment numbers and originating in the United States.

The original Canadian order applied only to preference rating orders and certificates, and, in June, 1943, following the adoption of more direct methods of allocation, the War Production Board requested a modification of the order which would also cover allocations, allotments, and other authorizations. The intent of this was to establish Canadian rules similar to those subsequently laid down in Priorities Regulation 22. However, the Canadian authorities were not keen to perpetuate the anomalies in the order and decided to leave it unchanged. Finally, the order was revoked on March 15, 1944.[4] At this time, it was replaced by an order of the Priorities Officer with roughly the same intent but a more sensible wording. The new order prohibited the use of any rating, words, figures or symbols by Canadians to designate a priority rating except when authorized by a general order or a specific authorization of the Priorities Officer of the Department of Munitions and Supply.[5] Later in 1944, the War Production Board amended Priorities Regulation 22 by deleting the phrase in the certification in which the Canadian purchaser guaranteed that his purchase was authorized under applicable regulations of the War Production Board.[6] The implication of the original regulations was that Canadians were legally bound to observe the letter of United States controls. In this case, the political forebodings of officials in the United States seem to have triumphed over common sense. The attempts to impose uniform compliance procedures in the two countries were relatively unimportant in comparison with the more general undertaking that Canadian controls over the use of scarce materials would be similar to those in effect in the United States.

In the negotiations around the end of 1941 relating to the extension of blanket preference rating orders to Canadian industry, the Department of Munitions and Supply agreed that it would supervise the use of general preference rating orders by Canadians. It was recognized that if controls over the use of critical materials in Canada were more liberal than in the United States, the Office of Production Management would be vulnerable to criticism both from Congress and from industry. The Canadian Priorities Officer noted that no great difficulty was anticipated in adjusting any cases of divergence. It must be remembered that the issue arose at about the time of Pearl Harbor when Canada had been at war for over two years and in most cases had progressed further than the United States in controls over the use of scarce materials. The Canadian officials concerned must have regarded their commitments concerning the imposition of comparable controls as rather unimportant. Certainly, it was never the Canadian view that formally identical controls would be adopted as the price of priority assistance from the Office of Production Management. Nevertheless, the internal instructions issued by the War Production Board outlining the agreement between Canada and the United States as well as a press release issued at the time gave the impression that Canada had undertaken to introduce parallel controls where necessary. For example, the administrative instructions issued by the War Production Board stated that persons administering general preference orders must be satisfied that substantially the same limitations and controls applied to a Canadian firm applying for participation as to users in the United States before approving its inclusion.[7] The press release, issued by the War Production Board explaining the agreement with Canada, stated:

Arrangements are being made between the United States and Canadian governments to insure that substantially the same enforcement and compliance controls are in effect, and that substantially the same restrictions are placed on the use of scarce materials in both countries.[8]

The fact that the extension of blanket priority ratings to Canadian applicants was conditional upon the existence of parallel controls was distasteful to Canadian officials and for this and other reasons a new agreement was negotiated in the summer of 1942. The original agreement was confirmed and extended at this time in an exchange of correspondence between the Priorities Officer of the Department of Munitions and Supply and the Deputy Director-General for Priorities Control of the War Production Board. A directive, embodying the agreement, was issued by the War Production Board stating again that Canada was to have "the right to participate in the benefits of United States preference ratings providing action has been or will be taken by Canada to obtain similar results in the control of scarce materials, enforcement and compliance."[9] It was clearly understood that precise alignment of controls was not to be a condition for the extension of blanket preference ratings to Canada. The priority benefits were to be extended to Canada automatically and immediately and any questions concerning divergent restrictions were to be considered afterwards. The directive of the War Production Board was explicit on this point, as the following quotations show, but there was some ambiguity concerning the precise steps which were to be taken:

Upon application by Canada for participation under a P order, it is the policy of the Division of Priorities Administration to permit such participation *immediately* upon approval by the Deputy Director General for Priorities Control subject only to setting up the procedure necessary to insure the proper clearance through the Priorities Officer in the Department of Munitions and Supply, Ottawa, the Canadian Section and the Administrator of the Order. . . .

After participation under a P order by Canadian companies has begun, a determination shall be made whether similar results have been obtained by Canada in the enforcement of specific limitations contained in the P order or limitations set forth specifically in the L and M orders referred to in the individual P order. . . .

If it is determined that Canadian controls do not appear to obtain the same results as those of the United States, such differences in results will be adjusted between the Priorities Officer of the Department of Munitions and Supply and the Deputy Director General for Priorities Control.[10]

The point which is not clear is the precise significance of the phrase, "such differences in results will be adjusted." The Canadian officials concerned understood this to mean merely that issues arising out of disparity of controls would be the subject of discussion between officials responsible for priorities in the two countries. If the divergence could not be readily resolved, it meant that differences would be referred to higher quarters for consideration. On the other hand, it was not the Canadian view that there had been any undertaking to match the controls of the United States to the letter. It is unfortunate, in the light of later events, that the limited nature of the agreement was not made clearer. Difficulties began to crop up as soon as the comparative analyses visualized in the priorities agreements were started.

As an essential feature of the agreement reached in January, 1942, a Priorities Specialist was to be appointed by the War Production Board to carry out comparative studies of controls in Canada and the United States and to assist in the processing of priority applications. Accordingly, shortly after the formal agreement was announced, an official of the War Production Board was attached to the Department of Munitions and Supply in Ottawa. By the time of the August agreement, a small staff of War Production Board officials had already been established in Ottawa. In the first six months of 1942, there was a rapid growth in the number of control orders and consequently in the volume of priority applications originating in Canada. Because of this increased volume of work, the War Production Board established a Canadian Branch of the Division of Priorities Administration, which absorbed the functions of the Priorities Specialist.[11] A Controls Co-ordinating Section was created to carry out the comparative analysis of controls in the two countries and the staff engaged in this work was expanded. The functions of the Canadian Branch of the Division of Priorities Administration were established by an administrative order of the War Production Board in the fall of 1942, which renamed the branch the Canadian Priorities Review Division.[12] This order specifically provided that the Canadian Division should carry out studies of Canadian regulations governing the use of materials "to ascertain whether such controls are parallel in effect to the controls imposed by War Production Board orders."

The work of those engaged in comparing controls was complicated by the informal nature of many of the Canadian restrictions. The Controllers of the Department of Munitions and Supply had been given wide grants of power, and, in some cases, control orders consisted simply of letters or directives issued to industrial concerns. It was not until August, 1941, that a system of central clearance of all orders was instituted and until early 1942, directives were still being issued by individual Controllers without review by the legal staff of the Department. Under these circumstances, a proper comparison of controls required a detailed knowledge of the informal controls which were in effect. Accordingly, a member of the staff of the Department of Munitions and Supply was designated to advise and assist the Canadian Division in its analyses. An agreement was also reached later between the Chairman of the War Production Board, the Chairman of the Wartime Prices and Trade Board, and the Priorities Officer of the Department of Munitions and Supply that any information relating to the control activities of the Wartime Prices and Trade Board would be made available to the Canadian Division. A representative of the Wartime Prices and Trade Board was appointed to carry out the necessary liaison work with the Canadian Division.

Even with full and detailed information on the controls in the two countries, it was difficult, in many cases, to decide whether the restrictions achieved comparable results. In some cases, Canadian controls had been introduced earlier than in the United States, and the effect of a restriction which had been in effect for some time was different from that of a newly imposed control, mainly because of the depletion of inventories. In view of the geographic and climatic differences in the economies, the same nominal restrictions might have rather diverse effects on civilian welfare. For example, it was clearly essential for Canada to retain a higher relative production of heating equipment than the United States. Another complication resulted from the fact that limitation or conservation orders restricting the use of critical materials, or the output of goods containing critical materials, generally permitted the consumption or manufacture of a specific percentage of consumption or output in a base year. The comparability of restrictions allowing the same percentage of consumption or production in the same base year depended on the similarity of conditions in the base year. Comparisons were therefore subject to a great many qualifications and assumptions.

One further difficulty which hampered the analysis of comparability of controls was the discretionary power sometimes given to persons administering control orders in both countries to grant special dispensations or licences. It was very common in Canada to prohibit completely the manufacture of certain products except under licence. The laxity or severity of the control, therefore, depended on the licensing policy and could not be determined adequately from any written order. Furthermore, there existed in the War Production Board an appeals procedure which permitted manufacturers to apply for relief from the provisions of particular limitation or conservation orders. The policy of the Appeals Branch of the War Production Board was consequently of some significance in assessing the actual effect of a restrictive order. Apart from this, evasions of the regulations were inevitable, although any attempts to compare the degree of compliance in the two countries were impossible. As a result of these factors, it was often hard to reach any conclusions about comparability of controls without relying heavily on personal judgments.

In a number of fields, the analysis of restrictions required expert knowledge of the technical aspects of different industries. It was necessary, as a result, for the Controls Co-ordinating Section of the Canadian Division to rely on the advice of specialists who were temporarily assigned by the War Production Board to assist in the work of comparison. This arrangement had the distinct advantage of familiarizing the administrators of control orders with conditions in both countries. It promoted, moreover, the personal contacts which were so valuable a stimulus to co-operative action.

It was perhaps intentional that the procedure to be followed when some disparity in controls came to light was left ambiguous. The undertaking on the part of Canada that differences in results would be "adjusted" certainly did not mean that Canadian regulations would always be modified to conform to the corresponding orders in the United States. There were, nevertheless, many cases in which Canadian restrictions were tightened

and new orders were issued as a result of representations made by the
Controls Co-ordinating Section. Sometimes, agreements were reached to
modify United States orders to parallel Canadian restrictions, but this
was relatively uncommon. It was not true, as was sometimes suggested
by the Controls Co-ordinating Section, that their function was a direct
outcome of the Hyde Park Declaration. The comparison of controls was
rather a result of an agreement between officials of the Department of
Munitions and Supply and the War Production Board. The Wartime
Prices and Trade Board which was responsible for the administration of
many control orders in Canada was apparently not aware of the implications
of the agreement at the time it was made. Later, when the responsibilities
of the Wartime Prices and Trade Board for consumption controls
increased, following the transfer of jurisdiction over end products
containing metals from the Department of Munitions and Supply to the
Co-ordinator of Metals,[13] the Wartime Prices and Trade Board inherited
many of the irritations engendered by the Controls Co-ordinating Section.

The activities of the Controls Co-ordinating Section of the Canadian
Division were strongly resented by a number of Canadian Administrators
and Controllers and other officials. To some extent, this was a result of
the fact that the discussions were conducted by representatives of the War
Production Board whose zeal sometimes outran their discretion. It was
not quite fitting that international negotiations involving matters of
Canadian domestic policy should be carried out in such a casual way.
There was, moreover, a fundamental difference of opinion concerning the
functions of the Controls Co-ordinating Section. Canadian officials
believed that the function of the group was to analyse the controls in the
two countries and to report their findings to the War Production Board.
The view of the Canadian Division was, at one stage, that it should
negotiate with Canadian officials for a revision of Canadian regulations in
any cases where controls appeared to be less stringent than in the United
States. The main objective of the Controls Co-ordinating Section in its
early phase was to assure the War Production Board that no disparities
existed. It should be noted that many of the Canadian officials concerned
were unfamiliar with the inner workings of the War Production Board
and were not in a good position to assess the importance of the thinly-
veiled threats of the Controls Co-ordinating Section that an adverse report
would mean a modification of the terms on which priority assistance would
be granted, if nothing worse.

Sometimes the Controls Co-ordinating Section was anything but
diplomatic in its written reports on the Canadian situation. Certain of

these reports did become available to Canadian officials, who were justly disturbed by some of the comments. Here, for example, is an excerpt from a report relating to the control of machine tools in Canada:

> The Canadian control of machine tools is not satisfactory. This was brought to the attention of the Steel Controller. He stated that the primary difficulty is organization; the blurred lines of authority between the Department of Munitions and Supply and Wartime Prices and Trade Board make any responsible control of this product impossible. To correct this, a fundamental change in policy is necessary.[14]

Quite apart from the correctness or incorrectness of this blunt appraisal of the situation, remarks of this sort could hardly be expected to promote a friendly attitude to the activities of the Controls Co-ordinating Section.

There were other instances where the Controls Co-ordinating Section interfered in matters which did not seem to fall within the scope of the original agreement. The Canadian understanding was that the agreement referred to products or materials which were being procured with priority assistance in the United States. The Controls Co-ordinating Section, on occasion, appeared anxious to deal also with materials for which the United States depended heavily on Canada. The two following quotations from a report on aluminum illustrate some of the absurdities which resulted:

> Canada is diverting more of its supply of aluminum to direct war than is the U.S. Despite this conclusion, it was suggested to the Controller that a formal order on aluminum would bolster his position should any case of compliance arise; it would also clarify his relationship with industry. As a working model, the U.S. Priorities Staff wrote an order combining all the limitations and restrictions of the U.S. Orders M-1-i and M-1-h. This model, with the few exceptions noted, was accepted by the Controller.[15]

> During the first six months of 1942, Canada kept for its domestic consumption less than 5 per cent of its output of primary aluminum. It has diverted about a third of its production to the U.S. through the Metals Reserve Corporation. . . .[16]

Sometimes the issues were minor. For example, it was noted by the Controls Co-ordinating Section, again in the report on iron and steel, that, in view of the lack of comparability, an agreement had been reached with the Department of Munitions and Supply to reduce the production of metal hair pins to 50 per cent of the 1941 output, and to allow the use of low carbon steel of one gauge less than .035 inches and to restrict the length of hair pins to two inches.[17] Other cases of comparable triviality could be cited.

The adoption by the War Production Board of formal controls over retail and wholesale inventories of consumer goods at the end of 1942 was regarded by the Controls Co-ordinating Section as a desirable precedent for similar action in Canada.[18] The attitude of the Wartime Prices and Trade Board was that inventory and distribution controls of a different sort had been in effect in Canada for some time and that the adoption of inventory regulations matching those of the United States would not be considered. The flat refusal of the Wartime Prices and Trade Board to modify its whole system of inventory control provoked the Controls Co-ordinating Section into making certain inappropriate and ill-considered suggestions which implied that Canada was not keeping faith with the agreement. In fact, the suggestions of the Canadian Division were in conflict with Priorities Regulation 15 of the War Production Board which had been issued in October, 1942. The text of this order was:

Exports and deliveries of material to be exported may be made regardless of any order of the Director General for Operations restricting inventories of material or uses thereof in manufacture or otherwise, or requiring certificates with respect to such inventories or uses, insofar as such inventories are maintained or such uses occur in the country to which such material is to be exported, but shall be subject to such restrictions with respect to inventories maintained or uses occurring within the United States prior to export.[19]

The disagreement over inventory controls crystallized the resentment of the Wartime Prices and Trade Board and seriously impaired relations with the Controls Co-ordinating Section. Unfortunately, the issue could not be disposed of with a harsh word. The upshot was that Canadian retailers and wholesalers wishing to replenish inventories of goods imported from the United States which required priority ratings had, for a period at least, to certify to their inventory positions on each priority application, a burdensome procedure which was not required for wholesalers or retailers in the United States.

Probably the most vexatious aspect of the whole scheme was the fact that Canadian officials were called on to defend their control orders and their control policy to officials of the United States. One expression of the rising irritation was the suggestion that Canada appoint a similar mission in Washington to investigate and uncover cases where controls in the United States did not parallel those in Canada. This was a direct result of the unilateral character of the comparisons. Perhaps the suggestion was not put forth very seriously, but at least it reflected a critical frame of mind. More careful reflection showed, in fact, that Canada had very little to lose as a result of the activities of the Controls Co-ordinating Section and a great deal to gain. It was of inestimable value from the point of view of procurement to be able to assure officials of the War Production Board that the Canadian situation had been investigated by their own representatives and that they could be assured that material or equipment assigned to Canada as a result of priority arrangements would be used for essential purposes. A little reflection made it obvious that the formal establishment of a counter-irritant in Washington would do little to promote co-operation or contribute to better understanding between the war agencies.

The realization that the activities of the Controls Co-ordinating Section were stimulating ill-will led to a substantial modification of the tone of its reports in the course of 1943, and finally, in September, 1943, the Section was withdrawn from Ottawa and reconstituted as the Research Section of the Canadian Division in Washington. The work was continued by correspondence, but specific instructions were issued that there were to be no more suggestions to Canadian officials that they revise or modify their regulations to parallel those of the War Production Board. If necessary, these matters could be discussed by senior officials of the two countries.

Although some of the unfortunate features of the work of the Controls Co-ordinating Section have been emphasized above, it must be admitted that its objective was both reasonable and beneficial. The War Production Board, despite the friendly feelings of its officials for Canada, was often required to defend its actions before Congressional committees or against criticisms from other rival groups in Washington. If there had been any conclusive evidence that critical materials were being dissipated in non-essential uses in Canada, there would have been no lack of persons eager to point with alarm to the relatively favoured position of Canadian industry. Under such circumstances, the terms on which Canadians got priority assistance might have been made more rigorous and the difficulties of procurement in the United States might have increased, possibly to the extent of disrupting Canadian production programmes. Also, the centralization of the comparison of controls was desirable. If each individual division of the War Production Board had undertaken to carry out its own comparisons, it is probable that a chaotic situation would have developed. The officials of the Canadian Division in Ottawa were at least in a position to familiarize themselves with the whole structure of Canadian controls and to see the individual orders in perspective. It is doubtful if this could have been done by anyone concerned with only one control or group of controls.

The close and friendly association between administrative officials of wartime agencies in both countries was a powerful influence in bringing about comparability of controls. There was a continual interchange of ideas on methods of dealing with common problems. The difficulties which might arise from unco-ordinated unilateral action were clearly recognized and, in most cases, administrators found it essential to keep in close touch with developments in the other country. The usefulness of the personal associations which grew up during the war is stressed in the following excerpt from a speech by an official of the Department of Munitions and Supply in January, 1942:

All Controllers keep in constant touch with their opposite numbers in Washington and make periodical trips there. The Department of Munitions and Supply maintains an office in Washington with excellent personnel which is constantly consulting with Washington officials and which keeps Ottawa fully informed as to new developments. In my own case in my own trips to Washington I meet the officials in the O.P.M. who control the same type of materials and products and secure the benefit of their advice and experience and give them the benefit of our experience and ideas. As Canada has been at war from the beginning, it is only natural that we have gone further than the United States in our control system, but from the rapidity with which the United States has moved since the Japanese attack it would appear that the American civilian will be asked to make sacrifices as severe as will be imposed in Canada.[20]

The administrators of control orders in both countries recognized that, in many cases, Canada and the United States were using the same pool of resources, and that the adoption of similar restrictions was desirable. Farm machinery is a good example. In this case, there was continual consultation between the Administrator of Farm Machinery and Equipment of the Wartime Prices and Trade Board and his counterpart in Washington throughout the period of wartime controls. Production limitations of similar severity were adopted in the two countries and when allocation controls were adopted later, the close association of the persons responsible for controls and their understanding of mutual problems prevented any significant divergence in the treatment of the agricultural community in the two countries. There were many other examples of parallelism resulting from informal influences. In 1942, when there was a critical scarcity of tin, the United States introduced a rule that no person could purchase anything packed in a collapsible tube without surrendering an old tube. The same rule was enforced in Canada because it seemed likely to yield useful quantities of tin, but not primarily because of the action of the United States. In general, it seems clear that the pattern of restrictions in the two countries naturally tended to be similar, with the result that the Controls

Co-ordinating Section was left to deal with essentially minor aspects of the problem.

The activities of the Controls Co-ordinating Section show one of the dangers of entrusting international negotiations to amateurs. There are certain niceties to be observed in applying pressure to another country. Canadians are particularly sensitive about the influence of the United States, and anyone familiar with the historical relations of the two countries might have recognized the desirability of negotiating a careful and specific agreement on comparability of controls. This kind of agreement is most conveniently handled through diplomatic channels. In the early phase of its operations, the Canadian Division apparently did believe that it was operating under the ægis of the Hyde Park Declaration, a notion which was both incorrect and unfortunate. The cool reception which undoubtedly met many of their proposals must have led to some wondering whether Canada was really willing to adopt "measures by which the most prompt and effective utilization might be made of the productive facilities of North America."

In retrospect, one conclusion is obvious An agreement such as that concerning the participation of Canadian industry in blanket preference rating orders should have been made the subject of formal intergovernmental negotiations. In fact, the Canadians in Washington sometimes threatened to refer questions at issue to the Department of State, knowing that some effort would be made by the war agencies to avoid this. Although the diplomats came to be regarded as bogies, it is doubtful whether the agreement in question could be adequately dealt with in an exchange of letters between two government officials. The agreement affected several branches of the Canadian government, and it appears that inadequate consideration was given to the possible effects of the agreement under circumstances where the control regulations in the two countries tended to diverge. One might also wonder what the status of the agreement would have been if the officials of the War Production Board who negotiated the agreement had been replaced by others less sympathetic or less interested. As it was, the agreement led to substantial benefits to Canada, but it also stimulated a certain amount of discord and friction. It must be emphasized, however, that any wrangling over controls was confined almost exclusively to junior officials. There is no evidence to indicate that senior officials of the War Production Board were ever seriously concerned over the issue of comparability. It might well have been possible to obtain the benefits of participation in the United States priority system and to avoid the minor irritations which were produced by that part of the agreement relating to the comparability of restrictions and controls.

2. THE SPECIAL CASE OF GOLD MINING

There were a good many controversies in the period when the economies of Canada and the United States were being mobilized for war over both the method and degree of curtailment of industries not contributing directly to the war effort. Gold mining was perhaps a natural target for critics who believed that the non-war sector of the economy was not being restricted sufficiently, and its continuation was often cited as an outstanding example of the misallocation of resources. However, the view was also held that gold production should be treated as a special case in view of the monetary functions of gold and the extreme localization of the industry. These issues were of particular importance in relations between Canada and the United States, not only because the United States purchased all newly-mined gold from Canada, but because Canada was partly dependent on the United States for machinery and supplies necessary to maintain the industry. The history of the restrictions which were gradually imposed in the two countries provides an interesting example of the adoption of co-ordinated restrictions which eventually diverged in the light of special circumstances in Canada.

In Canada, in 1940, efforts were made to increase gold production in an effort to alleviate the growing shortage of United States dollars, but the policy of encouraging gold mining was reversed after the Hyde Park Declaration when alternative solutions of Canada's exchange difficulties were formulated. By the summer of 1941 the increasingly grave shortage of materials affected the mining machinery industry as well as most other metal-using industries and stimulated discussion of the place of gold mining in a war economy. To protect the position of the mining industry in general in the United States, the Office of Production Management issued Preference Rating Order P-23 late in July, 1941.[21] This order permitted the use of an A-3 priority to facilitate delivery of materials needed in the manufacture of mining machinery. The order, while it applied to a specified list of manufacturers, did not discriminate against the production of gold mining machinery. For some items, such as drills, hoists, and cages, there was no difference between the machinery used in gold mines and other mines. However, when Preference Rating Order P-56, prescribing the priorities to be used for the maintenance and repair of mines, was issued in September,[22] gold mining was definitely discriminated against. This order provided that a mine, whose production was regarded as essential in the judgment of the Administrator of the order, could be issued a serial number entitling the operator to use an A-1-a priority for repair material in case of a breakdown and an A-8 rating for general supplies and repair parts Placer gold mines were specifically excluded from the benefits of the order while the applicability of the order to other gold-producing mines was dependent on the issuance of authorization in the form of a serial number by the Office of Production Management. However, any mines in the United States could use an A-10 rating for repairs under the terms of Preference Rating Order P-23, a privilege which was denied Canadian and other foreign mines. The Administrator of P-56 decided to withhold serial numbers from foreign gold mines, a decision which was concurred in by the Metals Controller of the Department of Munitions and Supply as far as Canada was concerned. Canadian mines without serial numbers could apply for permission to use an A-8 priority rating for repairs or operating supplies in specific instances, but the use of such a rating was in no sense automatic.

By around the beginning of November, 1941, a number of international complications had developed in this field and there was evidently a need for a clarification of the policy of the Office of Production Management respecting exports of mining machinery and equipment. In several instances, the Economic Defense Board had protested to the Office of Production Management over its refusal to release mining machinery to foreign countries on the grounds that these actions involved considerations of international policy.[23] Another pressing reason for the reconsideration of export policy was the fact that Preference Order P-23 was scheduled to lapse at the end of November at which time it was believed that exports of new mining machinery to Canada and South Africa would cease.[24]

So far as Canada was concerned, there had been almost continual discussions of gold mining in the Joint Economic Committees since their establishment. Canadian gold output in 1941 was slightly higher than in 1940 and sales of gold to the United States were an important factor in alleviating the Canadian balance-of-payments problem. Nevertheless, the question of diverting Canadian resources from gold mining and finding some other way of relieving the Canadian dollar shortage had considerable fascination for some of the United States representatives, although this enthusiasm was not shared by the Canadians. It was the Canadian opinion that while gold mining was a valuable source of foreign exchange this was an incidental factor and the important consideration was that gold mining was carried on in large and isolated communities and that the northern areas concerned would suffer an economic collapse if the mines were shut down. The whole question of diverting resources from gold mining to critical non-ferrous metal mining was reviewed by the Materials Coordinating Committee, but it was the opinion of the Canadian members that the possibility of expanding the output of non-ferrous metals was limited and the suspension of gold mining was not likely to help much. Despite this, considerable attention was devoted to the gold mining problem by the Joint Economic Committees during July, 1941. These deliberations received some attention in the press, and an Associated Press dispatch date-lined Washington, July 31, 1941, stated that the Joint Economic Committees had drawn up a plan to halt Canadian gold exports to the United States and to substitute strategic metals. This, however, was hurriedly denied.

In November, when interest in the priority treatment of gold mining heightened, the Joint Economic Committees returned to the issue and the Canadian view respecting gold mines was explicitly stated. It was noted that gold mining played an important rôle in the Canadian economy and that probably other sectors of the civilian economy would be cut back before gold mining. So far as the United States was concerned, imports of such requirements as supplies, equipment, and repair parts amounted to only about $3,000,000 a year. On the other hand, if large sections of the industry were shut down, this would mean economic ruin for a number of the isolated communities in Canada completely dependent on gold mining. The maintenance of closed-down mines in a condition that they could subsequently be reopened would be extremely costly and it might be impossible to prevent the destruction of very valuable mining properties and the bankruptcy of the mining companies involved. Among the United States representatives there was some fear that ill-considered priority action might impair the post-war status of gold with consequences that could not be easily foreseen. Moreover, despite the alternatives to gold purchases by the United States, these were not always practical from a political point of view. The discussions of the Joint Economic Committees finally led to the adoption of the following resolution on November 8, 1941:

(A) WHEREAS one of the purposes of the Hyde Park agreement was to remove the problem of exchange as a barrier to the combined defence effort of Canada and the United States; and

(B) WHEREAS the Hyde Park agreement is having this effect to a large degree; but

(C) WHEREAS the current production and refining of gold in Canada remain an important means to obtain exchange which is necessary to pay for a large volume of needed war supplies from the United States; THEREFORE, the Joint Economic Committees recommend that:

Although in the allocation of scarce supplies the gold mining and refining industry should in general be treated as a non-defence industry, wherever priorities or allocations would, through curtailing gold production, diminish the supply of exchange for vital imports, this prospective deficit should be prevented:

(1) By increasing the purchase of defence articles or by other methods which will maintain the exchange position in the spirit of the Hyde Park agreement; or

(2) By such particular modification of the system of priorities and allocations as will permit the continuance of gold production to prevent the deterioration of the exchange position.[25]

In the United States the resolution was forwarded by the President to the Supply Priorities and Allocations Board for its guidance. This Board was trying to clarify the policy problems raised by the manufacture and export of gold mining machinery while the Office of Production Management was engaged in the revision of the priority regulations covering mine machinery.

It was decided by the Office of Production Management to allow Preference Rating Order P-23, which governed priorities for material used in the manufacture of new mining equipment, to lapse and to extend the coverage of Preference Rating Order P-56 to include manufacturers previously under P-23. This was accomplished by the issuance of a supplementary order, P-56-a, on December 31, 1941, which allowed manufacturers of essential mining machinery to use an A-3 rating for their needs. New serial numbers were allotted on the basis of essentiality and gold mining machinery went to the bottom of the list. It should be appreciated that there was continuous consultation between the Office of Production Management and the Metals Controller in Canada who recommended the issuance of serial numbers to Canadian mines. No serial numbers for Canadian gold mines were being issued under either P-56 or P-56-a.

While the Office of Production Management was concerning itself with the domestic aspects of gold mining, the Supply Priorities and Allocations Board was attempting to outline a satisfactory international policy. One document prepared for consideration by the Supply Priorities and Allocations Board suggested the following treatment for foreign mines:

In lieu of any blanket privileges to foreign mine operators, all foreign mine needs could be reviewed continuously with the Economic Defense Board, so that considerations of inter-American and British American policy could be consistently applied to decisions authorizing or forbidding shipments of gold-mining machinery and repair parts. No serial numbers authorizing several purchases would be issued, but applications for individual shipments would be entertained. Here again, the specific quantities of burdened materials (which are not large) are not the issue, but the political considerations involved and the question of treating non-essential industries consistently are paramount. In the special case of Canada, the Joint Economic Committees could secure all relevant statistical data.[26]

Other government agencies were carrying out independent investigations of the problems involved in gold mining. The Economic Defense Board had devoted special attention to Canadian gold production and, in a memorandum prepared by staff members, notable more for its boldness than its accuracy, there were some unfavourable reflections on the fact that Canada was being credited with $35 for every ounce of gold delivered to the United States. The document, dated November 25, 1941, went on to remark that Canada was:

> finding it advantageous to apply previous labor, capital, supplies and power to gold mining, even giving to this industry substantial aid in the form of (a) Tax concessions, both under the corporation income tax and under the excess profits tax, and (b) Preferred priority ratings.

and continued,

> The question of exports of machinery for Canadian gold mines presents an opportunity to reduce now a problem raised by the very grave weaknesses of United States gold-purchase policy. . . . The Canadians have shown reluctance to reduce substantially their production of gold while United States gold producers are still going full blast. The Canadians point out, quite accurately, that there is no economic or financial reason whatever for the continuation of United States gold production, since there is no foreign exchange problem within this country. . . . We can assist Canada's war effort by declining to ship machinery for gold mines and at the same time making a financial arrangement which recognizes Canada's grave inability to pay now in useful goods and services.[27]

These comments, apart from the factual inaccuracies, reflect a somewhat unsophisticated approach to the problem of gold mining, particularly in Canada.

Somewhat less positive views had been reached in other agencies. Early in December, the Supply Priorities and Allocations Board appealed to the State Department, the Treasury Department, the Federal Reserve Board, and the Economic Defense Board for an expression of their official views on the question of exports of gold mining equipment and on alternative ways of meeting dollar deficits.[28] Shortly after, the Executive Director of the Supply Priorities and Allocations Board summarized the opinions as follows:

> (1) In a war economy, labor, materials and machinery applied to gold production are largely wasted. Moreover, dollars made available through Lend-Lease, R.F.C. and stabilization loans, etc., have made gold unnecessary as a provider of dollar exchange. Therefore:
> (a) Nothing should be allowed for expansion, although minimum amounts for maintenance and repair should to some extent be provided.

(b) Only high-grade ores or those yielding high percentages of other minerals useful in the war effort should be mined.

(c) Labor, materials and machinery should be converted to more vital production except where extreme political or economic hardship would result.

(2) In-the-ground purchase of gold is neither necessary nor desirable. It is an experiment which raises serious complications and not only fails to solve the present problem but also presents a new one for the post-war period.

(3) Agreements should be entered into with gold producing countries to the end that they do not divert labor, materials and machinery from more essential uses to gold production.[29]

These general principles were approved by the Supply Priorities and Allocations Board which, on December 23, 1941, was reported to have agreed that "in view of the military program only limited priorities and export licenses should be granted to the gold mining industry," and that "in granting priorities and export licenses for gold mining machinery, materials should not be allowed for expansion of production although minimum amounts for maintenance and repair may be provided."[30]

The Canadian policy with respect to gold mining did not depart materially from this from the time of the Hyde Park Declaration on. The tonnage of ore that gold mines could treat was restricted by the Metals Controller and the amount of development work was also limited. In general, gold mines were at the bottom of the list when it came to priorities for materials or labour. Substantial numbers of men were transferred from gold camps to non-ferrous metal mines but they tended to leave again so that the transfers may not have achieved a great deal. Despite various restrictions, the gold mines were allowed to continue at minimum operating rates, and where mines were about to be shut down for lack of labour, action was taken to divert enough manpower to them to allow their continued operation.

In the United States, the course of events was quite different. The continuation of domestic gold mining after Pearl Harbor stirred up a great deal of vehement criticism and, while the basic policy on exports was not revised, the War Production Board acted early in March, 1942, to eliminate any priority assistance for gold mining as well as silver mining.[31] If 30 per cent or more of the value of the output of a mine consisted of gold or silver, the mine was not eligible for priority assistance under P-56 as amended. This arbitrary definition of gold and silves mines was far from satisfactory, and provoked a storm of criticism, particularly from the gold mining areas in the United States. The clause in question was withdrawn around the middle of May, 1942, although this involved no essential change in the policy of the War Production Board since priorities to mines continued to be governed by the issuance of serial numbers. As a result of the episode, however, considerable doubt arose among the mining officials of the War Production Board of the possibility of defining a gold mine satisfactorily.

By the summer of 1942, shortages of labour in non-ferrous metal mines developed and the pressure on the War Production Board to cut out gold mining in the United States intensified. The Labor Production Division of the War Production Board urged this in order to divert labour and facilities to non-ferrous mines producing critically needed metals. This goal was supported by the War Manpower Commission and the War and Navy Departments. The War Department was particularly emphatic in view of the apprehended necessity to furlough soldiers for copper mining. Finally, after much discussion, the gold mines were ordered to be closed on October 6, 1942. This was effected by Limitation Order L-208, which prohibited the operators of either lode or placer mines from breaking ore or proceeding with any development work or new operations after October 15, 1942, and from carrying on any operations incident to gold mining except maintenance sixty days after October 6.[32] Despite the resultant wave of protest, the order was continued in effect.

The drastic action of the United States raises a nice question concerning the co-ordination of controls since similar restrictions were not adopted by Canada. It was unlikely that there was any pressure on Canada to follow suit from the Mining Equipment Division of the War Production Board, which would be charged with the ultimate responsibility for assessing the comparability of controls. The results of the order were, in fact, quite disappointing. The Deputy Administrator of L-208 stated in May, 1943:

The general effect of the Order has been to antagonize the individual and the communities dependent on gold mining, and caused large losses to the operators. To repeal it would not calm the situation, but would stir up increased resentment from the many who have lost their livelihood, relinquished leases, forfeited equity in equipment, or sold equipment in anticipation of no further need for the duration.[33]

The official history of the closing of the mines summarizes the effect of the closing of the gold mines in the following paragraph:

With regard to the question as to whether or not the results achieved by L-208 compare favorably with the results anticipated at the time the order was issued, the answer would appear to be in the negative. The actual benefits in labor and equipment obtained through closing the gold mines were small in proportion to the economic distress and individual hardship that ensued. Considerable confusion prevails as to the exact number of men transferred to essential nonferrous metal mines, but the number seems in any case to be very small. Here again, it is impossible to weigh the exact advantages, because many of the released gold miners, while they did not go into other metal mines, did engage in occupations, such as lumbering, that were beneficial to the war effort. Nevertheless, some did not go into any other occupation, and remained idle. There are opposing claims as to the amount of equipment saved, and the amount of equipment transferred elsewhere, by the closing of the gold mines.[34]

In view of these conclusions, some question may arise whether the argument, sometimes advanced by Canadians, that the continuation of gold mining in Canada was to be partly justified on the grounds that it alleviated a balance-of-payments difficulty, was not superfluous. It might also be borne in mind that gold production in the United States in the period 1938-41 was somewhat greater than in Canada although it was of relatively minor importance to the United States economy, compared to its significance in the Canadian economy. The divergence of the restrictions on gold mining in the two countries was clearly desirable in view of the different conditions in the two countries and demonstrates clearly, if such a demonstration is needed, that the strict comparability of controls was not necessarily something to be applauded.

REFERENCES FOR CHAPTER V

1. *18 U.S. Code* 80, Sec. 35a.

2. Wartime Industries Control Board Order No. 1, February 11, 1942.

3. War Production Board, Priorities Regulation No. 22, October 23, 1943, 7 *Federal Register* 14426.

4. Wartime Industries Control Board Order No. 1A, March 15, 1944.

5. Department of Munitions and Supply, Priorities Officer, Order No. P.O. 6, May 8, 1944.

6. War Production Board, Priorities Regulation No. 22 as amended, November 15, 1944, 9 *Federal Register* 13706.

7. War Production Board, Division of Industry Operations Memorandum No. 1, February 3, 1942.

8. War Production Board, Press Release No. WPB 188, February 10, 1942.

9. *Ibid.*

10. *Ibid.*

11. *Ibid.*

12. War Production Board, Administrative Order No. 20, October 8, 1942. It will be convenient to use the abbreviated term "Canadian Division" hereafter.

13. P.C. 504, January 23, 1943.

14. "Survey of U.S.-Canadian Wartime Controls and Co-ordination Agreements," October 27, 1942, part I, p. 65. This typewritten document originally consisted of twenty-six reports, which were supplemented by others during the period when the Controls Co-ordinating Section was active.

15. *Ibid.*, part II, p. 2.

16. *Ibid.*, part II, p. 9.

17. *Ibid.*, part I, p. 59.

18. Limitation Order L-219, December 29, 1942, 7 *Federal Register* 11065.

19. War Production Board, Priorities Regulation No. 15, October 10, 1942, 7 *Federal Register* 8188.

20. A. H. Williamson, in a speech before the Vancouver Board of Trade, January 5, 1942, reported in *British Columbia Lumberman,* January, 1942, p. 32.

21. Preference Rating Order P-23, July 29, 1941, 6 *Federal Register* 3775.

22. Preference Rating Order P-56, September 17, 1941, 6 *Federal Register* 4786.

23. Historical Reports on War Administration, War Production Board, Special Study No. 9, *The Closing of the Gold Mines, August, 1941, to March, 1944* (Washington: U.S. Government Printing Office, 1946) p. 6.

24. *Ibid.*, pp. 5-6.

25. "Minutes of the Fourth Joint Meeting of the Joint Economic Committees," November 7, 8 and 9, 1941.

26. Quoted in *The Closing of the Gold Mines,* p. 8.

27. The document, quoted in *The Closing of the Mines,* p. 9, is attributed to Ralph Turner, C. H. Burgess, and Warren S. Hunsberger, Economic Defense Board, and is entitled "Canada's Gold Mining Industry."

28. *The Closing of the Gold Mines,* p. 10.

29. Memorandum, Donald M. Nelson to the Supply, Priorities and Allocations Board, December 23, 1941, quoted in *The Closing of the Gold Mines,* pp. 10-11.

30. *Minutes of the Supply, Priorities and Allocations Board,* December 23, 1941.

31. General Preference Rating Order P-56 as amended, March 2, 1942, 7 *Federal Register* 1637.

32. Limitation Order L-208, October 6, 1942, 7 *Federal Register* 7992.

33. Quoted in *The Closing of the Gold Mines,* p. 51.

34. *Ibid.*, p. 53.

CHAPTER VI

THE ALLOCATION OF MATERIALS AND FINISHED PRODUCTS

BRIEFLY, the priorities system involved the issuance of instructions to producers or distributors that orders with a higher priority rating should be filled before orders with a lower rating. The obvious danger in such a system is that high priority ratings will be over-issued and that they will cease to assure delivery in the time required. This is exactly what happened in the United States in the spring of 1942. The problem was aggravated by the broad delegation of authority given by the War Production Board to the Army and Navy Munitions Board in February, 1942, for issuing priorities on all military contracts.[1] Partly as a result of the actions of the Army and Navy Munitions Board and contracting field officers, a rapid inflation of priorities occurred. New techniques of control were necessary, the introduction of which always raised the question of Canada's status in the new control system. This chapter first deals with the issues which arose with the adoption of formal allocation techniques in the United States and then goes on to consider the complementary problems arising out of purchases by the United States in Canada.

Underlying the method of allocating materials and finished products was the concept that certain sectors of the economy, including a foreign sector, had certain requirements and that the available supply should be handed out to agencies representing the different sectors. This general notion was originally embodied in the organization of the Supply Priorities and Allocations Board.[2] In this instance, the so-called "claimant agencies" were the War Department, the Navy Department, the Office of Price Administration and Civilian Supply, the Office of Lend-Lease Administration, and the Board of Economic Warfare. The claims of these agencies would presumably add up to the total requirements to be met from domestic supplies. Essentially, therefore, allocation meant that a specific quantity of a commodity would be reserved and made available to each of the claimant agencies.

1. ALLOCATIONS TO CANADA BY THE UNITED STATES

The right of Canada to participate completely in the priority system of the United States was of great assistance in the procurement of certain classes of materials and components. This should not be allowed to conceal the fact that, in some cases at least, Canadian production programmes were hampered by the inability or unwillingness of the United States to deliver adequate quantities of certain critical commodities. One can detect a certain undertone of dissatisfaction in the following comments by the Co-ordinator of Production of the Department of Munitions and Supply taken from a speech made on October 17, 1942:

> The most serious effect on our industrial war programme possibly came about with the advent of Pearl Harbor. Our neighbours to the South became a fighting nation instead of a neutral supplying the weapons of war. It becomes a different picture when you are defending yourself and supplying your own army.
> In the production of steel we had expected to receive so many thousand tons per month. With the great expansion of their programme and its tremendous size, it became obviously necessary that steel shipments emanating from that country be curtailed, and as a result of that curtailment Canada had to absorb its share. We went to Washington not once but twice, and I thought, and still think, presented an admirable case on behalf of our country and our fighting forces, and its war industries, but notwithstanding our case we were asked to give up thousands of tons of carbon steel and more thousands of tons of alloy steel in the last quarter of 1942.[3]

Some of the difficulties are illustrated by the Canadian merchant-ship-building programme. It was noted in the Hyde Park Declaration that Canada was in a position to produce and deliver ships urgently needed by the United States. Accordingly, a large-scale ship production programme was scheduled in Canada to fill the needs of the United Kingdom and the United States as well as Canadian domestic requirements. For example, the United States had ordered from Canada seventy-seven vessels for delivery between July 1 and December 31, 1942, comprised of sixty-seven ships of 9,300 tons and ten ships of 4,700 tons.[4] By the fall of 1941, the Canadian programme was being seriously hampered by the lack of wide steel plates. About two-thirds of Canadian requirements were produced domestically while the balance had to be imported from the United States. The Canadian programme had been undertaken, however, on the definite understanding that the United States would supply the deficit. By November, the President of Wartime Merchant Shipping Limited was quoted in the House of Commons as saying that the shortage of steel had slowed up the ship construction programme in all its parts. He was quoted further as saying, "There is not enough steel produced in Canada for all war purposes, and the United States defence programme, now gaining real momentum, has cut down the amount that can be got from there."[5] Although official statements were issued that the shortage was not as bad as it was pictured, it appears that shipments of steel plate from the United States were completely cut off between August and December. At that time, steel plate was subject to partial allocation by the Office of Production Management but because of the rather erratic control exercised by other government agencies in the steel plants, steel intended for Canada was subject to diversion to other users. In the course of a visit to Washington in the fall of 1941, the Minister of Munitions and Supply had requested shipments of 3,000 tons of steel plates per month from November, 1941, to June, 1942, a relatively small amount in the light of total United States production. The fact that a large part of Canadian production of merchant ships was scheduled for delivery to the United States seemed to the Canadian authorities to be an argument in favour of this allocation. Late in November, 1941, the question was referred to the Supply Priorities and Allocations Board, which agreed to the release of 5,500 tons of wide steel plate in December, any further releases to be held up pending a study of the possibility of using substitute material or drawing on other sources such as excess plate in warehouses.[6] This decision was reached despite the advice of the Vice-chairman of the United States Maritime Commission who was present at the meeting of the Supply Priorities and Allocations Board and who was reported to have said that shipyards in the United States could produce more rapidly and in greater volume than the Canadian shipyards. He then stated that steel needed by the United States Maritime Commission should not be shipped to Canada for ships already under construction.[7] The Canadian requirements of 3,000 tons a month seemed modest compared to United States Maritime Commission requirements which were nearing 200,000 tons a month at about this time.[8] The Canadians were naturally somewhat bitter about what was regarded as the niggardly attitude of the United States. It should be recalled, however, that it was in January, 1942, that President Roosevelt set the seemingly impossible goals of 8,000,000 dead weight tons of shipping in 1942 and 18,000,000 tons in 1943. Moreover, on January 1, 1942, producers of steel plate in the United States had a backlog of unfilled orders amounting to 4,500,000 tons.[9] This shortage threatened to delay not only the production of merchant ships but the Navy construction programme, as well as the expanson of facilities for aluminum, synthetic rubber, 100-octane gasoline, and steel itself.[10] These developments were unfortunate from the point of view of the Canadian ship-building programme and unfortunately fostered the idea among certain Canadian officials that joint planning with the United States was a risky venture.

The Joint Economic Committees had been concerned with the particular problem of steel plates and more generally with the question of integrating Canadian production into the developing priorities and alloca-

tions system of the United States. The attitude of the Canadian Section
was that the United States should establish specific allocations of materials
for Canada which would be distributed according to the needs of the
Canadian economy. This would have meant that the distribution of scarce
materials in Canada could be carried out independently of the United States
priority system. The contention of the Canadian Section of the Joint
Economic Committees is of interest from two points of view. In the first
place, the proposal betrays a certain unawareness of the internal political
situation in Washington during the war. It was true that certain specific
allocations had been established for Soviet Russia as a result of the Moscow
Protocol of October, 1941, but there was a wide difference between the
Russian and the Canadian bargaining position. At a time when there was
a major struggle between military and civilian interests going on in the
United States, it was hardly practical to suggest that Canada should be
given an absolutely preferential status. In the second place, the recommendations originating with the Canadian Section of the Joint Economic
Committees were directly at variance with the efforts of the Department of
Munitions and Supply to secure the fullest possible Canadian participation
in the priorities system of the United States.

Talk of allocations was in the air in the fall of 1941. It was pointed
out by the Executive Director in the first meeting of the Supply Priorities
and Allocations Board early in September, 1941, that the Office of Production Management believed an allocation system to be a necessary supplement
to priorities whenever more than 50 per cent of the supplies of any material
was required for the armed services.[11] It was again reported at the end of
October by the Under-Secretary of War that the Army and Navy Munitions
Board regarded the allocation of steel as essential if military needs were to
be met and a high rate of production maintained.[12] Accordingly, the Supply
Priorities and Allocations Board issued a recommendation to the Office of
Production Management that a system of allocating steel products be introduced as soon as arrangements could be made, particularly with a view to
controlling steel products used by industries producing for the Army, Navy
or Maritime Commission. In response to this, the Office of Production
Management issued an order, effective December 1, 1941, placing steel
plates completely under allocation.[13] This order authorized the Director of
Priorities to modify production and shipment schedules of producers of steel
plates and to allocate steel plates to defence industries without regard to the
priority ratings which had been issued.

The case of steel plates is an aggravated instance of the inadequacy
of a simple system of preference ratings to direct supplies when the volume
of high-rated requirements exceeds a certain level. By the spring of 1942,

this situation was becoming quite general. The volume of outstanding priority certificates had grown to the point where some new and more effective technique for channelling materials and equipment was essential. During this period, there was continual pressure on the Army and Navy to develop requirements which were balanced and reasonable in the light of whatever strategic plans they had, and, above all, to restrict their demands to levels which would be met by existing productive capacity.

While allocation methods for specific materials and equipment had been adopted in a number of cases, the first step in the development of an overall allocation scheme came with the announcement of the Production Requirements Plan early in December, 1941.[14] The essence of this scheme was that each manufacturer was to submit to the War Production Board a list of his products, their priority ratings, his prospective output, his inventory and future requirements of critical materials. The statements of the manufacturer were to show his requirements by months for a later three-month period. A tally of those schedules would show prospective requirements for critical materials which could then be reviewed by the War Production Board in the light of probable future supplies. The War Production Board allocated critical materials to the major production programmes and scaled down the requirements of individual plants to match the target output. The aim also was to allocate balanced quantities of materials and components to manufacturers.

Priority ratings for materials were to be assigned on the basis of the essentiality of the end products being produced. Delivery or acceptance of more than the rated quantity was prohibited. This meant that, under the Production Requirements Plan, priority ratings applied to specific quantities of materials. In this way, or so it was hoped, total requirements could be balanced against available supplies and the indiscriminate issuance of priority ratings stopped. Under the new system, the rating pattern which a firm could use in purchasing scarce materials reflected the ratings of orders placed with the firm, a fact which was of some importance for Canada.

Initially, participation in the Production Requirements Plan was voluntary but early in June, 1942, the War Production Board issued an order that the new system would become mandatory beginning with the third quarter of 1942.[15]

The War Production Board had made important changes in its internal administrative organization to deal with the increasingly important work of allocating critical materials. The most important of these was the creation of a Requirements Committee to decide on detailed allocations.[16] Representatives of government agencies responsible for military requirements, export and civilian requirements were appointed to this committee, which began operations in mid-February, 1942. The Requirements Committee was required to determine programmes for the production of over 200 end-products and to adjust these programmes to fit the available supply of materials. In effect, the Requirements Committee passed out allotments of materials to the various industry divisions of the War Production Board and to the military agencies. Under the Production Requirements Plan, it was the responsibility of the industry divisions to keep the amounts of materials released to individual companies within the overall allotments granted by the Requirements Committee. In addition, a residual of unallocated materials was retained to cover individual priority certificates, ratings assigned by P-orders, and unforeseen needs arising because of programme changes.

Arrangements were made by the Department of Munitions and Supply for the participation of Canadian firms in the Production Requirements Plan. Indeed, this was a natural consequence of the policy agreements which had been reached at the end of 1941. However, there was a special difficulty involved in Canadian participation in the plan since Canadian firms did not normally fill orders bearing priority ratings. As a result, complete rating patterns for Canadian firms did not usually exist. This was the same problem which had hindered Canadian participation in the Defense Supplies Rating Plan. Certain modifications of the Production Requirements Plan were adopted to include Canadian industry, and arrangements were made for full Canadian participation beginning in the third quarter of 1942. Fortunately, there were representatives of the War Production Board in Ottawa whose assistance was heavily relied on in adapting the plan to Canadian industry. To compensate for the fact that the output of Canadian firms did not usually bear priority ratings, arrangements were made to have the Department of Munitions and Supply recommend the percentage of the output of firms that could be regarded as essential and to suggest priority ratings to the War Production Board. The actual ratings and percentages in the highest priority band were obtained from a directive of the Army and Navy Munitions Board issued in February, 1942. Other ratings could be obtained on the basis of directives to the review staff of the War Production Board or from knowledge of ratings assigned for comparable end uses in the United States.

It was essential for Canadian firms importing large amounts of critical materials from the United States to operate within the framework of the Production Requirements Plan. As a result, a special order was issued by the Canadian Priorities Officer making it mandatory for any person using more than $5,000 worth of metals a quarter to qualify and operate under the plan.[17] By the fourth quarter of 1942, the Production Requirements

Plan controlled the flow of materials from the United States to Canada. For this period, signalling an important new development, Canada was given overall allocations of raw materials which were to be allotted to individual concerns under the supervision of the Department of Munitions and Supply. The processing of the applications and the allotment of materials to individual applicants was carried out in Washington by the War Production Board with the help of officials of the Department of Munitions and Supply. Responsibility was still further decentralized in making allotments for the first quarter of 1943, when the applications were entirely processed in Ottawa by the Canadian Division of the War Production Board with the advice and assistance of the Department of Munitions and Supply.

The priority ratings of allotments made to an individual firm under the Production Requirements Plan depended on the priority rating directly assigned to its output if the firm was a prime contractor, or, where the priority rating had been extended, by the ultimate output to which it would contribute. The rating pattern of a supplier was thus principally dependent on the ratings of his customers. Because of this, there was a marked increase in the use of priority ratings by Canadian industry when the Production Requirements Plan was operative. The use of priority ratings became quite general in Canada, although, of course, they had no legal status except for firms officially operating under the Production Requirements Plan. Despite their unofficial status, it seems quite probable that the use of such ratings may have exerted a significant effect on the distribution of materials in Canada.

In order to appreciate more fully the unusual place of Canada in the Production Requirements Plan and its descendants, it is necessary to examine in more detail the internal allocating machinery created by the War Production Board. The War Production Board itself was a high-level inter-agency committee concerned mainly with major policy problems, and, because of other demands on the attention of its members, not a suitable body to deal with the complex and technical issues involved in allocating materials. Shortly after the creation of the War Production Board, its Chairman announced that this work would be the responsibility of the Requirements Committee, also an inter-agency group whose Chairman was to be a senior official of the War Production Board. All claimants for United States supplies of critical resources were to be represented directly or indirectly on this Committee. Originally, its members included representatives of the United States Army and Navy, the United States Maritime Commission, the Board of Economic Warfare, the Office of Lend-Lease Administration, and the Division of Civilian Supply of the War Production Board, although the membership broadened somewhat later. The requirements of these different claimant agencies covered most of the military, export, and domestic civilian claims on the United States output of critical materials or commodities. The stated requirements of all the claimants were reviewed by this tribunal in the light of the known or forecast supply. When the sum of requirements exceeded supply, it was evident that the achievement of a balance would necessitate either a reduction in requirements or an increase in supply and it was the responsibility of the Requirements Committee to recommend either or both. The functions of the Committee were outlined succinctly when it was established formally on March 3, 1942. The order officially confirming its existence stated that its duties were to:

1. Determine the direct and indirect military, other governmental, civilian, and foreign requirements for essential and critical raw materials and industrial materials;

2. Ascertain the total available supply of such materials;

3. Determine the amount by which the available supply of such materials shall be increased to meet requirements;

4. Determine and approve programs for the allocations of such materials;

5. Determine and approve allocation programs for foreign requirements for fabricated and semi-fabricated products; and

6. Communicate such determinations and approvals to the Chairman of the War Production Board and to appropriate divisions of the Board.[18]

It will be clear from this description that the Requirements Committee was to play a central rôle in the determination of foreign, including Canadian, allocations.

It is important therefore to understand the basic policy of the Requirements Committee with respect to foreign requirements, especially for countries in the Western Hemisphere. The issue had been raised in April, 1941, and at that time a directive concerning Latin American requirements had been sent by President Roosevelt to the Director-General of the Office of Production Management. The President pointed to the possibility of serious dislocation in the economies of Latin American countries as a result of decreased shipments of industrial and consumer goods and went on to say that it was desirable to assign the "vital requirements of these Republics such priority as may be necessary to maintain their industrial and economic stability, provided there should be no prejudice to the national defense program of this country."[19] Action was taken by the Office of Production Management to carry out these instructions. This general policy was also adopted by the Requirements Committee and the so-called "parity" principle

was formally stated by the Chairman shortly after the formal establishment of the Committee.[20]   The principle was briefly that Latin American
requirements normally purchased in the United States should be treated on
a comparable basis with domestic non-military claimants.   Although the
original statement of policy did not specifically include Canada, it was clear
that Canada could expect treatment at least as good and possibly better than
Latin America.

The Canadian position with respect to the Requirements Committee
was obscure, at first, except for Canadian military requirements which were
included in the programmes of the United States armed services.   In view
of the general responsibility of the Board of Economic Warfare for the
requirements of foreign countries, except those represented by the Office of
Lend-Lease Administration, it might have seemed natural for the Board
of Economic Warfare to represent Canada.   However, since export controls on shipments to Canada had been almost completely eliminated by the
spring of 1942, the Board of Economic Warfare had only a minor interest
in Canada.   Over a period, the question of Canadian representation was
clarified, a development which is of extreme importance in the history of the
relations between the war agencies of Canada and the United States.   The
solution of this problem is intimately related to the methods which were
worked out to achieve adequate Canadian representation on some of the
subsidiary allocating committees of the War Production Board concerned
primarily with civilian products.

Shortly after Pearl Harbor, it was clear that civilian production would
have to be severely curtailed.   In the fall of 1941, there had been some more
or less spectacular curtailments of the output of such goods as automobiles,
washing machines, and refrigerators.   Because of the critical shortages of
metals and facilities which were developing as a result of the huge munitions programme in the United States, more drastic curtailment of civilian
output could easily be forecast.   Recognizing the important rôle which the
Division of Civilian Supply of the War Production Board would play in any
curtailment of civilian production, the Wartime Prices and Trade Board
arranged in May, 1942, to attach a representative to the Division of Civilian Supply to observe the rapidly changing situation.   Shortly before this
time, plans for the curtailment of civilian production had encountered an
obstacle.   The War and Navy Departments had presented to the War Production Board military requirements for typewriters whose magnitude
indicated that no significant reduction in the level of production of the typewriter industry would be possible if the requirements were to be met.   Since
the specialized facilities of the typewriter industry were urgently needed
for munitions production, it was recognized that some technique would have

to be developed to review and adjust the military or other demand for type-writers, and civilian products in general, in accordance with the overall production programme.

Accordingly, in April, 1942, the End Products Committee (later the Standard Products Committee) of the War Production Board was created for the purpose of allocating civilian-type end products to the various claimants for United States supplies.[21]   The attention of the committee was almost exclusively confined to products using critical materials. Originally, the Committee consisted of representatives of the Army, the Navy, the Office of Lend-Lease Administration, the Board of Economic Warfare, and the Division of Civilian Supply of the War Production Board.

A concise statement of the purpose of the End Products Committee by the first Chairman of the Committee is quoted in *Industrial Mobilization for War*. He says:

When the End Products Committee was first created . . . there had been up to that time no genuine allocations of end products to speak of as between the several claimant agencies. No one had been able to find a method of cutting back the typewriter industry, the office equipment in-dustry and a great many other so-called civilian products industries, the products of which were being mainly used by the Armed Forces. It was the End Products Committee which accomplished this result in several hundred different products which were important users of scarce metals and labor. It seems to me in retrospect that this job was of great impor-tance in setting the stage for over-all materials allocations at a later date and making it possible for such systems to be workable.[22]

The following comment by the next Chairman of the Committee explains its functions quite clearly:

The functions of the Standard Products Committee and related com-mittees are to determine the following as to end products (including parts and accessories) manufactured in the United States:

(1) The total requirements for such end product;
(2) The total available supply of such end product;
(3) The proper distribution of the available supply of such end pro-ducts among competing demands.[23]

The Committee met frequently to deliberate on the requirements presented by its member agencies with a view to reducing demands to essential levels, or to available supply for the period under consideration as estimated by the industry divisions of the War Production Board.

In the course of an internal reorganization of the War Production Board in July, 1942, the precise place of the Standard Products Committee in the organizational structure was clearly defined. It was established as a sub-committee of the War Production Board Requirements Committee which was directed by the Vice-Chairman on Program Determination. The decisions of the Standard Products Committee were subject to review by the Chairman of the Program Adjustment Committee, another but senior sub-committee of the Requirements Committee and, initially at least, by the Requirements Committee itself. The recommendations of the Standard Products Committee might be, either that the capacity of an industry should be expanded, or that production should be limited to quantities sufficient to meet the approved requirements of the different claimant agencies. The dominant concern of the Committee was with ways of achieving maximum economy in the use of critical metals by eliminating non-essential products completely, or by restricting output to the point necessary to satisfy essential demands. To implement the quotas established by its various programmes, the Standard Products Committee had to rely on agreements with procuring or licensing agencies such as the Army, Navy, Board of Economic Warfare and the Office of Lend-Lease Administration, or on distribution controls imposed by the War Production Board. Limitation orders of the War Production Board provided adequate controls only in those cases where purchases from manufacturers had to be approved on a priority certificate. In these cases, an industry division was in a position to restrict releases to amounts which had been approved.

While Canada was heavily dependent on the United States for certain classes of end products, the question of Canadian representation on the Standard Products Committee was apparently not explored at the time of its formation nor for some time after it had begun to function. The Board of Economic Warfare had assumed responsibility for presenting estimates of Canadian requirements, although it is not clear that this procedure was discussed with the Canadian authorities. It soon became apparent not only that the Board of Economic Warfare was not equipped to supply adequate information concerning Canadian requirements, but also that Canada's position was quite different from that of other countries under the jurisdiction of the Board of Economic Warfare. Consequently, direct requests for statements of Canadian requirements were transmitted to officials of the Department of Munitions and Supply in Washington. It was evident that some more permanent and formal method of securing and transmitting estimates of Canadian requirements was desirable.

Accordingly, in mid-June, 1942, a meeting was arranged with the Chairman of the Standard Products Committee, the representative of the Division of Civilian Supply on the Committee and several Canadian officials representing the Wartime Prices and Trade Board and the Department of Munitions and Supply. It was decided that Canadian requirements would be presented to the committee by the representative of the Division of Civilian Supply. Under this arrangement, Canada was not formally represented on the Committee, but the Chairman invited a Canadian representative to sit with the Committee as an observer.

The estimation of future requirements by most claimant agencies proved to be a formidable task. This was particularly true of the military agencies whose requirements were subject to rapid change as a result of the volatile state of military planning. Nevertheless, the basic policy of the Standard Products Committee was that adequate justification of requirements would be required from all agencies. This view was put forth by the Division of Civilian Supply and strongly supported by the Chairman of the War Production Board. In a memorandum dealing with this question, he stated:

> The Division of Civilian Supply or any other agency which contends that allocation should be made only on the basis of reasonable evidence of need and that unsupported assurance of need is not enough, should be vigorously upheld. Moreover, allocations should be granted only on additional adequate evidence of effective conservation of material and products, including efficient use thereof. . . .
> The Division of Civilian Supply has endeavoured to estimate civilian requirements on a rockbottom basis and at this stage of our mobilization of economic resources the Services can no longer make valid assumptions as to their ability to make large claims for their own use of materials earmarked for civilian supply. We have practically reached the stage where there is no longer distinction between civilian and military supply, and military estimates based upon any other premise may interfere with the direct war effort to a serious degree.[24]

The Standard Products Committee drew up a staggering agenda of products to deal with, in many of which Canada was vitally interested. The estimation of Canadian requirements in many cases proved to be exceptionally difficult. Sometimes the products dealt with were closely related to munitions programmes, for example, clocks and chronometers for merchant ships, in which cases requirements could be derived readily from production schedules. In the majority of cases there was no usable statistical information concerning previous imports and therefore no means of knowing what quantities represented "minimum essential" requirements. More often than not, the import statistics based on tariff classifications did not quite fit the product specifications needed by the Committee. One way of approaching the problem was to request all the firms in an industry concerned for a statement of requirements, divide by an arbitrary number and hope that the quotient was a reasonable indication of the need. This approach was not recommended, even by the Canadians concerned. In contrast, the Division of Civilian Supply, having better statistical resources and a large and well-trained staff, was able to present statements of United States civilian requirements which reflected their basic policy at the time. Despite the faltering beginnings, the techniques of estimating requirements improved in the course of time and the Wartime Prices and Trade Board, which was mainly concerned, became adept at determining Canadian requirements. The volume of work handled by the Standard Products Committee increased rapidly during 1942 and finally a number of sub-committees were created to deal with specific commodity groups, such as medical and health supplies and fire-fighting equipment. Although the Division of Civilian Supply continued to represent Canada officially on these sub-committees, the extent to which the Canadian observers participated increased, and in many cases experts from Canada were invited to be present to discuss technical aspects of Canadian requirements. On the parent committee, the Canadian representative did not participate in the deliberations except to explain certain aspects of Canadian requirements when this was necessary.[25]

Canadian relations with the Standard Products Committee raised a number of problems and established a number of precedents which were to become increasingly important as allocation controls became more widespread.

First, the regular attendance of Canadians at meetings of an allocating committee of the War Production Board was an important and unusual precedent. This was the thin edge of what was to become a substantial wedge!

Second, a special difficulty arose in the case of Canada because of the necessity of controlling the distribution of an item once the size of the allocation had been established and approved. Without distribution or other controls, there was no way of restricting a claimant agency to its precise allotment. The administration of quotas established for the United States civilian economy was the responsibility of the industry divisions of the War Production Board. For those products which could only be delivered on an approved priority certificate, the criteria of approval could be adjusted to control the total amount released. A case in point was office machinery such as adding and calculating machines, dictating equipment, and punch card machinery, the essential types of which were allocated by the Standard Products Committee. It was the view of the Committee that, once an allocation had been established, it was appropriate for the claimant agency concerned to determine how its allocation should be disbursed. This meant, for example, that the Board of Economic Warfare was free to dispose of its allocation as it saw fit. There was, nevertheless, a good deal of pressure leading to conformity to the rules and restrictions applicable to United States civilians.   Acting on the basis of the policy declaration of the Standard Products Committee, Canadian officials in Washington decided that Canada, too, should control the Canadian allocation, on the theory that the size of the allocation took care of the question of equality of treatment of civilians.   Despite this theory, it was essential to restrict the distribution of allocated commodities to comparable users in Canada and the United States. The case of office machinery again offers a good illustration.   An agreement was reached with the War Production Board that there would be close consultation on criteria of essentiality and that the Canadian Administrator of Office Machinery would undertake to restrict releases to those classes of users who would be approved in the United States.   Once this system was introduced, no Canadian priority applications for office equipment were denied by the War Production Board; the right to refuse applicants rested with the Wartime Prices and Trade Board.   This arrangement resulted in the adoption of almost identical control policies over the distribution of office machinery in Canada and the United States.   In the event of a difference of opinion, it would clearly have been appropriate for the Canadian Administrator to rule on individual releases without regard to the opinion of the industry division of the War Production Board. This general policy was applied in a number of important fields.   Its successful operation required the intimate and close co-operation of the control authorities in the two countries.

Third, a significant issue arose shortly after the formation of the Standard Products Committee in connection with the steps which were to be taken to enforce allocation decisions.   In some cases, it was relatively simple.   Commitments were given to the War Production Board by the War and Navy Departments that procurement would be limited to the stipulated quotas.   Similarly, there was centralized control over the purchase or release of exports by both the Office of Lend-Lease Administration and the Board of Economic Warfare.   But, except for those commodities whose purchase required an approved priority certificate, there was no obvious way of policing a Canadian allocation to prevent exports in excess of the established quota.   This question was naturally a matter of concern to the Division of Civilian Supply, which could visualize excessive amounts of scarce civilian items being drained off to Canada.   The Division of Civilian Supply suggested that Canada consider ways in which purchases in the United States could be limited to the amounts allocated.   The Canadian view on this question was that Canadian civilians were entitled to the same access to non-controlled goods in the United States as United States civilians, except when the restrictions tending to impair equality of access were adopted for Canadian reasons alone.[26] This issue was to become important later.

By the latter part of 1942, Canada had succeeded in obtaining informal but adequate representation on a number of the junior allocating committees of the War Production Board. Up to the end of the year Canada's position in relation to the parent Requirements Committee and the subsidiary Program Adjustment Committee remained ill-defined. On a number of occasions Canadian representatives appeared before the Program Adjustment Committee to explain Canadian requirements under the Production Requirements Plan and specific allotments were made to Canada. The possibility of arranging for full Canadian representation on the Requirements Committee had been explored informally, but some opposition had been encountered and the idea was temporarily abandoned. Formal membership was certainly not essential in view of the generally satisfactory treatment of Canadian requirements. The fact that Canada was able to gain the ear of the Requirements Committee was partly a result of the growing importance and influence of the Canadian Division of the War Production Board. The existence of this group meant that Canada had a very clear channel of approach to top-level allocating committees whose actions significantly affected Canada.

The importance of the Canadian Division had been considerably bolstered by the issuance of a directive in mid-November, 1942, assigning complete responsibility for priority and allocation matters affecting Canada to the Canadian Division.[27] In addition, in October, 1942, authority had been delegated to the Canadian Division to issue priority ratings on most PD-1A priority applications originating in Canada for items worth less than $500.[28] This decentralization of authority not only resulted in speeding up the issuance of priorities to Canadian applicants but greatly increased the responsibility of the Canadian Division.

The issue of Canadian representation on the Requirements Committee suddenly came to a head with the announcement of the Controlled Materials Plan early in November, 1942. This new scheme involved a wide extension of the use of allocations as a method of controlling the flow of materials. It was to be in full operation by the third quarter of 1943 after a transitional period in the second quarter. The essence of the plan was that the available supply of three controlled materials, carbon and alloy steel, copper, and aluminum was to be completely allocated by the War Production Board among the different claimant agencies. The determination of the requirements of the claimant agencies for controlled materials was to be based on bills of materials submitted by contractors producing finished items for the different claimants. Once the claims had been adjusted to the available supply, the claimant agencies themselves were to authorize prime contractors producing on their behalf to use their allocations. Prime contractors could then pass on allotments to their sub-contractors. The new scheme was designed to end the difficulties of the Production Requirements Plan arising out of the fact that production programmes were adopted with inadequate attention being paid to the availability of materials. As a result, manufacturers with low preference ratings were sometimes unable to obtain materials while excessive quantities could be accumulated by manufacturers with high priorities. The new scheme of vertical allocation would introduce centralized control over the supply of materials and yet decentralize control over the distribution to ultimate users.

Special arrangements were made to deal with the requirements of claimant agencies for end products and components. The Controlled Materials Plan specified a detailed list of what were called Class B products for which each claimant agency was to submit a statement of requirements to the War Production Board. The adjustment of these requirements to fit the available supply was the responsibility of the newly established Division Requirements Committees. These committees were modelled on the sub-committees of the Standard Products Committee but separate committees dealing with different product groups were established in the appropriate industry divisions of the War Production Board.[29] Each claimant agency was to have representation on the Division Requirements Committees. Other end products not included on the Class B lists but containing controlled materials were identified as Class A products, and allotments for these products were made directly to the claimant agency. This was in contrast to Class B products for which allotments were made by the industry divisions of the War Production Board.

Under the Controlled Materials Plan, claimant agencies were to play a central rôle in the direction of the flow of critical materials. The question immediately arose whether Canada was to become a full-fledged claimant agency with a status comparable to the United States Army or Navy or the Office of Civilian Supply. From the point of view of the mechanics of the Controlled Materials Plan, this would have been very convenient. On the other hand, there was a possibility that Canada would be precipitated into the arena of inter-agency rivalry and forfeit the advantages of an ill-defined but safe position. The arrangement, worked out with the Standard Products Committee, whereby the Office of Civilian Supply acted as the Canadian advocate, had certain distinct advantages, and, at one stage in the discussion of Canada's place in the new scheme, the Chairman of the Requirements Committee did designate the Office of Civilian Supply to act as a claimant agency on behalf of Canada.[30] However, there were some indications by the end of 1942 that the influence of the Office of Civilian Supply was declining and the Canadians were hesitant to become too closely dependent on an agency in its waning phase. The following appraisal of the Office of Civilian Supply, made subsequently, perhaps confirms the wisdom of the Canadian attitude:

This organization was maintained intact in spite of its paltry direct accomplishments, its continual friction with the Requirements Committee, with the industry divisions, and with the Army—this being its chief accomplishment—and the questions of the Bureau of the Budget as to whether the agency was still necessary.[31]

In any case, speculation on the advisability of placing responsibility for Canada in the hands of the Office of Civilian Supply was ended when the Office of Civilian Supply formally declined to act as a claimant on behalf of Canada.[32] This decision was a result of the changing rôle of the Office of Civilian Supply. Initially, it had been one of the centres of pressures for more rapid conversion and for the restriction of civilian needs to levels required in a war economy. Gradually, however, its predominant concern became the protection of the essential civilian economy against what were considered excessive and unrealistic military demands. Canada had also become a competitor for scarce civilian commodities under allocation, with the result that the Office of Civilian Supply could no longer act satisfactorily as a conscientious advocate of Canadian interests. Moreover, the Office of Civilian Supply was, around this time, the centre of serious organizational difficulties in the War Production Board and was probably glad enough to be relieved of any responsibility for Canada. A number of representatives of the Office of Civilian Supply urged, nevertheless, that Canada should press for full recognition as a claimant agency.

From any realistic point of view, the importance of allocations to Canada did not justify the establishment of an independent claimant agency. On the other hand, there was some risk that Canada might be inadequately represented in discussions on allocations unless the status of the body representing Canada were sufficiently important. Some compromise solution seemed to be asked for. Finally, after a good deal of discussion, agreement was reached to designate the Canadian Division of the War Production Board as a "technical claimant agency" on behalf of Canada.[33] This was partly in recognition of the growing importance of the Canadian Division, and was welcomed by the Canadians as a way of avoiding the possible dangers involved in complete independence. Not only was the Canadian Division to present Canadian requirements to the Requirements Committee and transmit the established allocations, but the Canadian Division was also to represent Canada on the Division Requirements Committees. Since the precedent had already been established, it was agreed that a native Canadian representative would attend the meetings of the Division Requirements Committees as well as a representative of the Canadian Division.

Provision was made for the adjustment of Canadian programmes in the event that Canadian requests had to be curtailed. So far as military requirements were concerned, questions of adjustment were to be referred to the Joint War Production Committee or its sub-committees.[34] Appeals of this sort were, of course, contemplated only if the action of the War Production Board appeared to endanger some significant war production programme. Normally, adjustments in the requirements of all claimant agencies were necessary and usually cuts were accepted with resignation if not with good grace. In practice, the Requirements Committee and the Division Requirements Committees did reduce Canadian allocations when this was necessary and it was exceptional when such decisions were appealed.

The Canadian position was somewhat unusual and liable to be misunderstood. This is unfortunately only too clear from the following quotation from the official history of the War Production Board, *Industrial Mobilization for War,* which, in referring to Canadian requirements, states:

Throughout 1942, the presentation of Canadian requirements proved especially troublesome. Canada declined to present its requirements through the Board of Economic Warfare because it objected to being considered a foreign country. It was willing to become a member of the Requirements Committee, but this was generally objected to by the committee on the ground that, although the Hyde Park Agreement of April 20, 1941, made Canada a part of the American economy, it was, in fact, a foreign country and foreign representation on the Requirements Committee was undesirable. A proposal that Canada accept the Lend-Lease Administration as its representative was rejected because Canada did not resort to lend-lease financing. A later suggestion that Canada accept the Office of Civilian Supply as its representative was rejected by the Canadians because it might lead to the erroneous inference that the bulk of its requirements was civilian. A proposal that the requirements of Canada be presented by all the claimant agencies on the Requirements Committee was tried but proved unsatisfactory. Finally, arrangements were made to utilize the Canadian and Foreign Divisions of WPB in a way which, in effect, treated Canada as a claimant agency without representation on the Requirements Committee.[35]

In view of some of the comments in this quotation, it may be well to notice again that Canada had divorced itself completely from the Board of Economic Warfare, so far as requirements were concerned, in June, 1942. By December, 1942, when the presentation of Canadian requirements became an issue for a short time, it seems unlikely that any authoritative person considered this channel, although the reason cited is rather trivial. Similarly, the proposal that lend-lease channels be used was not a responsible suggestion. The suggestion that Canada was willing to become a member of the Requirements Committee may convey the impression that the Canadian officials were anxious to see Canada treated as an independent claimant agency while, in fact, they were diffident about it. The statement that Canada rejected the Office of Civilian Supply as a representative is quite wrong; as already mentioned, the Office of Civilian Supply declined to act in this capacity. While it is true that a suggestion was made that Canadian requirements be split up and presented by the other claimant agencies, the suggestion was never adopted. The arrangements mentioned in the last sentence of the quotation went into effect before the proposal could be implemented.

Apart from the question of Canada's status as a claimant agency, there were other problems involved in the adaptation of the Controlled Materials Plan to Canada. The main difficulty was that Canadian prime contractors were not necessarily importers of controlled materials but were more usually dependent on suppliers mainly engaged in importing. In contrast to the United States, there was little point in passing out authorizations for controlled materials to Canadian prime contractors, except in the unlikely case that they imported their requirements directly from the United States. Consequently, in the modified version of the Controlled Materials Plan which was adopted in Canada, importers of controlled materials were issued preference ratings and allotment numbers authorizing imports from the United States directly by the Department of Munitions and Supply instead of receiving them from customers. However, imports of capital equipment continued to be allowed on the basis of preference ratings extended to the importer by his customers in Canada.

The necessary legal steps to implement the modified Controlled Materials Plan in Canada were taken by the issuance of two regulations by the Priorities Officer of the Department of Munitions and Supply. The first of these required principal Canadian users of critical materials to file reports with the Department of Munitions and Supply showing anticipated imports from the United States.[36] The second provided that any Canadian purchaser must identify any purchase valued at more than $25 from a Canadian supplier in accordance with a programme classification system.[37] This regulation permitted the classification of imports from the United States into twenty-four end-use categories. The purpose of this was to enable the Department of Munitions and Supply to identify the volume and essentiality of imports from the United States.

Fundamentally, there was a certain anomaly involved in Canadian participation in the Controlled Materials Plan since Canada was a net supplier of copper and aluminum and was dependent on the United States for steel only. Canada did import both copper and aluminum in fabricated form and complete participation in the Controlled Materials Plan did solve the mechanical problem of obtaining specialized imports from the United States. Steel was a different story. Approximately 30 per cent of Canadian steel requirements came from the United States during the war, only small amounts of special products such as tinned sheets and razor blade steel being imported from other countries. Canadian steel imports from the United States were about 1,800,000 tons in 1942, 1,500,000 tons in 1943, and approximately 1,000,000 tons in 1944. Because of their great importance to the Canadian war production programme, it was essential to adopt rigorous controls over steel imports from the United States. Early in October, 1942, the Steel Controller of the Department of Munitions and Supply issued a directive stating that any imports from the United States required his prior approval. With the inauguration of the Controlled Materials Plan, a formal order approval system was introduced by the Steel Controller requiring importers to submit their original purchase orders on their suppliers in the United States together with documentary substantiation of their need.[38] If approved, the order was then forwarded by the Steel Controller to the supplier in the United States. Similar order approval systems were in effect for aluminum and copper.

By mid-1943 Canada's status as a claimant on the United States had been firmly established and was to remain substantially unchanged until the end of the war and the relaxation of controls. Moreover, the rather minor adaptations of Canadian domestic controls necessitated by the Controlled Materials Plan had been made.

The problem of Canadian treatment did arise again in connection with efforts of the War Production Board to schedule the production of "critical common components." About the end of 1942, a presidential directive had been issued to the effect that programmes for the production of escort vessels, aircraft, high-octane gasoline, and rubber were imperative. Certain critical components such as propulsion machinery, boilers, valves, condensers, heat exchangers, and electrical equipment were common requirements for some or all of these items, and since there was a certain lack of coordination between the output of components and the products into which they were to be incorporated, vital production programmes were being handicapped. One difficulty was that manufacturers could not schedule their output effectively because of interference by representatives of various claimant agencies intent on improving their relative position on production schedules. To control this situation, the War Production Board issued General Scheduling Order M-293 which authorized the freezing of production schedules for critical common components.[39] Once a schedule was frozen, changes could be made only with the approval of the War Production Board. From the Canadian point of view, it was important to preserve the relative position of Canadian orders whenever production schedules were to be modified. An agreement was reached that the War Production Board would notify Canadian officials if any changes in production schedules affecting Canadian programmes were contemplated. Opportunity would thus be afforded to Canada to see that Canadian orders were not being discriminated against. This arrangement merely meant that Canadian programmes were placed on the same footing as those of other claimant agencies in the United States.

The general problems involved in the allocation of consumer goods to Canada can be illustrated by referring to the complex case of cotton textiles. Although textiles were not rationed in either Canada or the United States, critical shortages existed in both countries, particularly of cotton fabrics. Canada, traditionally dependent on the United Kingdom for cotton fabrics, was gradually compelled to depend more heavily on the United States. Canadian importers, who did not have the status of old customers in the United States, began to experience difficulties in purchasing in the United States in 1942 and 1943. The difficulties were aggravated by the decision of the United Kingdom in 1943 that exports to Canada would be limited to cotton yarns and fabric not obtainable either domestically or from the United States. Until the end of 1943, it had been possible to overcome most of the procurement difficulties as a result of the very close and harmonious co-operation between the Canadian Cotton Administrator and the Textile Division of the War Production Board.

One factor of some importance was the small additional export premium allowed to exporters of cotton fabrics to Canada by the Office of Price Administration. In general, exporters were allowed to charge, in addition to the domestic ceiling price, a premium equal to 125 per cent of the average export premiums charged in the period July 1 to December 31, 1940, or March 1 to April 15, 1942, whichever was lower, while for some commodities a specific premium was fixed. In the case of cotton fabrics, a premium of 7 per cent was allowed on exports to Canada by the export price regulations of the Office of Price Administration.[40] Such premiums were intended to compensate exporters for the extra costs involved in preparing export shipments, although the extra costs involved in selling in Canada were negligible. The export premium thus constituted some inducement to suppliers in the United States to sell in the Canadian market.

When the priority system was extended to cotton textiles in the summer of 1943, arrangements were worked out to provide for full Canadian participation. The War Production Board had issued General Conservation Order M-317, covering cotton broad-woven fabrics and requiring preference ratings for the delivery of these fabrics.[41] Any Canadian importer purchasing cotton fabrics covered by General Conservation Order M-317 was assigned a priority rating by the Canadian Division of the War Production Board, in conjunction with the Cotton Administrator of the Wartime Prices and Trade Board. Rigid control over imports was exercised by the Cotton Administrator who issued authorizations in the form of serial numbers to Canadian importers.

By the beginning of 1944, with the extension of the formal allocation system of the War Production Board to cotton and other textiles, Canada could no longer rely on the somewhat fortuitous effects of export premiums, priority ratings, and informal governmental assistance. However, by this time Canada had accumulated a good deal of experience in allocation problems. As a result of the activities of the Textiles Co-ordination of the Wartime Prices and Trade Board, and of the preliminary work carried out by the National Textiles and Leather Requirements Committee[42] which was responsible for the allocation of textile and leather supplies among civilian and military users in Canada, carefully prepared statements of Canadian requirements for cotton fabrics were available for submission to the War Production Board. The treatment of the Canadian claims for cotton fabrics for the first half of 1944 was somewhat disappointing since the allocation requested was reduced by 9 per cent. This was followed in the third quarter of 1944 by a further reduction to about 50,000,000 yards compared to requirements of 73,000,000 yards.

Despite these developments, Canadian imports of textiles from the United States had increased about four-fold over pre-war imports by the middle of 1944. At the same time, Canada was exporting specialized cotton fabrics to the United Kingdom for military purposes, a fact which gave rise to some misunderstanding of Canada's needs.[43]

During the spring of 1944, the position of civilians in the United States was somewhat weaker than that of other claimants. Manufacturers were required by regulations of the War Production Board to set aside a certain percentage of their output for export. Military claimants, on the other hand, were in a position to obtain either high priority ratings or firm allocations. In contrast, the United States civilian economy received merely a residual allocation whose volume was substantially below what was believed to represent minimum essential requirements. The Office of Civilian Requirements was naturally deeply concerned over the situation and pressed for a reassessment of export and domestic civilian needs. In line with this policy, the Office of Civilian Requirements persuaded the Office of Price Administration to eliminate the 7 per cent export premium on cotton fabrics shipped to Canada. The existence of the premium was something of an anomaly, and the Canadians were in no position to press for its retention even though its abandonment was unwelcome.

It was around this time that the Office of Civilian Requirements was pressing for a reconsideration of the "parity" principle originally enunciated by the Requirements Committee in the spring of 1942. Briefly, the principle was that civilian requirements of Canada and the Latin American countries which were normally obtained in the United States would be treated on a par with non-military domestic claimants in the United States. In July, 1944, the head of the Office of Civilian Requirements appealed to the Chairman and Executive Vice-Chairman of the War Production Board for an interpretation of the "parity" principle which would not jeopardize the living standards of civilians in the United States.[44] It is pointed out in the official history of the Office of Civilian Requirements that some confusion existed about the precise meaning of parity and that the Office of Civilian Requirements sometimes assumed that the principle referred to *all* civilian requirements of the countries concerned and not merely to imports from the United States.[45] In any case, the Office of Civilian Requirements, which had an important voice on the Requirements Committee, was far from sympathetic to the Canadian pleas for increased imports of cotton textiles.

By the fourth quarter of 1944, the balance of Canadian requirements and supplies was still further upset by a decision of the War Production Board to reduce the Canadian allocation of cotton fabrics by 29,000,000 yards below stated Canadian requirements. In view of unexpectedly heavy military demands during this period, the supplies available to Canadian civilians were approaching a dangerously low level. It should be emphasized, however, that the same percentage reduction in civilian requirements was imposed in both the United States and Canada. Despite the eloquent arguments of Canadian officials that equal percentage cuts were inequitable in view of the lower per capita consumption in Canada, the War Production Board would not alter its position. The principle of equal proportionate adjustments was maintained, more or less, until the allocation system was abandoned.

The elimination of the export premium in 1944 was not a serious threat to Canadian procurement in the United States so long as the War Production Board was in a position to underwrite Canadian allocations. But, by 1946, the implementation of textile allocations was becoming increasingly difficult, and the Wartime Prices and Trade Board undertook to persuade the Office of Price Administration to re-instate premiums on exports of cotton fabrics to Canada. Negotiations extended over several months during a period when exports to Canada were falling off substantially, and finally, by the summer of 1946, export premiums somewhat lower than those previously in effect were re-introduced. Since price ceilings in the United States were abandoned shortly after this time, the gains from the export premium were shortlived.

The rough concept of parity of treatment of civilians in both countries which governed allocations of cotton fabrics enabled the Wartime Prices and Trade Board to maintain supplies above the level where rationing would have been imperative. One reason for this was that the supply authorities in the United States recognized that the adoption of apparel rationing in Canada would probably have forced the United States to adopt it too, a prospect which was regarded with some dismay by all concerned. Apart from this argument, Canadian officials devoted a good deal of attention and statistical ingenuity to comparing levels of civilian consumption in the two countries. Since the determination of levels of civilian consumption of textiles is a technical matter, it is not surprising that comparisons were most commonly made by government officials and not by the public or the press.

2. ALLOCATIONS TO THE UNITED STATES BY CANADA

It has already been remarked that prices in the United States rose somewhat faster than in Canada in the early years of the war. This influence tended to stimulate Canadian exports to the United States and to support a natural predisposition of Canadian exporters to sell the maximum amount possible to the United States. There was, in addition, a general tendency to encourage exports to the United States to alleviate Canada's foreign exchange problem. Government intervention was usually necessary to maintain adequate supplies for domestic needs. This was in marked contrast to the situation in the United States where the principal difficulty lay in assuring a level of exports sufficient to meet official commitments.

The production and export of critical and strategic raw materials was, of course, one of the major contributions of Canada to the war production programme of the United Nations in general and of the United States in particular. It was natural that the Materials Co-ordinating Committee should play a central rôle in determining the policy concerning exports of Canadian raw materials to the United States. The committee was concerned with the problems involved in producing, distributing and transporting North American raw materials. This meant that the committee was not directly concerned with materials once they had been processed beyond primary shapes and forms. The fact that the members of the committee were senior officers of the Department of Munitions and Supply and the Office of Production Management or War Production Board meant that they were often in a position to implement their own recommendations, although the need for enlisting the co-operation of other agencies on some occasions was clearly recognized.

One of the first commodities to be dealt with by the committee was nickel, which, by the spring of 1941, was in critically short supply. In view of the essentiality of nickel in war production and the fact that Canada was the world's predominant supplier, there was obviously scope for concerted planning. Some expansion of Canadian capacity had already been planned but indications were that this was insufficient to meet the needs of the United States. Action in this field was certainly decisive, and at the second meeting it was agreed that Canada would initiate an immediate large-scale expansion plan for nickel production involving the opening of new mines, the construction of new plant facilities, and the exploitation of high-grade reserves. The wartime increase in Canadian nickel exports, shown in the table below[46] in thousands of pounds, must be partly attributed to the early recommendation of the Materials Co-ordinating Committee.

	Refined Nickel	Unrefined Nickel[47]
1939	137,400	98,400
1940	166,900	85,000
1941	172,300	101,900
1942	173,200	98,500
1943	192,600	83,900
1944	194,290	67,990

There were also serious shortages of zinc, lead, and copper developing in 1941 and the committee sponsored the expansion of Canadian output, particularly by the encouragement of sub-marginal mines. A good deal of attention had been devoted to this problem in the United States and a system of differential prices had been worked out to encourage the working of high-cost mines. Some thought was given to the payment of differential prices to Canadian mines, but this was discarded in favour of an alternative financing method worked out by the Materials Co-ordinating Committee and other government agencies. Briefly, the scheme involved a Master Agreement between the Metals Reserve Company, a subsidiary of the Reconstruction Finance Corporation, and War Supplies Limited. War Supplies Limited was to handle purchases from Canadian corporations and in turn would sell to the Metals Reserve Company. The essential feature of the contractual arrangements was that the Metals Reserve Company was to make capital advances to encourage the expansion of sub-marginal mining in Canada, the mines to be recommended by the Metals Controller. The agreement was eventually extended to cover at least five mining properties, two producing zinc and lead, two copper, and one copper and zinc, and there may have been others. As the output of these mines was sold to the Metals Reserve Company, the capital advances were gradually liquidated in accordance with the terms of the contracts.

Apart from such longer run planning, the committee also arranged for the diversion of raw materials in a number of emergency situations, often to meet critical needs which had developed at particular plants. One instance of this occurred early in the life of the committee. Shipments of cobalt metal were diverted from the United Kingdom to the United States pending the expansion of productive capacity in the United States. Many similar actions were taken during the war to relieve specific bottlenecks in both countries.

Probably the most outstanding achievement of the Materials Co-ordinating Committee was its action in facilitating the co-ordinated planning of the production of aluminum and newsprint and the use of hydro-electric power, especially in Quebec and Ontario and New York State. Recognition of the critical situation in aluminum was slow in developing but by early 1941, it was evident that there was a very serious shortage in prospect, particularly in the United States in view of the tremendous expansion of the aircraft programme. Canada was intimately involved in the problem in several ways. In the first place, the supply estimates prepared in the Advisory Commission to the Council of National Defense had assumed that monthly imports of 3,100,000 pounds of aluminum would be available from Canada. This source disappeared when the Canadian government suspended the issuance of export permits for aluminum going to the United States in January, 1941. Moreover, difficulties were being encountered in obtaining additional power from Canada to permit the expansion of output in the Massena, N.Y., plant of the Aluminum Company of America. An expansion of about 100,000,000 pounds in the annual capacity of this plant was planned but the Hydro-Electric Power Commission of Ontario, supported by federal officials, was unwilling to supply the enormously increased power needs.[48] This provoked some ill-will and it was even suggested by one official of the Office of Production Management that further exports of aluminum from the United States to the British Empire should be suspended until the issue was resolved.[49] It may have been this kind of problem the Minister of Munitions and Supply had in mind when, in referring to the formation of the Materials Co-ordinating Committee, he expressed the hope that "misunderstandings having to do with the situation of both our countries may be avoided through its agency."

In mid-April, tentative plans were made by the Office of Production Management to increase ingot supply by 200,000,000 pounds, one-half of which was to be produced by the Aluminum Company of America and the other half by Aluminium Limited, the corresponding Canadian company. On March 31, the Power Controller and representatives of Aluminium Limited had met with the chief power consultant of the Office of Production Management and had agreed that 44,000,000 pounds could be made available to the United States prior to April, 1942, and 110,000,000 pounds a year thereafter. However, the agreement was contingent on the completion of the Shipshaw development which was to yield 375,000 kilowatts, as well as on satisfactory arrangements relating to depreciation and purchasing arrangements.

Within two weeks, the Office of Production Management again revised its plans and sponsored a further increase of 400,000,000 pounds in aluminum capacity. On the following day, May 2, 1941, contractual arrangements were completed between the Aluminum Company of Canada, Limited, the operating subsidiary of Aluminium Limited and the Metals Reserve Company for the purchase of Canadian aluminum. The contract called for the delivery of roughly 375,000,000 pounds (170,000 metric tons) of aluminum ingot at a basic price of 17 cents.[50] The expansion of facilities required was to be partly financed by an advance of $25,000,000 by Metals Reserve Company. This advance was to be liquidated by deducting 6.67 cents for each pound delivered and, in addition, a financing charge of .295 cents per pound was to be made. The delivery schedule called for 20,000 tons before May 1, 1942, 50,000 tons in the next year, 65,000 tons in the year following and 35,000 tons between May 1 and November 1, 1944. One interesting feature of the contract was that deliveries were to be made to Metals Reserve Company "for the use of the United States Navy or for other purposes which would permit the importation of the aluminum, duty free, or subject to refund of substantially the entire amount of the duty."[51]

The expansion plans of the Aluminum Company of America had temporarily fallen through, which meant that the Office of Production Management still had to arrange for extra production of 400,000,000 pounds to meet its goal of an additional 600,000,000 pounds.

It was just about this time that the Special Senate Committee investigating the National Defense Program (Truman Committee) began a series of hearings to determine the reason for the aluminum shortage. This led to a good deal of publicity concerning the issues involved and made it quite clear that the government would have to finance the construction of new facilities and that publicly owned power would have to be made available.[52]

Before the end of May, the Office of Production Management had again revised its goal to a total of 800,000,000 pounds of additional capacity. The Metals Reserve Company was requested to renegotiate the contract with the Aluminum Company of Canada, Limited with a view to obtaining 200,000,000 pounds a year beginning as soon as possible. By mid-June, the Office of Production Management was counting on 200,000,000 pounds of aluminum from Canada.[53] The Office of Production Management also decided to ask Canada for 70,000 kilowatts of power for the Massena plant of the Aluminum Company of America, one of the plants which was to produce part of the domestic expansion of 600,000,000 pounds. On July 15, 1941, a new contract was signed between Metals Reserve Company and the Aluminum Company of Canada, Limited calling for supplementary purchases amounting to 170,000 metric tons, the same amount as specified in the original contract. An additional advance of $25,000,000 was also agreed to but this time it was to bear interest at 3 per cent. The price of 17 cents a pound specified in these contracts was very favourable since the domestic price in the United States was to drop to 15 cents a pound in October, 1941.

The domestic expansion programme in the United States which got under way slowly amid a good deal of controversy mainly concerned the production of primary aluminum and did not alleviate the serious shortage of fabricating facilities which had developed. Steps were taken to increase fabricating capacity and an arrangement was made between Metals Reserve Company and the Aluminum Company of Canada, Limited that any excess Canadian capacity would be made available to fill defence orders in the United States.[54]

It must be borne in mind that throughout this whole period Canada was attempting to meet the urgent needs of the United Kingdom for aluminum and that this sometimes involved the diversion of shipments intended for the United States. For example, United Kingdom representatives in Washington requested the Office of Production Management to agree to the diversion of 3,000,000 pounds due from Canada in May and 50 per cent of Canadian deliveries for the next few months. In this instance, the Office of Production Management did agree to a 50 per cent reduction in Canadian shipments.[55]

The entry of the United States into the war and the greatly increased production goals for aircraft announced by the President early in 1942 led to a complete revision of the estimates of supply and requirements of aluminum in the United States. On January 16, 1942, the War Production Board began to formulate plans for additional domestic capacity of 600,000,000 pounds of primary aluminum and for negotiations with Canada for an additional 100,000,000 to 200,000,000 pounds a year. Negotiations with Canada were instituted at once and new contractual arrangements were made on March 6, 1942, calling for 250,000,000 pounds to be delivered in 1942, 1943, and 1944. In addition, the Aluminum Company of Canada offered to make available a supplemental quantity of 370,000,000 pounds, an offer which was at once approved by the War Production Board.

The complex arrangements between Metals Reserve Company and the Aluminum Company of Canada, Limited involved in the two contracts have been summarized in the official publication *History of the Aluminum Policies of the War Production Board and Predecessor Agencies, May, 1940, to November, 1945,* as follows:

The first increment of 250,000,000 pounds was covered by a contract executed on March 6. Actually the third contract between the Metals Reserve Company and the Aluminum Company of Canada, the instrument superseded those of May and July, 1941, and embodied a modification of their provisions. Under the terms of this third contract 1,000,000,000 pounds of aluminum was to be delivered by the end of 1944, of which 800,000,000 pounds intended for use in the United States was priced at 15 cents a pound and the remaining 200,000,000 pounds, which was meant for lend-lease use, was priced at 17 cents. Both prices were retroactive to the first deliveries. The $25,000,000 down payment of the first contract and the $25,000,000 loan of the second were consolidated into an advance payment, without interest, of $50,000,000, the purpose of which was "to enable the seller to undertake the expansion of the productive capacity of its plants." Alcan also received credit up to $25,000,000 from the Export-Import Bank, without security and with interest at 3 per cent, this credit to be used to offset payments made against the advance at the rate of 5 cents a pound of aluminum delivered. The final 370,000,000 pounds of aluminum was covered by a fourth contract entered into on April 1, 1942, the terms of which were parallel to those of the third contract. Of the total amount 296,000,000 pounds were for use in the United States and were priced at 15 cents, while the remaining 74,000,000 pounds were designated for lend-lease at 17 cents. An additional advance of $18,500,000 and a further credit of $9,250,000 were provided on the same terms as those of the March contract. The third and fourth contracts represented a substantial price reduction from the straight 17 cents called for in the first two agreements, made before Alcoa's price cut of October, 1941.[56]

By the summer of 1943, the large-scale expansion programme had eased the supply situation with a vengeance. There were indications that surplus aluminum was accumulating and numerous relaxations of the strict end-use control over aluminum were permitted by the War Production Board over the following few months. In the meantime, perhaps influenced to some extent by the improved supply situation, the Truman Committee had vigorously criticized the terms of the contract of the Metals Reserve

Company with the Aluminum Company of Canada. There had also been a good many unfavourable comments in the press. No doubt partly in response to this criticism the Canadian contracts were renegotiated in September, 1943, and a uniform base price of 15 cents a pound was set for all aluminum delivered after November 1, 1943. Certain other features of the contracts were modified so that the Aluminum Company of Canada was to make retroactive interest payments of 3 per cent on all money advanced by the Metals Reserve Company and an escalator clause which had previously referred merely to transportation and labour costs was to apply retroactively to all costs. Despite its generally critical attitude the Truman Committee had this to say about Canadian aluminum production:

> In considering the contracts with the Aluminum Company of Canada and the extremely great benefits obtained by it, consideration must always be given to the fact that aluminum was produced in huge quantities and delivered at a time when we needed it. However, it is regrettable that the operations of the Aluminum Company of Canada, after the war, will not be subject to the jurisdiction of the laws of the United States.[57]

This was, unfortunately, not the end of the criticisms of the purchases of aluminum from Canada. During a later period, when primary aluminum production was being cut back in the United States, there was a new chorus of protests about the aluminum contracts. A detailed account of these developments is given later in the chapter dealing with the problems of reconversion in the two countries.

Despite the important rôle of the Materials Co-ordinating Committee in the early phases of the aluminum expansion programme, work in this field was later taken over by one of the committees of the Combined Boards, something which will also be dealt with later. However, the work of the Materials Co-ordinating Committee in its early stages was profoundly influenced by the aluminum problem. For one thing, the enormous power needs of the aluminum industry led to reallocations of power in Eastern Canada and the United States and to the construction of huge new sources of hydro-electric power such as those at Chute à Caron and Shipshaw. In February, 1942, it was recognized by the Materials Co-ordinating Committee that in view of the priority needs of war plants in both Canada and the United States, some power would have to be diverted from the newsprint industry. The resultant cut in the power available for newsprint production had major repercussions in the industry and, in consequence, on the relations between the two countries in the field of forest products.

There were other fields in which the Materials Co-ordinating Committee was immediately interested although the detailed work was assigned to four sub-committees which were to provide a medium for consultation between operating officials of the two countries. These sub-committees, established in the fall of 1942, were concerned with copper, zinc, ferroalloys, and forest products.

The principal purpose of the Copper Subcommittee was to provide a channel for the exchange of statistical data on the production, shipment, and stocks of copper in the two countries. The committee also aimed to encourage the most economical use of facilities for producing and fabricating copper.

Similarly, the Zinc Subcommittee was intended to review methods of increasing the joint production of zinc of different types and qualities. One of the important actions taken by this committee led to an exchange of certain types of high-grade Canadian zinc for a different type of zinc produced in the United States. This allocation of Canadian zinc to the United States necessitated important changes in the galvanizing techniques used by Canadian manufacturers.

The sub-committee which dealt with ferroalloys was established to arrange for the reallocation of fabricating capacity and for the diversion of raw materials and finished products such as ferro-manganese and silico-manganese, between the United Kingdom, the United States, and Canada, to economize shipping space, and to allocate capacity more efficiently.

The Forest Products Subcommittee was created in an attempt to work out some of the tangled problems involved in dividing the North American supply of pulpwood and Douglas fir logs between the two countries. Difficulties arose out of Canadian attempts to prevent excessive exports of pulpwood and logs to the United States where they tended to be drawn by differentially high prices. While a discussion of these problems belongs naturally in a chapter dealing with Canadian allocations to the United States, the issues in this field are complex and are dealt with in a separate chapter which describes, in some detail, the allocation techniques which were worked out.

Even without anticipating this later material, it is possible to draw some conclusions about the general considerations which influenced the allocations by one country to the other. From the point of view of Canada, the Canadian aim was always to obtain parity of treatment in the evolving systems of priorities, allocations, and scheduling in the United States. It was a slow process to achieve complete parity but, once the principles had been established in the case of priorities, Canada was accorded comparable treatment in the various allocation systems almost automatically. The complexity of the arrangements governing Canadian purchases in the United

States was a result of the heterogeneous composition of Canadian imports. In the converse situation, when the United States was purchasing in Canada, the nature of the imports into the United States was such that much simpler procurement and control mechanisms could be used. The problems in the latter case were essentially financial and technical. Once a contractual agreement was approved by the Canadian authorities, there was no necessity for detailed control over individual shipments. The fact that the United States was primarily interested in bulk purchases of homogeneous commodities such as non-ferrous metals meant that a complex administrative structure was not necessary to supervise or control the purchases. This contrasted sharply with the issues involved in Canadian purchases in the United States where the multiplicity of Canadian imports and the large number of importers meant that the question of parity was always in the foreground.

The issue of parity was important in other fields besides the control of materials. In particular, controls over exports, imports, and shipping raised complex problems of equality of treatment of the two countries. The next three chapters will be devoted to the techniques of co-operation and the principles of parity which were worked out in this important area of economic relations.

REFERENCES FOR CHAPTER VI

1. War Production Board, Industry Operations, Division Administrative Order No. 1, February 23, 1942.
2. Donald M. Nelson, *Arsenal of Democracy: The Story of American War Production* (New York: Harcourt, Brace, 1946), p. 156.
3. H. J. Carmichael in a speech before the Munitions Manufacturers' Meeting, October 17, 1942, *Industrial Canada*, November, 1942, p. 29.
4. U.S., Congress, House of Representatives, Subcommittee of the Committee on Appropriations, *Hearings on the First Supplemental National Defense Appropriations for 1943*, (77th Cong., 2d sess.), part 2 (Washington: U.S. Government Printing Office, 1942), p. 277.
5. *Canada, House of Commons Debates*, November 10, 1941, p. 4223.
6. Historical Reports on War Administration, War Production Board, Documentary Publication No. 3, *Minutes of the Supply Priorities and Allocations Board, September 2, 1941 to January 15, 1942*, November 26, 1941 (Washington: U.S. Government Printing Office, 1946), pp. 30-1. This will be cited hereafter as *Minutes of the Supply Priorities and Allocations Board.*
7. *Ibid.*, p. 30.
8. *Minutes of the War Production Board*, February 24, 1942, p. 18. The Maritime Commission had requested 200,000 tons of steel plates in January, 1942, and had received only 172,000.
9. Donald Nelson, *Arsenal of Democracy*, pp. 355-6.
10. *Ibid.*
11. *Minutes of the Supply Priorities and Allocations Board*, September 2, 1941, p. 2.
12. *Ibid.*, p. 22.

13. General Allocation Order No. 1, November 29, 1941, 6 *Federal Register* 6144.

14. Office of Production Management, Press Release PM 1635, December 3, 1941.

15. War Production Board, Priorities Regulation No. 11, June 10, 1942, 7 *Federal Register* 4423.

16. *Minutes of the War Production Board,* January 20, 1942, p. 2.

17. Department of Munitions and Supply, Priorities Officer, Order No. P.O. 2, August 1, 1942.

18. War Production Board, General Administrative Order No. 16, March 3, 1942.

19. The letter addressed to William S. Knudsen and dated April 5, 1941, is cited in *Industrial Mobilization for War,* pp.123-4.

20. *Requirements Committee Bulletin* No. 1, April 8, 1942.

21. The End Products Committee was established by Administrative Order 508-20 of the Division of Industry Operations on April 23, 1942.

22. Letter, John F. Fennelly to James W. Fesler, August 5, 1946, quoted in *Industrial Mobilization for War,* p. 438.

23. Memorandum, W. M. Black to E. R. Gay, August 24, 1942.

24. Memorandum, Donald Nelson to J. S. Knowlson, May 25, 1942. Quoted in Historical Reports on War Administration, War Production Board, Special Study No. 20, *The Rôle of the Office of Civilian Requirements in the Office of Production Management and the War Production Board, January, 1941 to November, 1945* (Washington: U.S. Government Printing Office, 1946), p. 106.

25. It may be noted that in almost all cases, Canadian statements were not subjected to the detailed scrutiny accorded the requirements of the other claimants. Partly this was a result of the fact that Canadian requirements were relatively small. Also this may be attributed to the fact that the Standard Products Committee met in the morning. Canadian requirements were usually presented last, and by that time, the Committee members were hungry and more interested in lunch than in haggling over minutiae.

26. The clearest example of a restriction of this sort was the War Exchange Conservation Act of December, 1940, which prohibited the import of a wide range of luxury and semi-luxury goods from the United States.

27. Memorandum from the Chairman of the War Production Board to all Divisions of the War Production Board, November 19, 1942.

28. Sometime later, the Canadian Division was authorized to rate PD-1A applications under $1,000, and in early 1944, the limit was increased to $2,500.

29. The direct contacts of the War Production Board with industry were handled through the Industry Divisions, a development of the Industry Branches set up originally under the Office of Production Management. The Industry Divisions were organized along commodity lines and were responsible for the control and maintenance of production in the industry.

30. Memorandum, F. E. Eberstadt to the Office of Civilian Supply, December 11, 1942.

31. Historical Reports on War Administration, Bureau of the Budget No. 1, *The United States at War* (Washington: U.S. Government Printing Office, 1946), p. 128.

32. Memorandum, J. L. Weiner to F. E. Eberstadt, December 16, 1942.

33. This decision was embodied in the form of a memorandum from F. E. Eberstadt, Program Vice-Chairman of the War Production Board to the Department of Munitions and Supply issued as Requirements Committee Document No. 1218, January 2, 1943.

34. Actually, on at least one occasion, a proposed reduction in the allocation of steel to Canada in the third quarter of 1943 was referred to the Combined Production and Resources Board for adjudication.

35. *Industrial Mobilization for War,* p. 342.

36. Department of Munitions and Supply, Priorities Officer, Order No. P.O. 3, January 21, 1943.

37. Department of Munitions and Supply, Priorities Officer, Order No. P.O. 4, May 19, 1943.
38. The modified system went into effect on April 22, 1943, with the issuance of a circular letter by the Steel Controller. The regulation was formalized by Order No. S.C. 28, June 28, 1943.
39. General Scheduling Order M-293, February 26, 1943, 8 *Federal Register* 2472.
40. Office of Price Administration, Second Revised Maximum Export Price Regulations, March 30, 1943, 8 *Federal Register* 4132.
41. War Production Board, General Conservation Order M-317, August 16, 1943, 8 *Federal Register* 11364.
42. The National Textile and Leather Requirements Committee was created by P.C. 3888, May 10, 1943.
43. *Minutes of the War Production Board*, May 2, 1944, p. 335.
44. Memorandum, W. Y. Elliott to Donald Nelson and Charles E. Wilson, July 25, 1944, quoted in *History of the Office of Civilian Requirements*, p. 303.
45. *History of the Office of Civilian Requirements*, p. 303.
46. Combined Production and Resources Board and Combined Raw Materials Board, *Combined Statistical Summary of Raw Materials and Finished Products excluding Munitions*, August, 1945, p. 127.
47. Unrefined nickel exports include the nickel content of exports of soft roasted sulphide, oxide, and monel matte.
48. Historical Reports on War Administration, War Production Board, Special Study No. 22, *Aluminum Policies of the War Production Board and Predecessor Agencies, March, 1940, to November, 1945* (Washington: U.S. Government Printing Office, 1946), p. 42.
49. *Ibid.*, p. 43.
50. U.S., Senate, Special Committee Investigating the National Defense Program, *Third Annual Report*, p. 68.
51. Quoted in *Aluminum Policies of the War Production Board*, p. 50. The question of duties on imports for war production is discussed in Chapter VIII which deals with trade barriers.
52. *Ibid.*, p. 54.
53. *Minutes of the Council of the Office of Production Management*, June 17, 1941, pp. 33-4.
54. Contract between Metals Reserve Company and Aluminum Company of Canada, Limited, in the form of a letter, August 26, 1941. Cited in *Aluminum Policies of the War Production Board*, p. 81.
55. *Ibid.*, p. 98.
56. *Ibid.*, p. 171.
57. U.S., Senate, Special Committee Investigating the National Defense Program, *Third Annual Report*, p. 68.

Chapter VII

THE CONTROL OF OVERSEAS EXPORTS

Government regulation of commercial exports was an important part of the system of wartime controls in both Canada and the United States. Initially, the aim was to stop the movement of strategic and other materials to enemy countries. As military requirements absorbed increasing propor- tions of the resources of the two countries and as conquering armies spread across the world, the objects of export control changed and became more diverse. Apart from its rôle in economic warfare, export control was used to stop excessive exports of goods which might hinder the production of munitions or deplete supplies of civilian goods unduly. In Canada, in par- ticular, any available export surpluses of many commodities had to be directed to meet contractual and other obligations to the United Kingdom. Export control was also a political device to encourage allegiance to the United Nations.

The first section of this chapter deals mainly with the administrative agencies responsible for export control in each country and with their adaptation to changing economic and political conditions. The second section is concerned with the formal and informal co-operation between the export control agencies in Canada and the United States. While the main aim is to describe the administrative background of co-operation, some attention is also paid to the official and unofficial attitudes which were important in determining the effectiveness of the liaison. Some aspects of co-operation between Canada and the United States in the field of economic warfare are discussed in the third section. The main features of this discussion are the use of the black list and the special treatment of Canadian exports through the United States to areas subject to blockade controls. The fourth section is concerned with the development of a co-ordinated export policy. The dependence of third countries on commercial exports from both Canada and the United States meant that, without the co-ordination of export restrictions, any attempts by one country alone to restrict overseas exports would be futile. The achievement of co-ordinated restrictions was not simple and, in some cases, involved major revisions of export regula- tions. In addition, some approach was made to the formulation of joint export programmes, particularly to Latin America. These programmes involved the establishment of allocations or quotas of commodities for certain countries and the determination of the share of the quotas to be assigned to Canada and the United States, and, sometimes, to other countries. Complex questions of equity, economics, and politics arose in fixing overall quotas for individual countries. Continuous negotiations on the sharing of quotas were conducted and required the most intimate co-operation. Sometimes these discussions were bedevilled by considerations of post-war commercial advantage, which, despite the war, remained in evidence. The final section of the chapter contains a relatively brief account of the relaxation of export controls in a period of expanding exports and growing commercial rivalry.

1. THE ADMINISTRATIVE FRAMEWORK OF EXPORT CONTROL

(a) Export Control Agencies in Canada

In Canada, export control of a limited kind had been in effect for several years prior to the outbreak of war. The power to impose such control stemmed from section 290 of the Customs Act,[1] which provides that the Governor-in-Council may require that no person shall export any specified article without first having obtained a permit, and that exports of munitions or other articles considered useful or necessary in war may be prohibited, restricted or controlled. In the summer of 1937, the growing tension in Europe and the "dangerous strife" in Spain led to the imposition of export control over munitions.[2] Shortly after the outbreak of war in September, 1939, the list of controlled items was extended to cover strategic raw materials such as aluminum, copper, nickel, cobalt, stellite, all kinds of scrap metal, and wool.[3] Export was prohibited unless a permit had been obtained from the Minister of National Revenue. Early in 1940, another group of materals was added to the list, including mica, radium and uranium salts, certain alloys and alloy ingredients, certain rare earths, and a number of iron and steel products.[4] These actions were taken to prevent strategic or critical materials from reaching enemy destinations, as well as to safeguard domestic supplies. Another important extension of export control occurred in November, 1940, when more iron and steel products, most machine tools, industrial diamonds and chrome ore were added to the list of controlled commodities.[5] From time to time, during the first eighteen months of the war, export controls were imposed over other commodities. Often the control was adopted at the request of agencies such as the Wartime Prices and Trade Board or the Agricultural Supplies Board, to assist in controlling an emergency supply difficulty or to facilitate procurement. Special emergency powers were also assigned by order-in-council to the Controllers of the Department of Munitions and Supply and the Administrators of the Wartime Prices and Trade Board to prohibit exports or to issue permits for exports of goods under their control.[6]

Although the actual issuance of licences was usually in the hands of the Department of National Revenue, responsibility for various other aspects of export control was rather widely scattered throughout the government by the spring of 1941. Individual Administrators and Controllers and special boards had been authorized to prohibit or license exports of certain commodities while other exports were under the jurisdiction of the Department of National Revenue. As a result, commercial exporters were confused by the diffusion of authority. Delays in the issuance of licences inevitably resulted. Moreover, with so many different agencies involved, it was difficult to make effective use of export control in economic warfare and blockade activities.

In consequence, it was decided to centralize export licensing powers in one department. Early in April, 1941, an order-in-council was passed conferrring on the Minister of Trade and Commerce the sole right to issue export licences.[7] At the same time, the creation of an Export Permit Branch in the Department of Trade and Commerce was authorized. The order-in-council withdrew from various Controllers, Administrators, and government departments the power to issue licences or permits for the export of goods, but the power to prohibit exports was not affected. The grant of powers to the Department of Trade and Commerce was, as a result, not as great as it seemed. It was still open to other departments or government agencies to issue a ministerial or a comparable order prohibiting exports. The power to prohibit exports was overriding, no matter what the mechanics of issuing licences were. The consequences of the continued diffusion of authority is illustrated by one instance of export control instituted by the Department of Agriculture. On August 25, 1941, two orders issued by the Minister of Agriculture prohibited exports of oats or barley, either alone or in combination with other feed grains, and low-grade wheat, except under permit by the Minister of Trade and Commerce. It was something of a surprise to the export licensing officials when applications for permission to export these commodities began to reach them, since they had previously been quite unaware of the issuance of the new regulations. The incomplete grant of power to the Department of Trade and Commerce thus contributed to the difficulty of establishing a unified policy of export control in Canada.

The order-in-council centralizing powers of export licensing recommended that the Advisory Committee on Economic Policy be asked for guidance on the principles to be followed in administering export control. The committee suggested the appointment of an Advisory Committee on Export Control and an Executive Subcommittee. Both of these bodies were accordingly created by order-in-council late in November, 1941.[8]

However, the senior committee was not very active and except in a few cases, the responsibility for determining Canadian export control policy rested with the Executive Subcommittee of the Advisory Committee on Export Control. This body will be referred to hereafter as the Export Control Subcommittee. Originally, the Export Control Subcommittee consisted of three members from the Department of Trade and Commerce, and representatives of the Department of External Affairs, the Department of Munitions and Supply, the Wartime Prices and Trade Board, and the Foreign Exchange Control Board. The Chairman was an official of the Department of Trade and Commerce. The number of committee members grew during the war and, from time to time, other persons concerned with export control problems attended the committee meetings by invitation.

During the early life of the Export Control Subcommittee there were indications that the Canadian shortage of United States dollars might have an important influence on export control policy. The Foreign Exchange Control Board was represented on the Export Control Subcommittee throughout its existence and the committee deliberated at length on the desirability of channelling exports to hard currency countries. While the policy was adopted by the committee that export control should operate to alleviate the shortage of United States dollars, this factor was always of secondary importance. Cases may have arisen in which exchange considerations were significant, but, in general, they did not influence Canadian export control policy to an appreciable extent. On the other hand, the Foreign Exchange Control Board had established its own system of licensing exports.[9] Foreign exchange regulations stipulated that a licence be issued for all exports requiring a customs export entry. The licence form and the customs export entry form were combined, and usually the Collector of Customs and Excise issued these licences on behalf of the Foreign Exchange Control Board as a routine matter. In certain special cases, approval of an authorized dealer in foreign exchange or the Foreign Exchange Control Board was required. The aim of the system was merely to provide records of exports for which payment would be made in United States dollars or in equivalent currencies. On the basis of these records, the Foreign Exchange Control Board was able to ensure that any United States dollar proceeds of exports would be sold to it and not improperly diverted. No control was exercised by this licensing system over the kinds of goods to be exported.

The Export Control Subcommittee met first on December 15, 1941, and immediately attempted to arrive at some policy concerning the respective places of export trade and domestic civilian trade. There seemed to be agreement that export and domestic trade should be treated equally, on the understanding that requirements arising out of the war effort were to be given absolute preference. Essential civilian needs in Canada and in other countries would be looked after next, while domestic and foreign civilian needs were to come last. It was also agreed that export trade was to be encouraged only with normal customers and only if political and commercial advantage would result either immediately or in the future. In commenting on the wartime policy, a senior government official later pointed out: "The Department of Trade and Commerce . . . did its best to see that such exports as were permitted were directed to maintaining trade with a continuing value and to see that historic markets were served."[10] The attitude of the Export Control Subcommittee reflected the view held by certain groups in the government, particularly in the Department of Trade and Commerce, that export control was to be a significant factor in the promotion of foreign trade.

Despite this attitude, it was difficult for the Export Control Subcommittee to establish a coherent and consistent policy. One reason was that the power to impose controls on specific commodities was widely diffused throughout the wartime agencies, even though the licensing machinery was centralized in the Department of Trade and Commerce. In addition, there was a statement in the governing order-in-council that the Export Permit Branch, which was the operating arm of the Export Control Subcommittee, should consult with, and secure the advice of, a responsible official of the agency established to deal with the supply of a particular product, before an export licence for that product was granted. In practice, this usually meant that the Controllers of the Department of Munitions and Supply and the Administrators of the Wartime Prices and Trade Board could effectively control the volume of supplies available for export. The division of authority was recognized as a possible source of difficulty in the early period of export control and the matter was referred to the Advisory Committee on Export Control. In July, 1941, this committee decided that the Administrators, the Controllers and other supply authorities should retain the power to fix the quantities of goods available for export. The officials responsible for civilian supply were naturally concerned principally with the maintenance of adequate supplies of scarce goods for home consumption and were not inclined to be sympathetic to generalized pleas concerning the welfare of foreign civilians or the benefits of export trade. As a result, inadequacy of domestic supply tended to dominate export policy and decisions concerning export applications were reached mainly on the basis of supply considerations. When the wartime agencies were relatively small, it had been possible to resolve disagreements by consultation, but, by 1942, the growing number of Administrators and Controllers, some of whom were stationed in Toronto and Montreal, meant that regular personal consultation was no longer practical.

The importance of export control grew rapidly after Pearl Harbor, and in the first few months of 1942 an increasingly large number of commodities were placed under export control. This was partly because of growing shortages of many goods, especially those containing metal, and partly because of the aggressive concern of supply officials for domestic needs. The imposition of export control over a commodity became almost automatic once a domestic shortage became noticeable. In addition, with the spread of the war, control had to be extended to more and more countries of destination. A major development of this sort occurred early in March, 1943, when an order was issued requiring permits for any exports to any country except parts of the British Empire and the United States.[11] The principal effect of the new ruling was that all exports valued at more than $5 to Latin American countries required a permit, and not merely certain specified commodities. The gradual extension of control over more goods and more destinations was accompanied by some disagreement among government officials on both the administrative and policy aspects of export control.

Since the initiative in imposing domestic and export restrictions remained with the supply authorities, it was inevitable that there should be some lack of co-ordination in export policy. This was not always the result of the unwillingness of Administrators or Controllers to approve exports. For example, in the spring of 1942, the Export Control Subcommittee was unwilling to release certain agricultural machinery to the United States despite the urging of the responsible Administrator that an export permit be granted. In this case, the Administrator had an understanding with the War Production Board which permitted certain definite quotas of special types of equipment to move between the two countries and the actions of the Export Control Subcommittee threatened to interfere with the agreement which had been reached. While this particular case was resolved by an appeal to higher quarters, it was symptomatic of the lack of adequate liaison on matters affecting export policy.

In general, the Administrators and Controllers were from industry and were usually more familiar with the supply situation than officials directly concerned with the administration of export control. In view of their more detailed knowledge of current conditions, the supply officials were better able to determine the volume of goods that could be made available for export. Gradually ceilings on the volume of exports of many commodities were established.[12] After the Administrators of the Wartime Prices and

Trade Board or the Controllers of the Department of Munitions and Supply had established an export ceiling, licences up to that amount were automatically approved by the Export Permit Branch of the Department of Trade and Commerce, provided that other aspects of the application, such as the consignee and the country of destination, were satisfactory. This method of operation was essential for the efficient administration of the export licensing system.

Usually, export quotas were merely ceilings on the level of exports and firm allocations for commercial exports were not fixed by the various supply authorities.[13] As a result, for many commodities, the amount available for export was a residual and the size of the residual fluctuated with changing supply conditions. The Chairman of the Export Control Subcommittee stressed this point in the following excerpt from a speech in June, 1942:

> Has the government any policy with respect to the allocations of definite quantities or percentages of supplies for export? The answer . . . is definitely "no." The constantly changing war manufacturing programme makes it impossible to establish any percentage of Canada's normal manufactures as available for either export or civilian use.[14]

One of the consequences of this policy in the early period of export control was that a disproportionate amount of time was spent by the Export Control Subcommittee in dealing with individual applications for export licences and with the assessment of the available supplies of specific commodities. The inadequacy of this system came to be recognized, and over the next two or three years, more sophisticated export programmes involving definite export allocations began to be developed.

In the spring of 1944, the scope and importance of export planning in Canada was substantially increased with the creation of the External Trade Advisory Committee.[15] This was a senior inter-departmental committee created expressly to clarify Canadian import and export policy and to make recommendations to the executive branches of the government concerned with external trade. At the time of the creation of this committee, export demands were high and it was recognized that urgent needs for relief and rehabilitation in liberated areas would have serious repercussions on civilian supplies. One of the major functions of the External Trade Advisory Committee was to determine the quantities of goods other than food to be made available for relief and rehabilitation.[16] The appointment of this high-level committee provided a channel for the resolution of issues involving domestic needs and export policy and programmes. Except in matters of policy, much of the detailed work of the External Trade Advisory Committee was assigned to its Standing Committee, which cooperated very closely with the Export Control Subcommittee. In fact, beginning in the middle of March, 1945, joint meetings of the two committees were begun and continued until the committees ceased to function.

(b) *Export Control Agencies in the United States*

Export control of a sort had been in effect in the United States for some years prior to 1939. Apart from the outright embargo on the shipment of munitions to belligerents imposed by the Neutrality Act of 1935 and similar related acts, a licensing control over exports to belligerents of other goods useful in war had been adopted in the late 1930's. For example, in the Neutrality Act of 1939, licences were required for the export of all arms, ammunition, and implements of war, and the President was authorized to proclaim lists of the articles covered.[17] In the meantime, the list enumerated in the proclamation of May 1, 1937, banning the export of arms to Spain, was to remain in effect.[18] Wartime export control of a more general type was authorized in the summer of 1940 by Congress in the Act of July 2, 1940.[19] The relevant section of the legislation provided that

Whenever the President determines that it is necessary in the interest of national defense to prohibit or curtail the exportation of any military equipment or munitions, or component parts thereof, or machinery, tools or material, or supplies necessary for the manufacture, servicing or operation thereof, he may by proclamation prohibit or curtail such exportation, except under such rules and regulations as he shall prescribe.

The President immediately issued a proclamation announcing the imposition of export control.[20] The proclamation stated that a licence was required before any person could export a long list of articles such as arms, ammunition and implements of war; a group of critical materials ranging from aluminum, antimony, and asbestos to vanadium and wool; certain specified chemicals; aircraft, armour plate, and optical materials; and machine tools.[21] In the regulations accompanying the proclamation, the power to issue export licences was assigned to the Secretary of State, who was to be guided by specific directives submitted to him by the Office of Export Control, a new agency under the direction of an Administrator. The administration of export control was regarded as "essentially a military function," and accordingly, President Roosevelt appointed an Army officer to act as Administrator of Export Control.[22] The Office of Export Control was originally almost completely staffed by military personnel.

The scope of export control was gradually broadened in an attempt to restrict exports of critical materials to the Axis powers. More positive measures were adopted in June, 1941, when an order was issued freezing all Axis assets in the United States. With the adoption of more forthright measures of economic warfare against the Axis, some realignment of the administrative structure of export control and economic defence, in general, was necessary.

This occurred with the creation, at the end of July, 1941, of the Economic Defense Board, whose function was "to co-ordinate policies, plans and programs designed to protect and strengthen the international economic relations of the United States in the interests of national defense . . . ."[23] The responsibilities of the new agency were to include the co-ordination of the programmes of different agencies concerned with exports, imports, economic warfare, preclusive buying, and related international economic activities. Not long after its creation, the Economic Defense Board absorbed the export control functions of the Office of Export Control and most of the related functions of the Division of Controls of the Department of State.[24] In addition, the Economic Defense Board was authorized to develop export programmes and to advise the Supply Priorities and Allocations Board of the quantities of materials required for export, and to notify the Office of Production Management of the priority ratings which would be required to meet its objectives. Shortly after Pearl Harbor, the Economic Defense Board was renamed the Board of Economic Warfare.[25]

The Board of Economic Warfare was explicit in its warnings to the trade that exports would be restricted to the minimum levels necessary. In one public release, exporters were advised not to submit applications for licences for critically scarce commodities needed in the United States war production programme.[26] It went on to say that applications would be considered only for "vital needs" in the country of destination and listed as examples requirements for national defence, and goods needed in the production of war materials, in essential public utilities and other industries.

In April, 1942, the functions of the Board of Economic Warfare were extended to include responsibility for carrying out directives of the War Production Board relating to the procurement of strategic and critical materials outside the United States.[27] The financial aspects of foreign procurement of these materials were to be handled by the United States Commercial Company or other subsidiaries of the Reconstruction Finance Corporation, which were to be subject to the direction of the Board of Economic Warfare.[28] The fact that the Board of Economic Warfare was responsible for the operation of the foreign procurement programme was of great importance in the determination of its export control policy, in view of the inter-relations of exports from the United States and imports from foreign countries. At the same time, the Board of Economic Warfare was authorized to advise the Department of State on the terms and conditions of lend-lease master agreements, and to arrange for the provisions of reciprocal lend-lease to the United States.

Some aspects of export control policy were also the concern of the Department of State. The plenary powers assigned to the Board of Economic Warfare in this field conflicted significantly with the traditional responsibilities of the Department of State. As a result, a presidential ruling was obtained which emphasized that the Department of State was primarily responsible for the formulation and conduct of foreign policy and for relations with foreign countries. The Board of Economic Warfare was to be mainly responsible for the technical and business aspects of foreign economic relations, but negotiations in foreign countries were to be under the ægis of the diplomatic representatives of the United States.[29] The detailed implementation of this ruling was agreed on in various discussions between the Board of Economic Warfare and the Department of State.[30] As a result, the Department of State kept a watchful eye on export control policy to minimize conflicts between the economic and diplomatic aspects of foreign policy.

A major reorganization of the United States agencies concerned with economic warfare took place in July, 1943, following a well-advertised dispute between the Chairman of the Board of Economic Warfare, who was also the Vice-President of the United States, and the Federal Loan Administrator, over the financial aspects of foreign purchasing. Out of the shakeup emerged the Office of Economic Warfare, which absorbed the Board of Economic Warfare, and assumed control over the foreign economic activities of the Reconstruction Finance Corporation and a number of its subsidiaries, such as the United States Commercial Company, the Rubber Development Corporation, the Petroleum Reserve Corporation, and the Export-Import Bank of Washington.[31]

Finally, all the agencies concerned with international economic relations were consolidated in the Foreign Economic Administration.[32] The new agency absorbed the Office of Economic Warfare, the Office of Lend-Lease Administration, the Office of Foreign Relief and Rehabilitation Operations, and many of the functions of the Office of Foreign Economic Co-ordination of the Department of State.

In the United States, internal administrative and political developments fostered a certain fluidity in the export control agencies. In Canada, some conflicts between different interests did occur, but they were not aired in the public press, nor did they stimulate the kind of factiousness which typified export control and related activities in the United States. The volatile character of the export control agencies in the United States was naturally a matter of some importance to Canada. Not only was there an ever-present possibility of significant policy changes as a result of the various administrative reorganizations which occurred, but there was a lamentable tendency to forget about Canada. This did not mean there was any un-willingness to co-operate with Canada. It was simply necessary in many cases to remind officials in the United States that despite their urgent domestic issues, Canada was also interested in exports and export controls and often intimately affected by the actions of the United States.

2. The Background of Co-operation

The close commercial relations between Canada and the United States strongly influenced the scope of export control in Canada as well as the policies followed by the Canadian authorities. For one thing, there was a strong impetus to establish Canadian export controls paralleling those in force in the United States. This was essential if Canada was not to become a "back-door" through which exports might be trans-shipped to other countries in contravention of the intent of the United States regulations. In view of this, the Canadian list of controlled commodities was revised and expanded continually to match the commodities subject to export control in the United States, so that the special exemptions applying to exports to Canada did not permit the circumvention of the United States regulations by unscrupulous exporters. Co-ordination in this case was semi-automatic, but the same could not always be said of a number of other aspects of export control. The fact that an identical list of goods was controlled was, of course, no guarantee of parallelism of control in view of the discretionary powers of the control authorities.

It must also be made clear that the willingness of the United States to export critical commodities to Canada depended to some extent on the willingness of Canada to accept certain definite criteria of export control. Such a consideration is unlikely to be expressed as an ultimatum, indeed, it it not likely to be expressed at all. Nonetheless, since Canada's production programme was vitally dependent on components from the United States, any export policy which tended to jeopardize the continued availability of essential ingredients from the United States was unlikely to be perpetuated.

In Canada, there were two special reasons for export control which were not of comparable importance in the United States. The first of these was a consequence of the extensive use of subsidies in Canada as a price stabilization device. Any goods which were subsidized were placed under export control to facilitate the recovery of the domestic subsidy. Since the issuance of an export licence was conditional on the repayment of the subsidy, there was no chance that the subsidy would accrue to the benefit of persons outside Canada. In the second place, export control was used to channel certain goods, particularly food, to specific export markets in fulfilment of Canadian contractual agreements. For example, rigid control was exercised over the export of such items as pork products and canned salmon to assure that the quantities needed by the United Kingdom would not be diverted to other, perhaps more lucrative markets.

The existence of independent export controls in Canada and the United States meant that there was ample opportunity for misunderstanding and confusion in this field. Although the export control officials of the two countries had reached a number of agreements covering specific commodities before the summer of 1941, no inter-governmental machinery existed to provide for regular consultation or for the exchange of information on operating policy. The lack of co-ordination between the export control systems of Canada and the United States was one of the first problems to be considered by the Joint Economic Committees. At the first joint session of the Committees, it was noted that the export control policies were uncoordinated and that in both countries there was misunderstanding of the methods and policies of the other. On July 16, 1941, the Committees formally recommended to the President and to the Prime Minister that steps be taken to provide for the alignment of export control policies and for the exchange of complete information by the officials concerned. The Committees recommended:

(a) that the Governments of Canada and of the United States give immediate consideration to the possibility of establishing a more coordinate policy in the field of export control wherever greater coordination would contribute to the defence effort of one or both countries;

(b) that appropriate steps be taken to facilitate and insure an accurate, complete and continuous transmission of information between the export control authorities of the two countries; and

(c) that the Department of State and the Department of External Affairs be directed to initiate whatever steps may be necessary to implement this recommendation.[33]

It was the opinion of the committees that, without improved liaison, the policies and procedures of the export control agencies might diverge sufficiently to prevent the attainment of this common aim.

The plea of the Joint Economic Committees for "a more coordinate policy" was only the first of many. Again and again, as the problems of co-ordination became more involved, there were suggestions that the solution was to be found in an international committee of some sort. Although there were committees created at different times to deal with special aspects of export problems, no joint committee with authority to co-ordinate all aspects of export control policy was ever created.

There was, nevertheless, close personal contact between officials of the two countries, which meant that effective agreements were often made informally. On a number of occasions, the Chairman of the Export Control Subcommittee and other members visited Washington to discuss problems of policy as well as administrative details. After his first visit to Washington, the Chairman of the Export Control Subcommittee reported to the Committee that his discussions had been extremely cordial and that he had left Washington with the belief that complete co-operation could be achieved if it did not already exist. He went on to refer to the friendly feeling and trust which Americans have for Canada and noted that there did not seem to be any divergence in the official attitude to exports in the two countries. On other occasions, United States export control officials attended meetings in Ottawa to discuss various aspects of both the policy and the mechanics of export control. The amicable attitude of the United States is illustrated by an excerpt from a letter written in January, 1942, by the Chief of the Office of Export Control of the Board of Economic Warfare to a member of the staff of the Canadian Legation, noting that certain proposals which would require individual licences for the export of a list of critical commodities to Canada had been abandoned. He wrote, "You know, of course, that we have no other desire than to promote to the fullest extent the cordial and co-operative relations already existing between our two countries."[34]

The greatest part of the liaison work between the Canadian export control agency and the comparable body in Washington was handled by members of the staff of the Canadian Legation or Embassy in Washington. The appointment of Canadian representatives in Washington was a clear recognition of the wisdom of the recommendation of the Joint Economic Committees "that appropriate steps be taken to facilitate and insure an accurate, complete and continuous transmission of information between the export control authorities of the two countries."[35] Much of the effectiveness of co-operation in export control was a result of the outstanding efforts of Canadian diplomatic representatives to achieve and maintain satisfactory working relations with the proper United States officials. All the good will in the world is not a substitute for effective and efficient co-operation on practical everyday problems.

Despite the amicable personal relations between the export control bodies in the two countries, there were occasions when the Canadians entertained some distrust of the motives of the United States, and when Canadian actions were regarded with some suspicion in Washington. For one thing, many of the persons administering export control in the United States had been engaged in private export business before the war, and, on the basis of this fact alone, there was some anxious wondering in Ottawa whether there was any relation between current export control policy and post-war commercial prospects in Latin American trade. Sometimes public utterances by United States officials did little to allay this suspicion. For example, the Executive Director of the Board of Economic Warfare, in testifying on export control operations before a Congressional committee, stated:

The whole job is complicated by the need to protect United States commercial exporters, just as far as it is physically possible to do so in a war economy. This is especially true of the smaller exporters. Just as in the case of importers, we need the trained services of exporters now; we shall undoubtedly need them much more to spearhead United States commercial activities abroad when the war is over. This means that the Government export control machinery must perform a lot of service functions in addition to merely licensing exports. It must help get the goods produced, moved to the seaboard and actually shipped.[36]

Canadian officials were also aware that the Economic Defense Board had been created "for the purpose of developing and co-ordinating policies, plans, and programs designed to protect and strengthen the international economic relations of the United States in the interest of national defense."[37] It was felt that this large responsibility might not exclude the outright promotion of United States commercial interests in Latin America.

Official Canadian statements of the aims of export control were even less reassuring. For example, the preamble to the order-in-council centralizing export licensing in the Department of Trade and Commerce contained the following comment:

Since the Minister of Trade and Commerce is the Minister chiefly responsible for the promotion of Canadian export trade and since the issue of export permits would provide the Department of Trade and Commerce with a great deal of information which would be of value in connection with their efforts to promote Canadian export trade, it is considered desirable in the opinion of the Advisory Committee on Economic Policy to establish an Export Permit Branch in the Department of Trade and Commerce to centralize the control over the issuance of export permits for all products for which permits are required.[38]

Moreover, some of the public utterances of Canadian officials concerned with export control might have been interpreted to indicate that Canada also was militantly seeking to maintain exports. The Chairman of the

Export Control Subcommittee remarked in a speech before the Canadian Manufacturers' Association in the spring of 1942:

The Government . . . has, in a broad sense, an export policy, which is to encourage the maintenance of legitimate trade to as great an extent as is possible in view of conditions imposed by the war. I think I can assure you that every one connected with export control in Ottawa, and the various Administrators of the Wartime Prices and Trade Board and the Controllers appointed by the Department of Munitions and Supply are unanimous in their recognition of the fact that export trade is vital to the normal Canadian standard of living and that they are doing all in their power to make supplies available to ensure that export trade is maintained at the highest possible level, having regard always for the necessity of recognizing that the war effort must have priority over all other considerations.[39]

There were significant differences in the machinery of export control in the two countries merely because of the large-scale operations in the United States. During 1942 and 1943, the United States agency concerned with the issuance of export licences had to process approximately 5,000-7,000 applications a day, compared to a few hundred a day in Canada.[40] This fact, combined with the need for detailed factual information about export programmes, meant that comprehensive statistical operations were an essential feature of export control in the United States. In both 1943 and 1944, the United States export control agency transferred nearly a million dollars to the Bureau of Foreign and Domestic Commerce of the Department of Commerce to pay the salaries of over 400 people engaged in statistical work relating to exports. Canadian export control depended more heavily on the expert knowledge of a few individuals, who had neither the staff nor the time to devote to detailed statistical analysis. It was naturally difficult for the Canadian authorities to furnish the mass of statistical detail which seemed always to be required before a joint programme could be worked out. Sometimes, requests for statistical information emanating from the United States were ill-considered, and the burden of preparing statistical reports of doubtful significance gave rise to some resentment and antagonism in Canada.

Minor dissatisfactions and grievances occasionally arose, but these were unimportant compared to the generally friendly tone of Canadian relations with the United States in the field of international economic relations. This was partly a result of the fact that in export control, the principles of economic co-operation were maintained unimpaired. It is worth noting that liaison with the export control authorities in Washington was the responsibility of the Canadian Legation or Embassy, whose normal approach to United States government agencies was through the Department of State. Friendly diplomatic relations were of incalculable benefit in facilitating agreement on the basic policies of export control. An indication of the official attitude of each country is contained in the exchange of notes of November 30, 1942, which reaffirmed the policy of economic co-operation in addition to sketching an agreement on basic post-war trade policies.[41] Shortly after, the Department of State instructed all diplomatic officers in Latin America that they should accord their Canadian counterparts the closest possible co-operation. The instructions went on to emphasize that the policy of the two governments was to restrict export trade to an equitable proportion of pre-war trade and to prevent any national of one country from taking any advantage at the expense of nationals of the other. It is evident that the affirmation of wide-spread feelings of cordiality in diplomatic agreements and statements was useful in establishing satisfactory operating procedures in the field of export control.

3. Co-operation in the Field of Economic Warfare

In both Canada and the United States, the cardinal aim of economic warfare was to bring economic pressure to bear on the enemy and, in particular, to prevent shipments of strategic materials to the Axis. The early export control measures in Canada were adopted with this object specifically in mind, and it was only in unusual circumstances that control was imposed for other reasons. Later, an increase in export prices which stimulated excessive exports became a common reason for the adoption of export controls. The efficient conduct of economic warfare required the services of skilled technicians and field operatives as well as current information about the political sympathies and activities of traders in neutral countries. Canada had neither the personnel nor sufficient independent interest in the blockade problem to justify the establishment of an economic warfare agency. Consequently, Canada relied on the example and advice of the United Kingdom in dealing with European neutrals. After the entry of the United States into the war, economic warfare operations in Europe were the joint concern of the United Kingdom and the United States while Canada continued to accept the joint policies which were adopted. So far as Latin America was concerned, Canada relied on the policy of the economic warfare agencies of the United States, particularly in assessing the desirability of consignees.

One of the principal weapons of economic warfare was the black list of Axis concerns or of persons in non-Axis countries known to be trading with the enemy. The black list, of course, supplemented the general rule forbidding relations with persons in enemy countries.[42] During the fall of 1939, the United Kingdom published at different times lists of persons living in neutral countries who were considered to be enemies within the meaning of the United Kingdom Contraband and Trading with the Enemy Act (1939). Canada followed suit late in 1939 by issuing lists of specified persons in neutral countries deemed to have "an enemy character" for the purposes of Canadian Regulations Respecting Trading with the Enemy.[43] Unless official consent had been obtained, any intercourse, commercial or otherwise, with persons or firms on the list was prohibited. In January, 1940, additional Canadian controls over the export of goods to neutral countries were adopted which required a licence for all exports to neutral countries contiguous to areas under enemy occupation and control.[44] Throughout the early months of 1940, export control was rapidly extended to cover other European neutrals. In February, licences were required for all exports to Bulgaria, Estonia, Finland, Greece, Latvia, Norway, Roumania, Spain, and Sweden,[45] and, in April, for exports to Albania, Iceland, Portugal, and Turkey.[46] After the fall of France, export permits were necessary for shipments to France and the French colonies, protectorates or other territories under French control.[47] A number of other relatively unimportant areas and territories were added to the list in the summer of 1940. Finally, in March, 1941, an overriding order-in-council was passed which required export licences for any goods destined to countries outside the Western Hemisphere exclusive of the British Empire or areas under British control.[48]

Initially, the United States relied on a licensing system established under regulations freezing the assets of designated countries in the United States. The authority for this type of control was contained in the Trading with the Enemy Act of 1917.[49] This financial control was first applied to Norway and Denmark on April 8, 1940, following the Nazi invasion of these countries, and was successively extended to other occupied countries.[50] Finally, by June, 1941, the regulations were extended to the whole of continental Europe, including Germany and Italy. With the invasion of Indo-China by Japan, the freezing control order was extended to include Japan and China. This type of control was originally designed to protect the assets of invaded countries, held in the United States, from falling into the hands of the aggressor nations. Gradually, the objectives of freezing control were widened to include the prevention of any financial, commercial or trade transactions between the United States and any country or any person likely to menace the security of the Western Hemisphere.[51] By the summer of 1941, more rigorous control was instituted over commercial intercourse which might benefit the Axis by the introduction of supplementary export licensing regulations. On July 17, 1941, President

Roosevelt authorized the Secretary of State, acting in conjunction with the Secretary of the Treasury, the Attorney General, the Secretary of Commerce and the Co-ordinator of Commercial and Cultural Relations between the American Republics, to prepare a list of persons who appeared to have any connection with Germany or Italy or their nationals.[52] At the same time, the President made public a preliminary Proclaimed List of Certain Blocked Nationals, covering about 1,800 firms. A wide range of goods could not be exported to any listed person without an export licence. The particular goods covered were any of those specified in the presidential proclamation of July 2, 1940 or in later proclamations or any forms, conversions or derivatives of military equipment or munitions or related components or machinery.[53] In effect, the list of articles controlled in this way included most scarce or critical materials. Moreover, if any listed person had any interest whatever in any export transaction being carried out by others, a supplementary licence was required from the Foreign Funds Control of the Treasury Department. It is of some interest to note that some firms in the United States had refused to export to anyone named on the United Kingdom black list before the issuance of the corresponding United States list. The promulgation of the United States list, however, meant that the paraphernalia of control was complete. Exports could be restricted to conserve scarce commodities and to prevent any trade with consignees associated in any way with the Axis.

The proclamation of July 17, 1941, also revoked any general licences, unlimited licences or general in-transit licences, i.e., licences not requiring the clearance of individual export shipments, for any exports consigned to persons on the proclaimed list. This suspension of general in-transit licences for any exports to consignees on the black list was of some importance to Canada. It meant that Canadian export permits covering shipments moving through United States ports of exit to black-listed consignees would require clearance from the United States authorities also. There was thus strong pressure on Canada to make the Canadian list of specified persons conform to the United States black list. As a result, a special committee in which both the United Kingdom and Canada were represented was established in Washington under the aegis of the Department of State to deal with black list problems and the issuance of uniform lists. The open black list published in Canada was thus based on information obtained from the economic warfare agencies of both the United Kingdom and the United States.

In addition to the proclaimed list, the United States compiled other unpublished lists containing the names of persons suspected or known to be aiding the Axis, the publication of which was not considered desirable, for diplomatic or other reasons. The Canadian export control authorities were informed of the contents of these lists and were scrupulously careful to check all consignees before issuing export licences to Latin America. As a result, there was complete co-ordination of United States and Canadian efforts to prevent shipments to undesirable consignees in Latin America.

There was also intimate co-operation between the United States and the United Kingdom in the field of economic warfare. Soon after the outbreak of war, the Ministry of Economic Warfare announced that the United Kingdom, as a belligerent, would exercise fully its rights to search neutral vessels. In order to avoid the delays involved in physical searches of cargoes at Contraband Control Bases, a certification system was eventually adopted, which required that all ships or goods consigned to ports from which goods could be trans-shipped to the enemy must be covered by navicerts, mailcerts, aircerts, or equivalent licences. The navicert system was an integral part of the War Trade Agreements which the United Kingdom had reached with the different European neutrals. The aim of these agreements was to limit overseas imports to quantities required for domestic consumption in the neutral country of destination and to prevent or limit the trans-shipment of goods to the enemy. A navicert was a certificate issued by a United Kingdom consular official in the country of origin that a cargo was in accordance with the terms of the applicable War Trade Agreement. This meant that the cargo was a normal import and was within the import quota which had been agreed on. In addition to a navicert covering the cargo, a ship's navicert was also needed before a voyage through the blockade controls could be undertaken. This system of screening exports was an essential part of the blockade and attempted to preserve neutral rights without weakening the blockade. Goods shipped without a navicert were liable to confiscation as prizes of war. The so-called navicert areas included Eire, Portugal, Portuguese Atlantic Islands, Portuguese Guinea, Spain, Spanish Atlantic Islands, Spanish Morocco, Sweden, Switzerland, Tangier, and Turkey.

In the United Kingdom, an inter-departmental Blockade Committee was established early in the war to co-ordinate several aspects of economic warfare against the Axis. This Committee, which operated under the aegis of the Ministry of Economic Warfare, exercised general supervision over such matters as black lists, navicerts, contraband, and agreements with neutral governments. With the entry of the United States into the war, the Committee was replaced by a Joint Anglo-American Blockade Committee in London. The Ministry of Economic Warfare and the United States economic warfare agency had equal representation on this body. The

Canadian Trade Commissioner for the United Kingdom sat on the Committee to represent Canadian interests. The Joint Blockade Committee became responsible for the issuance of navicerts, and the establishment and administration of quotas of commodities to be shipped to European neutrals. It also kept records of imports by neutrals from all sources.

The navicert system applied in a modified form to Canada. In addition to export permits, any Canadian shipments to European neutrals had to be covered by certificates from the consignee declaring that the goods would not reach enemy destinations before being cleared through the Contraband Control of the Ministry of Economic Warfare. Later, simplified techniques were developed for obtaining clearance of exports from Canada to navicert areas from the Joint Blockade Committee. A special problem arose in obtaining blockade clearance for Canadian exports being shipped through ports in the United States.

At first, contraband clearance of Canadian exports from United States ports was left to the individual exporter who could apply for a navicert either directly or through United Kingdom consular authorities, but this function was later absorbed by the Export Permit Branch of the Department of Trade and Commerce. Canadian export permit applications for shipment to navicert areas from United States ports were referred by cable to the Joint Blockade Committee which issued an Imperial Export License Number or "blockade number" for approved exports.[54] The approval was denoted by the endorsation of the blockade number on the Canadian export permit. By agreement, shipments from United States ports which were covered by export permits bearing a blockade number were automatically cleared by the United States authorities.

Originally, United States exports to navicert areas required a navicert issued by representatives of the United Kingdom as well as an export licence. However, the two governments agreed early in 1942 that, after March 31, 1942, navicerts, mailcerts, and aircerts were redundant and that a United States export licence would be sufficient.[55] In the case of Canada also, it was later decided that a blockade number was unnecessary and Canadian export permits alone were sufficient to obtain export clearance of any Canadian shipments from United States ports. This applied to exports to European neutrals and Latin American countries. The agreement reached on this point was of great benefit to Canadian exporters since it eliminated the necessity of double clearance of exports. From the Canadian point of view, moreover, this arrangement meant that export controls could be compared in general terms without the necessity of scrutinizing individual shipments. The Canadians were well aware that this favourable treatment was subject to revision if there were any indications that

Canadian exports were reaching Latin American consignees considered to be hostile to the United Nations.

In fact, the aims of export control as a tool of economic warfare were both clearly definable and common to both countries. There was, in consequence, whole-hearted and scrupulous co-operation between Canada and the United States not only in the policy to be followed but in the detailed methods to be used in putting the policy into effect.

4. THE DEVELOPMENT OF A CO-ORDINATED EXPORT CONTROL POLICY

(a) Agreements Concerning the Techniques of Export Control

By the fall of 1942, the system of controlling commercial exports from Canada and the United States to Latin America had developed a number of unsatisfactory features. In the first place, the twenty Latin American republics did not participate directly in the calculation of their estimated requirements. Since Latin America was an important source of such vitally needed materials as copper, lead, zinc, and manganese, there was a possibility that the volume of imports might be reduced unless the export control policy of Canada and the United States was liberalized. Moreover, unless the Latin American republics were consulted in the calculation of their needs, there was a danger that their changing pattern of requirements might diverge from the export programmes planned by the Board of Economic Warfare and the Department of Trade and Commerce. In the second place, the shipping shortage had become so severe that shipping space, rather than export allocations, imposed a ceiling on exports. In fact, shipping priorities were necessary to provide those parts of export allocations most critically needed by Latin America. Export programmes had usually been limited to scarce commodities, while a much more liberal export policy had been followed for goods which were available in ample quantities. Obviously, the use of scarce shipping for non-essential goods might reduce Latin American imports of essential and urgently needed goods. As a result, the United States introduced a major modification of the methods of export control.

The essence of the new scheme was that the Board of Economic Warfare, in co-operation with the Department of State, established a complex system of decentralized control over exports which was first to be applied to Brazil and later to the other Latin American countries. The Latin American governments were to participate completely in determining import requirements. In the case of Brazil, where the plan was to become operative on March 1, 1943, importers wishing to obtain commodities either from or via the United States were required to apply to the Bank

of Brazil for a preference request or *pedido de preferencia*.[56] The issuance
of a preference request signified official approval of the proposed imports.
A preference request, once approved, was to be turned over to the Board
of Economic Warfare and transmitted to the exporter for submission
with an application for a licence to export the designated commodities. It
was also proposed that, effective March 1, 1943, all general licences and
general in-transit licences to Brazil would be cancelled and that no freight
space applications would be considered after that date except for outstanding valid licences or those approved under the decentralization plan. This
was followed shortly afterwards by the announcement that the decentralization plan would be applied to the Argentine on April 1, 1943, and that
all general and general in-transit licences covering exports to the Argentine
would became invalid after that date.[57] It was forecast that the decentralization plan would be extended to all Latin American republics as soon
as practicable. In each country, plans were being made to designate a
"country agency," an official or quasi-official body whose primary responsibility would be to fix import quotas for different commodities. Provision
was made for the co-operation of representatives of the Department of
State and the Board of Economic Warfare stationed in each country in
screening the import recommendations of the country agencies. In determining import requirements, the supply position of the importing country,
the essentiality of the import in question, and the availability of shipping
space were to be taken into consideration. The original plan also visualized
that the import recommendations would be submitted to the Board of
Economic Warfare in Washington for further review.

Since the bulk of Canadian shipments to Latin America moved through
United States ports, any regulations of the United States covering in-
transit shipments were of great importance to Canada. The United States
was in a position to modify completely the Canadian controls on exports
to Latin America by insisting that in-transit shipments be covered by
United States export licences. The original United States regulations
adopted at the time export control was introduced in 1940 specifically
stated that articles or materials entering or leaving a United States port
in transit to a foreign country would not be subject to export control.[58]
This unlimited exemption was revoked in May, 1941,[59] but within a few
days, the Secretary of State issued a general exemption covering almost
all in-transit shipments from Canada through the United States.[60]

The benefits of the general in-transit licence were clearly recognized
by the Canadian authorities and the prospect of their general revocation as a
part of the decentralization plan was viewed with some alarm and indignation. The proposed cancellation of general in-transit licences would mean

that any Canadian exports to Latin America shipped via United States ports would require a supplemental export licence from the Board of Economic Warfare. This would, in effect, impose United States controls over Canadian exports to Latin America. The plan was regarded as something of an affront by the Export Control Subcommittee which felt strongly that Canadian export control policy was just as stringent as that of the United States.

In general, the rôle which Canada was supposed to have in the originally announced decentralization plan was obscure. The plan had been developed without consultation with Canada, although it was clear that Canadian co-operation was anticipated. Indeed, the new scheme had been presented to Canada informally and no effort had been made through formal channels to determine its acceptability prior to its announcement. The proposed elimination of general in-transit licences was not the only feature of the decentralization scheme which was distasteful to the Canadians. The fact that preference requests were channelled through the Board of Economic Warfare meant that an undue proportion of such requests might be assigned to exporters in the United States. It was considered, therefore, that the decentralization plan, as originally announced, offered a very real threat to Canadian trade with Latin America.

An official protest was submitted to the Department of State by the Department of External Affairs, and in addition, the Export Control Subcommittee drew up a resolution, outlining their objections to the proposals of the United States, to be forwarded to their representatives in Washington, for their guidance in discussions with the Board of Economic Warfare. The resolution emphasized the fact that Canada was to be considered a regular supplier of goods to Latin America, and that both trade and shipping space should be shared on the basis of performance in some representative period. In the determination of import requirements, it was proposed that an official Canadian representative should be appointed to the screening committees in Latin America, and, in the absence of Canadian representation, that the United States mission should consider the Canadian position in the light of the general principles of co-operation in international economic affairs which had been accepted by the two countries, particularly in the exchange of notes of November 30, 1942. It was further suggested that there should be a full discussion between interested officials of the two countries to work out revised administrative procedures.

The suggested conference on procedures was held in Ottawa and representatives of the Board of Economic Warfare, the Department of State, the Department of External Affairs, and the Department of Trade and Commerce agreed to certain modifications of the original plan. The modified scheme, known as Decentralization Plan A, was to become effective in the United States for most Latin American countries on April 1, 1943 and for a few countries on May 1, 1943. The plan was to go into effect for Canadian exports on June 1, 1943. One significant change provided that preference requests or import recommendations approved by the country agency would be returned to the importer who could place his order either with a Canadian or a United States exporter. However, the Export Control Subcommittee would give no firm undertaking that Canadian export licences would be issued for all goods covered by an import recommedation. The proposed cancellation of general in-transit licences was also revoked and a new procedure substituted which meant, in effect, that Canadian export licences would continue to be sufficient for the clearance of Canadian shipments to the twenty Latin American countries through United States ports.[61] When Brazil switched to the modified decentralization plan early in June,[62] the Canadian demands for equality of treatment had been fully met.

Preference requests or import recommendations or certificates of necessity in one form or another had been used for allocated commodities before the introduction of decentralized control over exports. They came to play a more important part in the decentralization plan since prior certification was required for all imports. The country agencies could administer the import quotas which had been agreed upon by the issuance or withholding of preference requests. Moreover, since such certificates were screened by United States representatives in the field, it became possible to exercise much closer control over exports which might reach undesirable consignees.

The decentralization plan was complex and inevitably gave rise to operating problems which had to be resolved by mutual consultation of the export control officials in Canada and the United States. The general framework of the plan was satisfactory and provided a basis for close cooperation in limiting and directing exports. The blundering way in which the plan was introduced illustrates the unfortunate consequences of unilateral action. The Canadian authorities felt that the original United States plan for determining the minimum requirements of Latin America and for establishing allocations of goods and shipping space might reduce Canadian exports and deprive Canadian exporters of their rightful share of the Latin American market. There is, however, little ground for the suspicion entertained by some of the Canadian export control officials and others that the tendency for the United States to pay inadequate attention to Canadian interests in the Latin American market was dictated by a desire to take over Canadian markets. In fact, total Canadian exports to the twenty

Latin American republics had been extremely small, amounting in 1940 to $26,000,000, or slightly more than 2 per cent of Canada's total exports in that year.[63] Moreover, newsprint alone accounted for about one-third of this small total in 1940.[64] To some extent, the fact that Canadian interests were sometimes overlooked by the United States was a consequence of Canada's relatively small share in the Latin American market. Canada's insistence on the right to share in exports to Latin America was not matched by any guarantee to ship specified quantities in any given period of time, except in the case of certain special commodities such as newsprint. Although there were estimates of the future volume of Canadian exports of specified goods, which were used as a guide in the administration of export control, the supply authorities were usually unwilling to give firm commitments on the quantities which would be forthcoming. The Board of Economic Warfare and its successors, on the other hand, were theoretically at least, in a position to direct supplies into Latin American channels through the priorities and allocation machinery of the War Production Board.

The main difficulty in the way of achieving complete harmony in the export policies of Canada and the United States arose out of fundamental differences in the methods of controlling the use of resources. The spirit was willing, but, in some cases, the flesh was weak.

(b) The Problem of Export Quotas and the Sharing of Markets

In the United States, responsibility for planning the allocation of materials among competing needs was centralized in the Supply Priorities and Allocations Board and later the War Production Board. The development of statements of requirements rested with the different claimant agencies. In particular, one of the important functions of the Economic Defense Board and its successors was to determine the materials required for export and to submit proposed export programmes to the supply agencies for review and approval. As a result, the formulation of detailed export programmes was an essential part of the allocation system. In Canada, the notion that firm allocations of materials should be set aside for commercial exports was never completely accepted with the result that export programming developed slowly. This meant that it was difficult to arrive at a co-ordinated joint programme of exports, particularly to Latin America.

Any such plan naturally involved some conception of what the level of exports ought to be. It has already been mentioned that the Export Control Subcommittee in Canada had agreed to the general policy of equivalent treatment for foreign and domestic civilians towards the end of

1941. The same decision had been reached in the United States earlier and a presidential letter had directed the Office of Production Management to provide appropriately for essential Latin American requirements for non-military goods and services. The policy of parity of treatment was later confirmed by the Supply Priorities and Allocations Board on the recommendation of the Economic Defense Board a few months before it became the Board of Economic Warfare. With this standard as a guide, the Board of Economic Warfare, as the claimant agency for commercial exports, was faced with the major task of preparing export programmes for scarce materials and finished products for all Latin American countries. This complex responsibility was assigned to the Interdepartmental Foreign Requirements Committee, which was set up in the Requirements Branch of the Board of Economic Warfare.

The Latin American export programmes recommended by the Interdepartmental Foreign Requirements Committee were originally based on Latin American imports from the United States in the period 1937-41, the availability of other supplies, and the supply situation in the United States. These proposed programmes were reviewed by special missions in each country as well as by diplomatic representatives, and were, of course, subject to change by the War Production Board before any priority ratings or allocations were established. The work of this Committee was naturally of great interest to the Canadian Export Control Subcommittee, whose staff and facilities were completely inadequate to carry out such a large statistical and analytical project. Arrangements were made early in 1942 by the Board of Economic Warfare to supply the Canadian authorities with copies of all United States export programmes.

Actually, the problem of implementing export allocations in the United States involved serious practical difficulties. It was not until May, 1942, when General Exports Order M-148 was issued by the War Production Board, that export allocations could be adequately controlled.[65] Originally, this order provided that a producer or distributor receiving a purchase order accompanied by an individual export licence for a specified list of critical materials or products was to accept the order and make delivery within a stated period provided the quantity was within the quota established by the War Production Board for the producer or distributor. An export licence for the commodities covered was equivalent to a certificate of absolute priority. The order thus assigned an overriding priority to export requirements, and meant that the Board of Economic Warfare could implement its export programmes simply by the issuance of export licences. At the end of July, 1942, the list of critical materials covered by M-148 was revised to include only materials under allocation to Latin

America for the third quarter of 1942.[66] This was to assist the Board of Economic Warfare in meeting its export commitments for this period. The basis for the scheme was revised, effective October 1, 1942, when the Board of Economic Warfare was authorized to assign preference ratings to certain purchase orders covered by export licences, subject to specific authorizations by the War Production Board for specified quantities of materials.[67] The applicability of the order was limited, since the authority delegated to the Board of Economic Warfare to assign preference ratings applied only to iron and steel products, the producers of which were assigned individual export quotas by the War Production Board.[68] Various expedients were adopted in this early period to apply the priority system to exports but the major difficulty was that the War Production Board could not delegate sufficient authority to the export control agency and still attain a nice balance between export and domestic priorities. Eventually, it became necessary to deal with the problem of export allocations within the framework of the Controlled Materials Plan. At the beginning of 1944, General Exports Order M-148 was replaced by Directive 27 of the War Production Board which clarified the priority powers of the Foreign Economic Administration.[69] This directive authorized the Foreign Economic Administration to assign specific priority ratings to commodities for which export allocations had been established by the War Production Board. In addition, priority ratings of AA-3 or lower could be applied to any export valued at less than $500 (later increased to $2,500), subject to a number of important restrictions.[70] On the whole, the extent to which the priority system was effective in implementing export commitments was limited except where specific export allocations had been established by the War Production Board.

Apart from the technical problems of implementing export allocations, there were a number of complex issues of policy involved in determining the way in which third country markets, particularly those in Latin America, were to be shared. These issues had been raised and widely publicized in the United States following the passage of the Lend-Lease Act. The discussion revolved around the propriety of the United Kingdom continuing to export to third countries materials which had been or were being received on lend-lease. The argument that exports by the United Kingdom were essential as a source of United States dollars was vitiated or at least weakened once the special foreign aid measures had been adopted in the United States. The fact that the United Kingdom continued to export after the Lend-Lease Act led to bitter denunciations and controversy in the United States, particularly in political and foreign trade circles. For example, in October, 1941, the *Chicago Daily Tribune* printed a news item headed "England's Toys to Compete in Holiday Trade," which read, in part:

> British-made toy soldiers, dolls, bicycles and stuffed animals will compete with domestic toys for a place in Christmas stockings, a survey of Chicago stores and manufacturers' representatives . . . indicated yesterday.
> Some of the toy manufacturers noted that British manufactured items, such as velocipedes and toy musical instruments, are made from materials which American makers can obtain only with difficulty.[71]

A few days later, the same theme was repeated in a story entitled "British Sales of Bicycles in U.S. Increasing," which began with the statement:

> British bicycle manufacturers are increasing their sales in the United States and other markets as American producers struggle with the problem of obtaining sufficient steel and other products to maintain plant operations. . . .[72]

There is no question that the criticism applied in some cases, at least, to goods which had been manufactured prior to lend-lease, but the allegations were awkward and tended to stimulate misunderstanding and discord. In view of this, there were discussions between the two governments, as a result of which the United Kingdom issued a White Paper on September 10, 1941, sometimes known as the Eden White Paper, setting forth the policy which would govern the domestic distribution and the export of lend-lease supplies. The Eden White Paper was in the form of a memorandum which referred to export policy as follows:

> 2. Lend-lease materials sent to this country have not been used for export and every effort will be made in the future to ensure that they are not used for export, subject to the principle that where complete physical segregation of lend-lease materials is impracticable domestic consumption of the material in question shall be at least equal to the amounts received under lend-lease.
>
> 3. His Majesty's Government have not applied and will not apply any materials similar to those supplied under lend-lease in such a way as to enable their exporters to enter new markets or to extend their export trade at the expense of United States exporters. Owing to the need to devote all available capacity and man-power to war production, the United Kingdom export trade is restricted to the irreducible minimum necessary to supply or obtain material essential to the war effort.
>
> 4. For some time past, exports from the United Kingdom have been more and more confined to those essential (I) for the supply of vital requirements of overseas countries, particularly in the sterling empire;

(II) for the acquisition of foreign exchange, particularly in the Western Hemisphere. His Majesty's Government have adopted the policy summarized below:

(I) No materials of a type the use of which is being restricted in the United States on the grounds of short supply and of which we obtain supplies from the United States either by payment or on lend-lease terms will be used in exports with the exception of the following special cases:

(a) Material which is needed overseas in connection with supplies essential to the war effort for ourselves and our Allies, and which cannot be obtained from the United States.

(b) Small quantities of such materials needed as minor though essential components of exports which otherwise are composed of materials not in short supply in the United States.

(c) Repair parts for British machinery and plant now in use, and machinery and plant needed to complete installations now under construction, so long as they have already been contracted for.

Steps have been taken to prevent the export (except to Empire and Allied territories) of such goods which do not come within the exceptions referred to in (a), (b), and (c) above.

(II) Materials similar to those being provided under lend-lease which are not in short supply in the United States will not be used for export in quantities greater than those which we ourselves produce or buy from any source.[73]

The restrictive commitments of this White Paper meant, in effect, that the United Kingdom had to abandon almost completely a number of important foreign markets, particularly in Latin America. While Canada had, in no sense, entered into any similar undertaking, the issue nevertheless existed with respect to scarce materials imported from the United States and, on other grounds, there were good reasons for discussion between the two countries concerning exports to Latin America.

Initially, the negotiations between Canada and the United States in this field were handled by the Joint Supply Committee for Latin American Republics. Canada and the United States were represented on this Committee, which was created in the spring of 1942 expressly to prevent duplication of exports to Latin America. Representatives of the Department of State, the Board of Economic Warfare, and the Canadian Legation sat on the committee. During the initial period of the Committee's activity, trade with the Argentine was being given special attention in view of the doubts then current concerning the sympathies of this country. Any economic sanctions imposed by the United States would have been seriously weakened unless Canada had agreed to act in unison. Because of this, a common policy was formally adopted to limit exports of such goods as asbestos, automobiles, calf upper leather, acetic acid, farm machinery, rayon yarn, woodpulp, ferro-manganese, nickel, and other base metals. In addition, special arrangements were adopted to keep exports of newsprint or woodpulp for newsprint out of the hands of pro-Axis newspapers anywhere in Latin America, a matter which is discussed more fully later. Superficially, there was a close resemblance between the Joint Supply Committee for Latin American Republics and the Combined Export Markets Committee, which is discussed in more detail in the chapter dealing with combined planning.

The question of the attitude of the United States to the continuation of Canadian exports containing either United States materials or components which Canada was importing from the United States had caused some concern to the Canadian Export Control Subcommittee after its creation. The concern was heightened by the rigorous White Paper restrictions adopted by the United Kingdom and the outspoken attitude of certain commercial groups in the United States. It was, therefore, a matter of considerable interest to the Canadian export control authorities to learn that the original export programmes of the Interdepartmental Foreign Requirements Committee of the Board of Economic Warfare were based on the assumption that Canadian exports to Latin America would continue at the pre-war level. On the basis of the procedures of the Interdepartmental Foreign Requirements Committee, it became clear that no interference with the disposition of Canadian supplies was visualized by the United States. The inadequacy of the assumption that Canadian exports would continue at pre-war levels was recognized, and arrangements were made by the Export Control Subcommittee to supply the Board of Economic Warfare with more realistic forecasts of Canadian exports.

While Canada was under no obligation to restrict exports of Canadian goods fabricated wholly or partly from United States materials, it was noted in the meetings of the Export Control Subcommittee, and elsewhere, that Canadian insistence on complete freedom to export critical materials without regard to the policy of the United States might stimulate discord. The issue was particularly clear with respect to Canadian exports of iron and steel products, the raw material for which was often imported from the United States. For example, Canadian agricultural implements contained screw stock, bearings, and steel sheets imported from the United States, and wire rope and pipe were fabricated in Canada from steel wire and skelp imported from the United States. The situation was particularly ticklish shortly after the entry of the United States into the war when a deficit of 2,000,000 tons of steel in the next year was forecast in Canada and there was some uncertainty concerning the volume of steel which would be available from the United States. Any exports merely added to the already serious steel shortage and increased Canadian dependence on the United States. The early submissions of Canadian steel requirements by the Department of Munitions and Supply to the War Production Board did not adequately deal with export programmes, a fact which led to some critical comments on Canadian policy by officials of that agency, despite the fact that Canadian plans for steel exports had been discussed with the Board of Economic Warfare. This served to emphasize to the Canadian officials concerned, the wisdom of full and frank discussion of Canadian export programmes with any United States officials who might conceivably be interested.

The negotiations between Canada and the United States concerning Latin American markets were mainly informal. Canadian representatives in Washington were in constant touch with officials of the Board of Economic Warfare and its successors in Washington. Information on export plans was exchanged as a matter of course and the negotiations on the shares of markets to be assigned to each country were generally most amicable. There were, however, instances where the views of some officials of the Board of Economic Warfare were coloured by their experience with lend-lease countries. There was some feeling that the United States might properly take over, totally or in part, the export markets of countries in receipt of lend-lease aid. Inevitably, this attitude sometimes crept into their views on Canadian exports. The officials of the Board of Economic Warfare were recruited largely from industry, and might not be expected to have a clear understanding of Canada's historic rights to share markets. In one particular case, involving watt-hour meters, some pressure arose in the Board of Economic Warfare to have Canada suspend exports, presumably on the grounds that branch plants of United States corporations could fill the need. This was a troublesome case and it was finally necessary to appeal to the Department of State for a clarification of the United States policy concerning Canadian trade with Latin America. This particular case must not be regarded as typical but it does illustrate the desirability of clear and formal understandings on issues of policy which contain the seeds of discord and misunderstanding.

A joint programme for the restriction of commercial exports involved more complicated problems than co-operative action in economic warfare. It was necessary to consider at once commercial policy, foreign policy, domestic supply conditions, and planning facilities. It was not usually possible to share markets on the basis of pre-war exports, because of the changing domestic supply conditions in the two countries. Nevertheless, deviation from normal trade patterns sometimes led to protests by one country or the other. Of greatest importance was the fact that wartime controls were dissimilar in the two countries, which meant that the determination of joint export programmes covering all scarce materials was difficult. In some cases, notable success was achieved, but co-ordinated action was not always attainable. This did not result from the unwillingness of either country to co-operate, but rather from the administrative difficulties met by the export control authorities.

5. THE RELAXATION OF EXPORT CONTROLS

One essential feature of the decentralized control over exports to Latin America was that the importing countries not only had a voice in the determination of import requirements, but, through official or quasi-official agencies, were largely responsible for the administration of the quotas. The regulation requiring that certificates of essentiality from the importing country accompany all applications for export licences was relaxed after a few months. Effective October 1, 1943, in both Canada and the United States, export licences and import recommendations were dropped for a large number of commodities in free supply.[74] This relaxation also permitted the wider use of general licences for exports from the United States to Latin America. The necessity for certificates of essentiality continued to apply to strategic goods or commodities in short supply as well as to any exports to Argentina (except newsprint). This relaxation was mainly a consequence of an easier shipping situation. The list of goods no longer requiring import recommendations was expanded effective January 1, 1944, to include certain classes of agricultural machinery, chemicals, drugs and health supplies, and most foodstuffs and communication equipment.[75] On March 15, 1944, goods such as automotive vehicles, office appliances, radio tubes and equipment, and petroleum products were added.[76] These exemptions were not always applied simultaneously to all Latin American countries, but a gradual process of liberalization was under way.

By the spring of 1944, a new type of blanket licensing procedure was adopted by the Foreign Economic Administration. Under the new system, an exporter was permitted to ship certain commodities to a specified list of consignees and purchasers in designated countries.[77] This obviated the necessity of submitting individual export licences and was another indication of the tendency to relax export controls in view of the improved materials and shipping situation. During this period, the policy of the War Production Board in relaxing restrictions on civilian production was unstable and this instability hampered the establishment of new and clear-cut export programmes.

The official attitude of the United States was clarified in the fall of 1944 in a letter from President Roosevelt to the Foreign Economic Administrator dealing with foreign economic policy, from which the following excerpt is quoted:

The following are the major policies which should be put into effect by the FEA within the scope of its present functions and responsibilities when the military resistance of Nazi Germany is overcome:

1. Export Control—With a view to encouraging private trade without interfering with the successful prosecution of the war against Japan, the FEA should relax control over exports to the fullest extent compatible with our continuing war objectives, particularly that of defeating Japan as quickly and effectively as possible.[78]

In the meantime, in Canada, the supply position of particular commodities, such as aluminum, had eased, and the Export Control Subcommittee was eager to find a formula which would permit a reasonable level of exports and still not conflict with the policy of the United States. Certain tentative relaxations, typified by the release of a relatively small quantity of aluminum to Cuba, had led to protests by the Foreign Economic Administration. The question was referred to the External Trade Advisory Committee which clarified a number of questions of Canadian export policy. In the first place, the issue arose whether Canadian exports containing United States components should be subject to special treatment. The opinion of the committee was that such articles should be exported at the discretion of the Canadian authorities when not covered by limitation orders in the United States, in the same way that the United States was free to export goods containing materials of Canadian origin. If limitation orders in the United States restricted domestic consumption, the level of Canadian exports should be comparable to that permitted in the United States. Second, the question arose whether it was reasonable for Canada to export goods whose manufacture in the United States was prohibited. On this point, it was noted that the pattern of Canadian production might well differ from the United States because of differences in the two economies and, in some cases, because of the earlier imposition of restrictions in Canada. From the Canadian point of view, the division of output between export and domestic uses was a matter of policy for Canada to decide, as long as war production was not impaired. Third, a decision had to be reached concerning Canadian restrictions on raw material exports to third countries for manufacture into end products whose production was banned in the United States. It was felt that exports could not reasonably be restricted to materials without end-use limitations in the United States. In particular, it was felt that aluminum exports should be permitted for the manufacture of utensils despite the prohibition in effect in the United States at that time. In general, the Canadian opinion was that exports which would not detract from the war effort should be permitted, provided that this did not involve unfair commercial advantages for Canadian exporters. It was also recognized that it would be desirable to avoid conflicts with United States policy in unimportant matters not involving any significant principles.

By the end of 1944, the pace of relaxation increased in accordance with the policy of eliminating export permit restrictions on commodities which were becoming more easily available. In December, 1944, a large number of articles were freed from control in Canada when exported to parts of the British Empire or the United States.[79] The list of exemptions was further extended at the beginning of 1945.[80] One reason for the relaxation of Canadian restrictions was that it already recognized that there would be a serious post-war shortage of Canadian dollars in the sterling area, and that substitute markets were essential.

In the spring of 1945, some disputation arose with the United States over Canadian exports to the Argentine. The opinion of the State Department was that Canadian actions tended to weaken the economic sanctions being used by the United States against the Argentine. It had been expected, as a result of the Act of Chapultepec, that the Argentine would liquidate any remaining Axis firms, but the official view in the United States was that this undertaking had not been completely carried out. In consequence, the United States had retained certain discriminatory features in its controls over shipments to the Argentine, mainly the continued use of certificates of essentiality in order to provide a check on consignees and end-uses. In the meantime, Canada had permitted some exports of whiskey and furs to the Argentine, in accordance with the Canadian view that refusal to permit shipments of such luxury goods would not seriously inconvenience the Argentine but would involve merely a loss of trade for Canada. It was not immediately apparent what the harmful effects on the policy of the United States would be if the Argentinians chose to wrap themselves in Canadian furs and debauch themselves with Canadian whiskey. The United States was somewhat worried by the Canadian action since complete co-operation had been anticipated. After some discussion of the question, the Canadian Export Control Subcommittee undertook to require certificates of essentiality for all exports except whiskey and furs.

There were prospects of a general improvement in the supply situation not long after VE-Day, evidenced by the relaxation of the Controlled Materials Plan and other regulations of the War Production Board. It was, therefore, appropriate to consider the relaxation of export controls and the abandonment of the decentralization plan shortly after VE-Day. Apart from prospective improvements in the supply situation, there had been an undesirable proliferation of import controls in several Latin American countries. Although such controls had been essential in the period of extreme scarcity of imports, there had been some tendency to adapt them to rather more general purposes with the result that the free flow of trade was being interfered with. In order to support requests for the removal of such impediments, the United States was anxious to dispose of its own controls.

One of the major aspects of Canadian relaxation was the redrafting of Export Permit Regulation No. 5 which had required permits for any shipment to any country except most of the Western Hemisphere,[81] and the British Empire. While the main feature was retained, the revised regulation exempted from export control all commodities except those specifically listed when consigned to destinations within the Western Hemisphere.[82] The Foreign Economic Administration was informed beforehand of the proposed relaxation of Canadian controls and expressed its full concurrence in the change.

Throughout the summer of 1945, plans were being drawn up for the liquidation of the decentralization plan. Finally, at the end of August, 1945, it was announced that the plan would be completely abandoned on October 1 by both Canada and the United States.[83]

The modified decentralization plan had become an important part of the export control mechanism in both Canada and the United States. Its primary aim was to provide realistic estimates of the import requirements of Latin American countries from Canada and the United States, which were the principal sources of supply. Despite its usefulness, its demise was not unwelcome in Canada. Its introduction had been attended by misunderstanding, its full operation was characterized by uneasy Canadian acquiescence, and even the easing of restrictions stimulated more discord. On the whole, the arrangement had some of the aspects of an unsuccessful marriage.

In general, Canadian co-operation was not always a result of adherence to the principles of justice and equity; a number of purely practical considerations were also important. First of all, the United States controlled most of the shipping space to Latin America. Second, the United States regulations governing in-transit shipments meant that Canadian export permits were sufficient clearance for shipments to Latin America through United States ports, a concession whose revocation would have clearly created difficulties. Third, Canada was dependent on the United States for essential components and raw materials. Under these circumstances,

Canada's unwillingness to co-operate might have had consequences detrimental not only to export trade but to the whole war production programme.

There were some noteworthy differences between Canada's relations with the Board of Economic Warfare or Foreign Economic Administration and with the War Production Board. The War Production Board seemed readier to make concessions to Canada and to recognize the existence of special Canadian problems. In part, this was a reflection of the strong and independent status of the War Production Board. It was freer from Congressional criticism or from pressure from powerful outside interests than the Board of Economic Warfare and its successors. As a result, the export control agencies were somewhat less willing to consult Canada or to make special arrangements which did not conform to the rules and regulations applicable in the United States. This attitude was reinforced by the consideration that any deviation was apt to involve changes in commercial relationships, something which was sure to be objected to by interested groups in the United States.

REFERENCES FOR CHAPTER VII

1. *Statutes of Canada,* 1 Geo. VI, c. 24, (1937).

2. P.C. 1838, July 20, 1937.

3. P.C. 2785, September 20, 1939 and P.C. 2735, September 20, 1939.

4. P.C. 287, January 23, 1940.

5. P.C. 5994, October 26, 1940.

6. For example, P.C. 6391 of August 19, 1941, establishing regulations concerning "supplies," conferred on the Controller of Supplies of the Department of Munitions and Supply the power to prohibit exports of any goods declared to be "supplies" except under authority of an export licence authorized by the Minister of Trade and Commerce. P.C. 3223 of October 21, 1939, which set forth certain regulations respecting sugar, stated that no person should export sugar except under authority of a permit issued by the Sugar Administrator of the Wartime Prices and Trade Board.

7. P.C. 2448, April 8, 1941. The Department of Trade and Commerce actually took over this function on May 5, 1941.

8. P.C. 9269, November 27, 1941. The members of the Advisory Committee on Export Control were the Deputy Minister of Trade and Commerce, the Deputy Minister of Agriculture, the Metals Controller, the Chairman of the Wartime Industries Control Board, the Special Assistant to the Deputy Minister of Finance, the Chairman of the Wartime Prices and Trade Board, the Under Secretary of State for External Affairs, the Commissioner of Customs, and an additional representative of the Department of External Affairs.

9. P.C. 2716, September 15, 1939.

10. Canada, House of Commons, Standing Committee on Banking and Commerce, *Minutes of Proceedings and Evidence No. 7*, March 13, 1947 (Ottawa: King's Printer, 1947), p. 202.

11. Department of Trade and Commerce, Export Permit Branch Order No. 63, March 2, 1943. Shipments by government agencies were not affected by this order, nor were newsprint exports to the British Empire or the Western Hemisphere, excluding French colonies or possessions.

12. This development was stimulated in the fall of 1942 as a result of the growing pressure to divert manpower to essential industry. At this time, the Wartime Prices and Trade Board, which was responsible for planning the reduction of non-essential output, requested the Export Control Subcommittee to prepare estimates of minimum essential requirements for exports, a request which focussed attention on export planning.

13. There were important exceptions such as newsprint and agricultural machinery and exports covered by contractual agreements with other governments or government agencies.

14. The speech was given to the 71st Annual Meeting of the Canadian Manufacturers' Association, June 8-10, 1942. Quoted in *Commercial Intelligence Journal*, June 20, 1942, p. 651.

15. P.C. 3059, April 27, 1944.

16. The External Trade Advisory Committee dealt with non-food requirements, while relief needs for food were the responsibility of the Food Requirements Committee.

17. *54 U.S. Statutes* 10-11; c. 2, Resolution of November 4, 1939.

18. Proclamation 2237, May 1, 1937, 2 *Federal Register* 776.

19. *54 U.S. Statutes* 714; c. 508, Act of July 2, 1940.

20. Proclamation 2413, July 2, 1940, 5 *Federal Register* 2467.

21. The list of arms, ammunition, and the implements of war continued to be that contained in Proclamation 2237 of May 1, 1937, 2 *Federal Register* 776.

22. Military Order of the President, July 2, 1940, 5 *Federal Register* 2491.

23. Executive Order 8839, July 30, 1941, 6 *Federal Register* 3823. The original membership of the Economic Defense Board consisted of the Vice-President of the United States, who acted as Chairman, and the Secretaries of State, War, Navy, Agriculture, Commerce, Treasury, as well as the Attorney-General.

24. Executive Order 8900, September 15, 1941, 6 *Federal Register* 4795. The licensing control over the export of arms, ammunition, implements of war, helium, and tinplate scrap was not transferred and remained the responsibility of the Department of State. Other export licensing regulations covering gold and narcotics remained under the jurisdiction of the Treasury Department.

25. Executive Order 8982, December 17, 1941, 6 *Federal Register* 6530.

26. Board of Economic Warfare, Export Control Branch, *Current Controls Bulletin No. 15*, April 8, 1942.

27. Executive Order 9128, April 13, 1942, 7 *Federal Register* 2809.

28. The Rules and Regulations issued by the Executive Director of the Board of Economic Warfare on April 16, 1942, made it clear that he was authorized to exercise complete supervision over any foreign procurement of strategic or critical materials (except munitions), any production or financing of production of such materials in foreign countries to be carried out by any of the following government agencies: Department of Commerce, Reconstruction Finance Corporation, Metals Reserve Company, Rubber Reserve Company, Defense Supplies Corporation, Defense Plant Corporation, United

States Commercial Company, Export-Import Bank of Washington, Treasury Department, Department of Agriculture, Department of State, Office of Lend-Lease Administration, 7 *Federal Register* 2935.

29. Clarification and interpretation of Executive Order 9128 of April 13, 1942, in respect of certain functions of the Department of State and the Board of Economic Warfare, May 20, 1942, 7 *Federal Register* 3843.

30. For example, see the Memorandum of Agreement dated January 8, 1943. U.S., Congress, House of Representatives, *Hearings before the Subcommittee of the Committee on Appropriations on the National War Agencies Appropriation Bill for 1944*, (78th Cong., 1st sess.) (Washington: U.S. Government Printing Office, 1944), II, pp. 368-9.

31. Executive Order 9361, July 18, 1943, 8 *Federal Register* 9861.

32. Executive Order 9380, September 25, 1943, 8 *Federal Register* 13081.

33. Minutes of the First Joint Meeting, Joint Economic Committees, July 15 and 16, 1941.

34. Letter, Col. F. R. Kerr to H. A. Scott, January 10, 1942.

35. Minutes of the First Joint Meeting, Joint Economic Committees, July 15 and 16, 1941.

36. U.S., Congress, House of Representatives, Subcommittee of the Committee on Appropriations, *Hearings on the National War Agencies Appropriation Bill for 1944*, (78th Cong., 1st sess.), part 2 (Washington: U.S. Government Printing Office, 1943), p. 322.

37. Executive Order 8839, July 30, 1941, 6 *Federal Register* 3823.

38. P.C. 2448, April 8, 1941.

39. *Commercial Intelligence Journal*, June 20, 1942, pp. 651-2.

40. U.S., Congress, House of Representatives, Subcommittee of the Committee on Appropriations, *Hearings on the Foreign Economic Administration Bill for 1945*, (78th Cong., 2d. sess.) (Washington: U.S. Government Printing Office, 1944), p. 422.

41. Canada, Treaty Series, 1942, No. 17, *Exchange of Notes (November 30, 1942) between Canada and the United States of America constituting an agreement respecting post-war economic settlements in force November 30, 1942* (Ottawa: King's Printer, 1944).

42. Authority to issue the lists of specified persons was granted by P.C. 4262, December 20, 1939, to the Secretary of State for External Affairs. The lists were to be concurred in by the Secretary of State for Canada and the Minister of National Revenue.

43. In Canada, the general prohibition against intercourse with the enemy was contained in P.C. 2512, September 5, 1939, as amended and consolidated by P.C. 3959 of August 21, 1940, and certain later minor revisions.

44. P.C. 286, January 23, 1940.

45. P.C. 885, February 29, 1940.

46. P.C. 1471, April 11, 1940.

47. P.C. 2833, June 27, 1940.

48. P.C. 2050, March 24, 1941. A previous regulation controlling exports to the colonies or possessions of France within the Western Hemisphere was confirmed by the new order-in-council.

49. *40 U.S. Statutes* 415; c. 106, Act of October 6, 1917.

50. The initial freezing order was contained in Executive Order 8389, April 10, 1940, 6 *Federal Register* 2897. This order was amended at various times in 1941 to include more countries.

51. U.S., Treasury Department, *Administration of the Wartime Financial and Property Controls of the United States Government* (Washington: U.S. Government Printing Office, 1942), p. 3.

52. Proclamation 2497, July 17, 1941, *55 U.S. Statutes* 1657.

53. The goods listed in Proclamation 2413 of July 2, 1940, were added to in later proclamations and a consolidated list was given in Export Control Schedule Z, issued by the Administrator of Export Control, July 19, 1941, *6 Federal Register* 3584.

54. Department of Trade and Commerce, Export Permit Branch Order No. 83, December 7, 1943.

55. *Commercial Intelligence Journal,* February 28, 1942. See also Board of Economic Warfare, Office of Export Control, *Current Controls Bulletin No. 9,* March 3, 1942.

56. Board of Economic Warfare, Office of Exports, *Current Export Bulletin No. 75,* February 25, 1943.

57. *Ibid., No. 77,* February 27, 1943.

58. Regulations accompanying Proclamation 2413, July 2, 1940, *5 Federal Register* 2469.

59. Executive Order 8752, May 6, 1941, *6 Federal Register* 2333.

60. *Commercial Intelligence Journal,* July 2, 1941. These general in-transit licence privileges, issued on May 9, 1941, did not, of course, apply exclusively to Canada. The general licence procedure did not apply, except for shipments from Canada to other parts of the British Empire, to certain ultra-critical commodities such as mesathorium, radium, uranium, silk, rubber, certain drugs, and technical data. See *Comprehensive Export Control Schedule No. 6,* issued by the Office of Export Control, Board of Economic Warfare, March-April, 1942.

61. The adoption of Decentralization Plan A was announced by the Office of Exports of the Board of Economic Warfare in *Current Export Bulletin No. 80,* March 5, 1943. The new in-transit procedure created a new general in-transit licence designated by the symbol GIT-C/V, applicable only to Canada. Initially, the new licence could not be used for certain specially critical commodities, but before long all restrictions on the use of the new licence were abolished. Board of Economic Warfare, Office of Exports, *Current Export Bulletin No. 95,* May 3, 1943.

62. Board of Economic Warfare, Office of Exports, *Current Export Bulletin No. 99,* June 7, 1943.

63. *Canada Year Book, 1942,* pp. 453-4. Gold exports are excluded.

64. Dominion Bureau of Statistics, *Trade of Canada, 1941,* Vol II, *Exports* (Ottawa: King's Printer, 1941).

65. General Exports Order M-148, May 12, 1942, *7 Federal Register* 3518.

66. Amendment 2 to General Exports Order M-148, July 29, 1942, *7 Federal Register,* 5864.

67. General Exports Order M-148, as amended, September 28, 1942, *7 Federal Register* 7730.

68. Supplement 1 to General Exports Order M-148, October 13, 1942, *7 Federal Register* 8279. Board of Economic Warfare, Export Control Branch, *Current Controls Bulletin No. 48,* October 1, 1942.

69. War Production Board, Directive 27, January 1, 1944, *9 Federal Register* 63.

70. For example, see Foreign Economic Administration, Office of Exports, *Current Export Bulletin No. 146,* February 12, 1944.

71. *Chicago Daily Tribune,* October 9, 1941, p. 27.

72. *Ibid.,* October 13, 1941, p. 26. It is of some interest to note that the same general theme has continued to be popular. On January 9, 1949, the *Chicago Sunday Tribune* printed a front-page story, one paragraph of which is: "The E.C.A. [Economic Co-operation Administration] found that it had been asking the American taxpayers to finance huge purchases of aluminum for Britain at 16 cents a pound, and British dealers were shipping aluminum back to the United States to sell for as much as 30 cents a pound. The aluminum was being bought for Britain from its own dominion, Canada."

73. U.S., Congress, *Report on the First Year of Lend-Lease Operations,* House Document No. 661, (77th Cong., 2nd sess.), Appendix IV (Washington: U.S. Government Printing Office, 1942), p. 53.

74. Office of Economic Warfare, Office of Exports, *Current Export Bulletin No. 124,* September 25, 1943.

75. Foreign Economic Administration, *Current Export Bulletin No. 137,* December 30, 1943.

76. *Ibid. No. 152,* March 14, 1944.

77. *Ibid. No. 153,* March 21, 1944.

78. White House Press Release, September 29, 1944.

79. Department of Trade and Commerce, Export Permit Branch Order No. 103, effective December 11, 1944.

80. Department of Trade and Commerce, Export Permit Branch Order No. 106, effective January 1, 1945. There were four classes of exemptions established by this regulation: (a) complete; (b) shipments of $25 or less; (c) shipments of $100 or less; (d) rubber under $5 to all destinations.

81. Colonies and possessions of France within the Western Hemisphere were excluded.

82. P.C. 4498, June 26, 1945.

83. Foreign Economic Administration, *Current Export Bulletin No. 274,* August 31, 1945.

CHAPTER VIII

TRADE BARRIERS

IN PEACETIME, there is a high degree of interdependence between Canada and the United States. In the 1930's, United States exports to Canada exceeded those to any other country and Canadian exports to the United States were exceeded only by those to the United Kingdom. The greatest part of Canadian exports to the United States was made up of the products of primary industries, typified by forest products and base metals, while, on the other hand, the bulk of United States exports to Canada consisted of manufactured goods and components to be used in Canadian industry. In the nineteenth century, there had been a brief period of reciprocity, but, since Confederation, the tendency had been to increase tariff barriers and to develop special impediments to trade when tariffs seemed inadequate. In the early 1930's, tariffs reached a new high with the Hawley-Smoot Tariff and the Ottawa Agreements but some progress was made in the reduction of tariffs immediately before the war as a result of the Trade Agreements of 1936 and 1939.

During the war, the usefulness of tariffs as a positive instrument of control was very limited. In Canada, tariff adjustments or closely related taxes were used as measures to conserve foreign exchange. There were some restricted reductions of tariffs to facilitate procurement of munitions in the United States and tariff suspensions were used quite generally as a price control device. Similarly, there were a number of interesting cases in which the United States permitted duty-free entry of off-shore purchases. The first part of this chapter deals with the wartime tariff changes which affected trade between Canada and the United States.

Old-fashioned trade controls had usually developed gradually so that the necessary adjustments in import and export practice could be made without serious disturbance. During the war, the imposition of export controls by both countries created obstacles to trade of a new and formidable type. These new controls raised important questions of equity and reciprocity and, in one period, seriously impeded the co-ordination of war production in the two countries. The second part of this chapter deals with the way in which export controls were modified in the light of emerging principles of economic co-operation. The concluding section refers briefly to measures taken to facilitate the exchange of information between the two countries.

1. TARIFFS AND ADMINISTRATIVE RESTRICTIONS

The lightning sweep of the German armies across the Low Countries in the spring of 1940 and the subsequent fall of France heralded new steps to protect Canada's diminishing reserves of United States dollars. It was evident that Canada would be required to meet increasingly heavy United Kingdom demands for finished munitions, as well as the growing needs of the Canadian armed forces. An increase in the Canadian munitions programme meant that requirements from the United States would grow correspondingly and throw further strains on Canada's balance of payments with the United States. As a result, immediate measures were introduced to conserve United States dollars by discouraging imports from the United States. The first of these, the War Exchange Tax, was introduced in the Budget of June, 1940, and was designed to restrict United States imports by adding a tax of 10 per cent to all imports not eligible for the British preferential rates of duty. At the same time, a progressive excise tax was levied on the manufacturers' price or value for duty of passenger automobiles amounting to 10 per cent up to $700 and increasing sharply to 80 per cent on values in excess of $1200. This new schedule replaced a flat excise tax of 5 per cent on the value in excess of $650. In July, 1940, further restrictions were introduced when it was announced that the Foreign Exchange Control Board would no longer furnish United States dollars to Canadians for pleasure travel. Import controls were extended by the passage of the War Exchange Conservation Act.[1] This act prohibited imports of a long list of commodities from countries outside the sterling area except under permit from the Minister of National Revenue. The intention was to ban completely imports of luxury goods from non-sterling areas and to encourage dependence on domestic or sterling area sources for other articles of a somewhat more essential character, such as components of machinery and various textiles.[2] The import restrictions introduced by the War Exchange Conservation Act were naturally a matter of keen interest to the United States, particularly in view of the understanding concerning the unilateral imposition of import controls embodied in Article X of the Canada-United States Trade Agreement of 1936.[3] The concurrence of the United States in suspending the provisions of Article X was obtained by an exchange of notes. In no sense, however, did the exchange of notes give Canada *carte blanche* to impose import restrictions at will, a fact which is brought out by the special attention paid to fresh fruits and vegetables. The Canadian government had given serious consideration to the inclusion of such imports on the prohibited list. In explaining the decision to leave fresh fruit and vegetable imports from the United States unrestricted, the Minister of Finance pointed out:

> While we had to weigh on the one hand the exchange that would be saved by the restriction of their importation, we had to weigh on the other hand the inevitable public reaction which there would be in many of the agricultural districts of the United States, the embarrassment this reaction would cause to a friendly and helpful government which has its own problems of agricultural surpluses, and the danger which would ensue not only to our own trade relations with the United States, not only to the market which our trade agreement with that country gives to so many of our primary producers, but to the whole trade agreement policy of the United States, a policy which affects the people of all nations and with which this government has consistently cooperated.[4]

He went on to say that a forecast by a Canadian trade association of the prohibition of imports of fresh fruits and vegetables had come to the attention of the United States government, which had expressed the opinion that such action would "gravely prejudice" the position of the Canada-United States Trade Agreement, meaning presumably that the United States would regard such an embargo as grounds for abrogating the agreement.[5] Throughout the discussion of the measure, the Minister of Finance was careful to emphasize that any element of protection in the import restrictions was accidental and temporary and that no vested interest in the restrictions would be recognized.[6]

Apart from the tariff modifications designed to reduce imports from hard currency areas and to encourage certain Canadian imports from sterling area sources, tariff changes were not used in either Canada or the United States as a positive instrument of control. When import restrictions were desired, licensing techniques were used. In other cases, when tariffs constituted an undesirable barrier, custom duties were suspended completely. The difficulty of predicting the quantitative effect of tariff changes meant that more incisive methods of control were necessary. Furthermore, increases in customs duties tended to impede governmental efforts to stabilize prices.

The introduction of the overall price ceiling in Canada on December 1, 1941, immediately gave rise to a number of problems relating to the prices of imported goods and led to several revisions in the administrative regulations governing tariffs. Dumping duties were indefinitely suspended except for fresh fruits and vegetables,[7] and provision was made for the general acceptance of the actual export price as a basis of valuation for duty rather than "fair market value as sold for home consumption," when recommended by the Wartime Prices and Trade Board and the Minister of Finance.[8]

It was also provided by a later order-in-council that import and excise duties and taxes of other countries were to be excluded in valuing Canadian imports from those countries for duty purposes.[9] In addition, orders-in-council were passed from time to time either lowering or removing altogether the duties on specific commodities, usually to assist in the maintenance of ceiling prices.

After the Hyde Park Declaration, it became evident that certain procurement regulations of the United States government were hindering the co-ordination of the war production and military supply programmes of Canada and the United States. As a result of the obstacles, it appeared improbable that Canada could supply munitions to the United States at the rate predicted in the Hyde Park Declaration. Procurement difficulties were encountered immediately, and by the end of 1941, progress had been disappointingly slow. One of the main difficulties was the so-called "Buy American Act" of 1933, which placed severe restrictions on foreign purchases by government procurement agencies of the United States.[10] The relevant section of this Act provided that:

Unless the head of the department or independent establishment concerned shall determine it to be inconsistent with the public interest, or the cost to be unreasonable, only such unmanufactured articles, materials, and supplies as have been mined or produced in the United States, and only such manufactured articles, materials, and supplies as have been manufactured in the United States substantially all from articles, materials, and supplies mined, produced, or manufactured, as the case may be, in the United States shall be acquired for public use.[11]

Similar restrictions on foreign purchases incorporated in the Merchant Marine Act of 1936 affected the United States Maritime Commission. Certain goods which were not produced in the United States in sufficient quantity or of a satisfactory quality or which were otherwise not readily available in commercial quantities were excluded from the restrictions of the "Buy American Act." With the growth of the defence programme and related domestic shortages, pressure was developing for the relaxation of these regulations during 1941. In August, 1941, a procurement regulation was issued by the War Department allowing the purchase of a long list of materials without regard to their country of origin.[12] It was stated that the listed materials, many of which were classed as strategic or critical, were not produced in the United States in sufficient and reasonable available commercial quantities or of a satisfactory quality. Among others, the following commodities on the list were of some interest to Canada: acetic acid, alpha cellulose, aluminum, cobalt and ores, copper and ores, fish oils, hides and skins, nickel and ores, pulp and paper, uranium and ores, zinc and zinc ores or concentrates.

It was not until after Pearl Harbor that the general restrictions of the "Buy American Act" were suspended for purchases in Canada. This was one of the "administrative barriers" which was inveighed against in the statement of war production policy of the Joint War Production Committee issued in December, 1941. In response to this, the War Department issued a directive on December 27, 1941 to its procurement officers that the provisions of the "Buy American Act" were suspended as far as Canada was concerned.[13] The text of the directive read, in part:

4. Under the provisions of the Act of March 3, 1933 (47 Stat. 1520), it is hereby determined to be inconsistent with the public interest to limit procurement of essential defense articles to those manufactured, mined or produced within the United States.

5. Any restrictions heretofore imposed on the placing of orders within the Dominion of Canada, or with War Supplies Limited (a Canadian corporation), are suspended, as are existing requirements for the clearance of orders in Canada or with Canadian corporations.[14]

A similar memorandum was distributed by the Under Secretary of the Navy on December 31, 1941.[15]

On March 13, 1942, the Under Secretary of War issued a generalized exemption from the provisions of the "Buy American Act" except for certain articles of food or clothing, although Canada was not affected by the rules governing food and clothing.[16] The War Department regulations on procurement cited the policy of the Joint War Production Committee and went on to say:

The President of the United States has directed that affected departments and agencies of the Government abide by the letter and spirit of the foregoing policy so far as lies within their power. It is directed that the chief of each technical service whole-heartedly co-operate in an effort to make such policy effective in action. Manufacturing facilities available in the United States and in Canada should be placed upon an equal basis so far as awards of production orders are concerned, having in mind that time is of the essence and that, other things being equal, production of essential war materials at the earliest practicable date is the immediate aim of the Army Service Forces.[17]

Late in July, 1942, a regulation was also issued by the War Shipping Administration waiving the restrictions of the "Buy American Act."[18]

The issue was to arise again in an appropriation restriction contained in the Military Appropriations Act, 1945, which contained a proviso that no part of the appropriation granted by the Act was to be used for the procurement of any article of food or clothing not grown or produced in the United States or its possessions unless the Secretary of War determined that such food or clothing was of unsatisfactory quality and could not be procured in sufficient quantities at reasonable prices in the United States.[19] Exemption from this restriction was duly accorded Canada by the Under Secretary of War.[20]

Apart from administrative restrictions, there were other instances where tariffs hindered procurement in Canada. Military procurement agencies in the United States were reluctant to place contracts in Canada because of customs duties on imported munitions. At various times, bills were introduced in Congress providing for the complete remission of duties on imports of goods needed for the war production programme, but there was a good deal of Congressional opposition to such legislation and little or no progress was made in this direction. The difficulty in the United States was a result of the fact that Congress retained control of the tariff, although limited reductions could be effected by executive action in accordance with the Trade Agreements Act of 1934. In the fall of 1941, there was considerable discussion of the possibility of a new trade agreement between Canada and the United States designed specifically to reduce tariffs on munitions and allied articles. However, the earlier trade agreements had exhausted most of the possibilities of reducing Canadian duties on imports from the United States and it was not clear what additional concessions Canada could offer in return for reductions in United States tariffs. The question was referred to the Trade Agreements Committee of the State Department which was not wholeheartedly in favour of a new agreement. This attitude was based on the fact that there was little possibility of increasing imports from Canada and also because of the necessity of extending to other countries any tariff concessions to Canada. This was a consequence of the most-favoured-nation clause incorporated in the various trade agreements of the United States.

Any tariff obstacles to military procurement were finally eliminated by channelling all United States military contracts in Canada through War Supplies Limited. Contracts were placed originally with War Supplies Limited and then by the Department of Munitions and Supply with the Canadian suppliers.[21] All purchases made through War Supplies Limited entered the United States duty-free..

In Canada, a provision of the Customs Act permitted the remission of duties on goods which could not be freely obtained from domestic sources.[22] Wide use was made of this provision to permit the duty-free entry of munitions and related articles from the United States. The suspension of tariffs was also used generally to stabilize or lower the prices of imported commodities.[23] In contrast to the situation in the United States, tariff adjustments in Canada could be made by order-in-council under the wide executive powers authorized by the War Measures Act. Tariff adjustments on United States imports to be incorporated in Canadian munitions were originally designed to reduce the cost of munitions produced in Canada for the account of the United Kingdom. In February, 1940, an order-in-council was passed authorizing the remission or refund of duties on imported articles or materials to be used in manufacturing munitions covered by contracts placed by the War Supply Board on behalf of the United Kingdom.[24] The regulation also applied to other Allied nations, but not to Canadian government contracts themselves. When the United Kingdom let the contracts directly in Canada, individual cases were to be considered on their merits by the Minister of National Revenue. As a practical matter, these regulations, after some revision, meant merely that the Department of Munitions and Supply, the successor of the War Supply Board, was to keep a record of all imports, and make appropriate credits to the United Kingdom account. It finally became clear that the accounting difficulties involved in isolating imports for the account of the United Kingdom were insuperable and, accordingly, authorization was granted to remit duties on imports by the Department of Munitions and Supply on Canadian account as well.[25] Similar exemptions were also extended to imports of the United States government into Canada,[26] and, effective April 1, 1942, to any imported goods to be used in the construction of the Alaska Highway.[27] It was also provided in an exchange of notes dated March 17 and 18, 1942, that Canada would waive import duties, tariff and similar charges on goods moving over the Alaska Highway between Alaska and the United States, and that there would be no discrimination against United States traffic moving over the Canadian part of the Highway or between the United States border and the Highway.[28] By themselves, tariffs did not constitute a significant barrier to imports required for Canadian war production and any adjustments which were made were designed to lessen the financial burdens on the United Kingdom or to facilitate inter-departmental accounting.

In the United States, it was possible to circumvent tariff hindrances in the case of purchases by the Reconstruction Finance Corporation and its subsidiaries but the scope of their purchases was limited. In general, the Reconstruction Finance Corporation could absorb the import duties and sell supplies purchased from foreign sources at domestic prices. Since the procurement of metals in Canada by the United States was handled by the Metals Reserve Company, a subsidiary of the Reconstruction

Finance Corporation, any tariff impediments in this important segment of wartime trade were eliminated. Short of extending the scope of purchases by the Reconstruction Finance Corporation, the applicability of this technique was limited.

The elimination of tariff impediments to trans-border movements of defence articles was a matter which received a good deal of attention from both the Joint Economic Committees and the Joint War Production Committee. It will be recalled that the Joint War Production Committee emphasized the desirability of a freer flow of defence articles and recommended the elimination of all legislative and administrative barriers, including tariffs, import duties, customs, and other regulations or restrictions of any character which would prohibit, prevent, delay or otherwise impede the free flow of necessary munitions and war supplies between the two countries. The fact that this statement was approved by both the President and the Canadian War Cabinet stimulated efforts to reduce special administrative impediments to trade between the two countries.

A solution to the United States problem was finally found by the extension of certain powers contained in an appropriations act of 1914, authorizing the Secretary of the Navy to make emergency purchases of war material abroad and to import this material into the United States free of duty.[29] The Navy Department, in co-operation with the Reconstruction Finance Corporation and its subsidiaries, had made extensive off-shore purchases of strategic materials for other government agencies to take advantage of this privilege.[30] Identical powers were granted to the Secretary of War, the Secretary of Agriculture, and the Reconstruction Finance Corporation at the end of May, 1942.[31] They were also extended to the United States Maritime Commission and the War Shipping Administration a little over two years later.[32]

While tariff adjustments were widely used in Canada during the war, the revision of tariffs was much less common in the United States. In a number of cases, certain classes of goods, such as personal or household effects of members of the armed forces of the United Nations in the United States or prisoners of war, were entirely exempted from duty. In few cases were the duty exemptions of much significance for Canada. From the Canadian point of view, one important revision of the United States tariff occurred when duty-free imports of feed grains and feedstuffs were permitted for a limited period in 1934-44. At the end of 1943, a serious shortage of livestock and poultry feeds developed in the United States as a result of drought conditions and the heavy drains on existing stocks attributable to the growth in the livestock population. Because of this, emergency legislation was passed about the end of 1943 permitting for about six months duty-free imports of wheat, oats, barley, rye, flax, cotton-seed, corn or hay or their derivatives or compounds for use as poultry or livestock feed.[33] This legislation was specifically designed to encourage imports of feedstuffs from Canada. One other interesting example of the granting of duty-free status to a particular commodity was the special treatment accorded thirty-pound newsprint in the Revenue Act of 1943, a matter which is discussed in a later chapter dealing with forest products.

2. OTHER RESTRICTIONS ON TRANS-BORDER TRADE

Tariff barriers and procurement restrictions were relatively minor obstacles to wartime trade compared to the special obstructions created by the adoption of export controls by both Canada and the United States. The importance of export controls between the two countries stemmed from the large volume of trade affected. The fact that Canada supplied the United States with basic materials such as forest products and base metals while Canadian imports were dominated by metal manufactures, strongly influenced the pattern of export controls over goods moving between the two countries.

The imposition of export controls in Canada over many commodities in 1941 and 1942 was often a direct consequence of the superior attractive-ness of the United States market. Not only did the general level of prices increase faster in the United States than in Canada, but, in numerous cases, sudden price increases for scarce commodities resulted from speculative purchasing. Any indication that a rapid drain on available Canadian supplies might occur was usually a signal for the adoption of licensing controls. It often happened that export control was introduced for some other reason, sometimes for purposes of economic warfare or to assist in controlling distribution between domestic and foreign buyers. It was the consistent policy of the Canadian export control authorities to exempt exports to the United States from control when the volume of exports was likely to be either normal or negligible. Accordingly, the Export Permit Branch of the Department of Trade and Commerce issued a long series of orders exempting certain specified goods from export control when destined for the United States (or the British Empire).[34]

So far as in-transit shipments were concerned, Canada offered no particular concessions to exports passing through Canada *en route* to the United States. An early regulation stated that a Canadian export permit was not required for shipments moving in-transit through Canada to a British Empire country[35] but this was later restricted to goods moving in-transit in bond.[36] In view of the small amount of exports passing through

Canada bound for the United States, the maintenance of Canadian export controls over shipments in-transit to the United States cannot be regarded as significant.

In the United States, by the spring and summer of 1941, export control covered a wide range of commodities but the restrictiveness of the control depended on the particular licensing arrangements affecting a commodity or commodity group. There were two main types of licences: "individual" licences, which required specific approval of each shipment to a destination; and "general" licences, which constituted a blanket authorization to ship specified commodities to designated countries.[37] Exports covered by general licences merely required the endorsation of the general licence symbol on the export declaration. In contrast, the individual licence procedure was apt to be onerous since it involved the submission of individual applications for review and approval by the export control agency.

In 1940 and 1941, it was a fairly consistent policy of the United States to extend the general licence procedure to an increasing number of exports to Canada, and to maintain these general licences when the use of individual licences for many other destinations was being extended. General licences were, however, not granted universally and the kind of problems that arose out of the individual licence procedure can be illustrated by reference to the case of machine tools. The original export control regulations in the United States, issued at the time the Office of Export Control was created, placed all exports of machine tools, and certain other machinery, under licence. No general licence was issued for machine tool shipments to Canada, with the result that from July 5, 1940, on, every shipment of machine tools or attachments to Canada required an individual licence. These export licences required the approval of the Division of Controls of the Department of State, the Office of Export Control, and the Tools Branch in the Production Division of the Office of Production Management. The processing routine was cumbersome and the resultant delays were serious. In the summer and fall of 1940, frantic efforts were being made to increase Canadian production capacity and the lack of a few cutting tools could sometimes immobilize a whole plant. Canadian officials in Washington concentrated their efforts on expediting particular applications, but since the number of applications was often as high as 1,000 a month, this was not a satisfactory solution. Some relaxation of controls over small items was agreed to around the end of 1940, but the major problem remained. Finally, in June, 1941, the Division of Controls of the Department of State was pressed to grant a general licence for exports of machine tools to Canada. The Canadian submission pointed out that such action would remove a heavy and costly burden from official bodies concerned with export control, the customs services, the railroads, and the machine tool industry. Moreover, more rapid and effective utilization of machine tools would result. Despite these gains, there would be no lessening of the effective control over the destination and use of critical machines. These reasons were expanded in the following excerpt from a Canadian memorandum on the subject:

A. *Removal of Administrative Burden*

Extension of general licenses to Canada would relieve the State Department of the necessity of processing some 800 or 1,000 applications a month. The clerical staffs of the manufacturers would be freed from a tremendous volume of paper work. Customs officials would assuredly welcome the lessening of their already onerous duties. Relief would be afforded to the heavily-taxed facilities of the railroads. A great saving in expense would be effected throughout industry and government departments.

B. *Increase in Efficient Utilization of Machine Tools*

Specific licenses inevitably cause delay in shipments. Such delays may be due to ignorance or neglect on the part of the manufacturers; necessity for customs officials to obtain rulings on border-line cases; last minute changes in specifications or values requiring amendments to licenses; sudden calls for small or used machine tools "off the shelf." Such delays result in congestion on shipping floors, tie-ups at the border, and machine tools idle, the seriousness of which cannot be overlooked. Nothing could be more futile than idle machine tools awaiting completion of a formality while production lags in the plants for which they are destined.

C. *No Diminution in Effective Control*

In practice the specific license is no longer used to control the export of machine tools to Canada. Such control is effected, when necessary, by allocation over and above the general priorities system. Control by allocation and priority which has been instituted since the inception of export control provides a more efficient means of meeting urgent requirements from the available supply of machine tools. License applications are submitted months in advance of delivery, and the delivery dates indicated can be no better than rough estimates. The most accurate source of information is the manufacturer's order boards which the Office of Production Management now uses as a guide to allocation.[38]

As a result of these impressive arguments, a general licence was granted for exports of machine tools to Canada on July 19, 1941.

In line with this favourable development, a substantial number of articles which were essential to the war production programme in both countries were granted general licences when shipped to Canada during the latter half of 1941. This was particularly advantageous in view of the increasingly heavy volume of imports required for war production in Canada in the fall of 1941. The general licence procedure made it possible to avoid the difficulties which were sometimes encountered in obtaining individual export licences. Often, it took weeks or months to obtain border clearances for components, repair parts, and other urgently needed articles. In addition, freight cars were held up at border points and substantial demurrage accumulated. Shipping facilities in United States plants were congested by machinery and equipment awaiting clearance. It was believed in Canada that the United States export control procedure resulted in unnecessary delays and was therefore burdensome and detrimental to the Canadian war effort. The Canadian authorities continued to press for the liberalization of the remaining controls over exports to Canada. Again, the declaration of policy of the Joint War Production Committee was cited to support the Canadian contention. Despite this emphatic declaration of policy, it was a long, slow process to achieve the goal of complete suspension of United States export controls on shipments to Canada.

For one thing, the situation was aggravated by the rapid tightening of export controls following the entry of the United States into the war. The case of rubber is revealing. On December 11, 1941, instructions were issued by the Economic Defense Board to all collectors of customs that all export licences for rubber tires or tubes, except those exported as components of new or used vehicles, and for crude and crepe rubber, had been cancelled and that no shipments were to be cleared to any destination except lend-lease shipments or consignments to the United States armed forces.[39] It was later announced that all general and unlimited licences covering rubber were revoked, effective March 7, 1942, and that individual export licences would be required for all shipments to all destinations.[40] The tightened restrictions on rubber exports caused serious difficulties for Canada. Despite the fact that an allocation of rubber had been established for Canada by the Combined Raw Materials Board, the Rubber Controller of the Department of Munitions and Supply found that the shipments making up part of the allocation were being held at the border awaiting clearance by the Economic Defense Board, by this time known as the Board of Economic Warfare. It finally required the intervention of the Minister of Munitions and Supply to have the rubber released. The recurrence of situations like this would obviously hamper war production in Canada. Because of this, the United States regulations were substantially modified early in April when it was announced that all rubber and rubber manufactures could be shipped under general licence to Canada.[41] This did not imply a slackening of control since all imports required a Canadian licence from the Rubber Controller, and detailed records were kept of the crude rubber content of all imports and their end-uses.

On December 23, 1941, all goods not already under control in the United States were made subject to export licensing regulations. In the case of Canada, this was not very important since most exports to Canada were already covered by general licences. The forecast that there might be a widespread revocation of general licences to Canada after Pearl Harbor proved to be ill-founded. At that time, only about a dozen articles required individual licences when shipped to Canada. An order of the Board of Economic Warfare which was to become effective January 20, 1942, listed some eleven commodities or commodity groups for which general licences to Canada were to be revoked, including certain types of industrial diamonds, some grades of mica, quinine, crude rubber, mercury, platinum group metals, rubber and balata belting, tin, tungsten, brass and bronze, and zinc. As a result of appeals by the Canadian authorities the proposed revocation was cancelled for all but the first four items on the list. This was a major achievement and reaffirmed the very favourable treatment accorded to Canada.

Throughout the spring and summer of 1942, the process of transferring the few remaining items requiring individual licences to the general licence list continued.[42] Finally, in October, 1942, the long-awaited abolition of all controls over commercial exports to Canada was announced by the Board of Economic Warfare. The text of the announcement read:

Effective immediately, all license requirements heretofore imposed by the Board of Economic Warfare on the exportation of articles, materials, supplies and technical data to Canada and that part of Labrador under Canadian authority are removed. Neither individual nor unlimited licenses nor other form of license will henceforth be required for such exportations. Furthermore, in the case of commodities, the general license symbol "G-1" need not hereafter be placed upon export declarations. Similarly, in the case of technical data, neither the symbol "General License TD-Canada" nor the release certificate heretofore required, need hereafter be placed upon or within the envelope or wrapper.[43]

The elimination of export controls over goods moving from the United States to Canada represented a major victory for a few Canadian officials, particularly those associated with the Department of Munitions and Supply, who recognized that the United States regulations were hampering the war effort and who worked long and hard for their abolition.

Since Canada did not reciprocate by removing all controls on exports to the United States, the special circumstances of Canada should be appreciated. In the first place, the claim for special concessions to Canada was based on the fact that Canadian industry was so closely linked with industry in the United States. Canadian war production was vitally dependent on industry in the United States for components and repair parts. In part, this was because many Canadian firms are branches of parent concerns in the United States and also because of the highly specialized equipment turned out only in the United States. It was customary for Canadian firms to order essential items by telephone or telegraph, particularly when any emergency need arose. As a result, any special barriers to the export of components or repair parts or machinery from the United States to Canada were much more onerous and hampering than similar controls over exports to other countries. In the second place, the Canadian officials who pressed for the revision of United States export controls argued that the licensing of exports was a superfluous control. It was pointed out that exports of scarce or critical articles required clearance through the priority system of the War Production Board. Under these circumstances, evidence of essentiality would be furnished to the War Production Board in the course of securing a priority certificate or some other form of release. The licensing of exports was, therefore, a duplicate control, and particularly hard to justify when it tended to slow down the joint war effort. As indicated by the statement of official policy with respect to the elimination of barriers to the flow of war materials, the United States agencies recognized the cogency of the Canadian arguments. The contention that controls over commercial exports to Canada were redundant did not generally apply to other countries, in particular to the Latin American republics. Overall exports to these countries were controlled by the War Production Board, but the control did not usually extend beyond the determination of overall export quotas and related quotas for individual manufacturers. In 1942 and later, control over individual export shipments of critical materials or allocated commodities was exercised by the Board of Economic Warfare. It could license exports only within the limits of its overall allocations, but once these allocations were fixed, the War Production Board was not responsible for reviewing the essentiality of proposed end-uses of individual export shipments.

The retention of export controls over goods going to the United States meant that Canada appeared to be less generous than the United States. The reason for the Canadian policy deserves to be examined in some detail. It resulted partly from the diffusion of responsibility for export control over specific commodities. The authority to impose export controls rested principally with the various Controllers and Administrators, even though they were not empowered to issue licences. One important aim of these officials was to see that domestic needs for essential civilian goods were satisfied. The first step in the face of a shortage accompanied by extraordinary exports was usually to institute export licensing control.

Such action was not wholly dictated by a desire to protect domestic supplies at the expense of exports. The main consideration was the disparity between price levels in Canada and the United States, as a result of which exporters might be tempted to sell excessive quantities in the United States. The lack of control over Canadian exports might lead to a very rapid depletion of domestic inventories. Moreover, a Canadian export licence did not duplicate priority and allocation controls similar to those imposed by the supply agencies in the United States. Again, it was not true that the Canadian system of export control had slowed down or damaged the war production programme in the United States. For one thing, the major requirements of the United States from Canada were for raw materials, such as nickel, newsprint, and aluminum, shipments of which were covered by contract or agreement, and which were outside the normal sphere of export licensing control. In view of the different types of exports involved, different types of controls were used, although this fact does not support the view that Canada's controls were, in general, less stringent than those of the United States. In a nutshell, the Canadian point of view was that each country should be able to buy its normal share of goods in the other country's market. If this state of affairs could be achieved, the retention of particular types of control was irrelevant.

Despite these arguments, there was an apparent absence of reciprocity in the treatment of civilian requirements; export licences were required for exports from Canada, but they were not required for exports from the United States. In view of the growing rigour of United States export controls by the end of 1942 and the beginning of 1943, it appeared to be necessary to defend the exceptional treatment of Canada. Shortages of consumer goods were growing and considerable interest was being shown in the quantities of scarce goods being exported. The attitude of Congress to exports was inclined to be watchful, if not unsympathetic, and there were widespread domestic shortages which necessitated a general tightening of controls, including export controls. As a result, the Executive Director of the Board of Economic Warfare had issued instructions that all possible loopholes were to be stopped, a directive which implied the cancellation of all general export licences. By the spring of 1943, there were a number of indications that the Board of Economic Warfare might be forced to re-impose border controls over exports to Canada.

The threat that export controls would be re-imposed was related to the introduction of the decentralization plan. Early in March, 1943, the Board of Economic Warfare announced the introduction of a system of programme licensing which was to be applicable to foreign government purchasing missions in the United States.[44] The scheme was worked out in co-operation with the Office of Lend-Lease Administration. Programme licences did not apply to countries included in the decentralization plan but were intended to tighten restrictions on other exports. A programme licence was to constitute blanket authorization for the export of commodities within a programme which had been agreed on. This meant that procedures, whereby such purchasing missions as Amtorg Trading Corporation, the Belgian Congo Purchasing Mission, the British Ministry of Supply Mission, the Netherlands Purchasing Commission, and the Universal Trading Corporation (China) could export under unlimited licences, general licences, and individual licences, were to be suspended. Any commodities covered by War Production Board controls would have to be covered by programme licences before they could be exported, while dollar and tonnage limitations would be imposed on exports of other commodities. Quarterly programmes of anticipated purchases by government purchasing missions would have to be prepared and presented for ratification to the War Production Board by either the Board of Economic Warfare or the Office of Lend-Lease Administration. Once a licence had been issued for a programme, an official declaration or release certificate from the importing country that any proposed export was within the programme, would be required. This system thus shifted the task of administering the quota or programme to the importing country. It appeared that the Board of Economic Warfare might be pressed to place exports to Canada under the programme licensing system. Once again, a full statement of the Canadian position was submitted to the State Department and other agencies re-iterating the Canadian arguments and explaining the reason for the absence of reciprocal treatment of exports. However, it was recognized by the Canadian authorities that the administration of export controls in Canada might, in some cases, lead to practical embargoes on legitimate exports. Accordingly, in the summer of 1943, as a part of a general review and analysis of Canadian export control policy with respect to the United States, a policy directive was sent to the different Administrators and Controllers by the Chairman of the Wartime Prices and Trade Board and the Chairman of the Wartime Industries Control Board, emphasizing the importance of the "share-and-share-alike" principle. This principle was merely that civilians in each country were to obtain the *normal share* of goods which they were accustomed to import from the other country. The concluding paragraph of this directive, quoted below, gives a concise statement of Canadian policy:

It should be understood that inadequacy of supply is not in itself a sufficient reason for stopping all export to the United States. Obviously, if Canada or the U.S. took this stand, there would be no interchange of really critical commodities whatsoever. In drawing this matter to your attention,

I do so because we are anxious to make sure that we are implementing in every way possible a policy which is today as mutually advantageous as it was at the time the Hyde Park Agreement was reached between the President and the Prime Minister.[45]

The obvious reasonableness of the Canadian position, coupled with the clear policy directives respecting exports to the United States, convinced the United States export control authorities that parity of treatment could well exist without formal identity of control mechanisms. Therefore, the Board of Economic Warfare and its successors dropped the question. The issue was revived by officials concerned with civilian supplies in the United States on a later occasion, but the problems involved were new.

The revival of the issue, curiously enough, was precipitated by the passage of an amendment to the War Exchange Conservation Act in 1944 repealing the prohibition of certain imports introduced in the original Act.[46] The Office of Civilian Requirements of the War Production Board, which had displayed increasing concern over the volume of exports of civilian goods to Canada, interpreted the revision of the War Exchange Conservation Act as a further threat to civilian supplies in the United States. Consequently, the Office of Civilian Requirements began to explore the question of re-imposing export controls. After learning of the development, Canadian officials in Washington hastened to point out to the Office of Civilian Requirements that any such action would be in conflict with established policy and practice. It was noted that controls in each country had been adapted to provide for the equitable sharing of civilian supplies and that Canadians customarily had the same freedom of access to United States markets as residents of the United States except for import restrictions imposed by the Canadian government. Moreover, many of the goods affected by the relaxation of import restrictions were either unimportant, no longer on the market, or would be imported in quantities insufficient to affect the supply situation in the United States. Faced by these arguments, the Office of Civilian Requirements abandoned its plans. The re-imposition of border controls was not seriously proposed again during the wartime period.

3. THE EXCHANGE OF INFORMATION

Control over the export of technical data such as blueprints or designs was an essential function of export control in view of the importance of keeping such information out of the hands of the enemy. It was a matter of great importance to Canada to have immediate access to both existing and new technical information in the United States in view of the close interrelations of war production in the United States and Canada. The export control regulations of the United States required licences for the export of technical data, which were defined as follows:

Any model, design, photograph, photographic negative, document or other articles or material containing a plan or specification or descriptive or technical information of any kind (other than that appearing generally in a form available to the public) which can be used or adapted for use in connection with any process, synthesis or operation, in the production, manufacture, or reconstruction of any of the articles or materials, the exportation of which is prohibited or curtailed.[47]

There was a gradual relaxation of the United States control over exports of technical data to Canada which followed much the same pattern as export controls over goods. At first, a general licence could be used only for the export of certain types of technical data to Canada. The retention of any type of control over the shipment of technical data to Canada was apt to be a burden and a nuisance because of the large volume of interchanges on technical matters between the two countries and the necessity of avoiding delay. In the spring of 1942, the control over exports of technical data was substantially liberalized by allowing exports under a general licence except for information officially classified as secret, confidential, or restricted.[48] In October, when export controls were abandoned altogether over export shipments to Canada, the vestiges of control over technical data were dropped also. An interesting sidelight on the exchange of technical information occurred in 1944, when the War Production Board issued two certificates, effective in 1942, stating that the exchange and use in Canada of technical information relating to butadiene, polystyrene, and synthetic rubber was for the common good.[49] This was evidently to obviate any anti-trust action which might arise out of such pooling.

Another remarkable instance of co-operation was the mutual lifting of the barriers restricting visits of production officials to war plants in the two countries. To supplement exchanges of technical information, it was often most useful or essential if technicians or others concerned with war production could inspect particular production processes or whole factories. The Joint War Production Committee recommended that arrangements be made to permit mutual visits in the interests of more efficient production.

The following excerpt from the regulations of the Navy Department indicates clearly the official attitude:

(c) The prevailing restrictions upon visits of Canadian nationals to domestic commercial plants are considered to be burdensome and to constitute an impediment to the progress of the joint war production of the

Governments of the United States and Canada. Imperative inspections, technical discussions, exchange of ideas and manufacturing processes, etc., must not be encumbered by delay, formalities and the inconvenience which foreign nationality necessarily evoked.

(d) Accordingly, effective March 1, 1943, and for the duration of the war, Canadian nationals will be considered as and accorded the same privileges as citizens of the United States with respect to the matter of visits to commercial manufacturing plants, engaged upon naval work or equipment. . . .

The policy . . . is founded upon an agreement of mutual cooperation for a common purpose. The benefits to be derived therefrom are intended to be bilateral and reciprocal. To insure these advantages in converse the Canadian Government, contemporaneously, is adopting a policy, comparable to that herein established, for the administration of visits of United States citizens to Canadian plants.[50]

The rapidity of changes in technical production processes during the war increased the desirability of a full and quick exchange of information between the two countries. The official steps which were taken to facilitate the exchange of data by the two countries tended to result in more efficient joint production. In another field, overseas shipping, the maintenance of good communication channels and the rapid exchange of information were absolutely essential if the shipping resources of the two countries were to be co-ordinated.

REFERENCES FOR CHAPTER VIII

1. *Statutes of Canada*, 4-5 Geo. VI, c. 2 (1940-1).

2. The War Exchange Conservation Act positively encouraged imports from sterling sources by completely eliminating import duties on many items, particularly textiles, and lowering duties on others.

3. Canada, Treaty Series No. 9, 1936, *Trade Agreement between Canada and the United States of America* (Ottawa: King's Printer, 1936).

4. *Canada, House of Commons Debates,* December 2, 1940, p. 556.

5. *Ibid.*

6. *Ibid.*, p. 557.

7. P.C. 9888, December 19, 1941.

8. P.C. 9889, December 19, 1941. Authority had already been granted to accept export selling prices as the basis of valuation for duty for goods produced or manufactured in the United Kingdom by P.C. 75/2980 of April 30, 1941.

9. P.C. 62/450, January 20, 1942.

10. *47 U.S. Statutes* 1520; c. 212, Act of March 3, 1933. The purchase of "strategic and critical material" from foreign sources was permitted subject to certain conditions by an Act of Congress of June 7, 1939.

11. *Ibid.*

12. War Department Regulations, Procurement of Military Animals and Supplies, August 9, 1941, 6 *Federal Register* 4001.

13. War Department, Office of the Under Secretary, P & C General Directive No. 94, December 27, 1941.

14. *Ibid.*

15. Memorandum, Under Secretary of the Navy to the Chiefs of Bureaus, Boards and Offices, Navy Department; the Major General Commandant, Headquarters, U.S. Marine Corps; Commandant, U.S. Coast Guard, December 31, 1941.

16. 10 CFR, 1944 Supp., 805.503, p. 894.

17. 10 CFR, 1944 Supp., 805.510, p. 898.

18. War Shipping Administration, General Order 18, July 27, 1942, 7 *Federal Register* 5880.

19. *58 U.S. Statutes* 579; c. 303, Act of June 28, 1944.

20. 10 CFR, 1944 Supp., 805.503, p. 894.

21. There was an exception to this rule in the case of purchases for the Alaska Highway. This procurement was handled through North West Purchasing Limited, another Canadian Crown Company. After the termination of North West Purchasing Limited on August 31, 1944, some contracts were let directly although the normal procedure was to use the local facilities of the Department of Munitions and Supply.

22. *Revised Statutes of Canada,* 1927, c. 42.

23. See Appendix H-2, *Report of the Wartime Prices and Trade Board, September 3, 1939 to March 31, 1943* (Ottawa: King's Printer, 1943), p. 109.

24. P.C. 68/537, February 8, 1940.

25. P.C. 1/8255, October 24, 1941.

26. P.C. 57/8600, November 5, 1941.

27. P.C. 84/3723, May 4, 1942.

28. U.S., Department of State, *Bulletin,* March 21, 1942, p. 238.

29. *38 U.S. Statutes 399;* c. 130, Act of June 30, 1914.

30. *Minutes of the Council of the Office of Production Management,* May 6, 1941, p. 18.

31. Executive Order 9177, May 30, 1942, 7 *Federal Register* 4195.

32. Executive Order 9495, October 30, 1944, effective August 1, 1944, 9 *Federal Register* 13035.

33. The original exemption was established for 90 days after December 23, 1943, by Public Law 211 of the 78th Congress *(57 U.S. Statutes* 607; c. 375, Resolution of December 22, 1943) and extended for another 90 days by Public Law 272 *(58 U.S. Statutes* 131; c. 144, Act of March 29, 1944).

34. See, for example, Department of Trade and Commerce, Export Permit Branch Order No. 4, June 17, 1941; Export Permit Branch Order No. 45, September 10, 1942; and many intervening orders.

35. Department of Trade and Commerce, Export Permit Branch Order No. 3, June 17, 1941.

36. See Department of Trade and Commerce, Export Permit Regulations (third revision), Regulation No. 40.

37. Authority was granted to the Secretary of State to issue general licences for controlled exports by Executive Order 8712, March 15, 1941, 6 *Federal Register* 1501.

38. Memorandum, Sydney Pierce for the Machine Tools Controller of Canada to Joseph Green, Chief of Division of Controls of the Department of State, June 5, 1941.

39. Economic Defense Board, Office of Export Control, Press Release No. 20, December 11, 1941.

40. Board of Economic Warfare, Office of Exports, *Current Controls Bulletin No. 10*, March 5, 1942. An exception was made for rubber moving through the United States under a general in-transit licence from one part of the British Empire to another.

41. Board of Economic Warfare, Office of Export Control, *Current Controls Bulletin No. 17*, April 18, 1942. The effective date of the relaxation was April 9, 1942.

42. For example, general licences were issued for agricultural machinery and track-laying tractors in March and for special quartz crystals in April. See Board of Economic Warfare, Office of Export Control, *Current Controls Bulletin No. 12*, March 25, 1942, and *Ibid., No. 19*, April 30, 1942.

43. Board of Economic Warfare, Office of Export Control, *Current Controls Bulletin No. 50*, October 6, 1942.

44. Board of Economic Warfare, Office of Exports, *Current Export Bulletin No. 81*, March 10, 1943.

45. Wartime Prices and Trade Board, *Bulletin No. 163*, "Re Hyde Park Agreement and Export Controls," July 20, 1943.

46. *Statutes of Canada*, 8 Geo. VI, c. 50 (1944).

47. Proclamation 2465, March 4, 1941, 6 *Federal Register* 1300.

48. Board of Economic Warfare, Office of Export Control, Press Release dated March 2, 1942. The order was effective on March 1.

49. War Production Board Certificate No. 204, June 26, 1944 (eff. October 15, 1942) and War Production Board Certification No. 205, June 26, 1944 (eff. March 26, 1942), 9 *Federal Register* 7234.

50. 34 CFR, 1943 Supp., p. 1616.

CHAPTER IX

THE CONTROL OF SHIPPING AND OVERSEAS IMPORTS

IT WAS soon evident that the war in Europe would throw heavy burdens on available shipping facilities. In Canada, immediate steps were taken to control merchant shipping and to align Canadian shipping controls with those established by the United Kingdom. But because of the small size of the Canadian merchant navy, Canadian demands for shipping were met to a considerable extent by the shipping facilities of the United Kingdom and the United States. The dependence of both Canada and the United States on a common shipping pool for certain routes, notably to Latin America, made it necessary to adopt parallel restrictions on ocean-borne imports and exports in both countries. For this reason, the administration of shipping priorities and import controls in the two countries were nearly indistinguishable and throughout the period when shipping space was scarce, the control authorities in the two countries worked together very closely. Immediately following a brief sketch of the organization and functions of the shipping control agencies in the two countries, the steps which were taken to achieve a co-ordinated shipping policy will be outlined.

1. THE ADMINISTRATION OF SHIPPING CONTROLS

(a) *Shipping Controls in Canada*

Control was instituted in Canada with the creation of the Canadian Ship Licensing Board early in September, 1939, by an order-in-council which provided, among other things, that any Canadian merchant vessel over 500 tons engaged in foreign trade required a permit before it could begin a voyage.[1] When the Canadian Shipping Board was formed in December, 1939, it absorbed the functions of the Canadian Ship Licensing Board, and was given additional extensive powers over Canadian shipping.[2] The Canadian Shipping Board was authorized to regulate ocean voyages of British ships registered in Canada and to fix priorities for the movement of certain classes of supplies by sea, as well as to establish liaison with the Ministry of War Transport of the United Kingdom with a view to facilitating Canadian export shipments. In the spring of 1940, the Canadian Shipping Board instituted a system of licensing the purchase of any vessel not registered in the British Commonwealth, or the charter of any sea-going vessel over 500 tons.[3] The charter-approval system was extended first to cover any vessel over 500 tons[4] and later any vessel over 150 tons.[5] With this control over charterings, the Canadian Shipping Board was able to

211

ensure the co-ordination of Canadian shipping facilities with those controlled by the Ministry of War Transport. In addition to the control over chartering, a system of Ships' Privilege Licences was adopted to match the control exercised by the Ministry of War Transport through its Ship Warrant System. Ship warrants were introduced in the United Kingdom in the summer of 1940 as a means of controlling neutral shipping or shipping not already under control of the Allies. The system was primarily intended to tighten the oceanic blockade of the European continent and, after the fall of France, this necessitated closer supervision of neutral shipping. The possession of a ship's warrant was helpful, if not essential, if a ship owner wished to use United Kingdom port facilities, such as bunkering, drydocking, repairing, insurance, stores, and minor services, and warrants were only issued to owners who would undertake to observe the blockade. The Minister of Shipping, in announcing the control, did not say that the possession of a warrant was a prerequisite to using port facilities but he suggested that each ship without a warrant would be subject to special investigation with resultant delays and inconvenience, which made the intention clear.[6] The fact that marine insurance could not be obtained in the United Kingdom without a warrant strengthened this control remarkably. With the introduction of ship warrants in Canada, the Canadian Shipping Board was able to withhold Canadian port facilities from any vessel not conforming to allied shipping policy.

Until the fall of 1941, the Canadian Shipping Board had attempted to meet all Canadian demands for shipping space, but in view of the relatively small tonnage under its direct control, it was becoming increasingly clear that a separate agency to determine the relative urgency of requirements for shipping space for imports was necessary. The determination of urgency or priority ratings was, however, not an appropriate function for the Canadian Shipping Board since its primary concern was with ship movements and allocations of shipping space.

The emergence of a system of priority ratings for shipping requirements emphasized the seriousness of the lack of co-ordination of Canadian and United States shipping which was becoming evident in the summer of 1941. The Office of Production Management had suggested that joint shipping problems be referred to the Materials Co-ordinating Committee in the absence of a more suitable agency. Although it had been concerned with shipping problems in one or two isolated instances, the Materials Co-ordinating Committee was not adequately equipped to deal with shipping problems in general. The proposal of the Office of Production Management was considered by the Canadian Section of the Joint Economic Committees, which recognized that the suggestion was unsatisfactory since it did not dispose of the problem of determining the relative importance of imports.[7] The Canadian Section of the Joint Economic Committees referred the matter, along with its recommendations, to the Economic Advisory Committee, which in turn recommended that a Shipping Priorities Committee be created. This was done at the end of October, 1941.[8] The new Committee began operations within a few days after its creation. Its main functions were to determine the volume of Canadian shipping requirements for exports and imports and to assign priority ratings to these requirements. The Shipping Priorities Committee was authorized to arrange with the Canadian Shipping Board for cargo space in vessels not of United States registry. The presentation of Canadian requirements to the United States shipping authorities was to be made directly by the Committee. A cautionary note in the order-in-council stated that the Shipping Priorities Committee was to ensure that Canadian shipping requirements were placed before the authorities in the United States responsible for overseas export and import priorities so that Canadian requirements would receive equal consideration with those of the United States. In the meantime, in the United States, control over shipping was divided.

(b) Shipping Controls in the United States

The regulatory powers assigned to the United States Maritime Commission by the Merchant Marine Act of 1936[9] were not adequate to deal with the urgent shipping problems which arose in the United States in 1941.

The main responsibility of the United States Maritime Commission was to plan the construction of vessels for the merchant navy, and under certain conditions, to carry out and to subsidize the construction of new merchant vessels. It had, in addition, various regulatory powers over shipping, although no provision had been made for the control of shipping space by the issuance of priorities. In view of the absence of statutory authority to take stronger measures, the President requested the United States Maritime Commission in February, 1941, to attempt to obtain the most efficient use of all merchant vessels of the United States.[10] The President suggested particularly that the United States Maritime Commission should co-operate fully with the Office of Production Management in facilitating imports of essential materials. The Commission at first relied on the voluntary co-operation of the shipping companies and carried on negotiations to arrange for the handling of export and import cargoes.

In June, 1941, the Office of Production Management established a Shipping Liaison Section and a Shipping Priorities Advisory Committee whose main function would be to draw up statements of import cargoes with associated priorities for presentation to the United States Maritime Commission. The Shipping Priorities Advisory Committee was an inter-agency body which was supposed to draw up an import programme which would meet the needs of various claimants. Eventually, the Shipping Priorities Advisory Committee consisted of representatives of the War Production Board, Tariff Commission, Army Service Forces, Office of Civilian Requirements, Bureau of Foreign and Domestic Commerce, Office of Procurement and Materials of the Navy, War Shipping Administration, War Manpower Commission, War Food Administration, and the Department of State, in addition to a Canadian representative. There was some doubt about which agency was to be responsible for import priorities following the passage of the Ship Warrants Act in July, 1941.[11] This Act empowered the President to authorize the United States Maritime Commission to issue ship warrants and the authorization was issued towards the end of August, 1941.[12] As in the United Kingdom and Canada, ship warrants were issued on the condition that ships would be used to further the defence effort, and could be used to control access to loading, discharging, and cargo handling facilities. This meant that the United States Maritime Commission could require the preferential handling of certain classes of cargo, and in effect, could allocate shipping space and assign shipping priority ratings in accordance with defence needs. These powers, however, conflicted with those of the Office of Production Management which had been reaffirmed in the executive order creating the Supply Priorities and Allocations Board.[13] Other problems of divided jurisdiction became of vital importance when the United States entered the war.

To resolve the administrative and other difficulties involved in divided jurisdiction, the President created the War Shipping Administration by executive order in February, 1942.[14] The War Shipping Administration absorbed those functions of the United States Maritime Commission relating to the operation, purchase, charter, insurance, repairs, maintenance, and requisitioning of vessels. The vessels under the control of the War Shipping Administration were to be regarded as a pool, available for allocation either to agencies of the United States government or to other United Nations. In addition, the War Shipping Administration was to co-operate with all other agencies concerned with overseas transportation to insure efficient utilization of shipping.

The new agency thus assumed responsibility for the control and direction of all shipping while the United States Maritime Commission turned its attention completely to the ship-building problem. In April, 1942, the scope of the War Shipping Administration was greatly extended when it took title to or reserved the right to use all ocean-going ships owned or controlled by the United States. Responsibility for imports was also clarified by the executive order creating the War Shipping Administration, which specified that the War Production Board would determine and submit to the War Shipping Administration import schedules for its guidance in allocating vessels and space.

In view of the somewhat diffuse and vague control over shipping in the United States in 1941, there is small wonder that there was some lack of co-ordination between the shipping operations of the United States and Canada.

2. Import Controls

Because of the predominant place of the North Atlantic route in Canadian shipping, it was natural that the Canadian Shipping Board should have very close associations with the Ministry of War Transport of the United Kingdom. So far as relations with the United States were concerned, the problems of co-operation concerned mainly the treatment of Latin American exports and imports. The dependence of Canada on United States shipping to handle Canadian trade with Latin America meant that the most careful arrangements were essential to ensure that civilians in both countries were sharing scarce imports equitably, and that the commercial exporters in each country were accorded comparable treatment. The general policy recommended by the Joint Economic Committees in August, 1941, after considering the question of a co-ordinated shipping policy, was that the governments of Canada and the United States:

A. *Accept* as basic policy the principle that United States and Canadian defence shipping requirements shall receive equal consideration and that United States and Canadian civilian shipping requirements shall receive equal consideration;

B. *Direct* the appropriate agencies in each country to enter into immediate consultation with a view to establishing an effective, convenient and continuing method for placing Canadian requirements before the United States agency or agencies responsible for deciding on overseas import and export shipping priorities.[15]

The responsibilities assigned to the Canadian Shipping Board clearly referred to the desirability of maintaining continual contact with the United Kingdom Ministry of War Transport and the appropriate agency in the United States "for the purpose of securing the fullest possible co-operation of the United Kingdom and the United States authorities towards meeting Canadian import and export requirements."[16] Accordingly, in 1941, representatives of the Canadian Shipping Board were appointed both in London and Washington where they served throughout the war. By mid-1941, it became clear that even with stringent control over shipping and the economical use of shipping resources, there was no possibility of meeting the total demands for shipping space. As a result, it became necessary to introduce a system of priority control to guide the shipping agencies in assigning cargo space for imports.

The determination of United States needs for imported commodities was one of the responsibilities originally assigned to the Office of Production Management, which operated primarily through its Interdepartmental Shipping Priorities Advisory Committee. Prior to the creation of the Canadian Shipping Priorities Committee in October, 1941, there was no Canadian body competent to furnish the Interdepartmental Shipping Priorities Advisory Committee with complete and authoritative information relating to the urgency of Canadian shipping needs, nor any clear-cut channel of approach to the United States agency. The suggestion that a joint sub-committee of the Materials Co-ordinating Committee be formed to channel Canadian shipping requests to the Office of Production Management was acted on but the joint sub-committee was shortlived. Until the late fall of 1941, Canadian requests for shipping were being submitted to Washington by the Canadian Shipping Board, the Transport Controller and other Controllers of the Department of Munitions and Supply, and private individuals. It was clearly essential that detailed information on Canadian shipping needs be available to the Office of Production Management before equitable treatment of the requirements of the two countries could be achieved. Apart from this, the United States Committee entertained the possibility that the United Kingdom Ministry of War Transport was attempting to shift an undue proportion of the burden of caring for Canadian shipping needs to the United States, a suspicion which could be allayed only by the presentation of Canadian requirements in detail.

With the establishment of the Shipping Priorities Committee in Canada, a forum for deciding on Canadian needs for ocean-borne imports and a channel for presenting them to the Interdepartmental Shipping Priorities Advisory Committee became available. Arrangements were made to appoint the Commercial Attaché of the Canadian Legation to the Interdepartmental Shipping Priorities Advisory Committee to represent the Shipping Priorities Committee and to submit Canadian needs for space.

The immediate problem facing the Shipping Priorities Committee was to review the different commodities imported into Canada from overseas sources, and to compile a priority schedule based not only upon essential Canadian requirements but also on knowledge of sources of supply and the availability of shipping. The overall Canadian import programme showing both quantities and priority ratings was presented to the Interdepartmental Shipping Priorities Advisory Committee so that individual requests for space could be properly assessed. So far as imports transported in United States vessels were concerned, individual requests originated with the Canadian importer whose application for shipping space required the approval of an Administrator or Controller before it would be approved by the Shipping Priorities Committee. Approved applications were forwarded to the Office of Production Management and later the War Production Board which, in turn, requested the War Shipping Administration to provide the necessary cargo space. While it is true that Canadian requests were subject to close scrutiny by the Interdepartmental Shipping Priorities Advisory Committee, sympathetic consideration was given to requests for space for imports from other parts of the British Commonwealth, even though this involved the uneconomic allocation of shipping resources. On the other hand, the general policy was to refuse space for imports from overseas sources if the only grounds for the request was that they were cheaper than similar commodities obtainable on the North American continent.

The main regulation governing imports into the United States was General Imports Order M-63, issued by the Office of Production Management at the end of December, 1941.[17] This order placed imports of strategic and critical material under a permit system designed to tighten control over private imports and to facilitate foreign purchases by government agencies. By early July, 1942, United States control over ocean-borne imports was extended and strengthened. The new regulations, embodied in amendments and revisions of General Imports Order M-63, prohibited imports of three specified lists of commodities (including imports in bond or in transit) unless purchased by a United States government agency or unless specific exemption had been granted by the War Production Board. The first two lists enumerated a number of strategic materials which had previously been subject to control, while the third list covered a wide range of civilian commodities. The purpose of the extension of the order to civilian goods was to eliminate the waste of shipping space involved in importing non-essential goods. The permit control exercised by the War Production Board over shipments moving through United States in bond or in transit immediately created difficulties for Canadian importers. The system of submitting individual import applications for clearance proved to be a time-consuming and cumbersome procedure. Nevertheless, the War Production Board insisted that blanket permits could not be issued to Canada unless it was demonstrable that Canadian restrictions on civilian imports were comparable to those of the United States.

Accordingly, early in February, 1943, an order of the Commissioner of Customs was issued establishing Canadian import controls similar to those in the United States.[18] The Canadian order, which was designated as WM-89, applied to specific overseas imports except from the United Kingdom, Newfoundland, and Labrador and provided that the long list of goods specified could be imported into Canada only with the permission of the Minister of National Revenue. The Shipping Priorities Committee recommended the issuance or denial of licences and, in effect, determined the policy. Agreements were reached with the War Production Board that Canadian quotas would be fixed by the Shipping Priorities Committee and that these quotas would constitute a ceiling on the amount of controlled imports. Once this system was in effect, the War Production Board agreed to assign blocks of in-transit permit numbers for issuance by the Canadian authorities. Periodically, reports were submitted covering the permits issued but the War Production Board ceased to review individual Canadian cases.

The first six months of Canadian experience in administering a joint import programme with the United States were marked by a good deal of dissension. This was not a result of any fundamental disagreement on policy but because the Canadian administrative machinery could not be adapted readily to fit the system imposed by the United States. The establishment of Canadian import quotas was a burden on the available analytical and statistical resources, and it took some time to convince the War Production Board that Canadian import requirements were reasonable. The fact that the United States was in a position to insist on the individual clearance of import shipments meant that Canada was left with no choice but to conform. On the other hand, once the Canadian import programme had been developed and cleared with the United States, the process of M-63 clearance was almost automatic and completely harmonious procedures were worked out. Of course, differences of opinion did exist on the adequacy of quotas for individual commodities but there were no basic differences which could not be resolved by discussion.

By early 1945, serious consideration was being given to the abandonment of import controls, a matter which was discussed fully between
Canada and the United States. Agreement was reached that import controls should be maintained on certain commodities subject to allocation
by the Combined Boards or in other cases where the resumption of private
trading would interfere with other government programmes. Accordingly, by the fall of 1945, the United States had abandoned most import
controls except those needed to implement allocations of the Combined
Boards or to assist in foreign procurement by United States government agencies. In Canada, there was a tendency to abandon import controls more slowly, partly because of problems relating to the subsidization of imports and the stabilization of prices. However, by the end
of 1945, the significance of import controls had sharply declined, along
with the necessity for continuous co-operation between Canada and the
United States in this field.

3. THE CONTROL OF SHIPPING SPACE FOR EXPORTS

The critical shipping shortage which developed in the winter of
1941-42, and which by the spring of 1942 was seriously threatening
Allied supply lines, necessitated the extension of shipping priorities to
exports as well as imports. Early in July, 1942, the United States announced the introduction of a system of shipping priorities on all ocean-
borne export shipments to Latin America of more than 2,240 pounds.[19]
The new system, to be effective on August 1, 1942, was to be administered
by the Board of Economic Warfare. Not being directly responsible for
the allocation of shipping space, the Board of Economic Warfare could
merely assign priority ratings which indicated the probability of freight
space being allocated but which did not guarantee space allocations.

Immediate steps were taken by Canada to co-operate with the Board
of Economic Warfare in developing a comparable system of shipping
priorities for Canadian exports. Again, co-ordination of the priority
systems of the two countries was obviously essential in view of Canadian
dependence on United States shipping to Latin America. The Canadian
regulations, which went into effect on August 15, 1942, provided that all
commercial shipments in excess of 2,240 pounds moving through United
States ports to Latin America required an export priority. Export priorities were necessary for all such shipments, whether subject to export permit
control or not. The Shipping Priorities Committee was responsible for
issuing export priorities and for forwarding applications for freight space
to Washington for action by the Board of Economic Warfare and the

War Shipping Administration. In the case of commodities requiring export licences, the Canadian procedure was to affix the shipping priority rating on the face of the export permit.

In the United States, the plan was that no shipments by sea freight would be permitted unless a shipping priority rating had first been assigned to the shipment by the Board of Economic Warfare, and that the priority rating would be endorsed on the export permit. However, no shipment could be moved to the port of exit until notice of tentative allocation of space, known as a Statement of Cargo Availability, had been received from the War Shipping Administration, as well as a permit to move the shipment by rail. Control over rail movements was exercised by the issuance of unit permits by the Office of Defense Transportation but, in practice, the War Shipping Administration acted for the Office of Defense Transportation in issuing permits for the rail shipments of exports from the interior to the port of exit.

In the administration of these controls over rail movements, the Transport Controller of the Department of Munitions and Supply issued unit permits on behalf of the Office of Defense Transportation for over-land movement through the United States.[20] The permit from the Transport Controller to move the shipment to the United States port of exit was sent to the shipper along with notification of a provisional allotment of freight space.

The United States regulations were modified so that any shipments originating in Canada moving in transit under a general licence through the United States automatically retained the shipping priority rating assigned by the Canadian government.[21]

Despite agreement between Canada and the United States on principles of co-operation in the shipping field, the early efforts to follow a common policy in controlling export shipping were marked by confusion and negligence. Difficulties arose immediately because of the failure of the Board of Economic Warfare to notify the Canadian export control authorities of procedural changes, particularly in the system of priority ratings. Moreover, although a system had been established for notifying the Shipping Priorities Committee when Canadian applications had been certified by the Board of Economic Warfare and submitted to the War Shipping Administration, the Board of Economic Warfare failed to convey the proper notification to the Canadian authorities. As a result, there were sometimes lengthy delays in filling Canadian requirements for freight space. These misunderstandings created particular difficulty for the Canadian flour-milling industry, which was forced to suspend shipments to Latin America almost completely in the last quarter of 1942 and early in 1943. It was only after extensive negotiations with the Board of Economic Warfare and the Department of State that a quota system was introduced to restore Canada's competitive position.

By early 1943, the backlog of freight space applications in the United States had grown to the point where increasingly rigorous restrictions were necessary. The policy of the Board of Economic Warfare had been to issue export licences even when there was no assurance that corresponding shipping space would be available. The result was that there had been a substantial over-issuance of export permits in terms of shipping space and some deflationary expedient was essential. To accomplish this, the Board of Economic Warfare imposed severe restrictions on licences for shipments to Argentina, Bolivia, Chile, Colombia, Ecuador, Peru, and Venezuela in the period January 11 to March 1, 1943. Except for a limited number of commodities, export permit applications were not to be submitted and any pending applications would be held for sixty days.[22] This drastic action was taken to provide a breathing space before the imposition of more rigorous controls over imports by Latin American countries. The action was closely related to the introduction of the decentralized control over exports which was discussed in the previous chapter. The action of the United States in imposing a virtual embargo on shipments to Latin America was something of a shock to Canada.

With the exception of newsprint, no provision was made for the shipment of Canadian exports under the interim scheme. The attention of the United States authorities was at once called to this omission, and arrangements were made to provide shipping space for Canadian exports of certain commodities, the share to be determined on the basis of the pre-war shipments by Canada and the United States. Beginning in March, Canadian shipping requirements were again incorporated completely in the allocation system.[23]

Once over, the preliminary difficulties, which were attributable to unintentional oversights rather than to a deliberate policy of discrimination, the relations of the authorities concerned with export shipping priorities were marked by amity and close co-operation.

Despite the gradual easing of the shipping shortage in 1943 and 1944, it was evident that the defeat of Germany and the subsequent concentration on the Pacific War would throw a serious strain on shipping facilities. It was therefore agreed by the Allied governments to continue shipping controls until six months after the end of the war. Apart from such general agreements, there were more specific agreements reached between the Canadian Shipping Board and the War Shipping Administration. The Canadian Shipping Board even undertook to carry certain imports in its own bottoms on behalf of the War Shipping Administration and to revise the priority status of imports if necessary to meet the needs of the War Shipping Administration. This was not the most usual situation.

By the summer of 1944, the regulations governing export shipments to Latin America were substantially relaxed. Announcements were made in both Canada and the United States that, after September 1, 1944, freight space applications would be required only for commercial shipments over 10,000 pounds (except for newsprint) to certain destinations in Latin America.[24] The allocation of space was dropped altogether for shipments to Costa Rica, Cuba, the Dominican Republic, El Salvador, Guatemala, Haiti, Honduras, Mexico, Nicaragua, and Panama, again except for newsprint. The relaxation, however, did not apply to the Argentine. It was later announced that Canadian freight space applications would not be required after October 15 for shipments to Bolivia, Colombia, Chile, Ecuador, Peru, Venezuela and after November 1 for shipments to Brazil, Paraguay, and Uruguay. The Argentine remained the exception, freight space applications being required for any shipments greater than 2,240 pounds.[25] This was paralleled by action of the United States which eliminated the corresponding Statement of Cargo Availability effective November 15 except for newsprint shipments anywhere weighing more than 2,240 pounds.[26] In effect, this meant the end of export shipping priorities to Latin America. Finally, shortly after VE-Day, the improved prospects for the availability of shipping space led to the complete abandonment of all freight space applications including those covering exports to the Argentine, except for newsprint to Latin America.[27] The effective date of the order was May 31, 1945, which marked the end of official control of shipping space for commercial exports by the Foreign Economic Administration and the Shipping Priorities Committee, except for newsprint to Latin America. The retention of control over newsprint is a significant example of the close and harmonious relations which were established by Canada and the United States in this field. It was not until the middle of January, 1946, that the allocation of shipping space for newsprint destined for the Latin American Republics was abandoned.[28]

REFERENCES FOR CHAPTER IX

1. P.C. 2524, September 5, 1939.
2. P.C. 4251, December 20, 1939. A proclamation of December 27, 1939 (P.C. 4357) brought the regulations into effect on the same day. The Canadian Shipping Board was to be an inter-departmental agency, made up of representatives of the Department of External Affairs, the Department of National Defence (Naval Services), the Department of Transport, and the Department

of Munitions and Supply, as well as the Director of Shipping. The Chairman was the Deputy Minister of the Department of Trade and Commerce. On December 23, 1941, the President of Wartime Merchant Shipping Limited, a Crown Company, was added to the Board by P.C. 9932.

3. Canadian Shipping Board Order No. 1 and 2, both dated April 6, 1940.

4. Canadian Shipping Board Order No. 3, November 15, 1941.

5. P.C. 6785, July 31, 1942.

6. Hansard, *Parliamentary Debates,* 5th series, vol. 364, July 30, 1940, pp. 1163-4.

7. Minutes of the Canadian Section, Joint Economic Committee, September 25, 1941.

8. P.C. 8487, October 31, 1941. The Shipping Priorities Committee was also inter-departmental in character, members being appointed to represent the Department of Trade and Commerce, the Department of Munitions and Supply, the Department of External Affairs, and the Wartime Prices and Trade Board, and including as well the Director of Shipping and the Commissioner of Customs. Although originally conceived of as responsible jointly to the Department of External Affairs and the Department of Trade and Commerce, its administrative functions were carried out solely by the latter department.

9. *49 U.S. Statutes* 1985; c. 858, Act of June 29, 1916.

10. National Defense Advisory Commission, *Defense,* February 18, 1941, p. 9, quoted in *The United States at War,* p. 145.

11. *55 U.S. Statutes* 591; c. 297, Act of July 14, 1941.

12. Executive Order 8871, August 26, 1941, 6 *Federal Register* 4469.

13. Executive Order 8875, August 28, 1941, 6 *Federal Register* 4481.

14. Executive Order 9054, February 7, 1942, 7 *Federal Register* 837.

15. Preamble to P.C. 8487, October 31, 1941. The original resolution of the Joint Economic Committees was dated August 9, 1941.

16. P.C. 6785, July 31, 1942.

17. General Imports Order M-63, December 27, 1941, 6 *Federal Register* 6796.

18. The order, authorized by P.C. 949, February 8, 1943, was issued as a Memorandum to Collectors of Customs and Excise dated February 11, 1943.

19. Board of Economic Warfare, Office of Export Control, *Current Controls Bulletin No. 33,* July 4, 1942.

20. Regulations of the Board of Economic Warfare, July 21, 1942, 7 *Federal Register* 5660.

21. Office of Defense Transportation, General Order O.D.T. No. 16, July 6, 1942, 7 *Federal Register* 5195.

22. Board of Economic Warfare, Office of Exports, *Current Export Control Bulletin No. 66,* January 11, 1943.

23. It was announced on February 25, 1943, that export permit applications would again be considered from United States exporters. See *Current Export Control Bulletin No. 76* issued by the Office of Exports of the Board of Economic Warfare.

24. Foreign Economic Administration, *Current Export Bulletin No. 185,* August 21, 1944. *Commercial Intelligence Journal,* August 26, 1944.

25. *Commercial Intelligence Journal,* October 7, 1944.

26. Foreign Economic Administration, *Current Export Bulletin No. 206,* November 3, 1944.

27. *Ibid. No. 244,* May 24, 1945.

28. U.S., Department of Commerce, *Current Export Bulletin No. 308,* January 16, 1946.

CHAPTER X

JOINT AND COMBINED PLANNING

FROM the Canadian point of view, partnership with the United States in a number of joint planning bodies turned out to be a step in the direction of full Canadian participation in the combined planning agencies originally begun by the United States and the United Kingdom. Before considering this development in a later part of this chapter, it may be useful to review some of the highlights of the activities of the three committees established in 1941 to deal with the economic problems of North America: the Joint Economic Committees, the Joint War Production Committee, the Materials Co-ordinating Committee, and one other special endeavour in the field of joint planning.

1. JOINT PLANNING

The Joint Economic Committees held their first meeting on July 15 and 16, 1941, and in less than a year, they had effectively ceased to function. During the course of their brief life, the Committees considered a large number of issues affecting economic relations between Canada and the United States. It was perhaps this diversity of interests which led indirectly to the weakening of the influence of the Committees. In other words, the Committees were inclined to venture into fields which had already been pre-empted by other government agencies or committees. The unfortunate consequence of this was that the intervention or the assistance of the Committees ceased to be very welcome in some cases, and without the complete co-operation of operating departments, the Committees could hardly be expected to be useful. Another important consideration was the fact that the members of the Committees were busy administrators with other pressing responsibilities and had little time to devote to long-range planning of the North American economy. One result of this was, and this was particularly true of the United States members, that the work tended to be delegated to subordinates without substantial authority. The lack of clearly defined and restricted terms of reference tended to stimulate the discussion of intellectually interesting issues which were often not of great practical importance. In fact, the Joint Economic Committees were pretty well barred from dealing with raw material problems because of the existence of the Materials Co-ordinating Committee, and, once the

Joint War Production Committee had been set up, from most war production problems. It was not until March, 1944, that the two governments formally disbanded the Joint Economic Committees. The announcement was brief, but kind, as is usual in such notices. Its full text is as follows:

It was announced on March 14 that the Governments of Canada and the United States have agreed to dissolve the Joint Economic Committees which were established in June 1941 to assist in the collaboration of the two countries in the utilization of their combined resources for the requirements of war. The Committees have been of great assistance, not only in the coordination of wartime measures and controls but also in surveying and advising on economic problems of common concern. It has been agreed, however, by the two Governments that the development of other agencies for coordination and exchange of views and the establishment during the past three years of methods of cooperation in production and the use of resources have rendered unnecessary the continued operation of the Committees.[1]

The Joint War Production Committee suffered from some of the same weaknesses as the Joint Economic Committees, but it was much stronger in other respects. The Committee consisted of top-ranking government executives most of whom had a crushing load of responsibilities for domestic problems and who therefore had little time to devote to the continuing study of the joint and perhaps remote problems of the two countries. Despite this, the Committee was able to work out satisfactory methods of delegating responsibility for particular problems to operating officials. The first meeting of the Committees, which took place about a week after Pearl Harbor, was important since it resulted in an emphatic statement of policy concerning the removal of trade barriers between the two countries. The beneficial results were apparent almost immediately. In addition, the Committee was instrumental in making available to the United States Canadian stocks of anti-aircraft guns, ammunition, bombs, and explosives urgently needed at a number of strategic bases and other exposed areas in the United States. The second meeting of the Committee was in January, 1942, and was devoted to a review of the progress that had been made in eliminating tariff and other impediments to purchases by the United States in Canada as well as to the establishment of sub-committees. The third meeting in the spring of 1942 led to the incorporation of Canadian war production requirements in the new military priority ratings created by the Priorities Directive of 1942. The activities of the Committee itself were unimportant after this date but its informal sub-committees played an important rôle in the integration of production plans right up to the end of the war. Altogether, nine sub-committees of the Joint War Production Committee were set up to deal with the following fields:

(i) tanks and automotive vehicles
(ii) artillery
(iii) ammunition
(iv) small arms
(v) chemicals and explosives
(vi) signals equipment
(vii) aircraft
(viii) naval and merchant shipbuilding
(ix) conservation

The members of the sub-committees were the two senior executives responsible for the production programmes in the two countries. The main importance of the sub-committees lay in the fact that they facilitated the exchange of information, ideas and plans and this very often led to more efficient use of available facilities in the two countries. In particular, in 1943 and 1944, Canada undertook to produce many of these items in large volume for the United States. One example of the usefulness of the sub-committees occurred in 1944 when a critical shortage of shell-manufacturing capacity developed in the United States, and Canada was able to make available quickly both shell lathes and shells for the United States Army.

There were naturally close relations between the Joint War Production Committee and its sub-committees and War Supplies Limited. This was the Crown company described briefly earlier whose function it was to handle Canadian orders placed by departments or agencies of the United States government in Canada. War Supplies Limited had been incorporated in May, 1941, specifically to facilitate purchases which were made in Canada in accordance with the terms of the Hyde Park Declaration. The company appointed representatives in Washington to negotiate with the procurement agencies of the United States and to keep them advised of the availability of Canadian supplies. The financial responsibility of War Supplies Limited was clarified when, through an exchange of notes, the Canadian government formally guaranteed the commitments of the company.

Some of the difficulties initially encountered by War Supplies Limited have already been described in the chapter dealing with administrative restrictions on off-shore purchases by agencies of the United States government. Another problem was to reach agreement with procurement agencies on the profit which would be permitted to Canadian contractors. It was agreed to limit profits to 10 per cent and, following the Contract Renegotiation Act of 1942, this agreement was further formalized. In addition to this ceiling on profits for private companies, the Canadian government was to make no profit on War Supplies Limited contracts, the rate of amortization on government-owned facilities was to be limited to 25 per cent per year and the Canadian customs or excise duties were not to be added to the cost.

Total sales by War Supplies Limited amounted to roughly one billion dollars, consisting of a wide variety of Canadian products. Its rôle was a significant one since it provided a practical means of making Canadian facilities available for production needed by the United States. It is likely that without a channel of this sort, it would have been difficult to arrange for the rapid placement of contracts, a factor of vital importance once production capacity became available.

The establishment of the Materials Co-ordinating Committee was announced on May 14, 1941, the day after the incorporation of War Supplies Limited. The Committee met for the first time in Montreal on May 21, 1941, and again in Washington on June 11. The main purpose of these initial meetings was to examine the supplies of raw materials in the two countries and to compare notes on rates of production and the existence of any excess capacity or the availability of new capacity. The supply situation for about fifty raw materials including all those of any significance for war production was reviewed but attention was principally devoted to scarce materials. This preoccupation with materials in short supply continued, naturally enough, throughout the life of the Committee. One result of these exploratory meetings was that Canada undertook to provide at once increased quantities of certain chemicals which were critically needed in the United States. In other fields, a further review of the supply situation was necessary before any commitment could be given. These preliminary negotiations were typical of much of the later work of the Committee which revolved around the problems of sharing scarce supplies between the two countries or attempting to alleviate the scarcity by increased production. Some examples of the work of the Materials Co-ordinating Committee have already been referred to in earlier chapters.

There was a great difference between the Materials Co-ordinating Committee on the one hand and the Joint Economic Committees and the Joint War Production Committee on the other. These latter were advisory committees whose recommendations were supposed to be approved by the President and the Prime Minister before implementing action was taken. This was not the case with the Materials Co-ordinating Committee whose members were the government officials responsible for the major commodities dealt with by the Committee. This meant that the implementation of agreements was generally left to those who had made the agreements, a state of affairs which is likely to result in more decisive action. In fact, the sub-committees of the Joint War Production Committees operated on much the same basis, and it seems unlikely that many of the day-to-day decisions of these sub-committees were ever submitted as formal recommendations for action by the governments. The Joint Economic Committees and the Joint War Production Committees, as such, became inactive relatively soon after their formation. The Materials Co-ordinating Committee continued to function until the end of the war, although an important part of its responsibilities was later absorbed by the Combined Boards, a development which will be described later in this chapter.

The main concern of the three joint planning agencies dealt with above was to promote internal economic adjustments in Canada and the United States. There were also certain fields where attempts were made to co-ordinate relations with third countries. One particular instance of this occurred in connection with lend-lease and mutual aid shipments by the two countries. In Canada, mutual aid, in its formal sense, was an evolutionary development which grew out of various devices designed to assist the United Kingdom in purchasing supplies in Canada. Prior to 1942, Canada was able to assist the financing of United Kingdom purchases in three main ways. The first method was the official repatriation of Dominion and Dominion-guaranteed securities held in the United Kingdom prior to maturity, in addition to which there was a substantial amount of private repatriation. The volume of such repatriated securities amounted to nearly $900,000,000 in the period 1939-42. A slightly smaller amount was accumulated in the form of sterling balances in London by the Canadian government and later converted to an interest-free loan. Canada also accumulated substantial book claims against the United Kingdom on different occasions, principally in connection with the operation of the British Commonwealth Air Training Plan. Apart from these forms of financial aid, Canada contributed one billion dollars outright to the United Kingdom in 1942. The preamble to the appropriation act, which is quoted below except for various "whereases," gives an interesting, if formal, account of the financial aid which Canada had thus far rendered to the United Kingdom:

Canada is at war with the German Reich, Italy, Roumania, Hungary, Finland and Japan; and the United Kingdom of Great Britain and Northern Ireland has been purchasing in Canada large quantities of foodstuffs, raw materials, munitions and war supplies; and the United Kingdom has not had an adequate supply of Canadian currency to make the said purchases and therefore Canada has made large sums of such currency available to the United Kingdom for the said purpose in exchange for sterling balances which in part have been utilized for the purchase of Canadian securities held by persons resident in the United Kingdom and in part are held in banks in the United Kingdom; and it is expedient that part of the said sterling balances be utilized to purchase Canadian securities held in the United Kingdom and that other such balances be converted into an obligation of the Government of the United Kingdom in Canadian currency; and it is necessary for the successful prosecution of the war that further substantial quantities of foodstuffs, raw materials, munitions and war supplies be made available to the United Kingdom and desirable that they be made so available on terms which will not result in an undue accumulation by Canada either of sterling balances or of indebtedness due from the United Kingdom.[2]

The principle was extended in 1943 when a further billion-dollar appropriation was authorized for "mutual aid."[3] Mutual aid thus became the Canadian counterpart of lend-lease, although it seems likely that the evolutionary development in Canada was speeded by the example of lend-lease. The Canadian scheme enabled any member of the United Nations to obtain munitions or agricultural products from Canada, provided they were to be used for the "effective prosecution of the war," the cost to be defrayed by Canada.

Once the mutual aid mechanism had been established in Canada, it was apparently felt to be desirable to provide some formal channel for the co-ordination of the aid programmes of the United States and Canada. Accordingly, negotiations were carried on between President Roosevelt and Prime Minister King at the QUADRANT Conference in Quebec City in August, 1943, and the creation of the Joint War Aid Committee was announced. The purpose of the Committee was "to study problems that arise out of the operations of the United States lend-lease and the Canadian mutual aid programmes and where necessary to make recommendations concerning them to the proper authorities."[4] The United States members of the Committee were military, diplomatic, and war production officials, while the Canadian membership consisted of various government officials stationed in Washington. While this Committee dealt with a few minor problems, it was largely inoperative and had no noticeable influence in co-ordinating lend-lease and mutual aid activities.

One of the issues in this general field which arose late in the war concerned the way in which the burden of overseas aid was to be shared between the United States and the British Commonwealth. It is understandable that there should exist in the United States a certain vagueness about the constitutional and financial relations of the countries within the

British Commonwealth. For this reason, there is a tendency sometimes to assume, for example, that the United Kingdom and Canada are united more closely than is, in fact, the case. As a result of this, it was felt by certain groups in the United States that the United Kingdom should not expect to obtain through lend-lease commodities which were available in Canada or other parts of the Commonwealth until these alternative sources of supply had been exhausted. For example, the Third Annual Report of the Truman Committee contained the following comment which could easily be misconstrued unless it were understood that the United Kingdom and the other Dominions were essentially independent:

> We should never forget that lend-lease was originally authorized by the Congress, solely because the English and others whom we desired to assist did not have sufficient American exchange to purchase materials needed by them. Lend-lease was never intended as a device to shift a portion of their war costs to us, but only as a realistic recognition that they did not have the means with which to pay for materials they needed.
> Before authorizing lend-lease, the Congress expressly requested and received assurance that lend-lease assistance would be extended only where the recipient was fully utilizing all of its own resources. Such resources, of course, include foreign-held American securities and foreign-held securities which control basic raw materials abroad.[5]

While this attitude was not altogether in harmony with the spirit of the Lend-Lease Act, it was held widely enough in Congress to lead the Foreign Economic Administration to espouse a so-called "residual policy" in the administration of lend-lease in early 1944. This policy was designed to divert United Kingdom lend-lease requisitions to Empire sources, if any. The policy was never widely applied although the issue did arise in connection with woodpulp in 1944. The Foreign Economic Administration advised the United Kingdom that it could not approve requisitions for any types of woodpulp which were available in Canada. The reason for this was not any inherent niggardliness on the part of the Foreign Economic Administration, but the attitude of Congress, which is clearly illustrated by the following excerpt from testimony before a sub-committee of the House Appropriations Committee in which Mr. Oscar Cox, the General Counsel of the Foreign Economic Administration, explained his agency's policy to a number of Congressmen:

> The Chairman: I note . . . that in 1942 the United States supplied 12 percent of the United Kingdom's paper-making raw materials and for 1944 we propose to cut that down to 5 percent, so it is evident that she has either found other sources, or has been able to tap other sources, or she must be rationing allocations very severely, as we are doing in the United States.

Mr. Cox: The United Kingdom rations newsprint, for example, far more strictly than we do here. Newspapers are only four pages and contain only the most important news. It is a very strict system of rationing of a very essential commodity.

Mr. Ludlow: Our newspapers get their supply mostly from Canada?

Mr. Cox: Most of it.

Mr. Ludlow: When we have to get our supply from Canada, why should we be sending wood pulp and paper to the United Kingdom?

Mr. Cox: The wood pulp here is not of the same character as that which can be obtained in Canada. It is a special type which comes only from American sources and is used only in making things which cannot be produced out of Canadian wood pulp.

Mr. Ludlow: Even so, the British Empire extends all around the world, and they have access to such material that can be produced in those countries that extend all over the surface of the earth. Why could not the United Kingdom get its wood supply from its dominions?

Mr. Cox: They do get most of it there, but this particular kind of wood pulp is not obtainable from Canada or any other place in the Empire.

Mr. Ludlow: I am not speaking particularly of the paper pulp, but there are other categories of hardwoods and softwoods and other lumber products, and you say those are of a character that cannot be obtained from the Dominions?

Mr. Cox: Or any part of the Empire; they are not obtainable there.

Mr. Wigglesworth: Do not they have any hardwoods in India, in North Africa, or Australia?

Mr. Cox: Of certain types, and the ones that the British obtain from those places are not provided under lend-lease. The only ones they obtain are the ones not obtainable from any place in the Empire.

Mr. Taber: A lot of those things, like pulpwood that goes into a lot of these papers, come in from elsewhere?

Mr. Cox: No; we have checked that. They are from domestic production.

Mr. Taber: You mean it is a temporary situation?

Mr. Cox: No; I do not mean that. There are certain types of woodpulp that are not produced in Canada of the character required for war purposes in the United Kingdom, which cannot be obtained in any part of the Empire.

Mr. Taber: I think that is true, but there are a great lot of those factories which produce a specialized paper in this country, but not of the types that are supplied by Canadian supply.

Mr. Cox: What is budgeted here is the residual minimum of material that they cannot get anywhere in the British Empire.[6]

In the specific case of woodpulp, the application of the "residual policy" apparently led to a decrease of United States exports of woodpulp amounting to about 60,000 tons and a corresponding increase in Canadian exports. The upshot of this was that there was a unilateral shift of financial responsibility from lend-lease to mutual aid. On general grounds, the policy was repugnant to Canada, not only because it was based on a misinterpretation of the inter-relations of the countries in the British Commonwealth but also because any consistent application of the policy would be a serious financial burden to Canada. The Canadians were aware of the political pressures involved and recognized that any outright reversal of the "residual policy" would not be very practical. Fortunately, a final determination of United States policy on the issue became unnecessary in view of the termination of lend-lease and mutual aid in 1945.

The issues arising in this particular case were typical in the sense that they involved the United States and Canada and the United Kingdom. It was difficult to segregate many problems which concerned Canada and the United States only; the United Kingdom was usually an interested party as well. This became particularly true after Pearl Harbor when joint planning by the United States and Canada tended to be superseded to a considerable extent by combined planning by the three countries.

2. THE COMBINED BOARDS AND RELATED AGENCIES

Combined planning was, in a sense, a formalization of the extremely close personal relationship between President Roosevelt and Prime Minister Churchill which developed long before Pearl Harbor. There had been close consultation on military, political, and economic problems not only between the two political chiefs but between senior military and civilian officials as well. With the entry of the United States into the war, it was possible to adopt more formal methods of consultation on common problems through the medium of special international committees.

On January 26, 1942, following discussions between the Prime Minister and the President in Washington in December, the establishment of a group of Anglo-American committees to be responsible for planning a co-ordinated war programme in a number of fields was announced.[7] The Combined Chiefs of Staff were to be responsible for the formulation of strategic plans. A subsidiary committee, the Combined Munitions Assignment Board, was concerned with the allocation of finished military items. Shipping and raw materials were to be the responsibility of the Combined Shipping Adjustment Boards and the Combined Raw Materials Board respectively. About six months later, on June 9, 1942, two additional committees, the Combined Production and Resources Board and the Combined Food Board, were set up.[8] The creation of these agencies visualized intimate co-operation between the United States and the United Kingdom in all spheres where the interests of the two countries touched. "Combined planning" became the watchword of a new philosophy of international planning. A grand joint military strategy was to be matched by the economic co-ordination of production, distribution, and shipping in the two member countries.

In Canada, the formation of these new super-agencies was viewed with considerable interest and some misgivings. It was obvious that, because of Canada's importance as a producer of food, raw materials, and munitions, the deliberations and decisions of these Boards might intimately affect Canada. Representations were therefore made to provide a place for Canada on those Boards dealing with matters of importance to Canada. As a result, Canada became the third member country on two of the Combined Boards. The significance of this will become clearer when the functions of the new agencies have been outlined.

(a) *The Combined Chiefs of Staff and the Combined Munitions Assignment Board*

The creation of a body such as the Combined Chiefs of Staff, whose members were to be jointly responsible for planning the strategy of the war against the Axis, was a remarkable symbol of the unity of purpose of the United Kingdom and the United States. The function of the new group was summarized by a statement issued by the Prime Minister and the President early in February, which read, in part:

The "Combined Chiefs of Staff" group has been established by the United States and Great Britain to ensure complete co-ordination of the war effort of these two countries, including the production and distribution of their war supplies, and to provide for full British and American collaboration with the United Nations now associated in prosecution of the war against the Axis powers. . . .

While the action of the Combined Chiefs of Staff on broad strategical questions will be in the form of joint recommendations to the heads of their respective governments, in minor and immediate matters relating to current operations they are prepared to take action without delay. The set-up, therefore, amounts to a combined command post for the conduct of all joint operations of the two governments in the war. It will be a control agency for planning and co-ordinating.[9]

The members themselves were the four top-ranking military and naval officers of the United States and a group of senior representatives of the Chiefs of Staff of the armed services of the United Kingdom. A number of sub-committees of the Combined Chiefs of Staff were created to deal with such subjects as planning, intelligence, meteorology, communications, military transportation, ship-building, civil affairs, and the assignment of munitions.

The last of these sub-committees, known as the Combined Munitions Assignment Board, was extremely important. Its responsibility was the vital one of allocating munitions to various countries and to the different theatres of war. This work was theoretically divided between a Washington and a London branch but, in practice, the Washington branch was of dominant importance. Subject, of course, to the strategic decisions of the Combined Chiefs of Staff, the influence of the Combined Munitions Assignment Board was tremendous in shaping the conduct of the war. It is of some interest to note that a civilian acted as chairman of each of the branches. In the United States, the chairman was the Special Presidential Assistant Supervising the Lend-Lease Program, while the chairman of the London Committee was the Minister of Production. It may be surmised that civilian control was retained in this way in order that proper weight would be given to international political considerations.

Since Canada was far from self-sufficient in military production, it appeared that the decisions of this Board would have a determining influence on the kind of military effort which Canada could undertake. Indirectly, moreover, the actions of this Board influenced the allocation of Canadian munitions output. It was natural, therefore, that Canada should seek membership on the Combined Munitions Assignment Board. Negotiations on this question were conducted over several months early in 1942, and judging from an announcement of the Canadian Prime Minister in the House of Commons, it seemed to be expected that Canada would become a member.[10] Early in June, 1942, it was decided by the two member countries that Canadian participation as a full member was not advisable. It would have created an awkward precedent to admit Canada in view of the heavy pressure on the United States and the United Kingdom to broaden the representation on the committee. Despite this, Canada did have access to the Combined Munitions Assignment Board through the Commander of the Canadian Army Staff in Washington who was consulted on matters which directly concerned Canada.

The Combined Munitions Assignment Board was necessarily a senior body whose principal concern was with matters of policy. Its allocating authority was, in practice, usually delegated to subsidiary committees, the most important of which was the Munitions Assignment Committee (Ground).[11] In February, 1942, soon after the formation of the Committee, a Canadian representative started to attend its meetings. At first, Canada was admitted under the wing of the British and requirements were stated through the British representatives. The pretense involved in this soon became evident and it was not long before the United States and even the United Kingdom accepted the practicability of Canada submitting requirements independently and supporting them directly. For all practical purposes, Canada was a member of the Committee, although, since it would set a precedent, the fact was not officially recognized at that time. It is important to bear in mind that Canadian participation was always limited to matters relating to Canadian requirements and did not extend to the sharing of responsibility for assignments of others.

Apart from the question of formal representation, it is interesting to note that Canada continued, throughout the war, to arrange for private procurement of non-common munitions from United States sources. This privilege was not extended to any other nation. This was a significant fact in view of Canada's relations with the Combined Munitions Assignment Board. The Board was in a position to control or direct the allocation of all munitions production in the United States, but far from limiting independent procurement activities by Canada, they were facilitated by the Munitions Assignment Committee (Ground).

Later, a Canadian Munitions Assignment Committee was created in Ottawa to handle the disposition or assignment of Canadian munitions output. The United States and the United Kingdom were represented on this Committee along with the Canadian domestic military services and the Mutual Aid Board. The fact that the United States and the United Kingdom were members of the Canadian Committee undoubtedly helped to strengthen the Canadian position with respect to the Combined Munitions Assignment Board in Washington.

In view of the importance of Canada as a producer of shipping, Canada did become a member of the Combined Shipbuilding Committee, another of the sub-committees of the Combined Chiefs of Staff which was mainly concerned with standardization of design and equipment in ship-building. Arrangements were also made to have Canada participate in a limited way in the work of the Combined Civil Affairs Committee, which was responsible for civil affairs policies in areas liberated from enemy control. This development will be described briefly later in this chapter in the section dealing with relief requirements.

The limited extent to which Canada participated in the work of the Combined Chiefs of Staff and the directly related agencies was a result of the fact that the Canadian armed forces were small in comparison to those of the United States and the United Kingdom. It was reasonable to expect that Canada's voice in the determination of overall military strategy would be correspondingly small. In certain other areas of combined planning, Canada's importance and bargaining power were greater and, as a result, Canada was able to attain a status formally equivalent to the other two countries.

(b) *The Combined Raw Materials Board*

The formation of the Combined Raw Materials Board, as well as the Combined Chiefs of Staff, was agreed on at the ARCADIA Conference in Washington a few weeks after Pearl Harbor. This Board was to deal with the serious threat to the raw material resources of the United Nations occasioned by the entry of Japan into the war. Important sources of rubber, tin, critical fibres, and other raw materials were completely cut off by the Japanese advance throughout the Southwest Pacific. In view of this, it was evident that combined action would be essential to obtain the most effective use of critical materials. This was explained in the joint statement issued by the political leaders of the two member countries at the time of the establishment of the Combined Raw Materials Board. The main responsibilities of the new Board would be to:

(b) Plan the best and speediest development, expansion and use of the raw material resources, under the jurisdiction or control of the two Governments, and make the recommendations necessary to execute such plans. Such recommendations shall be carried out by all parts of the respective Governments.

(c) In collaboration with other of the United Nations work toward the best utilization of their raw material resources, and, in collaboration with the interested nation or nations, formulate plans and recommendations for the development, expansion, purchase, or other effective use of their raw materials.[12]

In view of Canada's major rôle as a producer of raw materials for the United Nations, it was natural that Canada should be intensely interested in the action of the United States and the United Kingdom in creating the Combined Raw Materials Board. On the basis of the terms of reference, it was concluded by the Canadians concerned that the joint body would concern itself with the distribution of the Canadian output of raw materials and the amount of raw materials that Canada would receive among other things. It seemed that these decisions were going to be made in London or Washington and that Canada would not participate—altogether a disturbing outlook.

As a result, Canada made representations to the United States and the United Kingdom to the effect that Canada was a major raw material producer and was therefore entitled to complete participation in any decisions affecting the disposition of Canadian supplies. In reply, it was pointed out that the Canadian view was based on a misconception of the functions of the Combined Raw Materials Board and that the Board would certainly not attempt to improve the position of the member countries at the expense of Canada. Rather, the aim of the Board would be to allocate raw material supplies in such a way as to maximize the war effort of the United Nations, an aim which Canada naturally would support. The view was advanced that membership for Canada was really unnecessary since the requirements of the United States and Canada would be dealt with as a combined total by the Combined Raw Materials Board, and the allocation of raw materials between these two countries could be dealt with by the Materials Co-ordinating Committee. As a result of these persuasive arguments, the initial Canadian agitation for representation on the Combined Raw Materials Board was suspended and it was agreed that Canada would use the Materials Co-ordinating Committee as an alternative channel of approach.

Since the United States member of the Combined Raw Materials Board was also a member of the Materials Co-ordinating Committee, Canada was able to maintain very close liaison with the Combined Raw Materials Board. In general, the activity of the Materials Co-ordinating Committee continued without much change after the formation of the Combined Raw Materials Board although it operated on a rather informal basis. The recommendations of the Combined Raw Materials Board were transmitted to Canada by the United States member of the Materials Co-ordinating Committee. Similarly, Canadian data and statements of the Canadian views on proposed allocations were submitted to the Combined Raw Materials Board through this channel. Theoretically, the Materials Co-ordinating Committee was available as a forum to resolve disputed questions between the Combined Raw Materials Board and Canada, but in view of the close working arrangements of the representatives of the three countries, this could not be regarded as an important function. It is of some significance that the Canadian officials primarily concerned with the work of the Combined Raw Materials Board in Washington had their offices on the same floor of the same building as the corresponding United States and United Kingdom officials. As a result, there was a great deal of informal personal contact between these officials, which was a factor of considerable importance in facilitating inter-country adjustments.

The principal aim of the Combined Raw Materials Board was to keep under review the whole field of critical raw materials, to eliminate wasteful competition in purchasing and to allocate available supplies nationally. The Board relied on existing domestic agencies of the member countries to implement its recommendations for action, which were based on a continuing analysis of the total supply and demand situation in the non-Axis world. Early in 1942, there were the most pressing raw material problems to be faced, mainly because Japanese conquest had cut off vital supplies of such materials as silk, tin, rubber, tungsten, sisal and Manila hemp, among others. Apart from enemy conquest, there were serious shortages of non-ferrous metals arising because of the high demands of the military production programmes. There were also some indications that competitive purchasing of raw materials in third countries was stimulating price rises and demoralizing markets and that remedial action was essential.

In order to cope with material shortages, the Combined Raw Materials Board adopted different methods of allocation. In some instances, certain sources of supply were allocated to specified claimant countries although the quantities available were subject to periodic review. In other cases, overall country quotas were established. This was done, for example, in the case of shellac, mica, nylon, nickel, and hides. Conservation of shipping was sometimes of dominant importance. For this reason, Canada switched from the United Kingdom to the United States as a source for ferro-tungsten, and in another case, the United States undertook to supply the United Kingdom with phosphorus instead of rock phosphate, with resultant substantial saving in tonnage.

Traditional purchasing methods were not very satisfactory in the face of serious material shortages and some countries were quick to react to the competitive bidding of foreign purchasing missions. Consequently, the Combined Raw Materials Board encouraged the creation of monopolistic purchasing arrangements by which one country or a joint agency was assigned the responsibility for procurement abroad. Agreements were reached covering the assignment of responsibility for purchases of such commodities as mica, shellac, graphite, balsawood, sisal, balata, sheepskin shearlings, pyrethrum, and kapok.

The Combined Raw Materials Board was naturally vitally concerned with the rubber shortage which was of crucial importance in 1942. Responsibility for the international rubber programme lay with the Rubber Committee, made up of representatives of the Board and the Office of the United States Rubber Director. Rigorous allocations of natural rubber were developed and reviewed at intervals. Consumption quotas were fixed to prevent the dissipation of irreplaceable stockpiles, and each quarter adjustments were made by the allocation of the small quantity of Ceylon rubber becoming available.

One of the most serious and complex materials problems to be dealt with arose in the case of tin. Before the war, about 43 per cent of the world's supply of tin ore came from the Dutch East Indies and Malaya and another 10 per cent from Indo-China and Thailand. The principal remaining sources were in Bolivia, Nigeria, and the Belgian Congo, which produced around 27 per cent of the supply of tin ore. With the loss of Asiatic sources to the Japanese shortly after Pearl Harbor, more than half the world's supply of tin had been captured, not to mention the Malayan smelters which were the largest in the world. The Germans had taken over the smelters in Holland and Belgium, which left available the smelters in the United Kingdom and in the Belgian Congo, of which the latter were small. Ore *en route* to the United Kingdom was the target of submarine attack and the smelters were being bombed. After reviewing this desperate situation, the Combined Raw Materials Board issued a series of emergency recommendations for immediate action. It was agreed to speed the completion of a partially-finished smelter in Texas and to nearly double its planned size. All Bolivian tin concentrates except those needed in the United Kingdom were to be shipped to the United States. The capacity of the smelters in Nigeria and the Belgian Congo was to be increased and their output sent to the United Kingdom. These decisions cut squarely across existing trade relationships but the decisive action prevented any disruption of the United Nations war production plans arising out of a shortage of tin.[13]

Inevitably, these drastic measures had their aftermath. While a serious tin shortage could confidently be predicted in the immediate post-war world, there were also indications that world tin relationships would be seriously upset once capacity production was obtained. Primarily to deal with these problems it was decided to continue the work started by the Combined Raw Materials Board by perpetuating the Tin Committee after the dissolution of the Board itself. When the Combined Raw Materials Board lapsed on December 31, 1945, an autonomous Combined Tin Committee was continued. This Committee, whose membership was expanded to include the Netherlands, France, Belgium, China, India, and Canada, as well as the United States and the United Kingdom, has kept the international tin situation in the post-war world under review and has been responsible for the allocation of tin to both member and non-member countries. The Combined Tin Committee also sponsored the establishment of a Tin Study Group for the purpose of drawing up an international commodity agreement to prevent the disruption of the industry through price declines.

In most cases, the fact that Canada was not a member of the Combined Raw Materials Board was not a disadvantage from a practical point of view. Nevertheless, Canada's status was not equivalent to the other two countries, a matter which involved the question of national prestige. There may be some justification in the view that Canada's willingness to withdraw what appeared to be a legitimate claim for recognition was an unnecessary concession. On the other hand, the view was also held that it would have been contrary to Canadian interests to have been a member of the Combined Raw Materials Board. Even with the formal status, Canada would clearly have been a junior member of the Board and would have been committed to making all Canadian raw materials available to a common pool to be distributed under the direction of the Board. As it was, Canada was able to maintain a good deal of autonomy in deciding on the distribution of Canadian raw materials. It is conceivable that this autonomy might have been impaired if Canada had been subject to the overriding commitments which membership on the Combined Raw Materials Board implied. As time went on, Canadian relations with the Combined Raw Materials Board became increasingly close as a result of the creation of interlocking Committees of the Combined Raw Materials Board and the Combined Production and Resources Board. This facilitated Canadian participation in the work of the former Board in a manner which will be explained.

(c) *The Combined Shipping Adjustment Boards*

The creation of the Combined Shipping Adjustment Boards was announced by President Roosevelt and Prime Minister Churchill in January, 1942, at a time when the Allied shipping situation was critical. The general principle was enunciated at this time that the shipping resources of the United States and the United Kingdom were to be treated as a pool and that complete information on shipping would be exchanged. One Combined Shipping Adjustment Board was established in Washington and another in London. The existence of the two Boards was an obstacle to the establishment of a real shipping pool. Despite the acceptance of the principle of pooling, the fact was that decisions concerning United Kingdom shipping remained with the Ministry of War Transport and decisions concerning United States shipping were made by the War Shipping Administration. Thus, while these Boards provided a valuable channel for the exchange of information, the goal of a combined shipping pool was not achieved.[14]

Canada was not a member of the Combined Shipping Adjustment Boards, although liaison arrangements were created through Canadian shipping representatives in Washington and London. However, Canada was a charter member of the United Maritime Council, established on August 2, 1944, an international agency which was to commence operating at the end of the war with Germany. The principal object of the new agency was to provide for the efficient use of shipping before and after the defeat of Japan.

(d) The Combined Production and Resources Board

About five months after the formation of the original combined agencies, two additional boards were set up to deal with war production and with food. The creation of the Combined Production and Resources Board and the Combined Food Board was announced on June 9, 1942, and, originally, membership was confined to the United Kingdom and the United States.[15] For convenience, consideration of the Combined Food Board will be postponed to the chapter dealing with agricultural planning. The purpose of the Combined Production and Resources Board was to promote the co-ordination of war production in the light of the strategic objectives laid down by the Combined Chiefs of Staff. The new Board was essentially advisory and, since it came into existence after most of the wartime agencies had been established, it did not attempt to usurp responsibilities which had already been assigned. More specifically, the memorandum from President Roosevelt to Donald Nelson, the United States Member, which became the Charter of the Combined Production and Resources Board, stated:

The Board shall . . . combine the production programs of the United States and the United Kingdom into a single integrated program, adjusted to the strategic requirements of the war, as indicated to the Board by the Combined Chiefs of Staff, and to all relevant production factors. In this connection, the Board shall take account of the need for maximum utilization of the productive resources available to the United States, the British Commonwealth of Nations and the United Nations, the need to reduce demands on shipping to a minimum, and the essential needs of the civilian populations.[16]

Although the precise rôle of the Combined Production and Resources Board must have been somewhat obscure shortly after its formation, Canada recognized the potential importance of this Board and again asked the United States and the United Kingdom to include Canada as a full member. In view of the importance of Canada in the field of war production, and the close relations between war industry in Canada and the United States, any co-ordinated production planning would be weakened without the concurrence and participation of Canada, a factor which was recognized by the member countries. The Canadian request was formally agreed to by the United Kingdom and the United States on November 7, 1942, and, a few days later, an announcement was issued by Prime Minister Churchill, President Roosevelt, and Prime Minister

King that Canada was to be a full member of the Combined Production and Resources Board. This was an important and early stimulus to the development of a theory of functional representation on international bodies which was to be put forward by Canadian officials on a good many later occasions. Briefly, the Canadian view was that the rôle of a country in any international organization should depend on the importance of the country in the particular matters being dealt with by the international organization and not on considerations of the size or power of the country in general.

As noted above, it was the original intention that the Combined Production and Resources Board should carry out combined economic planning in concert with the strategic planning of the Combined Chiefs of Staff. On this point, the charter stated explicitly:

> The Combined Chiefs of Staff and the Combined Munitions Assignment Board shall keep the Combined Production and Resources Board currently informed concerning military requirements, and the Combined Production and Resources Board shall keep the Combined Chiefs of Staff currently informed concerning the facts and possibilities of production.[17]

The kind of problem which the Combined Production and Resources Board was supposed to deal with may be illustrated by referring to the question of the optimum use of fabricating capacity in North America and in the United Kingdom. Manufacturing capacity in the United Kingdom could be used to full capacity provided adequate supplies of North American raw materials were made available. Alternatively, North America could concentrate on the production of finished munitions for shipment to the United Kingdom which would involve some under-utilization of fabricating capacity in the United Kingdom. Or, again, the problem could be handled piecemeal, and production of individual items allocated on the basis of relative efficiency and shipping considerations. Such matters involved a complex blend of economic, strategic, and political issues.

Aircraft production was a case in point. Both the United Kingdom and the United States were producing heavy bombers and fighters. It was believed, in some quarters at least, that the United States was relatively more efficient in the production of heavy bombers and that a better distribution of resources could be attained if heavy bomber production were to be concentrated in the United States and if facilities in the United Kingdom were used for producing fighter airplanes. One consequence of such a move would obviously be to augment the dependence of the United Kingdom on the United States and to increase the influence of the United States on strategic plans, many of which were vitally dependent on bomber aircraft. Production plans in the two countries would be seriously upset during a period of readjustment and conversion of facilities. Moreover, such action would have a considerable influence on the post-war competitive position of the two countries in the field of air transport. It would, perhaps, have been somewhat unrealistic to expect that the recommendations of combined planners based on productive efficiency would outweigh political and strategic considerations and possibly adverse effects on post-war conditions.

In other cases, the issues were more clear cut. For example, at a time when submarine losses were imperilling Allied shipping, the production of escort vessels was of critical importance. The Combined Production and Resources Board carried out an investigation of the production schedules in the three member countries, as a result of which production was increased in all three countries. The support of the Board was useful to production authorities in establishing authoritatively the urgency of the need for escort vessels and their components.

The high hopes for combined production planning held out in the Charter of the Combined Production and Resources Board were unfortunately never realized. Not only were there almost insuperable difficulties inherent in the planning it was to undertake, but a host of organizational, statistical, and forecasting difficulties arose to inhibit the Board's development. A concise statement of the weaknesses of the Board is contained in the following excerpt from the official history of the War Production Board:

Despite early efforts, CPRB did not engage in comprehensive production planning or in the long-term strategic planning of economic resources. The American and British production programs for 1943 were not combined into a single integrated program, adjusted to the strategic requirements of the war. CPRB's isolation from the sources of decision regarding production objectives, its failure to develop an effective organization, its deference to other agencies and its tardiness in asserting its jurisdiction, the inadequacy of program planning by the agencies upon whom CPRB relied for forecasts of requirements, the delay of the Combined Chiefs of Staff in formulating strategic objectives for 1943—all these contributed to a result that saw adjustments in the American and British production programs for 1943 made by the appropriate national authorities in each case, rather than through combined machinery. [18]

It would be incorrect to assume that the Combined Production and Resources Board did not fulfil a useful function, even if it turned out to be different from that originally visualized. For example, the Combined Production and Resources Board made an outstanding contribution in the field of military production by integrating and co-ordinating munitions statistics of the United Kingdom, the United States, and Canada. An elaborate set of documents was published reviewing the progress of completed production and showing forecasts of the future output of munitions. Some of these publications were issued periodically while, on other occasions, special studies of the combined munitions programmes were undertaken. This material was the only comprehensive source of this vital information. Actually, the primary emphasis of the Board shifted during its lifetime from military to non-military production problems. Much of the work in the field was carried on by a series of committees.

(e) *Committees of the Combined Boards*

As the war progressed, problems began to arise in the production and supply of non-combat munitions and civilian goods such as medical supplies, textiles, and boots and shoes. It was recognized that there was a need for some group which could deal with civilian supply, particularly the difficult questions involved in dividing available output between military and civilian users. As a result, the Combined Production and Resources Board, not wishing to deal with these questions itself, appointed a Non-Military Supplies Committee early in 1943. This was a relatively junior committee compared to the Board itself. The Non-Military Supplies Committee was given general responsibility for recommending the reduction of non-military production to minimum levels consistent with the efficient prosecution of the war, and for the allocation of productive capacity among the member countries. Most of the work of the Committee was exercised through three sub-committees, the Medical Supplies Subcommittee, appointed January 22, 1943, the Textile Subcommittee. appointed February 13, 1943, and the Boots and Shoes Subcommittee, which was established about the middle of May, 1943.

Prior to the fall of 1943, the membership of the Non-Military Supplies Committee had been confined to the staff of the Combined Production and Resources Board, representatives of United Kingdom Missions in Washington, and representatives of the Wartime Prices and Trade Board and the Department of Munitions and Supply. In September, 1943, it was decided to expand the membership of the Committee to include representatives of about ten national or combined agencies. At about the same time, the sub-committees of the Non-Military Supplies Committee were reconstituted directly under the Combined Production and Resources Board. It became usual, when new committees were created, to make them responsible directly to the Board itself. As a result of these developments, the Non-Military Supplies Committee rapidly became superfluous. Most important commodity problems were assigned to other committees, and by the end of 1943 the Non-Military Supplies Committee was dormant. In April, 1944, it was disbanded. The accomplishments of the Committee were relatively minor. It did, however, pave the way for the establishment of more powerful and more effective committees which played an important part in the work of the Combined Production and Resources Board. A review of the work of some of these committees will show more precisely the nature of the problems encountered in combined planning.

The *Textiles Committee,* when it was originally created under the aegis of the Non-Military Supplies Committee, was designed to explore the proposals of the United Kingdom that apparel rationing be adopted in the United States. Although this particular goal was never achieved, the Committee performed notable work in co-ordinating the export programmes of the three countries. Much of the earlier work of the Committee was concerned with the development of standardized questionnaires to be used for the collection of information on production and requirements of textiles in almost all countries in the non-Axis world. On the basis of these forms, a detailed statistical picture of the world textile situation was obtained for planning purposes. The bulk of the time of the Committee was devoted to cotton broad-woven goods, for which a combined world supply and requirements programme was developed.[19] Considerable attention was devoted to wool and rayon fabrics. An agreement was reached by the Combined Production and Resources Board that the national agencies concerned with textile exports in the three countries would clear their proposed textile export programmes with the Textile Committee through the country's representative on the Committee. Supply problems in this field became particularly acute during the period when the requirements for European liberated areas had to be dealt with. Since Canada exported limited quantities of cotton textiles, and was, on balance, a large net importer, the agreements reached did not seriously affect Canada, although the Committee was a valuable source of detailed statistical information concerning the world textile situation.

The *Tires and Tubes Committee* was created in October, 1943, to review the critical shortage of tires in the United States, the United Kingdom, and Canada, and particularly to review the inventory position of the United Kingdom, which had become a subject of disagreement between the United States and the United Kingdom. The serious shortages which had developed in the fall of 1943 were intensified, and by the first half of 1944, total output fell short of requirements by one-third. The deficit was even more serious in truck and bus tires. The shortage arose because of inadequate manpower, lack of specialized facilities, and technical difficulties in converting from crude to synthetic rubber. The principal activity of the Tires and Tubes Committee was to recommend the distribution of the output of truck and bus tires between the United States, the United Kingdom, and Canada. The Committee adopted a "parity principle" on which its recommendations were based. This principle was that if a country's requirements amounted to a certain percentage of combined requirements, it would receive the same percentage of combined new supply. The underlying assumption was that all requirements were stated on a comparable basis. In effect, Canadian and United States production were lumped together so that the real problem of the Committee was to divide available supplies between North America and the United Kingdom. Canada did not play a very active rôle on this Committee, since the major problems concerned the United States and the United Kingdom. From the Canadian point of view, the Committee's main function was to apportion Canadian surplus production between the United States and the United Kingdom.

The responsibility of the *Transportation Equipment Committee* was to collect all relative information concerning the supply, production, and utilization of transportation equipment which was required to maintain or to re-establish railway, port, and inland waterway transportation facilities and services in areas outside the member countries, principally liberated areas. The Committee was not formed until the spring of 1944, although the Board had been concerned with the production of loco-motives as early as the summer of 1942. In practice, despite its broad terms of reference, the Committee restricted its attention to locomotives and rolling stock and was instrumental in increasing and reallocating locomotive production to take care of urgent needs arising in India and in other areas. The Committee also directed attention to the urgent needs of liberated areas and made a significant contribution in arranging for the allocation of this critically needed equipment to European countries.

The *Truck Committee,* established in November, 1942, was called on to deal with the critical shortage of trucks which developed during the war, although it was never able to review requirements and production plans, and its scope was correspondingly limited. In fact, the Committee restricted its attention to the distribution of trucks for civilian use and to the provision of spare parts. It was not until relief requirements became important that the Truck Committee was able to exercise some influence. It was at this time that the shortage of heavy trucks was very acute. In 1944, certain components, including foundry and forge products such as axles, transmissions, and housings, were critically short, mainly because of the lack of manpower. In the United States, it was expected that the 1944 production of heavy trucks might fall 20 per cent below schedule. Canadian production was also affected by shortages of components imported from the United States, but since output in Canada was concentrated on light-heavy and light vehicles, the problem was not of dominant importance. The most significant aspect of the work of the Truck Committee was in arranging for the apportionment of trucks to liberated areas.

The *Machine Tools Committee* was created in October, 1943, after the initial critical scarcity had subsided and techniques had already been established to work out international allocations. As a result, the Committee served mainly as a clearing house for information on machine tools, a function of some importance during later periods of acute, but transitory, shortages arising, for example, out of the rapid expansion of the United States production programmes for heavy artillery, large calibre ammunition and tanks during 1944. The Committee also sponsored studies of the possibility of relocating idle or excess machine tools during the later period of the war.

The *Internal Combustion Engines Committee* was created in September, 1943, and was faced with the gargantuan task of attempting to co-ordinate the supply and requirements of a wide variety of internal combustion engines. The Committee was created to provide a forum for the consideration of the United Kingdom requirements in the United States since it was believed that the United Kingdom was relatively worse off than the United States. The statistical data available did not substantiate this view. For this reason, and also because of the serious problems involved in computing requirements, the Committee became inactive after two meetings.

Two other Committees, the *Public Utilities Committee,* formed in January, 1944, and the *Medical Supplies Committee,* a descendant of the Medical Supplies subcommittee of the Non-Military Supplies Committee, were primarily concerned with relief requirements. The former Committee was specifically set up for this purpose, while, in the case of medical supplies, the initial problem of shortages had largely disappeared and did not become important again until it was necessary to provide for the requirements of liberated areas.

In addition to the committees which operated solely under the auspices of the Combined Production and Resources Board, other committees were formed jointly with the Combined Raw Materials Board and with the Combined Food Board. In another case, the Combined Food Board and the Combined Raw Materials Board established a combined committee. The great advantage of these combined committees was that their scope was not nearly as restricted as the committees of the Combined Production and Resources Board. The Combined Committees described below, were of some importance from the Canadian point of view since they gave Canada a direct voice in the deliberations of the Combined Raw Materials Board.

The *Combined Aluminum and Magnesium Committee* was created in March, 1943, particularly to review the question of repayment of certain quantities of Canadian aluminum which had been diverted temporarily from the United Kingdom to the United States, and generally to examine the supply and requirements of the United Nations for aluminum and magnesium. Within a few months after the formation of the Committee, the supply position had improved greatly and by 1944, the major problem to be dealt with by the Committee was the orderly reduction of output in the three countries. From the Canadian point of view, membership on this Committee was important because it permitted Canada to participate in the work of the Combined Raw Materials Board in a field of great significance for Canada. The new Committee, in effect, replaced the Materials Co-ordinating Committee as a forum for the consideration of the aluminum problem.

The *Combined Coal Committee,* formed in August, 1943, was concerned with coal supplies originating in either the British Empire or the United States. A corresponding committee was established in London. One of the major problems facing the Combined Coal Committee was to reverse the downward trend of coal production in the United Kingdom. Under the sponsorship of the Committee, a technical mission was sent to the United Kingdom from the United States to examine coal mining methods and to explore the possibility of increasing output by increased mechanization of mining methods. Strenuous efforts were made by the Committee to meet the needs of the United Kingdom for machinery for both underground and strip or open-face mining. In view of the heavy burden on shipping resulting from international movements of coal, the Combined Coal Committee recommended that importing countries rely on the closest sources of supply as much as possible, a consideration which became of great importance after the liberation of Europe. Canada, not being a net coal exporter, was not vitally concerned with most of the complex and important operations of this Committee, which was faced with some of the most tangled problems in the whole field of combined planning.

The *Combined Conservation Committee,* which was associated with an Anglo-American Conservation Committee in London, was originally concerned with saving critical materials. As time went on, its attention shifted from the substitution of less critical for more critical materials to the achievement of greater efficiency in production methods. Even after the metals situations had improved, the Committee continued to concern itself with the conservation of critical materials such as leather, and carried out investigations relating to reclaimed battlescrap, gasoline drums, and rubberless adhesive tape. The functions previously assigned to the Conservation Subcommittee of the Joint War Production Committee were absorbed by the new Committee. Under the sponsorship of the Combined Conservation Committee, a Screw Thread Mission visited the United Kingdom, and a conference on the Unification of Engineering Standards was held in Ottawa in the fall of 1945 to discuss the standardization of screw threads in the member countries and to consider other standardization problems as well. These exploratory meetings culminated in an important agreement on the standardization of screw threads in 1948.

Although it was created after the main problems of the international supply of copper had been settled, the *Combined Copper Committee* was faced with serious difficulties as a result of falling production in 1944, when copper requirements arising out of the ammunition programme were rising sharply. The main reason for the decline was the shortage of manpower in the mines in the United States which had resulted from a more rigorous draft deferment policy and the discontinuance of furloughs for soldiers to work in copper mines. Agreement was reached through the Combined Copper Committee to maintain the output of Northern Rhodesian mines at high levels, and to divert some of this production to Russia and to the United States. As a result of the decision of the United Kingdom to reduce imports of copper from Canada in 1944, it was agreed that any Canadian surplus was to be shipped to the United States. Once the Combined Copper Committee had been formed, the Copper Subcommittee of the Materials Co-ordinating Committee became superfluous and was disbanded.

The *Combined Footwear, Leather and Hides Committee,* which was established in August, 1943, constitutes a particularly interesting example of combined planning. The major work of this Committee concerned the international distribution of cattle hides. Canada had a vital interest in this problem because of Canadian military requirements for certain types of South American hides to be manufactured into sole leather. The fact that Canada had not adopted shoe rationing and the Canadian military specifications for shoes were more restrictive than those of the other two countries led to a certain lack of harmony in the workings of the Committee so far as Canada was concerned. In an attempt to clarify the basis of allocation, a draft agreement was drawn up by the Combined Raw Materials Board, setting out a formula to govern the future distribution of hides. Essentially, the formula was designed to maintain each country in the same relative position as in a specified base period. All purchases of South American hides were to be centralized in a single buying organization operated jointly by the United States and the United Kingdom. It might be noted that, since Canada was not represented on the Combined Raw Materials Board itself, there was no adequate method of presenting the Canadian point of view in the early stage of the negotiations of the hides agreement. The unfortunate aspect of the draft agreement was that, if the domestic production of hides in a country reached a high enough level, the country would be obligated, in theory at least, to export hides under the formula. This was precisely the situation which developed in Canada particularly when the output of domestic hides in Canada was seasonally high. A monthly adjustment was supposed to be made under the formula, and as a result of fluctuations in Canadian production, Canada owed a somewhat theoretical debt of hides to the other two countries in several instances. The debt of hides accumulated and was forgiven on different occasions, but the arrangement was unsatisfactory for the Canadian industry since it upset normal purchasing practices. The Canadian official attitude was that the distribution formula was in fundamental conflict with the principles of combined planning since it did not focus on the central problem of adjusting supplies and requirements. The hides agreement itself was never formally ratified and finally, early in 1945, Canada withdrew, primarily on the grounds that the effect of the formula was to deprive Canada of foreign hides completely. However, Canada continued to participate in the other work of the Committee, which also dealt with leather used for gloves, linings, and garments. Despite the admission of several other countries to the Committee after the cessation of hostilities, countries which were not represented on the Committee disrupted the South American market for hides by exceeding the agreed price scale, and succeeded in obtaining practically all available supplies.

The *Combined Agricultural and Food Machinery Committee* was established jointly by the Combined Production and Resources Board and the Combined Food Board in December, 1943. This Committee was of special interest to Canada not only because of the importance of farm machinery but because the Chairman of the Committee was the president of a Canadian farm machinery company. One of the main tasks of the Committee was to obtain a combined statement of the production of farm machinery as well as domestic and export requirements for the United Kingdom, the United States, and Canada for the two periods July 1, 1943, to June 30, 1944, and July 1, 1944, to June 30, 1945. Although some work was done by the Committee in recommending the allocation of productive capacity to normal export markets, its main function was to recommend sources of supply for the needs of liberated areas. This question was complicated by the Canadian anxiety to export a high proportion of total production. Before the war, Canada had normally exported a higher proportion of output than the United States, and it was the Canadian view that this relationship should be maintained, partly because of the desirability of increasing exports to normal markets as soon as possible after the war. It was finally agreed that Canada should supply 27,000 tons out of a total of 186,000 tons needed for relief while the United States and the United Kingdom should supply 127,000 and 32,000 tons respectively, subject to the condition that this would not interfere with the production of farm machinery for other essential purposes. The Canadian programme was of great interest to the United States because of Canadian dependence on imported components. There was considerable difficulty in meeting the export goal in the United States and the allocations to liberated areas were reduced in both Canada and the United States for the year ending June 30, 1946. With the termination of hostilities in Europe, it was felt that relief requirements could be dealt with by the appropriate agencies within the member countries, and the Committee ceased to function actively on July 1, 1945.

A *Combined Steel Committee* was established toward the end of 1942, and was active for a period in dealing with international problems of steel supply. In particular, the Committee was asked at one time to review the adequacy of steel allocations of the Requirements Committee of the War Production Board to Canada and the United States. By the beginning of 1944, this Committee had become dormant.

The committees of the Combined Production and Resources Board and the other Combined Boards were sometimes a useful instrument for resolving supply problems which arose in connection with particular commodities. The United Kingdom on several occasions requested the establishment of a committee to deal with cases where it was felt that the national agencies of the United States were giving inadequate consideration to the needs of the United Kingdom. In at least one case, the Combined Pulp and Paper Committee, whose operations are discussed in the next chapter, Canada was mainly responsible. While this particular

Committee was disbanded after its work was completed, this was not the usual practice and many committees continued in inactive existence after the need for them had passed. Nevertheless, the committees were a convenient administrative device for relieving the Members and Deputy Members of the Combined Boards of responsibility for detailed commodity problems.

3. COMBINED EXPORT PLANNING

Mention has already been made of a number of ways in which the United States and Canada attempted to co-ordinate North American exports. In addition, export allocation problems were also considered by the United States, the United Kingdom, and Canada together. The early attempts to allocate export markets on the basis of combined export planning were intimately related to the troublesome issue of exports from the United Kingdom of commodities containing ingredients which were being imported from the United States on lend-lease. In the summer and fall of 1941, there had been bitter complaints that exporters in the United Kingdom were supplying materials obtained under lend-lease to foreign markets in competition with exporters in the United States. Despite the inaccuracy and injustice of many of the charges, the United Kingdom agreed to adopt a ban on exports which were likely to stimulate further criticism in the United States. As already noted, the commitment of the United Kingdom was contained in the so-called Eden White Paper of September, 1941.[20] This did not mean necessarily that exports of any commodities containing materials or components similar to those obtained under lend-lease would be stopped. Instead, the agreement meant that clearance procedures would be established to satisfy the United States that the White Paper commitment was being lived up to.

Although the Canadian authorities refused to accept any kind of White Paper commitment, implicit or explicit, Canada was drawn into the negotiations between the United States and the United Kingdom on this subject. In the spring of 1942, following conversations between the State Department and the British Embassy, the Combined Export Markets Committee was established to deal with the problems raised by exports of raw materials and semi-finished products from the United Kingdom to third countries. At the request of the Assistant Secretary of State, the Combined Raw Materials Board agreed to assume jurisdiction over the Committee, and staff members of the Combined Raw Materials Board were appointed Chairman and Secretary. Continual pressure was exerted by the United Kingdom to have the Combined Export Markets Committee extend its jurisdiction to manufactured goods but, in view of its lack of jurisdiction over finished products, the Combined Raw Materials Board refused to broaden the scope of the Committee. An impasse resulted and the functions of the Combined Export Markets Committee were transferred back to the State Department and a new committee created late in 1942, when the Combined Raw Materials Board ceased to be directly concerned with its activities.

The State Department Committee, which was patterned on the Combined Export Markets Committee, was called originally the Interim Committee for the United States and United Kingdom—Export Programme Co-ordination: Standard Products and later the Combined Export Markets Committee (Finished Goods). The chairman was an official of the State Department. On this Committee were represented, in addition to the State Department, the British Embassy, the British Board of Trade Delegation, the War Production Board, the Board of Economic Warfare, the Office of Lend-Lease Administration, the Office of Price Administration, the Department of Commerce, and the Canadian Legation or Embassy when Canadian interests were affected. The reconstituted Combined Export Markets Committee was primarily concerned with special waivers of the White Paper commitment, and the ability of the United States to take over certain United Kingdom markets in cases where exports from the United Kingdom were curtailed. The committee dealt with a number of commodities such as incandescent lamp bulbs, photographic film, crown closures, typewriters and bicycles, not to mention machetes, a commodity which received an extraordinary amount of attention from the Committee. It seems clear, in retrospect, that the work of the Committee was slowed down greatly because of the attempt to apportion markets in too great detail, and further hampered by the difficulties of altering traditional channels of trade.

Despite the unsatisfactory experience of the Combined Raw Materials Board, it was the view of the State Department that the Committee should operate under the auspices of the Combined Boards. Accordingly, on December 23, 1942, the Assistant Secretary of State requested that arrangements be made to establish the new committee as an adjunct of the Combined Production and Resources Board. The Combined Production and Resources Board declined to assume complete jurisdiction over the Committee, but agreed to review cases where the Committee was unable to agree upon a source of supply; or where a national agency refused to approve the proposed export programme. At the same time, the Combined Raw Materials Board was asked to review disputed questions about commodities under its jurisdiction but the invitation was declined. It appears that the Combined Export Markets Committee was able to agree in almost all cases, so that the review function of the Combined Production and Resources Board was rarely exercised. In August, 1943, the Combined Production and Resources Board was requested to consider the tortured machete problem and to decide upon the most appropriate source of supply. The Combined Production and Resources Board refused to intervene and commented that there was no shortage of world production capacity, and that the amount of steel and labour involved was insignificant. For this reason, the Board concluded that the combined war programme would not be affected by a transfer of production from one country to the other.

The decision of the Combined Production and Resources Board to avoid becoming involved in the allocation of markets was made at a time when its attention was absorbed by pressing problems of munitions production. During this early period of its existence, the Combined Production and Resources Board was hesitant to concern itself with the allocation of production. As explained above, the Board was supposed to work closely with the Combined Munitions Assignment Board whose function was to direct the allocation of assignable munitions. Because of these prior arrangements, it was the view of the Combined Production and Resources Board that it was not responsible for the allocation of output. Its function was simply to arrange for the best use of productive resources in the member countries.

The Canadian position in relation to the Combined Export Markets Committee was somewhat delicate. On the one hand, representation was essential if Canada's commercial interests in the markets of third countries were to be properly taken into account. On the other hand, the Committee was mainly concerned with White Paper problems in which Canada had no direct interest. Moreover, it had been the consistent aim of Canadian representatives in Washington to disabuse the United States of the notion that Canada was bound by a White Paper commitment of any kind.

In the spring of 1944, an attempt was made to revive the Combined Export Markets Committee, which had become inoperative following its inability to deal satisfactorily with the allocation of third country markets for certain commodities, notably machetes. The plan was to establish a new Combined Exports Committee to provide a substitute for the procedure by which the United Kingdom requested United States concurrence in the suspension of its own restrictions for individual export shipments. This Committee was to be concerned only incidentally with the apportionment of markets; its primary function would be to handle questions which would arise if the United Kingdom achieved its aim of scrapping its rigorous restrictions on exports embodied in the White Paper. In fact, it was planned that the detailed allocation of markets would not be undertaken, probably in view of the unhappy experience of the original committee, but that attention would be restricted to problems of export policy and only in relation to commodities in international short supply.

Canada had been invited to participate in the Combined Exports Committee, although it was evidently intended that Canadian participation would be limited to those matters affecting Canada. This junior status was not acceptable to Canada which pressed for full membership, while reserving the right to limit attendance to meetings dealing with matters of concern to Canada. The prolonged negotiations, however, yielded no substantial results and the final decision was to abandon the whole idea.

The history of this Committee seems to demonstrate that the formation of a combined committee is not necessarily the best way to resolve a problem in international economic affairs. There is little evidence that the early attempt at combined planning in the export field had a perceptible influence on the direction or volume of export trade of any of three countries involved.

4. The Combined Boards and Relief for Liberated Areas

Since Canada and the United States became the major exporters of goods to the world during the war, it was natural that they both should play important rôles in the relief of liberated areas. Economic co-operation in this field lost its bilateral character and was carried on within a larger framework of tripartite or international organizations. The aim of this section is to sketch briefly the machinery which was set up to handle relief and to indicate the rôle of the Combined Boards, which has already been hinted at in the description of the functions of several of the Combined Committees.

As early as the middle of 1940, the conquered peoples of Europe were offered a definite promise by the British Prime Minister that once the Nazis were driven back, European needs for food would be provided by the victors.[21] Not long after this, Sir Frederick Leith-Ross was appointed chairman of a Committee on Surpluses which was to be responsible for stockpiling relief goods in surplus supply. About the end of September, 1941, the United Kingdom issued invitations to the Allied governments to participate in discussions in London of a co-ordinated solution of the relief problem. The Inter-Allied Committee on Post-War Requirements was established after this conference, again under the chairmanship of

Sir Frederick Leith-Ross. The main aim of this Committee during the year and a half of its existence was to formulate estimates of the relief requirements of a liberated Europe.

Concrete planning for the provision of relief supplies for liberated areas was begun in the United States with the creation of the Office of Foreign Relief and Rehabilitation Operations within the Department of State early in December, 1942.[22] This new agency was to be responsible for planning for the provision of the necessities of life in any areas conquered by the armed forces of the United Nations.

It was abundantly clear that the relief and rehabilitation problem was going to be complex and that a chaotic situation would develop if provisions were not made for co-ordinated action by all countries concerned. After preliminary conversations and agreements between the Foreign Office and the Department of State, it was proposed that all members of the United Nations should be invited to participate in a single relief organization to be financed by the contributions of the member countries. A draft agreement was submitted to all the United Nations by the United States, and after various amendments had been adopted, representatives of the forty-four member nations met in Washington on November 9, 1943, to sign the Agreement establishing the United Nations Relief and Rehabilitation Administration. An international convention was held in Atlantic City for about the last three weeks of November, at which the administrative structure of the new relief organization rapidly took shape. Agreement was reached that each country, except those which were or had been occupied, should make an initial financial contribution equivalent to approximately one per cent of its national income in the year ending June 30, 1943.

The United Nations Relief and Rehabilitation Administration, being a civilian organization, was not a suitable agency to direct relief operations in areas immediately after their liberation. On grounds of international law and also for military reasons, the responsibility for the security of civilian populations rested with the military commander of an invading army. The military aim was to prevent disease, unrest, or any interference with supply lines and to achieve this, it was essential that the Theatre Commander have complete jurisdiction over all relations with civilians in liberated areas. Accordingly, responsibility for relief in liberated areas was vested solely in the military authorities who were to invite civilian relief agencies to take over after the lapse of a suitable period. For planning purposes, the period was assumed to be six months after liberation. General authority for the determination of policies relating to civil affairs in territories conquered as a result of combined military operations lay with the Combined Civil Affairs Committee, a sub-committee of the Combined Chiefs of Staff. The Combined Civil Affairs Committee acted through its Supply Subcommittee, as far as relief supplies were concerned, and was primarily interested in relief as a means of preventing disease, unrest, and riot among civilians.

It was necessary, however, that some attention be paid to such fundamental needs as fertilizer, electric power, and agricultural machinery which were required to maintain the liberated economies in running order. As a result, a Combined Liberated Areas Committee, representing the United States and the United Kingdom, was established to review relief needs which would not be looked after so long as military relief was designed only to prevent disease, rioting, and unrest. The terms of reference of the Combined Liberated Areas Committees stated that its function was to provide a forum for the consideration of problems arising in liberated and conquered territories in which the two governments had a mutual interest as a result of combined machinery, supply, shipping, or financial responsibilities and which were outside the scope of the Combined Chiefs of Staff. In this case also, a Supply Subcommittee was created to match the Supply Subcommittee of the Combined Civil Affairs Committee.

Since Canada was not a member of the Combined Chiefs of Staff, no provision was made for Canadian representation on the Combined Civil Affairs Committee. But, because of Canada's direct concern with combined military operations and with the provision of relief supplies, negotiations were begun with the United Kingdom and the United States to provide for Canadian membership on the Combined Civil Affairs Committee. This question was tied in with complicated arrangements between the United Kingdom and the United States concerning their shares of the cost of military relief and the financial contribution which Canada would make. It was finally agreed that Canada would be given representation on the Supply Subcommittee of the Combined Civil Affairs Committee on the understanding that Canada would make some financial contribution to the net cost of military relief. Canada also became a member of the Supply Subcommittee of the Combined Liberated Areas Committee.

Provision was made for the close co-ordination of military relief and relief directed by the United Nations Relief and Rehabilitation Administration. The agencies concerned agreed to exchange information on the nature of relief programmes and the progress of procurement. It was also agreed that if military relief should terminate in less than six months, military relief supplies would be turned over to the United Nations Relief and Rehabilitation Administration, and on the other hand, if the military relief period should extend beyond six months, supplies procured by the United Nations Relief and Rehabilitation Administration would be made available to the military authorities, with appropriate financial adjustments being made in each case.[23]

The agreement for the establishment of a United Nations Relief and Rehabilitation Administration visualized an important place for the Combined Boards in the machinery of procuring relief supplies. It was provided in Resolution No. 1 of the Council, adopted at Atlantic City, that requirements for relief and rehabilitation were to be presented to the Combined Boards for recommendations as to sources of supply. This resolution, referring to the Combined Boards as "inter-governmental allocating agencies," stated in part:

> The Director General will present before the inter-governmental allocating agencies the overall requirements for relief and rehabilitation of all areas liberated and to be liberated in order to permit a global consideration of these needs with all other needs.[24]

This meant that the Combined Boards were to be responsible for integrating relief requirements submitted to them by the United Nations Relief and Rehabilitation Administration into the world supply and demand situation.

In addition to this, Resolution No. 17 of the Council stated that all requirements of liberated areas, including those which were able to pay for their requirements, were to be submitted to the Combined Boards. At the time of the Atlantic City meeting, there were no governments or other recognized authorities in any liberated areas which could make accurate appraisals of relief needs. Accordingly, the United Nations Relief and Rehabilitation Administration prepared interim estimates of need in conjunction with the governments-in-exile. Despite the Council recommendation that all governments should submit their relief programmes through the United Nations Relief and Rehabilitation Administration, several of the paying countries became unwilling after liberation to admit that the relief organization had the power to limit or revise their requirements. The disputes which developed between the paying countries and the United Nations Relief and Rehabilitation Administration tended to increase the responsibility of the Combined Boards for the apportionment of goods in short supply.

Agreements were reached with the military authorities that the Combined Boards should perform the same functions for relief needs during the period of military control. A directive was issued early in 1944 to the staff of the War Production Board that military relief programmes originating with the Combined Civil Affairs Committee were to be submitted to the War Production Board Division Requirements Committees concerned, for their recommendations concerning the extent to which the requirements could be met from the United States.[25] An agreement was subsequently reached that copies of all Combined Civil Affairs Committee programmes would be transmitted simultaneously to the Combined Production and Resources Board. It was provided, in the memorandum referred to, that the United States Members of the Combined Boards were to accept the recommendations of the Division Requirements Committees so far as recommendations specifying the United States as a source of supply were concerned. The military relief programmes of the Combined Civil Affairs Committee were passed on to the responsible committees of the Combined Boards, to be dealt with in the same manner as the requirements for the United Nations Relief and Rehabilitation Administration. As a result, Canadian representatives on the committees were given an opportunity to ensure Canadian participation wherever it was possible or desirable. Once the combined position was determined, the Boards' recommendations were to be returned through appropriate channels to the military authorities concerned.

In Canada, decisions on the availability of non-food supplies from Canadian sources were the responsibility of the External Trade Advisory Committee. In the case of food, similar responsibility was exercised by the Food Requirements Committee, a matter which is discussed later in the chapter dealing with agricultural planning. By the summer of 1944, it was evident that requirements for military relief and for relief dispensed by the United Nations Relief and Rehabilitation Administration would throw a heavy strain on Canadian supplies, a fact which was one of the main reasons for the appointment of the External Trade Advisory Committee. This Committee maintained close contact with Canadian representatives on the Combined Production and Resources Board.

Some administrative reorganization of the Combined Boards was necessary to deal with the urgent problems of relief requirements. A Central Section for Relief and Rehabilitation was set up under the joint auspices of the Combined Production and Resources Board and the Combined Raw Materials Board to handle requirements for liberated areas for both the military and other phases of relief. The function of the Central Section, which was composed of representatives of the three member countries, was to see that programmes submitted by the United Nations Relief and Rehabilitation Administration, or the requirements for military relief, were submitted to the appropriate national supply agencies. Apart from advance programmes, spot requests were received from the various

Theatre Commanders which were of a more urgent character than either the Combined Civil Affairs Committee or United Nations Relief and Rehabilitation Administration relief programmes. Within a matter of days, the Boards were required to make a decision concerning the source of supply in order that immediate procurement action could be initiated.

The procurement of relief supplies was beset with many difficulties. One problem which was particularly acute in the United States was the inadequate relief allocations of some commodities in short supply, such as textiles. The whole question of United States policy received serious consideration from President Roosevelt prior to his death. A mission, headed by Judge Samuel Rosenman, was sent to Europe to investigate relief needs and as a result of the recommendations of this mission,[26] President Truman wrote to the Chairman of the War Production Board and the heads of three other agencies concerned with relief needs in May, 1945, that the United States would be expected to furnish civilian supplies to liberated areas. His letter said, in part:

It is the established policy of this Government to accept this responsibility as far as it is possible to do so. As a matter of national policy, therefore, I request your agency to grant the priority necessary to meet the minimum civilian requirements of those of our allies who have been ravaged by the enemy to the fullest extent that the successful prosecution of military operations and the maintenance of our essential domestic economy permit.[27]

In Canada, the situation was somewhat different since Canada was not as large a supplier of scarce civilian items. The Canadian authorities were able to arrange for the use of the procurement machinery of the Mutual Aid Board for the purchase of relief supplies by the United Nations Relief and Rehabilitation Administration. In general, Canada was able to make substantial contributions of such items as wheat, hides, woollen clothing, and food to liberated areas. From the point of view of Canada and the United States, the essential importance of the Combined Boards in this field lay in the fact that they furnished a forum for the consideration of the share of North American relief supplies which would be furnished by Canada and the United States.

5. GENERAL COMMENTS

Planning for the end of the war introduced new and complicated problems for the Combined Boards as emphasis shifted from war production to reconversion and relief. One major problem to be faced by the Combined Production and Resources Board in the period of shrinking military requirements related to the production of essential non-military goods in the member countries in the best possible way. The fact that the pace of reconversion and the problems of maintaining reasonable stability in employment levels were apt to be different in each country indicated the desirability of planned distribution of military cutbacks and resumption of civilian production. While the Combined Production and Resources Board was the repository of the fundamental information necessary to plan the reduction of military output and the resumption of civilian production, domestic financial and political considerations in the member countries limited the extent to which reconversion could be planned in concert. Roughly the same considerations applied to the operations of the Combined Raw Materials Board.

One issue which hastened the liquidation of the Combined Boards was the question of representation of other countries besides the United States, the United Kingdom, and Canada. It became clear that the Combined Production and Resources Board, for example, would have to collaborate more closely with other members of the United Nations, and to take into account the utilization of their resources, as far as possible. In the early period of its operations, the Combined Production and Resources Board relied on informal arrangements between one of its members and other nations, when the co-operation of non-member countries was needed to carry out its recommendations. The United States, on behalf of the Combined Production and Resources Board, was in a position to reach agreements with Latin American countries and the United Kingdom could transmit Combined Production and Resources Board recommendations to British Empire countries, such as India and South Africa. Later, the arrangements for dealing with non-members became more formal. For example, arrangements were made to have the import programmes of French Colonial Territories submitted to the Combined Production and Resources Board by the Combined Policy Committee of the French Empire Economic Committee. Negotiations were also carried on by the Combined Production and Resources Board with Brazilian and Mexican Missions for mutual action in planning the production and export of cotton textiles. In addition, an informal India Committee was created under the sponsorship of the Combined Production and Resources Board to deal with problems in which India had a major interest.

Despite these moves, the Combined Boards had some of the qualities of large-scale cartels. The exclusive character of the Combined Boards came to be regarded with disfavour by the Department of State which looked to the establishment of a post-war international organization on which all the United Nations would be represented. The quasi-monopolistic character of the Boards no doubt inspired some resentment among non-member nations in addition. The influence of these considerations was evident in statements on the future of the Combined Boards issued by the President and the two Prime Ministers in January, 1945.[28] So far as the Combined Production and Resources Board and the Combined Raw Materials Board were concerned, it was agreed at this time that they would not be dissolved until after the termination of hostilities with both Germany and Japan. It was also suggested that the working committees of the Board should be expanded to include other countries whose importance as producers or consumers appeared to warrant it. On August 29, 1945, a further announcement was issued by the three governments that it had been decided to continue the Combined Production and Resources Board in existence temporarily to preserve some continuity in the methods of dealing with critical commodities. At the end of September, all the committees except the Textiles Committee, the Combined Coal Committee, and the Combined Footwear, Leather and Hides Committee were disbanded. Finally, on December 10, 1945, after most of the work of the Combined Production and Resources Board and the Combined Raw Materials Board had been disposed of, the President and the Prime Ministers announced that the Boards would be dissolved on December 31, 1945.[29]

Combined planning covered a very wide field of activity and it is not easy to draw any uniform conclusions which would apply throughout. In some ways, the combined planning of military operations is more difficult than the combined planning of production or food distribution or the allocation of shipping. Combined military action was essential and plans had to be agreed upon. At worst, planning in the civilian sphere could degenerate into argumentation from which no concrete results emerged. In the short run, at least, such a course would merely lead to inefficiency. Moreover, the acceptance of the principle was a far cry from the achievement of concrete results. Combined planning involved techniques which were not something to be learned overnight. On this point, Major-General John R. Deane, at one time United States Secretary of the Combined Chiefs of Staff, has the following comment:

Joint planning as between nations and to some extent as between the armed services within a nation was a development of the war. We were forced to learn the technique of planning between nations by reason of our close alliance and combined operations with the British, and that of planning between our separate services, because of the amphibious character of our Pacific operations. We were new at the game in the early stages of the war, and as a result, plans were delayed and were characterized by ineffective compromises. The most difficult part of the procedure was to be able to organize a group of planners who could and would study their problems objectively and endeavour to reach the best solution with regard to national or service interests. They could do this only when their respective superiors allowed them to approach the problem with open minds and unhampered by prior instructions from which they could not depart. Planning was best when it was accomplished with complete objectivity and when it was left to those responsible for approval of the plan to adjust the demands of special interests.[30]

Some of the difficulties of combined planning evident in the work of the Combined Production and Resources Board have already been referred to. It was of great importance that there was a lack of internal co-ordination between strategic and production plans in the United States. While there is necessarily a close relationship between strategy and production, there tended to be a separation of responsibility with the result that decisions were made in both spheres more or less independently. Moreover, care should be taken not to over-estimate the closeness of the relation between strategic and production plans. It appears that it was not until May, 1943, that the Allies were firmly committed to a plan for the invasion of Northern Europe, a fact which means that a good deal of war production in the early period of the war was not tied to any very definite strategy.[31] As matters developed, the War Production Board had no voice in the determination of strategic plans, although it had over-riding responsibility for the war production programme. In short, the absence of a focal point in the United States where strategic and production planning could be dealt with as a whole meant that the combined planning visualized in the Charter of the Combined Production and Resources Board was not an immediately practical goal. The best that could be done was to deal with special problems, some of them limited in scope, as they arose.

It is natural also that an agency such as the Combined Production and Resources Board with a grant of broad, but not very specific powers, should encounter operating difficulties. This was particularly true in the United States where the activities of the Combined Production and Resources Board sometimes conflicted with those of existing domestic agencies which were naturally jealous of their prerogatives. For example, it was difficult for the Combined Production and Resources Board to avoid becoming involved in questions of foreign economic policy, and this led immediately to jurisdictional difficulties with the agencies already charged with the responsibility for carrying out that policy. The implementation of decisions of the Combined Production and Resources Board depended principally on the fact that the Board was composed of the chief production authorities in the member countries. There were many instances where the recommendations of the Board involved other agencies, such as those responsible for manpower, and in these circumstances, the force of the recommendations was less obvious. In Canada, where the Minister of Munitions and Supply was the Canadian Member, the recommendations of the Board with respect to production problems had the force of a ministerial directive or otherwise reflected the wishes of the government.

The star of the Combined Production and Resources Board was in the ascendant during the phase of rising military requirements and serious shortages of productive capacity. Circumstances demanded co-operative action and planning. Once the supply of a critical commodity became easier, the necessity of combined planning became less evident and the pressure for autonomous action increased. For this reason, combined planning was apt to be most effective in a period of crisis. Moreover, to be fully effective, combined production planning must take into account the overall pattern of resource-use and not merely one segment of it.

Canada's membership on the Combined Production and Resources Board was symbolic of Canada's importance as a producer and supplier. Nevertheless, Canada never had quite the same concern with the problems of combined planning as the United States or the United Kingdom. The United Kingdom used the Combined Production and Resources Board as a high-level forum for the discussion of questions which could be dealt with inadequately so long as the United Kingdom was a claimant, operating mainly through lend-lease channels. It must be remembered that the United Kingdom did not have direct representation on the Requirements Committee of the War Production Board or on the other allocating committees of that agency. The Combined Production and Resources Board therefore constituted a kind of court of appeal which was of immense value to the United Kingdom. Similarly, the Board was potentially important to Canada in this connection.

In the case of Canada, the Combined Production and Resources Board tended to absorb or overshadow the special committees of the United States and Canada which had been established in 1941. Partly this was a result of the fact that during the most active period in the existence of the Board, the Canadian Deputy Member was also, for a time at least, Director-General of the Washington office of the Department of Munitions and Supply and one of the Canadian members on the Materials Co-ordinating Committee as well as Associate Metals Controller. This was an accidental aspect of the basic structure of the Combined Production and Resources Board but one which greatly strengthened the Canadian side of the Board.

From the point of view of formal status and authority, the Combined Production and Resources Board was very important. However, most of the business having to do with Canadian requirements, allocations or procurement in the United States continued to be handled through other channels. This was particularly true of negotiations concerning allocations to Canada which were dealt with by the Requirements Committee of the War Production Board as well as by junior allocation committees established in various divisions of the War Production Board. Canada was in a position to obtain special concessions with respect to allocations in some cases, sufficient at least to maintain some rough parity between the civilian economies of the two countries. This was more satisfactory than dealing through the Combined Boards where Canada could scarcely expect to be treated more favourably than the United Kingdom.

The administrative organization of the Combined Production and Resources Board provides an interesting comparison with both the Joint Economic Committees and the Joint War Production Committee. The Joint Economic Committees were dominated by officials primarily concerned with research. They were therefore not directly concerned with operating problems involved in relations between Canada and the United States. They had an advisory function only and were not in a position to interfere with or supervise the activities of operating agencies which were inevitably influential in determining policy. For this reason, the Joint War Production Committee or, more specifically, its sub-committees, constituted a more effective instrument of economic co-operation. This was mainly because the sub-committee members were in comparable administrative positions, and, by consultation, were able to solve production problems without the complex rigmarole of recommendations and resolutions. It becomes clear that any attempt to assign the responsibility for policy to one group and the responsibility for action to another is likely to be ineffective. By its very nature, the Combined Production and Resources Board was admirably adapted to the translation of policy decisions into action.

Some more specific aspects of the work of the Combined Production and Resources Board are considered in later chapters dealing with pulp and paper and reconversion problems. It will be seen in the next chapter, which deals with forest products, that combined planning was in no sense a panacea for international dislocations or disagreements.

REFERENCES FOR CHAPTER X

1. U.S., Department of State, *Bulletin,* March 18, 1944, p. 264.

2. *Statutes of Canada,* 6 Geo. VI, c. 8, March 27, 1942. The War Appropriation (United Kingdom Financing) Act, 1942.

3. *Statutes of Canada,* 7 Geo. VI, c. 17, May 20, 1943. The War Appropriation (United Nations Mutual Aid) Act.

4. *New York Times,* August 23, 1943, p. 1.

5. U.S. Congress, Senate, *Third Annual Report of the Special Committee Investigating the National Defense Program, November 5, 1943* (Washington: U.S. Government Printing Office, 1944), p. 401.

6. U.S., Congress, House of Representatives, *Hearings before the Sub-committee of the Committee on Appropriations, Foreign Economic Administration Appropriation Bill for 1945,* (78th Cong., 2nd. sess.) (Washington: U.S. Government Printing Office, 1944), pp. 125-6.

7. U.S., Department of State, *Bulletin,* January 31, 1942, p. 87.

8. *Ibid.,* June 13, 1942, p. 535.

9. *New York Times,* February 7, 1942, p. 4.

10. *Canada, House of Commons Debates,* April 29, 1942, p. 1977.

11. Similar committees existed for the assignment of naval items and for aircraft and more or less formal arrangements were made for Canadian participation in the work of these committees. Canada was always in a position to present requirements to these committees.

12. U.S., Department of State, *Bulletin,* January 31, 1942, p. 87.

13. The source of the information relating to the Combined Raw Materials Board's action in the case of tin is a speech by W. L. Batt, United States Member before the Controller's Institute in New York on September 14, 1944.

14. *The United States at War,* p. 151.

15. U.S., Department of State, *Bulletin,* June 13, 1942, p. 535.

16. *Ibid.*

17. *Ibid.*

18. *Industrial Mobilization for War,* p. 225. Mention of Canada is conspicuously lacking in this quotation.

19. For one reason or another, it was not possible to collect statistical data for the continent of Europe, the Union of Soviet Socialist Republics, China, and enemy-occupied territory in the Orient.

20. U.S., Congress, *Report on the First Year of Lend-Lease Operations,* House Document No. 661, (77th Cong., 2nd. sess.), Appendix IV (Washington: U.S. Government Printing Office, 1942), p. 53.

21. Hansard, *Parliamentary Debates,* 5th series, vol. 364, August 20, 1940, p. 1162.

22. The new organization was announced by the White House in a press release on November 21, 1942, and was actually established on December 4, 1942. It was later absorbed by the Foreign Economic Administration by Executive Order No. 9380, September 25, 1943.

23. *Report of the Director General: Second Session of the Council of the United Nations Relief and Rehabilitation Administration, September, 1944* (London: His Majesty's Stationery Office, 1944) part 1, pp. 16-17.

24. United Nations Relief and Rehabilitation Administration, *Resolutions and Reports Adopted by the Council at its First Session, Held at Atlantic City, New Jersey, U.S.A., November 10 to December 1, 1943* (London: H.M. Stationery Office, 1943), Cmd. 6497.

25. Memorandum, W. L. Batt to All Officers of the War Production Board, February 26, 1944.

26. *New York Times,* May 1, 1945, p. 15.

27. *Ibid.,* May 23, 1945, p. 9. The presidential letter was also sent to the War Food Administration, the Solid Fuels Administration for War, and the Foreign Shipments Committee.

28. *Ibid.,* January 20, 1945, p. 5.

29. White House Advance Press Release, December 8, 1945.

30. John R. Deane, *The Strange Alliance* (New York: The Viking Press, 1947), p. 258.

31. *The United States at War,* p. 131.

CHAPTER XI

THE SPECIAL CASE OF FOREST PRODUCTS

THE whole forest products industry is one of great consequence to the North American economy and particularly to trade between Canada and the United States. It is for this reason that the wartime relations between the two countries in this field are revealing. The wartime history of developments in forest products is significant because of the importance of the commodities concerned and not primarily because it is an interesting or convenient case study. To recognize the importance of forest products to Canada, it is only necessary to note that in the period 1936-45, Canadian exports of forest products to the United States made up about one-third of the total value of exports of Canadian produce to the United States (excluding gold). The annual figures for this period are as follows :[1]

	Total Exports of Canadian Produce to the United States (millions of dollars)	Total Exports of Forest Products to the United States (millions of dollars)	Percentage of Exports of Forest Products to Total
1936............	334	143	43
1937............	360	180	50
1938............	270	140	52
1939............	380	166	44
1940............	443	215	48
1941............	600	286	48
1942............	886	309	35
1943............	1,149	283	25
1944............	1,301	300	23
1945............	1,197	329	28

The issues which arose between Canada and the United States in dealing with forest products show clearly that the integration of the economies, even in a limited field, was a complex and difficult task.[2] The commodities included under forest products—logs, lumber, pulpwood, woodpulp, and newsprint—each exhibited special features, although the general pattern of Canadian relations with the United States was the same. The United States was dependent on Canada, to a greater or less degree, as a source of supply. This was not unusual in itself, since Canada was an important source of other imported raw materials. One important difference arose from the higher degree of United States dependence on Canada for pulp and paper products, particularly newsprint. Again, the United States importers were numerous, influential and vociferous, a

268

fact which created problems not met in the quiet procurement operations of government agencies buying base metals, for example, in Canada. Much of this chapter is devoted to a discussion of the difficulties and misunderstandings which occurred in the pulp and paper field. This emphasis should not be allowed to obscure the fact that the contentious issues were essentially marginal and residual. Because of political factors, they tended to assume a distorted significance. Basically, the North American problem was to parcel out scarce supplies of forest products so as to meet the varied and urgent demands of foreign and domestic consumers. To appreciate the serious shortages which began to develop in 1941 and 1942, some of the background developments in the early years of the war must be understood.

1. EARLY SUPPLY DIFFICULTIES

Before the war, about 85 per cent of world exports of woodpulp came from Scandinavia. In 1940, disturbed conditions in the Baltic, followed by the conquest of Norway and Denmark in April, indicated that this source of supply would be cut off from the non-Axis world. At the same time, the demand in the United States was rapidly growing as a result of expanded industrial needs for containers and speculative purchases of paper. The growing demand, supplemented by marked increases in the cost of woodpulp imported from overseas, led to rapidly rising domestic prices in the United States. At the end of July, 1940, following a detailed investigation by the Advisory Commission to the Council of National Defense, President Roosevelt issued an optimistic statement to the effect that there was no immediate danger of a serious shortage of woodpulp in view of the unused capacity in the United States and the fact that imports from Canada could be expected to increase.[3] The changing pattern of supply in the United States in the period 1939-42 is indicated in the following table which shows both domestic production and imports of woodpulp by the United States, in thousands of short tons:[4]

	Domestic Production	Imports from Canada and Newfoundland	Total Imports	Total New Supply
1939.......	6,986	638	2,026	9,012
1940.......	8,960	828	1,225	10,185
1941.......	10,375	1,145	1,158	11,533
1942.......	10,783	1,236	1,236	12,019

The situation remained relatively quiet in the latter half of 1940, but by the spring of 1941, a serious shortage of unbleached sulphate pulp developed. This grade of pulp is used mainly in making Kraft wrapping paper and paper board for containers, two commodities urgently required for packaging war materials, particularly lend-lease shipments. Shipments for overseas required special packaging, and beginning early in 1941, there was a move to substitute containers manufactured from woodpulp, such as fibreboard and multi-walled paper bags, for other standard packaging materials such as lumber, metals or burlap. The Office of Production Management, which was in existence by this time, concentrated its efforts on expanding domestic facilities and encouraging waste paper collection. It also assisted the Office of Price Administration and Civilian Supply and its forerunner, in attempting to control prices. By the early fall of 1941, demands for paper again soared, partly as a result of large government purchases, and serious price and supply problems in this field seemed to be imminent. In an attempt to compensate for the disappearance of Scandinavian pulp, imports of unbleached sulphate pulp from Canada were increased from 74,000 tons in 1938[5] to 171,000 tons in 1941.[6] Production capacity was also expanded in the United States around the middle of 1941. The domestic demand for Kraft-grade pulp declined somewhat after specifications for shipping containers were relaxed and the effects of voluntary conservation of paper containers became noticeable. As a result, the critical shortage of unbleached sulphate pulp eased around the end of 1941.

A comparable shortage had developed in the supply of bleached sulphite or nitrating pulp, a high-grade pulp consisting almost entirely of cellulose, and used in the manufacture of fine papers, rayon yarn, cellophane, smokeless powder and plastics. In 1941, the requirements of the rayon industry expanded rapidly when, as a result of the beginnings of economic warfare with Japan, silk imports from that source were cut off. The substitution of nitrating pulp for cotton linters in the manufacture of smokeless powder had also stimulated an enormous new and urgent military demand for nitrating pulp.

In the winter of 1941-42, the cut of pulpwood in both Canada and the United States was abnormally low, particularly in the Pacific Northwest where weather conditions had hindered cutting. Also, the supply of woods labour was becoming seriously depleted in both Canada and the United States largely as a result of the drain of manpower into war industries. United States pulp and paper mills in the Pacific Northwest stepped up their demands for pulpwood from British Columbia to make up for the diminishing local supplies. The level of pulpwood exports from British Columbia increased from an average of 72,000 rough cords in 1935-39 to 270,000 rough cords in 1941. East of the Rockies, exports of pulpwood rose from a pre-war average of 1,306,000 rough cords to 1,842,000 rough cords in 1941.

This high level of exports was creating difficulty in Canada. About three-quarters of the pulpwood used in Canada was cut by the pulp and paper manufacturers while the remainder was obtained from settlers, farmers or dealers who cut pulpwood on Crown or freehold timber lands. The high level of exports and the withdrawal of woods labour meant that the supply of pulpwood being offered on the domestic market was falling seriously below normal levels in the early winter of 1941. About the middle of December, 1941, the situation suddenly became critical. The price ceiling imposed in Canada on December 1 froze domestic pulpwood prices in Eastern Canada at about $9 a cord, while exporters were offering up to $15 a cord for pulpwood to be shipped to the United States. It was evident that any marketable pulpwood in Canada would soon disappear if exports were not checked. The Chairman of the Wartime Prices and Trade Board, concerned with the influence of price disparities, referred the problem to the Canadian Section of the Joint Economic Committees to see if a solution and a satisfactory precedent could be devised.

The question of pulpwood exports was also being considered in other quarters. Jurisdiction properly rested with the Timber Controller of the Department of Munitions and Supply, although very little action had been taken to regulate pulpwood up to this time. As a result of the critical developments in December, the Deputy Timber Controller initiated discussions with the pulp and paper officials of the Office of Production Management who suggested that the Materials Co-ordinating Committee should sponsor a meeting of interested officials in the two countries to discuss the export of pulpwood. The Materials Co-ordinating Committee had been concerned with pulp and paper problems on a number of occasions in the latter half of 1941. This Committee had undertaken to study the problems of shifting from the production of newsprint to the production of paperboard and wrapping paper and later had recommended the use of Canadian shell-casing board by the United States. In the meantime, the Wartime Prices and Trade Board notified the Canadian Section of the Joint Economic Committees that it was withdrawing its earlier request for an investigation and intimated that any decisions were the responsibility of the Wartime Industries Control Board and the Timber Controller. The next development was in mid-January, when, on the recommendation of the Wartime Industries Control Board, export control over pulpwood was introduced effective February 1.[7] The action was taken, according to the preamble of the order-in-council imposing export control, "in order to conserve supplies essential for Canadian requirements."

A precedent for such action had been established earlier by a regulation of the Timber Controller issued early in July, 1940, temporarily prohibiting the export of Douglas fir sawlogs to non-Empire countries.[8] The necessity for export control in the case of Douglas fir sawlogs arose because of price premiums on export shipments to the United States which ranged from $10 to $20 per thousand board feet. The prevention of excessive non-war exports was essential in view of the urgent needs of the United Kingdom for lumber and rapidly increasing domestic requirements stemming from war construction in general, and the needs of such special military projects as the British Commonwealth Air Training Plan in particular. In view of the relatively easy supply position of lumber in the United States at the time, and the fact that United States mills in the Pacific Northwest usually imported only about one per cent of their Douglas fir logs from Canada, the Canadian action was not regarded as a serious matter. In fact, legislation to prohibit the export of high-grade Douglas fir logs from the United States was under consideration in Congress in the summer of 1940. One member of Congress, in urging passage of this legislation, referred approvingly to the Canadian example and was quoted as saying that Canada had effectively put into practice a sensible step in timber conservation which United States interests in the Pacific Northwest had unsuccessfully sought after for years.[9]

The Canadian decision to extend export control to pulpwood made it even more desirable to proceed with the international conference under the sponsorship of the Materials Co-ordinating Committee. The Joint Economic Committees were invited to participate in the discussions between officials of the two countries which were to be held in Montreal and to consider the problems of determining the most equitable way of administering the export permit system. At the Montreal meeting, the Canadians made it explicitly clear that pulpwood shipments which represented normal exports to mills in the United States would not be interfered with, and that the main purpose of the control would be to prevent abnormal purchases for export occurring because of lower Canadian price and wage levels. This general policy was discussed later in the Joint Economic Committees and was agreeable to both the United States Section of the Joint Economic Committees and the Pulp and Paper Branch of the War Production Board. The understanding, in more specific terms, was that the export permit system would not be used to reduce total exports to the United States below the percentage of the total pulpwood cut which it had been customary to export over the past few years. It was also agreed that it would be the responsibility of the United States to direct imported pulpwood to domestic mills.[10]

There was certainly no intention on the part of Canada to be selfish about the supply of pulpwood; the aim was merely to control a disorderly situation. In spite of the efforts which were made to arrive at a mutually satisfactory control of exports, the Canadian action was unpopular in the United States, particularly among Western consumers of Canadian pulpwood. A number of pulp and paper mills in the Puget Sound area had become heavily dependent on Canadian imports and in some cases had acquired large pulpwood limits. The export control restrictions were particularly galling to this group. The Army and Navy in the United States were also concerned because of the threat to the production of nitrating pulp. The attention of various members of Congress was directed to the inequities of a situation in which the Canadian ceiling price on pulpwood was $11.50 a cord compared to the United States price of $17, but the amount available from Canada was limited by governmental action. This state of affairs was particularly unpalatable to United States users of pulpwood whose products competed with those made in Canada. Protests were submitted to the Secretary of State by several members of Congress who considered that the situation was "a glaring example of the laxity in our State Department," and reflected the "lack of sympathetic coordination of our war efforts between this country and Canada, particularly when we are so generous and liberal in supplying our allies with materials."[11] The Secretary of State referred the matter to the Chairman of the War Production Board, who, after investigation, reported to the interested members of Congress that inventories of pulp mills in British Columbia had decreased more than the inventories of the Puget Sound mills and that the difficulties arose out of the reduced pulpwood cut in British Columbia and not because Canadian export controls were being used to discriminate against United States mills. The shortage of pulpwood in Puget Sound was recognized by the Canadian authorities as a serious matter and some adjustments were made to permit a higher level of exports. The Canadian price ceiling on hemlock logs was increased in April, 1942, and an additional 10,000,000 board feet of pulping logs were released for export. These actions were only a temporary palliative and evidently did not convince producers in the United States that the Canadian attitude was anything but selfish and grasping.

During the first half of 1942, the demands of the war began seriously to affect operations in the pulp and paper industry in both countries. The industry consumed large quantities of critical materials such as copper, chlorine, power, gasoline, and rubber, in addition to being a large employer of men of military age. Apart from restrictions on the use of specific critical materials, it would clearly be necessary to introduce curtailment measures to limit the output of relatively non-essential paper products. Planning was started by the pulp and paper officials of the Office of Production Management to reduce future production of pulp and paper to levels ranging from 40 to 80 per cent of current production, depending on the degree of austerity required in the economy.

The complex structure of the industry made a simple limitation of the level of output difficult. Some of the firms in the industry were integrated units which produced their own pulp, often from their own pulpwood limits, and manufactured it into paper products. Other firms depended wholly or in part on market pulp, which was imported or purchased from domestic pulp mills for conversion into paper or paperboard. The shortage of pulpwood was more serious for the non-integrated or semi-integrated mills in view of the diminishing supply of domestically produced market pulp. The integrated mills were naturally anxious to fill their own needs and to reduce their offerings of market pulp. In addition, Scandinavian sources which previously supplied large quantities of market pulp had been completely cut off. In view of the internal structural differences in the industry, it was decided by the War Production Board to allocate pulp to individual mills, whether integrated or not. An allocation scheme was introduced by Conservation Order M-93 which went into effect May 1, 1942.[12] The order gave the War Production Board authority to direct all deliveries of woodpulp in the United States, including imported woodpulp once it crossed the border. Canadian pulp and paper officials as well as the Canadian industry agreed to co-operate fully with the War Production Board and to modify delivery schedules whenever this was required to implement the allocations which had been fixed. The control was extended in 1943 when pulp producers were required to set aside 20 per cent of their monthly output as a pool for emergency allocations by the War Production Board. In the same regulation, the War Production Board was also authorized to restrict or direct the end-use of allocated pulp.[13] The woodpulp allocation scheme proved to be a very satisfactory method of control throughout the period of its operation.

Despite the value of such controls over distribution, the basic difficulty continued to be a shortage of pulpwood and woodpulp. To make matters worse, the shortage of lumber was becoming acute by the early summer of 1942. Action was taken by the War Production Board to set aside sufficient lumber to fill military needs in the United States.[14] Draft deferment was also granted by Selective Service for loggers performing certain types of work, but the deferment order did not include persons

engaged in cutting pulpwood. This was in accord with the policy of
certain groups in the War Production Board who felt that the maintenance
of a high level of pulp and paper production, particularly in the Pacific
Northwest, could not be defended in view of the serious labour shortage
which existed in shipyards, aircraft and aluminum plants, and in logging.
In response to the growing volume of protests, the Pulp and Paper
Branch of the War Production Board prepared a comprehensive programme for the limitation of pulp and paper production, and plans were
drawn up for the concentration of the industry in the Pacific Northwest
region.

Prior to the summer of 1942, the Canadian policy in administering
the control of pulpwood exports had been to allow the export of pulpwood
cut on Crown-grant lands by United States companies. But, in August,
1942, it was decided to ban further exports of hemlock pulping logs
because of declining inventories in Canadian mills and the expectation
that the situation would become worse. This action was a signal for
another vituperative outburst from United States consumers of Canadian
pulpwood in the Puget Sound area. It was alleged that Canada was
attempting to maintain woodpulp production at the expense of the United
States mills and that the export control would probably not increase
lumber output in British Columbia. The Canadian representatives replied
that the output of United States pulp mills had increased substantially
and that Canadian production would have to be cut because of declining
log inventories, a condition which was common to both countries. The
Assistant Timber Controller, however, agreed to lift the export control
if the mills in the United States could demonstrate that their output was
more essential than the Canadian output or if the inventory position of
Canadian mills improved. In the meantime, the Canadian authorities
refused to postpone the decision to broaden the scope of export control.
The additional restrictions went into effect in September, 1942. It was
believed that the additional embargo would reduce log supplies of the
Puget Sound mills by 20 per cent, a fact which immediately heightened
the necessity for concentration of the industry. This proposal was strongly
supported by the War Manpower Commission and the War and Navy
Departments. Accordingly, near the end of October, the War Production
Board issued regulations providing for the compulsory concentration of
the pulp and paper industry in the Pacific Northwest.[15]

Sometime prior to this, the unhappy relations between Canada and
the United States on the subject of pulpwood exports had again come to
the attention of the Materials Co-ordinating Committee, which proposed

in a meeting late in August that it should create a Forest Products Subcommittee to review the whole question. Such a committee was established and met early in October, 1942, to consider the various issues involved. The United States contended that the Canadian export control system had left United States mills with very small inventories of pulpwood, and was forcing concentration of the industry and making drastic curtailments of paper consumption in the United States necessary. Simultaneously, some Canadian pulp mills were increasing their exports to the United States. The Canadian reply to this charge was that any increase in Canadian pulp exports was a result of earlier efforts of the United States to stimulate Canadian output as a substitute for Scandinavian pulp. The Canadian representatives also pointed out that lumber exports from British Columbia to the United States had quadrupled since before the war, and that Canada had to meet not only the demands of the domestic war production programme but also urgent needs of the United Kingdom. In view of the current shortage of manpower, any attempt to supply the virtually unlimited demands of the United States would seriously disrupt other Canadian commitments and would involve an unwise and uneconomic distribution of resources. While it was generally agreed that the logs of the two countries should be regarded as a pool for consumption in a way that would maximize the joint war effort, agreement could not be reached on a formula covering log exports from Canada which would achieve this purpose. The discussions of the Forest Products Subcommittee of the Materials Co-ordinating Committee did not lead to any change in the Canadian decision to maintain the embargo.

The Canadian policy was thoroughly aired and criticized by the Truman Committee in November, 1942. Senator Wallgren of Washington, having been supplied with evidence by mill operators in the Puget Sound area, remarked:

They [the Canadians] are just conserving their timber and forcing our operators or owners up there, American owners, to put their logs into the market. That is exactly what is happening at the present as far as this lumber thing is concerned, and it looks to me like the War Production Board ought to get a little bit tough about this thing and see that we get that timber into this country. . . . There is no question but that these people in Canada now cutting logs that are owned by American owners in British Columbia have timber of their own that they are just holding, while these men are forced to cut their timber at the present time.[16]

Mr. Wallgren, in questioning Mr. Ben Alexander, Lumber Coordinator of
the War Production Board, again indicated in the following exchange that
a change in tactics seemed to be indicated:

Senator Wallgren: Why don't you get a little bit tough about it?
Why don't you tell these Canadian people that we have to have this stuff?
We have lifted all the embargoes ourselves. By an order recently we
removed all tariffs [sic] against anything, as far as Canada is concerned.
Why don't they loosen up a little bit?

Mr. Alexander: We have been tough and we have talked tough
and we have talked just as tough as you are, but we haven't got any
logs. I think it will take a bigger brass hat than I have got to do the
job.[17]

The submissions of the Puget Sound operators did not all condemn
the Canadian action. The president of one company pointed out:

Referring to . . . testimony that Canada should lift the embargo on
logs in order to assist lumber production, such repeal would not materially affect the importation of Douglas fir which is the bulk of the lumber
required. Out of an approximate total of seven hundred million log
importations from January 1, 1939, to the date of the embargo on August
11, approximately five hundred million feet were hemlock logs intended
for the pulp mills. The bulk of Canadian lumber production is for war
requirements, over sixty percent being shipped to the United Kingdom
and other British possessions, the balance in Canadian war work. I am
thoroughly familiar with the industry on both sides of the line and think
it unfair to criticize British Columbia for restricting her raw material
exports when she needs it so badly herself.[18]

It is evident that the situation was thoroughly confused.

The issue of Canadian policy on the export of pulpwood continued
to dog the increasingly vexing problems which were arising in the
forest products field. The question arose at a later date in connection
with the actions taken in the two countries to limit the consumption of
the so-called cultural papers, including book papers, writing papers and,
above all, newsprint.

In an attempt to explain the rather turbulent relations between
Canada and the United States in this field, the problems and the related
negotiations are dealt with in some detail. The issues were complex and
contentious and tend to become obscured unless the fundamental features
of the production and consumption of forest products, particularly pulp
and paper, are kept in mind.

The difficulties between Canada and the United States were essentially
a result of the inability of either country to make adjustments in a
situation which inherently lacked flexibility. This was particularly true

in the case of newsprint, which accounts for the prominent and vexatious place of newsprint in the negotiations between officials of the two countries. Canada, as a major supplier of forest products, had the largest segment of the industry producing newsprint, a standardized good produced by highly capitalized, technical processes specially adapted to this product and not suited for the production of substitute products. Newsprint typically consists of about 85 per cent groundwood pulp and 15 per cent low-grade sulphite pulp. The average mill is designed to produce these grades in these proportions in a continuous process of conversion into a final product. Groundwood pulp was never a critical or significant item in the overall pulp shortage. Moreover, the grade of sulphite pulp used for newsprint could not normally be diverted from the average Canadian mill since facilities for drying and handling pulp as a separate operation did not usually exist. Even if it could, the larger proportion of groundwood pulp would be sterilized and, in effect, wasted. Substitution at an earlier stage of production by re-allocating pulpwood provided no solution because the wood moved to the mills by water in most cases and because the newsprint producers could not be expected to make extraordinary efforts to encourage pulpwood cutting if they were not to be allowed to reap the benefits.

In the United States, the basic adjustment problem centred around consumption. The principle of equal treatment in limiting the use of cultural papers necessitated equal percentage cuts in terms of base period tonnage consumption for different classes of consumers. This unavoidably discriminated against the newspaper publishers. Again, there was no simple remedy because they, like their suppliers in Canada, were using a highly standardized product while their competitors in the magazine field were free to increase circulation by using lighter and cheaper grades of paper than they had used in the base-period. As a result, the newspapers actually lost millions of dollars of advertising to the magazines. Under these circumstances, it became more and more necessary for the War Production Board to insist on the principle of non-discrimination. Unfortunately, application of the principle tended to foster the inequities which it was intended to prevent.

The historical development of the paper industry in the United States was also an important conditioning influence. Generally speaking, the industry had been steadily moving out of the newsprint field during the twenty years prior to the war. Under tariff protection a large and widely varied assortment of mills had developed, producing all types of paper products and relying on an extensive open market for pulp to be used as raw material. When Scandinavian sources were cut off, and when

later the expanded military uses of pulp in the United States gave rise
to greatly increased requirements for high-grade pulps, the resulting
demand on Canada was something quite new in the experience of both
countries. Unfortunately, the demands simply did not fit the structure
of the Canadian industry, although, in fact, larger quantities of high-
grade pulps were supplied from the mills equipped to produce them than
anyone might have expected in the circumstances.

Thus, on the production side, the industry in the United States
was flexible in terms of end-product facilities and final output but lacked
raw material. The Canadian industry was inflexible in its largest sector,
newsprint, and was not adapted to intermediate diversion of a semi-finished
product, pulp, in the grades required. At the same time, the consumption
pattern in the United States was flexible only in marginal respects. This
basic pattern of production and consumption was at the root of the
problems involved in trying to control the output and use of cultural
papers.

2. THE ADOPTION OF PRODUCTION AND CONSUMPTION CONTROLS AND RELATED PROBLEMS

Cultural papers include the almost infinite variety of papers designed
for printing or writing. The product is highly differentiated for competitive reasons and, in wartime, the retention of a wide variety of grades,
sizes, and weights of paper diverted resources in an undesirable way.
In addition, general price ceilings stimulated the elimination of relatively
costly special papers. As a result, government agencies in Canada and
the United States, and the paper industry itself, began making plans for
the standardization and simplification of paper about the end of 1941.
After a period of relying on the voluntary co-operation of the industry,
compulsory simplification measures were introduced in the spring and
early summer of 1942.[19] By mid-1942, concerted pressure for more
drastic reduction of pulp and paper consumption in the United States
was being exerted by the Army and Navy Munitions Board and by certain
groups within the War Production Board itself. Various proposals and
programmes to reduce paper consumption were discussed in the summer
and fall of 1942. The Pulp and Paper Branch of the War Production
Board originally recommended that production be limited to 65 per cent
of the 1941 level, a reduction of approximately 20 per cent below the level
then current. The Office of Civilian Supply of the War Production Board
proposed a reduction of at least 50 per cent below the 1941 output to be
accomplished by differential limitation of the major classes of paper.
This contrasted with the view of the Pulp and Paper Branch which,

because of the serious difficulties in fixing satisfactory quotas for the different classes of paper, favoured a flat horizontal cut.

During September, 1942, news of the curtailment proposals leaked out and caused a good deal of speculative purchasing. About this time, public announcement was made of a system of allocating newsprint production in Canada, a step designed to lessen the dislocations resulting from enforced cuts in Canadian output.[20] Hydro-electric power was being diverted from newsprint mills to the United States or to war industry in Canada, and woods labour was becoming increasingly scarce. The prospective reduction in Canadian output occurred at a time when Canada was being called on to supply the United Kingdom with pulp and paper normally imported from Scandinavian sources. As a result of these influences, a serious paper shortage seemed to be developing in the United States by September, 1942.

It became necessary to take immediate action, and a compromise agreement was reached among the United States agencies concerned to adopt the plan of the Pulp and Paper Branch which involved curtailment to 65 per cent of the rate of production in the base period October 1, 1941, to March 31, 1942. By this time, the cut would amount to a reduction of 10 per cent below the current level.

Compulsory reduction of the consumption of cultural papers in the United States was a particularly delicate issue inasmuch as it involved some limitations on the complete freedom of newspapers. An impartial observer might have had grounds for believing that an appreciable proportion of newsprint consumption was non-essential. For example, it was not clear that display advertising, comic strips, and Sunday supplements were essential in a war economy. Recognition of this fact did not mean that it was politically practical to restrict newsprint consumption to essential uses, as determined by some government agency. Scrupulous care was taken by government officials in both Canada and the United States to avoid establishing any criteria of essentiality. In the minds of the publishers, government action which affected advertising revenue was automatically an infringement on the "freedom of the press." Anyone espousing a different point of view was handicapped in publicizing it, to say the least. The Chairman of the War Production Board was naturally anxious to avoid disputes with the industry in view of its tremendous influence on public opinion. For this reason, every effort was made to avoid any action which might appear to discriminate against the use of newsprint as opposed to other cultural papers, especially book and magazine papers. The upshot of this was that non-discriminatory limitations were initially adopted as a matter of policy even though it was evident that the maintenance of uniform restrictions would cause difficulties.

Canada had a vital interest in any steps taken by the United States to limit paper consumption in view of the fact that about 70 per cent of the newsprint requirements of the United States were obtained from Canada. The Canadian pulp and paper industry was specifically adapted to producing newsprint for export, while the industry in the United States was able to diversify its output more readily and could shift to the production of essential nitrating pulps, photographic papers, wrapping papers, and paperboard without unduly disrupting its operations or impairing its efficiency. Any paper curtailment programme in the United States would have serious repercussions on the Canadian newsprint industry in view of the limited possibilities of shifting to other pulp and paper products. The proposal of the United States to curtail paper production by 10 per cent was a shock to the Canadian industry and to the Wartime Prices and Trade Board. The War Production Board first informed the Canadian Newsprint Administrator of the decision twenty-four hours before it was scheduled to go into effect. The Wartime Prices and Trade Board protested against this precipitate action and urged temporary postponement, which was agreed to. After about two weeks, during which time Canadian officials discussed the details of the technique of restriction, the Wartime Prices and Trade Board gave its reluctant concurrence to the plan and agreed to impose similar restrictions in Canada.

The Chairman of the Wartime Prices and Trade Board, in explaining Canadian reluctance to endorse the War Production Board plan, pointed out that the restriction scheme was ill-planned, and unlikely to be effective. He emphasized that any reduction in output must be carefully scheduled in advance to avoid the inefficiencies resulting from part-time operation. Moreover, the base period chosen coincided with a seasonally low rate of operations in Canadian newsprint mills with the result that the effective rate of curtailment in Canada would be nearer 17 per cent than 10 per cent. He also expressed some doubt concerning the effectiveness of the curtailments unless they were accompanied by simultaneous limitations on end-use. He concluded by making a plea for co-ordinated action in the future, saying:

In this particular case, we were confronted with a decision of your officials. It seems obvious to me that as soon as any matter arises in your country which significantly affects our trade, our policies or our plans, there is only one proper procedure and that is for us to get together and work through to a common decision after giving due consideration to our several problems and our joint responsibilities as partners in war. I venture to suggest that we could make a real contribution in that way.[21]

Recognizing the force of the Canadian arguments, the War Production Board somewhat tardily arranged for a conference between the government officials of the two countries in mid-October to consider long-run aspects of the curtailment programme. As a result of these discussions, it was agreed to change the base period originally proposed—October 1, 1941, to March 31, 1942—to the eight weeks prior to October 4, 1942. The major difference between the Canadians and the representatives of the War Production Board, particularly the Office of Civilian Supply, concerned the way in which the ultimate reduction was to be achieved. The Office of Civilian Supply sponsored an immediate reduction of newsprint output to about 45 per cent of the current level with accompanying concentration of the industry.

It might be mentioned that enthusiasm for the concentration of industry was reaching its peak in the Office of Civilian Supply around this time. Late in August, the Deputy Director of the Office of Civilian Supply had been appointed Chairman of a Committee on Concentration of Production created by the War Production Board and two senior officials of the Office of Civilian Supply returned from the United Kingdom in September after having looked into the wartime experience with concentration there.[22] The Office of Civilian Supply were eager to draw up a concentration plan for the North American pulp and paper industry. Since, in Canada, the pulp and paper industry is located mainly in areas which are remote and sparsely populated except for the pulp towns themselves, such an experimental programme was not looked on with much favour by the Canadian officials concerned. In fact, it was their view that it would be difficult to find a less suitable industry for concentration.

The counter-proposal of the Canadians, which was supported by the Pulp and Paper Branch of the War Production Board, was a scheduled curtailment which would allow mills to use up their accumulated inventories of pulpwood in order to avoid disorderly and uneconomic operations. It was agreed, finally, that an immediate reduction of 10 per cent below current production levels would be adopted in both countries and that further reductions would be imposed to reach a maximum reduction of 40 per cent by mid-1943. The Canadians emphasized throughout that their concurrence in this scheme depended on the adoption of end-use limitations in the United States. There were some last-minute changes in the War Production Board curtailment order which, when it became effective on November 1, provided that production of paper and paperboard should be limited to 100 per cent of the rate in the six months from April 1, 1942, to September 30, 1942.[23] The Wartime Prices and Trade Board issued comparable orders at about the same time limiting the production of newsprint paper and magazine papers for delivery in Canada or the United States to the rate prevailing in the same base period.[24]

These were essentially temporary measures, which were inadequate to relieve the more serious shortages which were forecast for the future. The Canadian pulpwood cut in the wood-year ending May 1, 1943, was expected to drop sharply with a consequent reduction in pulpwood exports to the United States. Pulpwood production in the United States was also falling off because of the diversion of labour to other industries. On the basis of this pessimistic forecast of supplies, the Pulp and Paper Branch reported to a meeting of the War Production Board about the middle of November that paper and paperboard output would have to be cut from the current annual rate of 15,250,000 tons permitted under Conservation Order M-241 to 13,200,000 tons. It was also noted that the contemplated curtailment of newsprint to 60 per cent of the peak production rate would cut domestic output to 604,000 tons and imports from Canada to about 1,812,000 tons annually, which would preserve the historical ratio of imports to domestic production.[25] Plans were initiated shortly after this to draw up a series of orders which would reduce overall paper consumption to the annual rate of 13,200,000 tons.

Experience with Conservation Order M-241 had been disappointing. The base period was characterized not only by seasonally low levels of operation, but by considerable variability among different mills. The resultant inequities led to a large number of appeals to the War Production Board for relaxations of the order with the consequence that the order was not effective in reducing overall production levels. Although the original version of Conservation Order M-241 was supposed to freeze production at the rate of 3,800,000 tons per quarter, a revised order issued early in January, 1943, provided for an increase to 4,100,000 tons a quarter, which, in the opinion of some groups in Washington, was not an effective way to reduce paper consumption.[26] The new order again changed the base period to October 1, 1941, to March 31, 1942, and provided for a small percentage reserve to be distributed by the War Production Board, and complex restrictions on inventories.

Meanwhile, steps were being taken to limit the consumption of cultural papers. The Canadian preference for a gradual reduction up to mid-1943 which was supported by the Pulp and Paper Branch of the

War Production Board and representatives of the newspaper publishers, became the basis of the curtailment programme which was to be carried out by four limitation orders. Limitation Order L-240 was designed to limit the use of newsprint to 1941 rates, equivalent to about 90 per cent of 1942 consumption. Limitation Order L-241 proposed to cut the use of paper by commercial printers to fill civilian orders to 90 per cent of 1941 consumption. Limitation Orders L-244 and L-245 were intended to limit the consumption of paper by magazine and book publishers to 90 per cent of 1942 levels. The limitation orders governing newsprint and magazine paper became effective on January 1, 1943,[27] and the other two orders covering commercial printing and books were issued about a week later.[28] The newsprint order limited the output of newspapers during each quarter of 1943 to 100 per cent of the net paid circulation in the corresponding quarter of 1941 plus a 3 per cent allowance for production wastage.

Comparable restrictions covering newsprint and magazine paper were introduced in Canada by the Wartime Prices and Trade Board by an order prohibiting any person from acquiring or using paper for newspaper or periodicals without a permit from the Administrator of Publishing, Printing and Allied Industries.[29] Similar restrictions were introduced for book, writing, and specialty papers shortly after.[30] The permit system was designed to have the same effect as the limitation orders in the United States. Production and deliveries of newsprint in each quarter of 1943 were further restricted to 90 per cent of three times the monthly average in the period October 1, 1941 to March 31, 1942.[31]

In the meantime, in the fall and early winter of 1942-43, raw material shortages in Canada were becoming more serious. This was the period of Stalingrad and El Alamein, not a propitious time to divert resources to the production of pulpwood. In accord with the prevailing attitude, the Wartime Prices and Trade Board announced detailed plans for the general curtailment of civilian industry late in October.[32] One difficulty arose out of the uncertain applicability of National Selective Service regulations granting draft deferment to workers normally engaged in agriculture who worked in the woods in the winter. This tended to decrease the available supply of casual woods labour. Moreover, in British Columbia, labour had to be diverted to cut lumber urgently needed by the United Kingdom or for domestic war industry, particularly aero-timber. In view of these conditions, the Timber Controller advised the War Production Board around the end of 1942 that a maximum of 1,300,000 cords of pulpwood could be exported to the United States from east of the Rockies in 1943, a drop of about 600,000 cords from the 1942 level. He also pointed out that the pulpwood supply in British Columbia was so serious that none could be exported to the Puget Sound area in 1943. This provoked an immediate protest from the War Production Board, which began negotiations with the Canadian authorities for larger quantities. The threatened loss of pulpwood for Puget Sound mills was particularly serious, since about 35 per cent of their output was nitrating pulp required for military explosives and propellants. After a series of meetings, the Canadians agreed to try to increase exports in 1943 to 1,550,000 cords of pulpwood east of the Rockies, and 1,170,000 tons of pulp. Apart from this, every effort would be made to ship 90,000,000 board feet of pulp logs from British Columbia, or, failing this, an amount sufficient to maintain comparable production rates and inventories in mills on both sides of the border in that area. Despite these undertakings, the Canadians had serious misgivings about the possibility of meeting the target and anticipated that this export programme would mean shutting down pulp and paper mills in British Columbia.

This was the prospective supply situation when the War Production Board began to make concrete plans for the second 10 per cent cut in paper consumption which was scheduled to become effective in the second quarter of 1943. Despite the fact that the War Production Board had appointed a Newspaper Industry Advisory Committee in the hope of securing the full co-operation of the industry, the prospects of a second cut provoked immediate and emphatic protests from the publishers and from Congress. In the midst of the wranglings between the War Production Board and the publishers, the Canadian Newsprint Administrator arrived to explain the Canadian position, bringing with him revised estimates of prospective newsprint supplies for 1943. He reported that the newsprint supply was somewhat improved and that the second 10 per cent reduction would be unnecessary. This was a mixed blessing since it would be impossible to cut other cultural papers and not newsprint. The War Production Board was not only irritated by the conflicting advice obtained from different Canadian sources, but felt that Canada should make available more pulpwood and woodpulp instead of newsprint to enable the restrictions to be applied evenly in the United States. Following two meetings of the officials concerned in Montreal on March 2 and 3, and April 15, Canada agreed to supply an additional 107,000 tons of pulp in order to make a differential reduction in papers other than newsprint unnecessary. As a result of these agreements, it was announced about mid-April, 1943, by the Chairman of the War Production Board that additional restrictions on newsprint or other printing paper would not be adopted before October 1. This decision was premised on the undertaking given by Canada to deliver 210,000 tons of newsprint per month during the second and third quarters of 1943. The Chairman of the Wartime Prices and Trade Board, in referring to this commitment, was careful to point out that forecasts were subject to qualification. He wrote in a letter to the War Production Board:

> In making any statement in relation to production and shipments during the third quarter of 1943, it must be realized that wartime conditions introduce a very considerable measure of uncertainty. No one can predict with accuracy the developments of labor supplies, electrical power requirements and the general development of the course of the war. Any statement must therefore be subject to these underlying qualifications.[33]

One outstanding feature of the limitation programme for cultural papers during the early phase of its operation was its ineffectiveness. During the first five months of 1943, for example, the reduction in newsprint consumption under L-240 was less than 5 per cent below 1942 levels. Inadequate attention had been paid to the substantial geographic shifts of the population which had occurred since 1941. Newspapers serving congested production areas were granted additional newsprint on appeal with the net result that newsprint consumption initially increased rather than decreased under L-240. The inability or unwillingness of the War Production Board to limit newsprint consumption effectively was a source of difficulty and embarrassment to the Canadian industry. Although Canada had undertaken to supply newsprint at the rate of 210,000 tons a month, which was sufficient for consumption authorized by L-240, orders placed by United States publishers were consistently 30,000-40,000 tons a month higher than the level agreed on. This question was the subject of continual protests by Canadian officials who were forced to devise some method of allocating shipments to United States publishers. For one thing, the Canadian authorities had to enforce gratuitously the restrictions imposed by the United States which they were neither authorized nor equipped to do. For another, the inability of Canada to fill the orders of United States publishers led to a good deal of unfavourable comment which sometimes amounted to abuse in the newspapers in the United States. In an effort to restore some order to the situation, the Newsprint Administrator instructed Canadian newsprint mills to cut all United States orders scheduled for July delivery by 12 per cent, which, at best, was an unsatisfactory method of dealing with the problem.

It was clearly recognized by senior War Production Board officials in the spring of 1943 that drastic steps were necessary to protect rapidly disappearing reserves of woodpulp, and that major administrative changes were necessary before this could be done effectively. A detailed set of recommendations was submitted in June by the Operations Vice Chairman to the War Production Board proposing a general tightening of the conservation and limitation orders governing pulp and paper products.[34] Following the approval of the War Production Board, the necessary steps were initiated to revise the control orders. Of particular importance from the Canadian point of view was an amendment of Limitation Order L-240 early in July, providing for a reduction of newsprint consumption to 95 per cent of the 1941 level during the third quarter of 1943.[35] In September, a still further reduction of newsprint consumption of 5 per cent in the fourth quarter of 1943 was ordered by the War Production Board.[36] Other orders governing paper products were similarly tightened.

As a part of the general overhauling of the control mechanism, a Forest Products Bureau was established in the War Production Board in October, 1943, with centralized control over the Pulp and Paper, Containers, Printing and Publishing, and Lumber Divisions.[37] One of the major aims of the reorganization was to establish a more effective liaison with Canadian pulp and paper officials. There was clear evidence that this was desirable in view of new difficulties between the two countries which had arisen since the spring of 1943.

As a result of the agreements reached in January, 1943, between the two countries, to maintain an equitable distribution of pulpwood between the mills in British Columbia and in the Puget Sound area, export permits were granted from time to time for shipments of pulpwood from British Columbia. In general, a smoothly working arrangement had been achieved in this area. This was not the case east of the Rockies. Individual importers of pulpwood in the United States had been assigned import quotas by the War Production Board in order to restrict imports to the level of 1,500,000 cords which had been agreed on. The regulations of the War Production Board affected actual imports rather than the volume of contractual commitments which United States importers could make. The consequence of this was that excessively high orders at agreeably high prices were placed with Canadian suppliers. Pulpwood in Canada which was owned by United States concerns but in excess of their import quotas was thus immobilized and available neither to Canadian nor United States manufacturers. Excessive purchases of this type meant that Canadian pulp and paper mills were faced with a serious shortage of raw material during the second quarter of 1943. In order to protect the position of Canadian consumers, the Timber Controller issued a directive early in June, prohibiting any company from exporting more pulpwood than 80 per cent of its exports in 1942. Many Canadian shippers had already exhausted their 80 per cent quota with the result that their customers in the United States were suddenly cut off from further Canadian supplies. Nor was this all. The prospects of a serious shortage of fuelwood in Canada in the winter of 1943-44 resulted in a campaign to encourage the use of men and facilities for cutting fuelwood. The encouragement given to farmers to cut fuelwood rather than pulpwood would clearly reduce the supply of pulpwood for export. The Timber Controller warned the War Production Board in mid-1943 that not more than 1,000,000 rough cords of pulpwood could be expected from Canada east of the Rockies in the next year, and explained:

It has, of course, always been our attitude to ship the largest possible quantity we can, but as it is absolutely essential that we immediately fix a quota for our exports to cover 1944 operations, we are sending out instructions based on a quota of one million cords for 1944. To accomplish this, we are passing an order that no one may operate in the business of acquiring pulpwood for export unless he has a permit from the Timber Control, and the permits when issued will specifically set the quantities which he may acquire to be exported in 1943 and 1944.

Because of the much higher prices that were being paid for pulpwood for export, we found that all wood was being bought by exporters and that none was available to Canadian industry in certain districts, and I am hopeful that the arrangements we are making will correct this situation, and at the same time make it possible for you to know the specific quantities which you can count on securing from Canada.[38]

To implement this plan, Timber Control Order No. 20 was issued about the middle of July, 1943.[39] The new order provided that any person dealing in pulpwood for export had to obtain a licence before September 1, 1943. The licensing feature of the regulation was intended to control United States dealers in pulpwood. Initially, it was decided that export permits would not be granted for quantities in excess of two-thirds of the exporters' shipments in 1943. These actions were immediately denounced by industry in the United States as a crowning example of Canadian cupidity. At this point, the pulpwood situation seemed to be back where it had started.

In the early fall of 1943, relations between Canada and the United States in the pulp and paper field were quite friendly despite the shadow of Timber Control Order No. 20. Near the end of October, a mission of senior pulp and paper officials came to Ottawa to urge the cancellation of this order and to discuss other problems. As a result of these conversations, an agreement was reached by the Chairman of the Wartime Prices and Trade Board, the Timber Controller, and the Co-ordinator of the Forest Products Bureau of the War Production Board, that Canada and the United States would divide equally the available Canadian supply of "purchased" pulpwood after proper provision had been made for other export commitments. "Purchased" pulpwood referred to pulpwood offered for sale to domestic or foreign consumers and excluded pulpwood cut by Canadian plants for their own use. It was anticipated that this agreement would involve the shipment of at least 1,250,000 cords of pulpwood from Canada to the United States, and that any quantities in excess of 2,500,000 cords would be divided equally between the two countries. For purposes of discussion and planning, the Canadians had made two hypothetical forecasts of the Canadian pulpwood cut in the current season, one of 6,000,000 cords and the other of 6,500,000 cords. Even the larger of these two estimates would mean a reduction in newsprint exports to the United States from 210,000 tons a month to 182,000 tons a month. Although the estimates of the total cut of pulpwood were based on the best information available at the time, the cutting season was just beginning and firm estimates could not be made until early in December. The Canadians had cause later to emphasize that their estimates of the future wood supply were hypothetical and conjectural.

The forecasting problem was complicated by a change in the labour priority assigned pulpwood cutting as a result of recommendations of the Interdepartmental Labour Priorities Committee of the National Selective Service Advisory Board. On October 29, 1943, the Minister of Labour announced that pulpwood cutting operations had been assigned a "B" priority rating, a high rating exceeded only by such industries as ship-building, aircraft, and munitions production.[40] The effectiveness of the revised regulations in channelling more labour into pulpwood cutting could not be assessed until later in the cutting season.

Despite the absence of reliable estimates of newsprint exports, the War Production Board felt obliged to report to its Newspaper Industry Advisory Committee in mid-November that additional restrictions on the use of newsprint would have to be imposed in the first quarter of 1944 on the assumption that imports from Canada would be cut from 210,000 to 182,000 tons a month. In explaining the situation to the Committee, the spokesman of the War Production Board said:

We are satisfied that Canada, within the limits of equity and production ability is endeavouring to supply the United States with pulpwood, pulp and newsprint in proportions and quantities that suit us best. Nevertheless, our overall appraisal of the situation, having regard to the fact that all inventories are down in both the United States and Canada, is that we should not count on Canada being able to maintain current rates of supply. Therefore, we have decided that it will be necessary to limit consumption while at the same time making it possible to take from Canada all the pulpwood, woodpulp and newsprint that she can supply to us in such proportions as are required for war and essential civilian requirements.[41]

The Newspaper Industry Advisory Committee concurred in the proposed cut and plans were drawn up for comparable reductions in the end-use of other cultural papers. Then, early in December, the Wartime Prices and Trade Board informed the War Production Board that newsprint prospects had improved and that exports of 200,000 tons a month could be maintained. The announcement was made public about ten days later.[42] The press release forecast a monthly output of newsprint of 252,900 tons in 1944, of which 200,000 would go to the United States, 15,400 tons could be for domestic consumption, and 37,500 would be exported to overseas markets.

This news was received with some bitterness in the War Production Board since it disturbed the plans for non-discriminatory limitation of cultural papers, and seemed to demonstrate that Canada was seeking the commercial advantages of exporting newsprint rather than woodpulp or pulpwood. The War Production Board immediately announced that it would stockpile newsprint imports in excess of 182,000 tons a month to achieve balanced restrictions of all cultural papers. In a press release, the War Production Board commented:

We prefer that Canadian authorities allow us the benefits of this increased wood production proportionately in pulpwood, pulp and newsprint. This would give us more flexibility in meeting the shortages which are serious in other paper products and certain highly important military non-paper uses. This the Canadians agreed to do in November and with that understanding, the War Production Board is imposing the necessary restrictions on all the graphic arts industries on an equitable basis.[43]

On the question of stockpiling, the statement of the War Production Board went on to say:

By so doing, we will in a large measure remove the disheartening uncertainty caused by steadily declining inventories and consistent deterioration in the wood supply under which our graphic arts industries and other industrial groups dependent on Canadian imports have labored in the last year.[44]

The improvement in the newsprint supply situation was embarrassing to the War Production Board and awkward from the Canadian point of view in view of its disturbing effect on efforts to preserve a balanced production of cultural papers and specialized pulps. In answer to suggestions that the favourable position of the newsprint industry was dictated by commercial considerations, the Timber Controller pointed out to the War Production Board:

> No advantages have been granted to producers of pulpwood for newsprint companies that have not also been granted to other pulpwood producers. All producers are subject to the same wage ceilings, to the same income tax regulations, and to similar conditions of work. The differences in results attained lie in the fact that the newsprint companies are exceedingly well organized, and that they have at their own expense kept a large number of canvassers continually scouring the country to get men into their camps, which cannot be done to anything like the same extent either by lumber operators or pulpwood operators who are not organized in the same manner as the large newsprint corporations.[45]

Despite the element of confusion introduced by the revision of the Canadian supply forecast, the Requirements Committee of the War Production Board established an overall allocation pattern for pulp and paper products in mid-December, 1943. The resultant Program Determination required a complete revision of Limitation Order L-240 covering newsprint.[46] Under the new order, large publishers were to have their newsprint consumption cut roughly 25 per cent below base period consumption and a sliding scale of proportionately smaller cuts was introduced for smaller consumers. Comparable action was taken by the War Production Board to restrict the use of other cultural papers and paper products. The new techniques of control based on Program Determinations of the Requirements Committee represented a major advance over the somewhat chaotic set of regulations which had developed piecemeal.

Early in 1944, meetings were held in Washington between senior officials of the War Production Board and the Wartime Prices and Trade Board to review the misunderstandings and difficulties which had arisen in December. As a result of the very frank discussions at that time, the personality conflicts which had developed were largely allayed and the way was cleared for the more satisfactory conduct of negotiations in the future.

The troublesome problem of administrative restrictions on exports of pulpwood, typified by Timber Control Order No. 20, remained. In the course of the discussions between the pulp and paper officials of the two countries in October, it had been agreed to cancel Timber Control Order No. 20, if the United States would impose price ceilings on imported Canadian pulpwood to lessen the wide price differential in the two countries. Although the War Production Board had undertaken to make appropriate representations to the Office of Price Administration, there had been a series of delays and, at one point, a change in the attitude of the War Production Board. Canadian domestic ceilings on pulpwood were increased early in February, 1944,[47] but it was not until May 1 that the Office of Price Administration fixed maximum prices on pulpwood imported into the United States from Quebec, New Brunswick, and Nova Scotia.[48] Timber Control Order No. 20 was accordingly revoked on May 1, 1944.[49] The cancellation of this order belatedly marked the end of a difficult and confusing period.

By about the end of 1943, the mechanics of controlling pulp and paper had been fairly well developed, and for the balance of the wartime period, it was possible to make the minor adjustments in the programmes of the two countries without arousing the animosity and mistrust which had characterized the period of adjustment. The attention which has been paid to discord and difficulties should not be allowed to obscure the fact that very satisfactory working relations were achieved in the balance of the wartime period. Before commenting briefly on general developments in 1944 and later, the intervention of the Combined Boards in the pulp and paper field will be discussed briefly.

3. THE EXCURSUS INTO COMBINED PLANNING

By the summer of 1943, quite an array of national and international agencies had intervened at one time or another in the pulp and paper problem. The Joint Economic Committees, for example, had attempted to lay down the basic principles which should govern the allocation of North American forest products but they were either ignored or long since forgotten. The Wartime Prices and Trade Board, which had appealed to the Joint Economic Committees in late 1941, again decided in the spring of 1943 that it would be useful to have some impartial and authoritative body review the whole range of problems involved in the consumption of pulp and paper in North America. It was the Canadian view that the root of the difficulties was the inability or unwillingness of the War Production Board to achieve the cuts in consumption imposed by limitation orders. This was particularly awkward in the case of newsprint for which orders from publishers in the United States were higher than the levels permitted under Limitation Order L-240 throughout the wartime period. It was not the function of the Wartime Prices and Trade Board to enforce compliance with War Production Board orders. Moreover, Canadian inability to supply the inflated demands of United

States buyers stimulated a good deal of adverse comment in the United States press. Paper curtailment was a contentious issue in the United States, and the United States side of the Combined Production and Resources Board welcomed the possibility of high-level support for the curtailment programme of the War Production Board. Therefore, primarily at the instance of the Wartime Prices and Trade Board, it was recommended at a meeting of the Combined Production and Resources Board on July 15, 1943, that a committee of the Combined Boards be constituted to study, and report on, the requirements, supplies, uses, production and distribution of the products of the pulp and paper industries of the United Kingdom, the United States, and Canada. As a result, the Combined Pulp and Paper Committee, consisting of a New York industrialist, a Canadian financier, and the United Kingdom Member on the Combined Raw Materials Board, none of whom had previous connections with the pulp and paper industry, was appointed on August 23.

After a series of meetings during the summer and early fall, the Combined Pulp and Paper Committee submitted a preliminary report early in October to its parent committees, the Combined Production and Resources Board and the Combined Raw Materials Board. In this report, considerable attention was given to conservation and extension of raw material supplies by reducing the weight of paper, particularly newsprint, using less sulphite pulp and more mineral filler and wastepaper. It was also urged that the manpower authorities give special consideration to deferring workers in the woods, and that efforts be made to recruit casual labour and prisoners-of-war for pulpwood cutting.

The recommendations about the reduction in the demand for paper products were not startling. It was proposed that wasteful methods of packaging be eliminated and that a widespread salvage campaign be initiated. Without becoming very specific, the Combined Pulp and Paper Committee recommended that further steps be taken in curtailing the non-essential use of paper and, in general, limiting the consumption of paper, paperboard, and woodpulp.

By early 1944, after several more months of deliberation, the Committee prepared a final report which, from the Canadian point of view, contained several fundamental weaknesses. The main objection was that the draft report recounted the real or fancied inadequacies of Canada's performance as a supplier, although a number of the charges had not been considered by the Committee. Finally, after the elimination of the features of the report objectionable to Canada, it was approved by the parent Boards in February, 1944.

In its final report, the Combined Pulp and Paper Committee gave strong encouragement to the diversion of pulpwood from the production of newsprint to the production of pulp, and to the further substitution of pulp production for newsprint production in newsprint mills in both Canada and the United States. It was also recommended that pulpwood supplies in the Pacific Northwest should be allocated so as to make the best use of the capacity of dissolving pulp mills on both sides of the border.

Another important suggestion was that the representatives of the wartime agencies concerned with pulp and paper in both countries should continue to explore the possibilities of achieving amicable working arrangements for the settlement of their problems, and that improved administrative co-ordination should be striven for. In particular, it was agreed that the operating officials of both countries should try to reach a satisfactory agreement on the operation of Canadian export controls, particularly Timber Control Order No. 20.

The Combined Pulp and Paper Committee also made recommendations, discussed in a later section of this chapter, concerning the supply of woods labour. Immediately following the acceptance of its final report, the Committee was dissolved, in accordance with its own wishes.

It was hoped originally, at least by the Canadians concerned, that the Combined Pulp and Paper Committee would make specific recommendations concerning restrictions on the consumption of paper. Apart from some general statements on the desirability of limiting non-essential end-uses, the Committee conspicuously failed to do this. To this extent, the excursus into combined planning under formal auspices was a complete failure. Much of the attention of the Committee, particularly in its early stages, was devoted to technical matters of relatively minor significance which might better have been left to administrative officials. Despite its disappointing performance, the Committee managed to establish very clearly that there was an alarming shortage of pulp and paper products, a point which had often been challenged by influential, it not authoritative, groups. This conclusion, in itself, was useful to the War Production Board in providing independent support for conservation measures. In another way, the Committee had a certain cathartic value; it clarified, if it did not resolve, certain issues between officials of the two countries by providing a forum for the recital of various inequities and inadequacies. Probably the most important result of the deliberations of the Combined Pulp and Paper Committee was to call attention to the importance of woods labour and to the urgent necessity for government measures to increase the manpower available for the forest products industry.

4. THE ADJUSTMENT OF SUPPLY AND DEMAND

Relations between pulp and paper officials of Canada and the United States were more satisfactory after the administrative reorganization of the War Production Board which led to the establishment of the Forest Products Bureau. Although there were misunderstandings and disagreements which culminated in a series of heated exchanges in late 1943 and early 1944, co-operative arrangements improved steadily thereafter.

During the whole of 1944 and the first half of 1945, newsprint shipments from Canada continued at the steady rate of 200,000 tons a month, while woodpulp shipments were reduced somewhat to the rate of approximately 1,000,000 tons a year from 1944 to 1945 as a result of the increased pulp requirements of the United Kingdom. The agreement providing for the equal sharing of supplies of "purchased" pulpwood with minimum exports of 1,250,000 cords continued on into 1945. After a slight relaxation in Limitation Order L-240, newsprint shipments from Canada were raised to 220,000 tons a month beginning in the third quarter of 1945.[50]

By October 1, 1945, all controls over pulp and paper had been lifted in the United States with two exceptions. Conservation Order M-241 which required pulp producers to set aside a proportion of their output continued in effect. Newsprint consumption continued to be regulated by Limitation Order L-240, although the restrictions were relaxed. In the fourth quarter of 1945, Canadian exports of newsprint to United States were increased to 230,000 tons a month and, finally, control over the use of newsprint, except for inventory restrictions, was removed at the end of 1945.[51] The corresponding control in Canada was lifted at the same time.[52]

To devote so much attention to the detailed difficulties which arose prior to 1944 and to dismiss the equally long period during which relations were marked by complete co-operation with a few summary comments may give a distorted picture of the relations of Canada and the United States in the pulp and paper field. The mere fact that the supply and demand relations between the two countries were adjusted satisfactorily means that any problems which arose were essentially residual. They did not raise new issues of policy nor did they threaten to impair good relations between the two countries. The machinery of co-operation which had been created was adequate to deal with the issues which did arise. Some of the special problems which arose were merely special aspects of the central supply problems. Others concerned mainly technical and political questions. A discussion of newsprint export prices, overseas exports of pulp and paper, thirty-pound newsprint and woods labour will throw useful light on relations between Canada and the United States.

5. SPECIAL ISSUES

(a) *Export Prices for Newsprint*

The price of newsprint paper was a bone of contention between the United States and Canada during and immediately after the first world war. In 1920, the price of newsprint in New York rose to over $120 a ton, a fact which publishers in the United States remembered with bitterness. During the second world war, the price of newsprint again became a contentious issue. To complicate matters, agencies of the two governments became involved and the actual buyers and sellers watched their bargaining being carried out for them by government negotiators. From the Canadian point of view, the welfare of the newsprint industry was a matter of some official concern. It was not only an immediate source of hard currency, but a hope for the future as well. In the United States, which normally purchased about 90 per cent of the Canadian output of newsprint, the newspaper publishers felt that it was appropriate for their government to protect them from exorbitant price increases, this being interpreted rather narrowly.

Although prices of other pulp and paper products had risen substantially since the outbreak of war, the price of Canadian standard newsprint had remained unchanged at $50 a ton in New York from the beginning of 1938 until the end of 1941. Early in December, 1941, the International Paper Company announced that newsprint prices would be increased to $53 a ton beginning in the second quarter, an announcement which was echoed by other Canadian producers.[53] At this time, a bill designed to give the Office of Price Administration statutory authority to fix prices was the subject of stormy debate in the United States Congress.[54] It can be surmised that the Office of Price Administration feared that the prospective increase in newsprint prices would antagonize the press in the United States and might stimulate an intensified publicity campaign damaging to the whole price control programme, including the legislation before Congress. The Office of Price Administration took immediate steps to analyse the cost-price structure of the industry to determine whether the proposed price increase was justified. Any such investigation would be inadequate unless accountants of the Office of Price Administration could make detailed analyses of the books of Canadian firms, a procedure which was rejected as improper by the Canadian industry and the Wartime Prices and Trade Board. The fact that Canadian newsprint companies and executives were being threatened with anti-trust proceedings in the United States at this time may have had some bearing on the Canadian attitude. Following discussions with the Office of Price Administration, the Wartime Prices and Trade Board undertook to have a detailed analysis of costs of production prepared in support of the Canadian case. The action of the Wartime Prices and Trade Board in sponsoring the increased price was unusual. Normally, price ceilings on Canadian exports to the United States were accepted as a matter of course although the Wartime Prices and Trade Board was willing to take an interest in commodities of which Canada was a major source of supply. Newsprint and asbestos are cases in point. In this particular instance, the Wartime Prices and Trade Board intervened partly in order to submit cost data on the Canadian industry and partly because it was believed that the well-being of the industry was in danger. While negotiations were still in progress between the two agencies the Office of Price Administration imposed a temporary price ceiling of $50 a ton for a sixty-day period beginning April 1, 1942, pending the completion of the cost studies.[55] After examination of data from both Canadian and United States mills, the Office of Price Administration concluded that profits in the industry had not fallen below the 1936-39 level and that costs had not risen to such an extent that they could not be absorbed. The temporary ceiling price was therefore confirmed in a new price regulation issued at about the end of April, 1942, the preamble to which stated:

In the judgment of the Price Administrator, the price of Standard Newsprint Paper is threatening to rise to an extent and in a manner inconsistent with the purposes of the Emergency Price Control Act of 1942.[56]

The Wartime Prices and Trade Board recognized the political difficulties involved in adjusting ceiling prices in the United States and, without concurring in the decision of the Office of Price Administration, did not press the issue of newsprint prices until the end of 1942. The Canadian industry had been seriously affected by various measures restricting not only output but power, transportation, and labour, with the result that average production costs were increasing. The Wartime Prices and Trade Board again approached the Office of Price Administration early in 1943 requesting an increase of $8 per ton in the price of newsprint. After some delay, occasioned by the appointment of a new Price Administrator, the Office of Price Administration agreed to an increase of $4 a ton effective March 1, 1943, although it was clearly stated that this decision did not preclude reopening the price discussion later.[57] At the same time, the Canadian domestic ceiling on newsprint prices was increased $4 a ton over basic period prices.[58] In April, the Wartime Prices and Trade Board did reopen the question of newsprint prices, proposing an increase in the United States ceiling price to $60 a ton. The Office of Price Administration was not willing to raise the ceiling beyond $58, despite Canadian protests that the increase of $4 a ton was inadequate. Effective September 1, 1943, the ceiling price in both countries was increased $4 a ton.[59] There were two later increases in United States newsprint ceiling prices but these were not the result of representations by Canada. The first of these, effective April 1, 1945, raised the price to $61 a ton,[60] and the second, which increased prices to $67 a ton, went into effect on December 11, 1945.[61] The Canadian domestic ceiling was not changed to conform to these revisions and remained in effect until May 1, 1946, when the ceiling on newsprint prices in Canada was suspended.

The intervention of the Wartime Prices and Trade Board in the newsprint price negotiations was justified on the grounds that Canada was a principal source of supply for the United States. Except under such circumstances, the Canadian government did not question price ceilings established in the United States. The desirability of such a policy of non-intervention is amply shown by the difficulties which bedevilled the Canadian efforts. The original reason for governmental intervention was to preserve the confidential nature of information about Canadian costs, but it was almost inevitable that the Wartime Prices and Trade Board should also act as a partisan bargaining agent. This meant that a Canadian government agency was deeply involved in controversial issues between the newsprint industry and the publishers, and that the animosity of the publishers in the United States tended to be directed towards Canada instead of the newsprint industry. Fortunately, the Canadian negotiations were handled by mature and reasonable officials who were anxious to avoid unilateral action by either country. Canada was consistently disappointed in the outcome of the negotiations, but it was never seriously proposed that concessions should be forced from the United States by withholding supplies. This might have been a natural line for negotiators from the industry to take, but any prospective embargo would have immediately involved the two governments. Under these circumstances, or any other circumstances where the national interest is sufficiently involved, it may be preferable to have the government intervene from the beginning rather than at the point where private negotiations have broken down amid angry press releases in an atmosphere of bitterness and recrimination. An unsatisfactory compromise reached after confidential negotiations is probably more satisfactory than the same agreement arrived at after much drum-beating and sabre-rattling in the newspapers.

(b) Overseas Exports of Pulp and Paper

When the overseas exports of Scandinavia stopped, Canada and Newfoundland became the only net exporters of pulp and paper products in the non-Axis world. About 75 per cent of total domestic production of pulp and paper products was exported and nearly 95 per cent of the output of newsprint was exported. Although the United States absorbed the bulk of Canadian exports, particularly of newsprint, the Latin American countries and Australia and New Zealand depended on Canada for 80 per cent of their newsprint needs.

Because of the importance of newsprint as a weapon of political warfare, Canadian newsprint shipments to Latin America were carefully controlled and directed. Arrangements were worked out between the Department of State and the Canadian export control and shipping authorities in late 1942 to furnish the needs of friendly newspapers in Latin America and, at the same time, to prevent the diversion of newsprint to pro-Axis publishers. The Department of State, with the advice of United States missions in the different Latin American countries, established quotas of newsprint each quarter for each country and for each newspaper. The policy was to provide newspapers with sufficient newsprint to maintain operations, although this normally involved a reduction below peacetime consumption levels. Obviously, unfriendly newspapers were given no quota. Canadian suppliers continued to export to their old customers and the needs of newspapers previously dependent on Scandinavian supplies were filled by various mills under the direction of the Newsprint Administrator with the co-operation of the Canadian Newsprint Association.

The technique of controlling shipments of newsprint to Latin America was unusual since it was exercised during most of the wartime period through the allocation of freight space and not by the more usual system of issuing export permits. Newsprint was exempted from the export permit regulations early in November, 1942, when shipped to any part of the Western Hemisphere except the colonies or possessions of France.[62] Newsprint quotas for Latin America were administered by the Canadian Shipping Priorities Committee, which, by granting or withholding shipping priorities, could effectively direct the movement of newsprint to approved customers. The quotas of both newspapers and countries were revised periodically in accordance with changing requirements. The operation of this system was marked by the most intimate and harmonious co-operation between the United States and Canada which continued until the suspension of shipping controls after the war. Control over newsprint was not abandoned until the middle of January, 1946.[63] The end of the war meant that it was no longer so essential to maintain newsprint supplies to Latin America. In the immediate post-war scramble for newsprint, some Latin American countries found their imports dwindling instead of growing, a fact that was very disappointing, but perhaps understandable.

There was also very close co-operation between the Wartime Prices and Trade Board and the War Production Board in arranging for newsprint exports for liberated areas. The division of supply responsibility had originally been worked out at the end of July, 1944, in connection with procurement of newsprint by United States government agencies. At that time, it was agreed that 70 per cent of such newsprint requirements would be obtained in Canada and 30 per cent in the United States. Any quantities purchased in Canada under this agreement were to be deducted from the amounts which Canada was committed to supply to the United States. The scheme was intended to make procurement and scheduling of production easier and was based on the fact that about 70 per cent of United States supplies of newsprint were imported from Canada. Early in October, 1944, it was decided to extend the same scheme to cover the requirements of liberated areas for the first six months of 1945. This meant that 30 per cent of liberated area requirements were to be supplied by the United States, while the remaining 70 per cent was to be deducted from Canadian exports to the United States. The fact that Canada was already committed to exporting 95 per cent of its output of newsprint meant that there was no real inequity in shifting the burden of supplying the needs of liberated areas to the United States.

(c) Thirty-Pound Newsprint

Techniques of conserving virgin pulp fibre by using waste paper and other extenders had been emphasized from the beginning of the paper shortage. The reduction in the weight of newsprint seemed to be a natural application of these methods. The agitation for lighter weight newsprint was started by publishers in the United States around the end of 1943, and considerable direct and indirect pressure was brought to bear on the Canadian industry to change its product. Standard newsprint weighs thirty-two pounds per 500 sheets 24" x 36" and Canadian mills were adapted to making newsprint of this type. Not the least important reason was the fact that standard newsprint was entitled to enter the United States free of duty. From the point of view of the United States publishers, thirty-pound newsprint had the alluring feature that it yields 6 per cent more yardage per ton than standard newsprint. Under pressure from the newspaper publishers, the War Production Board supported the change to the lighter grade. Unfortunately, the production of thirty-pound newsprint involved technical difficulties sufficient to outweigh the superficial increase of yardage per ton. The Wartime Prices and Trade Board, officially recognizing the clamour for thirty-pound newsprint, advised the War Production Board that the change would probably involve a decline in both the tonnage and yardage available from Canada. For one thing, the high-speed machines used for standard newsprint would have to be run at less than capacity to avoid excessive tearing and breaking of the lighter paper. For another, wood extension methods could not be used effectively for producing mixed weights because the proportion of filler and other extenders used for the two grades varied. There were also managerial difficulties involved in producing the two grades in the same plant. Pulp and paper officials of the War Production Board came to Canada to determine the validity of the claims of the Canadian industry and were able to see that the technical difficulties outweighed any apparent gains.

Despite this, the campaign of the newspaper publishers was well under way. The United States tariff was amended by Congress, effective February 26, 1944, to allow the duty-free entry of thirty-pound newsprint.[64] To allow time for consideration of the problems involved, the Newsprint Administrator, with the concurrence of the War Production Board, issued an order at the end of February prohibiting the manufacture of thirty-pound newsprint for North American consumption during March and April.[65] Near the end of April, the pulp and paper officials in the two countries agreed to permit the industry to produce both thirty-two- and thirty-pound newsprint as an experiment during May and June.[66] Production was to be scheduled in accordance with orders certified by the War Production Board. Price ceilings were adjusted in both Canada and the United States by allowing thirty-pound newsprint an increase of $4 per ton over the ceiling for standard newsprint after May 1, 1944.[67]

The results of production in the experimental period were carefully examined in June by officials of the Wartime Prices and Trade Board, the War Production Board, the Canadian producers, and a committee of the newspaper publishers in the United States. It was seen that the production of thirty-pound newsprint was resulting in a loss of about 10,000 tons a month and that the initial warnings of the Canadians had been amply borne out. The committee of the publishers recommended that the export target of 200,000 tons of standard newsprint per month be reinstated and that anyone ordering thirty-pound newsprint have his tonnage quota reduced to maintain his yardage quota unchanged. At the end of June, the War Production Board officially announced that users of thirty-pound newsprint would have their quotas reduced 6¾ per cent below the amounts allowed under Limitation Order L-240.[68] This effectively eliminated any advantage to the consumers of thirty-pound newsprint with the result that normal trade in standard newsprint was quickly resumed.

This whole episode illustrates the suspicious attitude of the newspaper publishers to the Canadian newsprint industry. Canadian assurances, based on a detailed technical knowledge of industry operations, that thirty-pound newsprint could not be produced satisfactorily, were rejected and it was necessary to carry out a complex, troublesome, and costly experiment with the net result that the operations of Canadian mills was impaired and exports reduced. Refusal by the Canadian industry to supply thirty-pound newsprint would certainly have been regarded as an attempt to preserve commercial or financial advantages at the expense of the rationed newsprint users in the United States. The Canadian willingness to experiment, if it did nothing else, probably convinced the publishers that the Canadian industry was co-operative even if, in their eyes, it was saddled with outmoded ways of producing newsprint. Unfortunately, it was a hard, technical fact that newsprint machines can be run at maximum speeds when producing standard newsprint and that lighter paper can be produced only at slower speeds and hence more inefficiently.

(d) Woods Labour

Toward the end of 1941, the Joint Economic Committees became concerned about the movement of woods labour from Quebec and New Brunswick into Maine. Although a seasonal movement of this sort was usual, the number of migrants had increased markedly in the winter of 1941, partly in response to higher wage rates in the United States and the imposition of a wage ceiling in Canada. In particular, the movement of several thousand Canadian lumbermen to Maine to work on the manufacture of shell-casing boxes was disturbing to Canada. The only limitations on such outflows of labour at the time were the immigration regulations of the United States which were of negligible effect since the United States customarily waived passport and visa requirements for seasonal workers crossing the border if they were bonded. It was the opinion of the Joint Economic Committees that it would be more satisfactory to exercise the control in the country of origin in order to prevent excessive migration which might reduce the manpower available for essential production. Accordingly, about the middle of January, 1942, a formal recommendation was prepared by the Joint Economic Committees, the essential clauses of which were:

1. Each country should permit the departure of labour to the other subject only to the military service regulations of the respective countries and to such safeguards as are necessary to ensure that labour is not withdrawn from its own war industries or essential civilian industries;

2. There should be a continuous exchange of information between the employment services of the two countries concerning the available supply of labour in border areas with a view to its more effective utilization; and that for this purpose direct communication between neighbouring employment offices in the two countries should be encouraged; . . . .[69]

The number of these migratory workers had increased to about 7,400 prior to the summer of 1942. This outflow was recognized as a drain on the dwindling supply of Canadian manpower and negotiations between the Department of Labour and the War Manpower Commission in July, 1942, resulted in an agreement to fix a quota of 3,700, one-half the number in the previous year.

This severe reduction led to a serious shortage of woods labour in the Northeastern United States. The situation was particularly acute in Maine, where a mill had just been reopened to cut airplane spruce. The need for loggers to work in the spruce forests was urgent and the War Manpower Commission recommended the release of 1,250 Canadians to work in the Maine woods. At the same time, it was being proposed that loggers from Washington and Oregon should be permitted to enter British Columbia to cut hemlock, unless the Canadian export ban could be removed. Local political interests were heavily involved in both these proposals, and, in the East, the Canadian authorities yielded and increased the quota of migratory woods labour by 500, on the understanding that the border would be closed to these movements after mid-January.

Bitter opposition to the policy of the government in permitting the exodus and especially in increasing the quota was expressed because of the shortage of men in the Canadian woods.[70] There were also suggestions that the logging interests in New England had influenced the Canadian decision but the Minister of Labour pointed out that the War Manpower Commission had conducted the negotiations on behalf of the United States. He went on to say:

We take what I might call a broad view of the question. We felt it was a duty as good neighbours at least in part to comply with the request of the United States.[71]

In the spring of 1943, a new agreement was reached between the Department of Labour and the War Manpower Commission to allow 3,500 Canadians to enter the United States to work in the woods in the period June 15 to October 31. Canadian producers cutting in the United States were to be assigned 800 of the migrant workers. These arrangements were naturally of keen interest to the United States producers and the erroneous impression was gained that the Canadian authorities had specified that the men were not to be allowed to cut pulpwood for newsprint. This would have involved flagrant interference with manpower controls in the United States and, in fact, was not true. The understanding between the two government agencies was that the bulk of the Canadians were to be engaged in cutting airplane timber. Despite the quota which had been agreed on, the Canadian authorities suspended the issuance of further exit permits on July 22, 1943, when about 2,550 Canadians had crossed the border. The United States producers and the War Production Board considered this action to be unduly restrictive and in conflict with the general understanding that resources of all kinds would be pooled. During the fall and winter, the restrictions were relaxed sufficiently to fill the quota.

In February, 1944, Canadian policy was subject to spirited newspaper attack in the United States. A correspondent of the *Boston Herald* had claimed that hundreds of men were idle in several small border towns in Quebec because they could not get exit permits to go to the United States.[72] The mayor of one of the small towns was quoted as saying that 500 men could be recuited in a few hours to work in the New England woods. The Truman Committee became involved in the question and implied that the Canadians were not being very co-operative. In its *Third Annual Report,* the Committee stated:

The committee is advised that surveys made by experienced recruitment officers indicated 2,500 or more workers are now available in Canada and could be immediately employed by logging operators in the Northeast. Statements have been obtained from mayors on the Canadian side of the border indicating that such workers are available. However, this is not admitted by the Canadian Government. Officials of the State Department have been endeavouring to bring about more favourable consideration by the Canadian Government.[73]

The Minister of Labour commented on these claims in the House of Commons and stated that a careful investigation of the border countries had failed to disclose any pool of surplus labour.[74] Rather, the labour shortages in the area affirmed the necessity of restricting the migration to the quota of 3,500.

The whole question was re-examined in the spring of 1944 and another agreement was reached between the manpower authorities of the two countries to allow Canadian woodsmen to remain in the United States after April 30, the normal expiry date of the exit permits.[75] The arrangement was that 3,500 men would be allowed to remain in the United States for an indefinite period. The situation did not change appreciably during the rest of the wartime period.

The adoption of controls over the migration of Canadian woods labour to New England exemplifies the problems which arose in preventing an undue drain on Canadian supplies as a result of the disparity in price levels in the two countries. Export controls over commodities were necessary to prevent excessive exports of goods which could command higher prices in the United States. Similarly, the device of exit permits was necessary to counteract the allure of higher wages in the United States which tended to deplete the supply of manpower available for agriculture and for woods operations on the Canadian side of the border. The control over migratory woods labour was complicated by local political pressures. At least one of the politically powerful pulp and paper companies in New England conducted a campaign to influence the manpower and pulp and paper officials in both countries to liberalize the border restrictions on migrant workers.

6. Lumber

The unhappy events of the spring of 1940 led to a sudden large-scale increase in the needs of the United Kingdom for Canadian softwood lumber. Scandinavian sources of supply were cut off and requirements of lumber for specialized uses and for war construction in general rose rapidly. Canadian domestic requirements had also expanded under the impetus of the accelerated war production programme beginning in the early summer of 1940. In order to prevent the disorganization of the lumber market and particularly to protect the needs of the United Kingdom, a Timber Controller was appointed under the Department of Munitions and Supply late in June, 1940.[76] As noted earlier, one of the first acts of the Timber Controller early in July was to prohibit the export of Douglas fir sawlogs to the United States, on the grounds that the total Canadian supply was needed to fill United Kingdom and domestic orders. Despite the crudity of an embargo as a method of control, this established a precedent for similar action by the Timber Controller on a number of future occasions.

During the first six months of 1941, the domestic demand for lumber slackened and Canadian lumber exports to the United States increased as a result of the growing demands there and the relatively attractive export prices. From 1939 to 1941, Canadian lumber exports to the United States doubled, a fact which may have encouraged the view that lumber would be available in the United States in almost limitless quantities. It was true that there was an ample supply in 1940 and 1941, and that wood tended to be used as a substitute for more critical materials on almost all possible occasions. By the spring of 1942, difficulties began to develop in the military procurement of lumber. As a result, the War Production Board issued a limitation order in May, giving the Army and Navy priority in the purchase of softwood construction lumber.[77] The Timber Control co-operated fully in arranging for the compliance of Canadian exporters by the issuance of two directive letters by the Timber Controller on June 5 and June 18, 1942, prohibiting exports to the United States of softwood lumber covered by Limitation Order L-121 unless the purchase was allowed by the order. This meant that the Canadian supplier had to obtain a declaration from his customer in the United States that the order had been specifically approved by the War Production Board or was otherwise authorized by the regulation. This arrangement was continued under General Conservation Order M-208 which replaced L-121 in August and established a general system of priorities for construction lumber.[78] Demands of the United States for Canadian lumber continued to be high throughout the summer of 1942 and threatened to disrupt the flow of lumber going to the United Kingdom and to the domestic market. The Timber Controller emphasized his intention of protecting domestic requirements in a letter to the trade in June, 1942, in which he stated:

While we are fully aware of the needs in the United States for lumber from Canada and while it is our desire to meet this need where we can, nevertheless, we must first take care of Canadian requirements both direct and indirect.[79]

By the fall, the Canadian supply situation, particularly in British Columbia, had deteriorated badly. In an analysis of the British Columbia situation in October, the Timber Controller noted that there was a backlog of 95,000,000 board feet in unshipped orders for Canadian war projects. The United Kingdom Timber Controller urgently needed lumber in quantities which would absorb half the monthly output. No new orders for shipment to the United States had been accepted since early in July but there remained an unfilled backlog of 40,000,000 board feet for essential projects in the United States. To make matters worse, production had fallen by about 15 per cent in the previous four months.[80] Production in British Columbia was under allocation by the Timber Control but the basic problem was one of a serious overall shortage.

Action was taken early in November, 1942, to impose export control over all lumber shipments to the United States and other non-Empire destinations.[81] Despite the existence of priority restrictions, the volume of potential rated orders was so large that this system did not provide an effective upper limit on exports, however useful it may have been to the War Production Board in implementing priorities. The issue was the familiar one. Prices in the United States were appreciably higher than in Canada, which meant that the overall volume of exports had to be limited and the permissible exports allocated equitably among the Canadian producers. The plan for controlling British Columbia output in 1943 was announced by the Timber Controller early in the year. The target was to export 40 per cent of output to the United Kingdom, 5 per cent to other British Dominions, 12 per cent to the United States, and to retain 43 per cent for domestic consumption. However, the announcement went on to say that no Douglas fir sawlogs were to be exported to the United States in 1943. Pulping logs were not to be exported until later in the year when the export of some hemlock and balsam from Crown-grant lands might be allowed. Even then, according to the announcement:

> The intention is to grant permits only for logs 19″ and under and to endeavour to grant such permits for logs that can best be spared from the Canadian market and on the most equitable basis possible.[82]

Further restrictive action was taken in the spring of 1943, when all lumber exports to the United States from the three Prairie Provinces and the interior of British Columbia were banned, the domestic producers being granted price increases to compensate them for the loss of this market.

From the point of view of the United States, certain aspects of Canadian policy were to be deplored. The major cause for complaint was the restrictive regulations governing exports from British Columbia. While the original embargo on the export of Douglas fir sawlogs had been replaced by an export permit system, there were long periods when all export permits were refused. This policy came to the attention of the Truman Committee which served as a convenient sounding-board for United States operators who were pressing for more generous exports from Canada. The record of Canadian performance in supplying the United States with Douglas fir sawlogs was none too prepossessing. In 1939, about 34,000,000 board feet of these logs were exported to the United States, while the quantity dropped to about 430,000 board feet in 1943. It is perhaps understandable that several members of the Truman Committee should be disturbed by the Canadian action in restricting Douglas fir exports to the United States. Actually, when it is recognized that Canadian exports usually amounted to less than one per cent of the total annual production in the Pacific Northwest, the quantitative effects of the Canadian embargo were not very important. The matter was discussed at length by the Department of Munitions and Supply and the War Production Board and finally, in April, 1944, it was agreed to set an annual export quota of 17,500,000 board feet.[83]

The existence of export controls when export prices were higher than domestic prices raised a number of difficult problems of equity which could not be resolved satisfactorily without fixing export quotas for individual producers on the basis of performance in some base period, an unsatisfactory device at best. In an effort to cope with this problem, as well as others, the Timber Control introduced a complex system of export credits in May, 1944.[84] Under the new system, a lumber producer in western Canada earned an export credit for lumber delivered to the three Prairie Provinces and part of northwestern Ontario. For every three cars shipped to this region, the producer earned the right to export either one and one-quarter or one and three-quarter cars, depending on the particular part of the region to which the lumber was delivered. Certain additional credits were given for deliveries into these areas in the six months prior to May 1 when the scheme was inaugurated. In June, 1944, the rules were modified and the credits liberalized, to allow for a credit of one car for every four cars shipped to eastern Canada.[85] The system meant, in effect, that a producer could obtain permission to export quantities of lumber which varied directly with the amounts he had made available for the domestic market. This system provided for a sharing of available supplies and was not subject to the criticism levelled at more drastic methods of preventing excessive exports.

Criticism of the lumber controls was not restricted to the United States. The Canadian lumber producers were naturally keenly interested in the price ceilings fixed by the Office of Price Administration and were often quite bitter about what they considered to be the niggardly attitude of the United States. One offending regulation was issued in May, 1943, and established ceilings on Canadian lumber sold in the Northeastern states.[86] One editorial from a Canadian trade magazine lamented this unfriendly action as follows:

No government department either in Canada or the United States is in a position to accurately estimate the price requirements of an industry located in a foreign country and operating under a set of laws and conditions over which the governmental authority of such department has no control. . . . We cannot believe that they [the American people] will fail to see the inconsistency in their lashing themselves into indignation on the subject of Germans riding rough-shod over German enemies while condoning an action by one of their own government departments which cavalierly disregards the rights of their own closest friends and allies. Especially can we not believe it when it is so obviously apparent that such action would be so crippling to U.S.A. war effort.[87]

The stir which was created over Canadian export policy was symptomatic of the critical lumber shortage which developed in the United States in 1943. One reason for this was the changing character of the war and the enormous requirements for lumber for packaging material to be sent to theatres of war all over the world. Between 1942 and 1943, requirements for boxes, crates, and dunnage rose from nine and one-half billion board feet to sixteen billion board feet and were expected to continue increasing in 1944. By the end of 1943, inventories were declining, production was falling, and, in general, it was clear that a vigorous and tight control system was essential. As a result, in the spring of 1944, a complete allocation system was adopted for lumber, effective August 1. The regulations contained in Limitation Order L-335, provided for quarterly allocations to military and export claimants, large industrial consumers, and other groups.[88] The major users required the prior approval of the War Production Board before purchases against their quotas could be made. This order represented a determined effort to balance supply and requirements. It was a good deal more inclusive than any of the control schemes which had been introduced in Canada, according to an editorial in the *Canada Lumberman*, which commented:

It is far broader in its application and more rigid in its controls than any restrictions or regulations which have been applied in Canada for practically all producers, distributors and consumers come under some of its many and varied applications.[89]

Arrangements were made between the Department of Munitions and Supply and the War Production Board for the complete participation of Canada in the new control system before it became effective. The Timber Controller circularized the Canadian industry with a warning that no purchaser in the United States was authorized to import lumber from Canada except in accordance with the terms of L-335 and that export permits would not be granted unless accompanied by a properly certified purchase order.[90]

The new limitation order also affected Canadians importing either hardwood or softwood from the United States. Directive letters were issued by the Timber Controller to Canadian importers pointing out that no one could import lumber from the United States unless the order had been approved by the Timber Controller, the Priorities Branch of the Department of Munitions and Supply, and the Canadian Division of the War Production Board.[91] The total Canadian quarterly allocation was set at the same rate prevailing in 1943 and individual importers were also assigned individual quotas limiting them to their 1943 rates. This system continued in effect until the allocation of lumber was suspended in the United States at the end of September, 1945.[92]

This detailed intermingling of controls is a good example of the co-operation of administrative officials in Canada and the United States. From the beginning the mechanics of co-operation worked very smoothly, although, at times, the Canadian policy appeared to depart rather widely from the principles of the Hyde Park Declaration. The imposition of restrictive export controls was justified by the fact that there were urgent domestic and export needs which had to be met before any surplus could be made available for export to the United States. It was precisely this reasoning that Canadian officials most intimately concerned with export controls between the United States and Canada resisted most strenuously throughout the war. The equitable sharing of scarce supplies was a much more valuable guide from the Canadian point of view. It would have been unfortunate to establish the principle that domestic scarcity justified an export embargo of forest products of any kind. The natural extension of the principle to iron and steel products would have been greeted with great alarm in Canada.

7. Conclusion

The manufacture of forest products is an enormous North American industry and production is sufficiently specialized in Canada and the United States to allow a large volume of two-way trade. The character of this trade, and production and consumption patterns in North America, had to be adjusted to meet special wartime needs and the adjustment seemed to offer an ideal opportunity to apply the general principles of economic co-operation which had developed early in the war. Resources could be pooled and the economies integrated, or so it seemed. Integration, unfortunately, is apt to be a painful process in a contracting sector of the economy. In the case of pulp and paper and forest products generally, there were technical, historical, and political reasons why the adjustment process should be uncomfortable. The rigidities which existed account for the difficulties encountered in the period of adjustment prior to 1944.

In the United States, the demand for pulp and paper products was dominated by enormous demands for pulp, particularly dissolving pulp. This kind of pulp was used in the manufacture of rayon, plastics, explosives, cellophane, paints, lacquer, and photographic paper, the wartime demand for which soared to unprecedented levels. Much of the demand stemmed from military requirements of a high urgency. Civilian requirements for pulp products, such as cultural papers, could be restricted by government order. But, for reasons of equity, or, more bluntly, of politics, the restrictions on cultural papers could not be applied unevenly. Books, magazines, and newspapers had to be cut back impartially, which meant that the supply of book and magazine paper and of newsprint had to be adjusted accordingly. Canada, which supplied about three-quarters of the newsprint needs of the United States, was automatically drawn into the problem of adjusting exports to fit the fixed pattern of demand.

The adaptability of the Canadian output of pulp and paper was limited. The Canadian industry was designed to produce newsprint primarily and there was a definite limit on the extent to which pulp exports could be substituted for newsprint exports. The reasons were partly technical and partly financial. Since newsprint mills are not designed to produce pulp, the substitution of pulp for newsprint is uneconomical and a financial burden to the industry. During the early years of the war, the price concessions to the industry had been small and it was hardly reasonable to force the industry to revamp its pattern of output, unless it could be shown to be a necessary wartime measure. Above all, the difficulty arose from variability of raw material supplies. Forecasts of the pulpwood cut had to be made well in advance to permit plans to be made, but these forecasts were necessarily hazardous because of fluctuations in the supply of woods labour, not to mention the weather. Once conditions in the industry had stabilized, it was possible to predict with considerable precision the future pulpwood cut. Before this time, there were fundamental reasons why there should be "disheartening uncertainty" about Canadian exports.

Normally, the output of an industry producing civilian goods could be limited to a level sufficient to supply what were considered to be essential needs. Allocation or rationing procedures could be devised to distribute the output to these essential needs. This procedure was reversed in the case of pulp and paper; consumption limitations were adjusted periodically to varying supply conditions. In view of the influence of the newspaper publishers, any attempt to restrict paper consumption below the quantities available would have been rigorously resisted. The root of the difficulties between Canada and the United States was the fact that the pattern of Canadian exports did not match the pattern of United States demands. It is also true that some Canadian officials were apt to take the detached view that the problem of non-discriminatory restrictions on the consumption of cultural papers was a problem for the United States to deal with. A more sympathetic attitude might not have altered the basic disequilibrium but some unnecessary recrimination might have been avoided. Fortunately, a series of marginal adjustments of both supply and demand occurred early in 1944 and from that time on, satisfactory relations were restored in the pulp and paper field. It must be emphasized that, in the later years of the war, when the two economies were satisfactorily adjusted, relations were marked by complete friendliness and co-operation.

It would be incorrect to attribute the maladjustments which occurred solely to the basic structure of the industry or to the pressure of consumer groups. At least part of the difficulty arose from the glare of publicity with which all domestic and international negotiations were afflicted. The newspapers in the United States were particularly prone to attribute base motives to the Canadian pulp and paper industry, a fact which was mildly irritating to Canadian officials, not to mention the Canadian industry itself. It was also unfortunate that a number of Canadian actions seemed contrary to the general policy which was supposed to govern trade between the two countries. In particular, the Canadian action in mid-1942 in imposing outright embargoes on exports of certain types of logs, from British Columbia, was ill-advised. No doubt domestic demands were urgent, and possibly more urgent than in the United States. Even if this is true, a formula is preferable to an embargo, and an appropriately devised formula will achieve the same results. Moreover, embargoes invite retaliatory embargoes as well as tough talk.

The political and economic power of the groups concerned with forest products in each country was sufficient to ensure that the governments themselves became involved in the difficulties and the disputes.

The political pressures which developed at different times did not make it easier for the administrative officials to achieve the kind of compromises which characterized all the international agreements relating to forest products.

REFERENCES FOR CHAPTER XI

1. These figures are taken from the annual reports of the Dominion Bureau of Statistics on Canadian exports for each of the years mentioned. The export category includes wood, wood products, and paper.

2. The historical and background material contained in Historical Reports on War Administration, War Production Board, Special Study No. 7, *Pulp and Paper Policies of the War Production Board and Predecessor Agencies, May, 1940, to January, 1944* (Washington: U.S. Government Printing Office, 1946) has been used extensively in this chapter. This document will be referred to hereafter as *Pulp and Paper Policies of the War Production Board.*

3. *New York Times,* July 31, 1940, p. 7.

4. Combined Production and Resources Board and Combined Raw Materials Board, *Combined Statistical Summary of Raw Materials and Finished Products,* Issue No. 14, August, 1945, p. 28.

5. Dominion Bureau of Statistics, *Trade of Canada,* 1940, II, p. 232.

6. *Ibid.,* 1941, II, p. 242.

7. P.C. 328, January 16, 1942.

8. Timber Control Order, July 6, 1940, effective July 10. The order was originally limited to a three-month period but was later extended for another two months to December 10, 1940. The outright prohibition was relaxed when the order of the Timber Controller was replaced by P.C. 7156 of December 4, 1940, which declared Douglas fir sawlogs to be "munitions of war" and "supplies" and placed all exports under permit.

9. Representative John M. Coffee (Wash.), quoted in *Canada Lumberman,* August 15, 1940, p. 22.

10. The policy discussions of the Joint Economic Committees were of some theoretical interest but the fact that they had no direct control over operating officials meant that their conclusions and agreements had little or no influence on later developments.

11. Letters, Representative Charles H. Leavy and Senator Homer T. Bone to the Secretary of State, April 1, 1942, quoted in *Pulp and Paper Policies of the War Production Board,* p. 56.

12. Conservation Order M-93, March 12, 1942, 7 *Federal Register* 1978. This order replaced Conservation Order M-52, a more specific allocation order dealing with bleached sulphite pulp issued on January 9, 1942, 7 *Federal Register* 204.

13. Conservation Order M-93-a, May 4, 1943, 8 *Federal Register* 5801.

14. Limitation Order L-121, May 13, 1942, 7 *Federal Register* 3574.

15. The authority to concentrate production was contained in General Preference Order M-251, October 19, 1942, 7 *Federal Register* 8424, and the regulations became applicable to the Puget Sound and Columbia-Willammette areas with the issuance of Schedules 1 and 2 of this order, both dated October 26, 1942, 7 *Federal Register* 8686-7.

16. U.S., Senate, *Hearings before the Special Committee Investigating the National Defense Program,* part 15 (Washington: U.S. Government Printing Office, 1943), pp. 6226-7.

17. *Ibid.,* p. 6228.

18. *Ibid.,* Telegram, J. H. Bloedel, President, Bloedel Donovan Lumber Mills to Mon C. Wallgren, November 25, 1942, pp. 6332-3.

19. In Canada, a number of orders were issued by the Wartime Prices and Trade Board for this purpose, including Administrator's Order A-50, Paper, April 15, 1942, and Administrator's Order A-179, Book, Writing, Bond, and White Specialty Papers, May 20, 1942. In the United States, the War Production Board issued Limitation Order L-120 on July 4, 1942, providing for the simplification and standardization of five major groups of writing and bond papers, 7 *Federal Register* 5119.

20. Wartime Prices and Trade Board, Press Release 0189, September 3, 1942.

21. Letter, Donald Gordon to Donald Nelson, October 7, 1942.

22. Historical Reports on War Administration: War Production Board, Special Study No. 20, *The Rôle of the Office of Civilian Requirements in the Office of Production Management and the War Production Board, January, 1941, to November, 1945,* pp. 147-9. The Committee on Concentration of Production was created by War Production Board General Administrative Order 2-50, August 26, 1942.

23. Conservation Order M-241, October 31, 1942, 7 *Federal Register* 8859.

24. Wartime Prices and Trade Board, Administrator's Order A-454, Respecting production and delivery of newsprint, October 28, 1942, and Administrator's Order A-455, Respecting production and delivery of paper for magazines and other periodicals, October 28, 1942.

25. *Minutes of the War Production Board,* November 17, 1942, pp. 156-7.

26. Conservation Order M-241, as amended, January 8, 1943, 8 *Federal Register* 352. Another regulation, Conservation Order M-241-a issued at the same time limited or prohibited the use of paper products for certain articles, 8 *Federal Register* 355.

27. Limitation Order L-240, December 31, 1942, 8 *Federal Register* 6, and Limitation Order L-244, December 31, 1942, 8 *Federal Register* 7.

28. Limitation Order L-241, January 8, 1943, 8 *Federal Register* 357, and Limitation Order L-245, January 8, 1943, 8 *Federal Register* 358.

29. Wartime Prices and Trade Board, Order No. 223, December 30, 1942.

30. Wartime Prices and Trade Board, Order No. 227, January 21, 1943.

31. Wartime Prices and Trade Board, Administrator's Order A-547, December 30, 1942.

32. *Canada Gazette,* October 21, 1942.

33. Letter, Donald Gordon to Donald Nelson, April 16, 1943.

34. *Minutes of the War Production Board,* June 22, 1943, pp. 249-50.

35. Limitation Order L-240, as amended, July 5, 1943, 8 *Federal Register* 9194.

36. Limitation Order L-240, as amended, September 28, 1943, 8 *Federal Register* 13231.

37. War Production Board, General Administrative Order 2-127, October 19, 1943.

38. Letter, A. H. Williamson to A. G. Wakeman, July 16, 1943. Quoted in *Pulp and Paper Policies of the War Production Board and Predecessor Agencies,* p. 108.

39. Department of Munitions and Supply, Timber Controller, Order No. Timber 20, July 15, 1943.

40. *Labour Gazette,* November, 1943, p. 1475.

41. Extract from Statement of Harold Boeschenstein, Director, Forest Products Bureau to Newspaper Industry Advisory Committee, November 16, 1943.

42. Wartime Prices and Trade Board, Press Release 0726, December 20, 1943.

43. War Production Board, Press Release WPB 4713, December 21, 1943.

44. *Ibid.*

45. Letter, A. H. Williamson, Timber Controller, to Harold Boeschenstein, Acting Director, Forest Products Bureau, January 13, 1944. Quoted in *Pulp and Paper Policies of the War Production Board,* p. 110.

46. Limitation Order L-240, as amended, December 24, 1943, 8 *Federal Register* 17343.

47. Wartime Prices and Trade Board, Administrator's Orders A-1078 to A-1081, referring to pulpwood cut in Ontario, Nova Scotia, Quebec, New Brunswick, all dated February 2, 1944.

48. Maximum Price Regulation No. 530, April 26, 1944, 9 *Federal Register* 4478.

49. Department of Munitions and Supply, Timber Controller, Order No. Timber 20-C, May 1, 1944.

50. Limitation Order L-240 as amended, July 3, 1945, 10 *Federal Register* 8210.

51. Limitation Order L-240 (Revocation), December 27, 1945, 10 *Federal Register* 15415.

52. Wartime Prices and Trade Board, Administrator's Order A-1837, Revocation of Administrator's Orders A-451, A-457, and A-1124, December 15, 1945.

53. Office of Price Administration, Press Release PM 3005, January 8, 1942.

54. H.R. 5479 was submitted to Congress on July 30, 1941, and became the Emergency Price Control Act of 1942 on January 30, 1942, 56 *U.S. Statutes* 23, c. 26.

55. Temporary Maximum Price Regulation No. 16, March 26, 1942, 7 *Federal Register* 2395.

56. Maximum Price Regulation 130, April 28, 1942, 7 *Federal Register* 3183.

57. Amendment 2, Maximum Price Regulation No. 130 (revised), March 1, 1943, 8 *Federal Register* 2670. See also Office of Price Administration Press Release OPA-1840, February 27, 1943.

58. Wartime Prices and Trade Board, Administrator's Order A-628, Respecting the price of newsprint paper, February 27, 1943.

59. Maximum Price Regulation 130, Amendment 4, August 14, 1943, 8 *Federal Register* 11382. Wartime Prices and Trade Board, Administrator's Order A-820, Respecting the price of newsprint paper, July 21, 1943.

60. Maximum Price Regulation No. 130, Amendment 10, March 29, 1945, 10 *Federal Register* 3435.

61. Maximum Price Regulation No. 130, Amendment 12, December 6, 1945, 10 *Federal Register* 14819.

62. Department of Trade and Commerce, Export Permit Branch Order No. 49, October 22, 1942, effective November 2, 1942.

63. Department of Commerce, *Current Export Bulletin No. 308,* January 16, 1946.

64. 58 *U.S. Statutes* 73, c. 63, sec. 507, Act of February 25, 1944.

65. Wartime Prices and Trade Board, Administrator's Order A-1124, Respecting production of 30-pound newsprint, February 28, 1944.

66. Wartime Prices and Trade Board, Press Release No. 0824, April 21, 1944.

67. Wartime Prices and Trade Board, Administrator's Order A-1193, Maximum Price of 30-pound Newsprint Paper. Amendment 7, Maximum Price Regulation 130, April 28, 1944, 9 *Federal Register* 4540.

68. War Production Board, Press Release, June 29, 1944.

69. Minutes of the Sixth Joint Meeting of the Joint Economic Committees, January 26, 1942.

70. *Canada, House of Commons Debates,* February 9, 1943, pp. 278-9.

71. *Ibid.,* February 10, 1943, p. 303.

72. *Ibid.,* February 1, 1944, p. 70.

73. U.S., Congress, Senate, *Additional Report of the Special Committee Investigating the National Defense Program Pursuant to S. Res. 71,* Report No. 10, (78th Cong., 2nd. sess.), part 16 (Washington: U.S. Government Printing Office, 1944), p. 82.

74. *Canada, House of Commons Debates,* February 7, 1944, pp. 206-8.

75. Joint Statement, War Manpower Commission and Department of Labour, April 22, 1944.

76. P.C. 2716, June 24, 1940.

77. Limitation Order L-121, May 13, 1942, 7 *Federal Register* 3574.

78. General Conservation Order M-208, August 21, 1942, 7 *Federal Register* 6637.

79. Letter, Timber Controller to Lumber Manufacturers in Northern British Columbia and in the Provinces of Alberta, Saskatchewan, and Manitoba, June 30, 1942.

80. Circular letter of Timber Controller, October 24, 1942.

81. Department of Trade and Commerce, Export Permit Branch Order No. 50, October 28, 1942, effective November 9, 1942.

82. Timber Controller, Announcement to the Pacific Coast Lumber and Logging Industry, January 30, 1943.

83. War Production Board, Press Release WPB 5541, April 24, 1944.

84. Letter, Timber Controller to Lumber Manufacturers in the Prairie Provinces and in British Columbia excepting the Vancouver Forest District, and to the Wholesale Lumber Trade, May 5, 1944.

85. *Ibid.,* June 23, 1944. In October, 1945, the regulations were again modified to allow export credits of 50 per cent of the amount of softwood lumber delivered domestically and 82 per cent of the amount of hardwood lumber. Timber Letter 42-45, October 1, 1945.

86. Amendment 1, Maximum Price Regulation 219 (revised), May 18, 1943, 8 *Federal Register* 6620.

87. *Timber of Canada,* June, 1943, p. 4.

88. Limitation Order L-335, March 22, 1944, 9 *Federal Register* 3144.

89. *Canada Lumberman,* July 15, 1944, p. 34.

90. Letter, Timber Controller to all Canadian Shippers of Lumber and Lumber Products to the United States, July 10, 1944.

91. Letters to this effect were sent to Canadian importers of hardwood and softwood on July 15, 1944.

92. Limitation Order L-335 (Revocation), September 12, 1945, 10 *Federal Register* 11742.

CHAPTER XII

AGRICULTURAL PLANNING AND CO-OPERATION

THE basic aims in redirecting and controlling wartime agricultural and industrial production in Canada and the United States were the same. The production of specific kinds of foods or agricultural products became urgently necessary to maintain domestic and foreign civilians or military forces while other farm crops became relatively non-essential. The techniques of industrial and agricultural planning and control were different, in general, because of inherent differences in the organization of the two sectors of the economy. Moreover, differences between the agricultural economies of Canada and the United States as well as strong nationalistic influences imposed narrow limits on the area where co-operative planning of production was likely to be effective. In agriculture, the area of co-operation was quite different from that encountered in forest products. In the latter case, the United States was heavily dependent on Canada for raw materials and finished products, while Canada and the United States were largely independent so far as their domestic needs for agricultural produce were concerned. Co-operative agreements, often of an informal type, were made by the two countries to assume responsibility for specific overseas markets or areas. This was the main aspect of agricultural co-operation which was of great importance despite the fact that production adjustments were essentially marginal and unimportant.

1. THE CONTROL AND DIRECTION OF NORTH AMERICAN AGRICULTURAL OUTPUT

In both Canada and the United States, serious agricultural difficulties had existed during the decade before the outbreak of the second world war, arising mainly out of the agricultural depression of the 1930's and centering around surpluses, low prices, and the loss of foreign markets. In both countries, there had existed Departments of Agriculture for many years which had been organized to deal with the quasi-emergency situation of the 1930's and which were capable of being adapted to cope with the food problems of the second world war. A brief outline of the administrative structure which was developed in Canada and the United States to handle wartime food planning may be useful to the understanding of the co-operative ventures of the two countries.

317

(a) *Canada*

The federal government is given wide powers by the British North America Act to make laws in relation to agriculture, and it is the main function of the Department of Agriculture to administer such legislation. Since the dominant Canadian crop was wheat in the inter-war period, it is not surprising that government control agencies for wheat should have been created. In fact, the Board of Grain Supervisors had been established in 1917 in the midst of the first world war, followed by the Canadian Wheat Board in 1919 with compulsory price-fixing powers. In the mid-1930's, the Canadian Wheat Board was re-established to stabilize Canadian wheat prices and to handle the overseas marketing of Canadian grain. Such an organization was an obvious guide to the administrative organization needed to deal with the food problems encountered early in the second world war. On September 9, 1939, an Agricultural Supplies Committee was created within the Department of Agriculture to direct food production and marketing in Canada. This Committee, or Board as it was later called,[1] was composed of senior officials of the Department of Agriculture and was given the power to buy and sell agricultural supplies and to control exports.

There was no sudden and general increase in the overseas demand for Canadian agricultural produce in the initial phase of the war although the Ministry of Food negotiated two agreements with the Canadian government calling for substantial quantities of bacon and cheese. The procurement of these commodities was turned over to two new boards, the Bacon Board,[2] which commenced functioning in January, 1940, and Dairy Products Board,[3] which operated under the general guidance of the Agricultural Supplies Board. With the military reverses of the spring and early summer of 1940, continental European markets were lost to Canada and the United Kingdom became by far the most important overseas market. At the same time, the food requirements of the United Kingdom increased markedly and Canada was called on to supply increasing quantities of bacon, cheese, and evaporated milk. Canada was a favoured source for such commodities in view of the relatively short distance to the United Kingdom and the necessity of conserving both shipping space and the United Kingdom's dwindling supply of United States dollars. During 1940, the Ministry of Food took over the procurement of Canadian eggs. To supervise egg production and shipments, as well as flax and dehydrated foods and other agricultural products, a new agency, the Special Products Board, was created.[4] The principal function of these commodity boards was to determine, after negotiation with the Ministry of Food, the price and quantity of various foodstuffs to be supplied by Canada. Early in 1943, serious domestic shortages were developing for certain foods, and there was some jurisdictional overlapping between the Wartime Prices and Trade Board and the Department of Agriculture. Steps were taken to clarify the responsibilities of the two agencies and it was agreed that the Department of Agriculture should exercise supervision over food production goals, should divert essential foods to essential users and should recommend the level of subsidies to producers. To carry out these functions, the Agricultural Food Board was established on March 1, 1943.[5] This Board was also to act in a liaison capacity with the Wartime Prices and Trade Board and to co-ordinate the activities of the different commodity boards of the Department of Agriculture.

Canada's rôle as a food producer for the United Nations during the war was a source of pride to Canadians and showed the efficacy of prices and propaganda in redirecting agricultural production. This is particularly true of shipments to the United Kingdom. The contracts with the Ministry of Food specified fixed prices for the term of the food contracts with the result that one of the main elements of risk in agricultural production was removed. The rapid expansion of Canadian production can be illustrated by referring to the following tables which show contractual exports of bacon and eggs to the United Kingdom:

BACON

(*millions of pounds*)

	Minimum Contract	Actual Shipments
1939-1940.............	291.0	331.0
1940-1941.............	425.6	425.6
1941-1942.............	600.0	600.0
1942-1943.............	675.0	675.0
1944-1945.............	900.0	1,103.8[6]

EGGS

(*dozens of equivalent shell eggs*)

	Shipments
1941............................	15,336,000
1942............................	37,535,940
1943............................	33,642,810
1944............................	79,929,750
1945............................	89,945,100[7]

The Canadian view was that contractual agreements would not only stimulate wartime production but would offer farmers some guarantee that the bottom would not drop out of their export markets with the cessation of hostilities. On this point, the Canadian Minister of Agriculture said, in a statement to the House of Commons in 1942:

Ever since the war started I have been of the opinion that we should have long-term contracts with Great Britain covering all farm products. I based that opinion on the experience of Australia and New Zealand during the last war. As I recall it, their contracts extended for the period of the war and one year thereafter and we have attempted continuously to make that type of contract with the British Food Ministry to cover food products.[8]

The production of food, particularly to fill export contracts, and the protection of the interests of the farmers were the main concern of the Department of Agriculture while the Wartime Prices and Trade Board was responsible for domestic food consumption problems. The Board directed the food price control programme, as well as food rationing, and dealt with the question of subsidization of food imports as well as bulk purchasing of imported food. The mechanics of paying subsidies and bulk purchasing were handled by the Commodity Prices Stabilization Corporation, a Crown company which operated under the direction of the Wartime Prices and Trade Board. In view of the disparity in the interests of the two Canadian agencies mainly concerned with food it is not unnatural that there should have been points of difference between them. On certain occasions, the Wartime Prices and Trade Board was critical of the procurement methods for export shipment which, it was claimed, unnecessarily disrupted domestic supplies. More fundamental differences arose over price ceilings for agricultural commodities, which were a reflection of age-old disputes between producers and consumers over what constituted fair and reasonable prices. In the United States, the same issues received wide publicity and exerted an important influence over the whole price stabilization programme.

(b) *United States*

In the United States, administrative direction of the food programme was more widely diffused than in Canada. The first step in building up the gigantic wartime food organization of the United States came in May, 1940, with the appointment of the Advisory Commission to the Council of National Defense, which included an Agricultural Adviser. This new officer was quite independent of the Department of Agriculture and was to advise the President on the place of agriculture in defence preparations, including the disposal of surplus commodities, the stimulation of the production of raw strategic agricultural commodities, and the place of agricultural manpower in the defence programme. After about a year of existence, the Agriculture Division of the National Defense Advisory Commission was abolished and in its place the Office of Agricultural Defense Relations was set up in the Department of Agriculture under the immediate direction of the Secretary.[9] Although the new Office was assigned very broad responsibilities within the growing defence organization of the United States, it confined its attention principally to negotiations with the Office of Price Administration and the War Production Board on problems relating to prices of agricultural products and priorities for farm machinery and equipment.

The reassignment of responsibility for food production to the Department of Agriculture was obviously a desirable move since this Department had accumulated many years of experience in food production problems and thus had an organization capable, potentially at least, of redirecting agricultural production. Despite this, responsibility for specific aspects of the food problem was scattered widely throughout other government agencies with the result that jurisdictional problems became acute, particularly during 1942. The War Production Board, for example, had been assigned overriding responsibility for economic mobilization and had taken over several important aspects of the regulation of food, such as the formulation of industrial needs for agricultural products, control of the manufacture of farm machinery and similar equipment, and the allocation of shipping for imported foods. Control over food prices was the responsibility of the Office of Price Administration which also administered the rationing system for scarce foods under directives from the Chairman of the War Production Board. Other agencies such as the Board of Economic Warfare and the Office of Lend-Lease Administration were concerned with the procurement of foreign and domestic food supplies respectively. The Army and the Navy were also purchasing food on a very large scale.

The rôle of the War Production Board was clarified with the creation of the Food Requirements Committee early in June, 1942.[10] The Chairman of this Committee was the Secretary of Agriculture, although the Committee was to report to the Chairman of the War Production Board. The other members of the Committee represented the Army, the Navy, the Department of State, the Board of Economic Warfare, the Office of Price Administration, and the Office of Lend-Lease Administration, as well as the War Production Board. The function of this Committee was to determine requirements for food and to allocate available supplies to the different claimant agencies represented on the Committee. Organizationally, the Food Requirements Committee was a sub-committee of the parent Requirements Committee which had been created some months earlier and which retained control over the materials and machinery required for food production. Difficulties were encountered in absorbing the new responsibilities for food into the administrative framework of the

War Production Board, and there were numerous delays in obtaining decisions on matters of food policy. At the same time, disputation over food prices between the Department of Agriculture and the Office of Price Administration had become more frequent and contentious.

There was, as a result, some agitation for the consolidation of control over food and a variety of suggestions were made concerning the appropriate place to lodge these powers. Finally, on December 5, 1942, the President directed that responsibility for nearly all food problems be transferred to the Department of Agriculture and assigned to the Secretary of Agriculture several of the functions which had been previously vested in various agencies.[11] These functions included the calculation of foreign and domestic food requirements, the direction of a food production programme to meet these needs, the development of priority or allocation methods to control the distribution of existing supplies, and the procurement of food for military and other governmental purposes. These various operating functions of the Department of Agriculture were assigned to two major divisions, the Food Production Administration and the Food Distribution Administration.. The Food Requirements Committee of the War Production Board was abolished and personnel primarily concerned with food production were transferred to the Department of Agriculture. The executive order transferring responsibility for food to the Department of Agriculture raised some questions concerning the jurisdiction of the Secretary of Agriculture and other officials such as the Chairman of the War Production Board, but eventually a series of informal agreements were concluded between the agencies concerned to clarify the division of responsibility.

The basic pattern of food control was established by the food order of December, 1942, and the subsequent inter-agency agreements. However, late in March, 1943, responsibility for wartime food operations was taken away from the Secretary of Agriculture and assigned to the War Food Administration which was set up in the Department of Agriculture, but whose Administrator was directly responsible to the President.[12]

It will be seen that there were serious jurisdictional and administrative problems involved in the wartime control of agriculture and food in both countries, although they were considerably more complex and difficult in the United States than in Canada. In part, these were symptomatic of the substantive problems involved in controlling and directing the agricultural segment of the North American economy.

Canada had some advantages over the United States in contending with wartime agricultural problems. For one thing, Canada had a substantial backlog of experience with the administrative machinery involved in stimulating the output of specific products for export and in government marketing. For example, steps had been taken in the 1920's to develop the Canadian bacon industry with a view to selling greater quantities to the United Kingdom, and the many years of experience with the Canadian Wheat Board and similar agencies were invaluable. Canada had also started to adjust agricultural production to wartime demands in 1939, and thus had several years of grace before the world food situation became really critical. In contrast, the mobilization of agriculture in the United States had to be carried out with very little notice. There were serious difficulties involved in redirecting agriculture in the United States because of the influence of habit and custom in farming, uncertainty concerning production goals, and legislative bars to the efficient use of prices to encourage readjustment. In Canada, the dominant rôle of export contracts and their related prices simplified the management problem considerably. While the Canadian policy with respect to the production of some commodities such as wheat, bacon, and cheese was clear-cut, there were other cases, of which beans and canned and dried milk may serve as examples, where this was not invariably true. In the United States, the problem of redirection of agriculture was a larger and more complicated task, and, towards the end of the war, enormous progress had been made. Some of the particular problems involved will be illustrated by the early efforts of Canada and the United States to work out a co-operative solution of their agricultural problems.

2. JOINT PLANNING—INITIAL PHASES

In the early stages of the war, the main objective of Canadian agricultural planning was to stimulate the output of bacon, cheese, and evaporated milk and to curtail the production of wheat. The extremely large wheat crops of 1938-40 resulted in the accumulation of large surpluses in Canada, so large, in fact, that there were inadequate facilities for storage available. By mid-1940, moreover, the export market for wheat had nearly disappeared except for the United Kingdom. The Canadian government therefore intervened directly to support the price of wheat and to encourage the production of other crops. Legislation was enacted in 1941 authorizing the payment of compensation for acreage diverted from wheat which was similar in many ways to the farm legislation passed in the United States in the heyday of the New Deal.[13] The subsidiary aim of the wheat acreage reduction scheme was to encourage the raising of coarse grains, such as oats and barley, and grass to support larger numbers of livestock. This was particularly desirable in view of the expanded overseas and domestic demand for bacon, cheese, butter, milk, and meat. Despite the difficuties involved in persuading farmers to shift to new crops or to revise drastically their normal methods of operation, the government was able to offer assured markets and guaranteed prices for alternative products destined for export to the United Kingdom. The prices, however, were very favourable in relation to feed costs with the result that expansion of agricultural output along desired lines was very rapid.

In the United States, the extent to which prices could be used to divert agricultural output from less essential to more essential foodstuffs was limited by the complex legislation which governed farm prices. The support of farm prices had been one of the cardinal objects of government policy in the mid-thirties and as early as 1933, the Commodity Credit Corporation had been authorized by Congress to purchase agricultural products in the open market or to lend money to farmers up to a specified percentage of the "parity" price of the crop in question. Although the Secretary of Agriculture had been authorized to determine the loan rates prior to 1938, Congress in that year passed the Agricultural Adjustment Act which fixed mandatory loan rates of from 52 to 75 per cent of parity for corn, cotton, and wheat. The minimum loan rates for basic commodities were subsequently raised to 85 per cent in May, 1941.[14] In October of the following year, the Stabilization Act of 1942 provided for an increase of the loan rate to 90 per cent in certain cases. Meanwhile, in July, 1941, Congress acted to extend the same system to non-basic commodities and instructed the Secretary of Agriculture to support the price of any agricultural commodity for which increases in production were to be officially encouraged as a war measure. Such prices were to be supported until they reached 85 (later 90) per cent of parity or comparable levels. One result of these manoeuvres was to hamper the extent to which differential prices could be used to direct and influence production. Since the floor under the prices of basic crops was 90 per cent of parity, price support for alternative products had to be established at impractically high levels. The issues have been summarized succinctly in an official statement prepared by the War Records Section of the Bureau of the Budget, which reads as follows:

Congressional inflexibility towards modification of the parity structure compelled the country to operate under a price system wherein the relations between the prices of various commodities were determined by patterns existing in 1910-14 rather than by current requirements. Upward adjustment of the loan rates from 75 percent to 90 percent of parity and rejection of incentive payments meant high prices for produce for which there was little need and even higher prices for products of significant wartime value. Moreover, market prices seldom indicated the essentiality of crops because prices were controlled for the purpose of holding down the cost of living, a policy which Congress had likewise approved. As a result, commodities which provided the most nutrients for the man-power, fertilizer, and land expended, such as fresh vegetables and dairy products, were the commodities for which stable prices were sought. As increased purchasing power pushed up the prices of luxury foodstuffs, such as watermelons, farmers and processors were encouraged to allot acreage and facilities to products which probably should not be grown in wartime. Fruits needed for canning and freezing were taken out of the markets at high prices for immediate consumption or for use in making ice cream. Conflicting legislative policy made it virtually impossible to use price effectively as an instrument of production management.[15]

From the Canadian point of view, the almost automatic increases in the prices of farm products resulting from legislative action in the United States was of great significance in assuring the almost continuous disparity of prices of agricultural products in the two countries. For example, the basic price offered by the Canadian Wheat Board for the 1941 crop was 70 cents a bushel while the comparable loan value in the United States was 97 cents.[16] As a result of this situation, the United States was a very attractive market for Canadian produce. Substantial tariff concessions had been agreed to in the 1939 Trade Agreement and, during the early period of the war, Canadian exports of food to the United States increased rapidly. There were, however, several omens of future problems.

The first of these was the decision of the United States to restrict imports of Canadian wheat. In May, 1941, the Department of State pointed out officially and regretfully in a note that action would have to be taken to limit imports from Canada since there already was a wheat surplus in the United States.[17] The reply of the Canadian government was that it appreciated the problem fully and would undertake to avoid any measures which would disrupt the United States programme. In due course, the United States imposed an annual import quota of 800,000 bushels on Canadian wheat.[18]

It was also mentioned in this exchange of notes that the wheat problem was really an international one and that action would be taken in the near future to consider ways and means of stabilizing the world wheat trade. In the summer of 1941, an international conference on wheat was held in Washington by officials of the Argentine, Australia, Canada, the United States, and the United Kingdom for the purpose of reaching an agreement on international trade in wheat. This concluded the wheat discussions which were initiated immediately prior to the outbreak of war and resulted in a Memorandum of Agreement which was signed on April 22, 1942.[19]

The action of the United States in introducing quota limitations on imports of Canadian wheat was to have repercussions at a later date. The phenomenal growth in the North American livestock population led to serious shortages of feed grains and negotiations were undertaken as early as the summer of 1942 for additional supplies of wheat from Canada. At this time, the Secretary of Agriculture noted in a meeting of the Civilian Requirements Policy Committee, an inter-agency committee set up in the Office of Civilian Supply, that "trade relationships are currently obstructing the importation of one million bushels of wheat from Canada."[20] The need for imported feedstuffs became particularly acute towards the end of 1943 and at that time the United States Congress passed special legislation authorizing duty-free imports of Canadian wheat and coarse grains and other feedstuffs for a ninety-day period. The period was later extended for an additional ninety days.

There was a haunting and persistent fear in Canada that, after the passage of the Lend-Lease Act, the United Kingdom might initiate large-scale procurement of agricultural supplies in the United States through lend-lease channels and thus damage the relative security of Canadian producers. The food contracts which had been concluded with the United Kingdom offered Canadian farmers a secure market for enormous quantities of hogs, cheese, and other produce. Any suspicion that the United Kingdom might switch orders from Canada to the United States for a significant fraction of its food imports was a disturbing thought in Canadian agricultural circles.[21] The following comment by a member of Parliament in June, 1942, is indicative of this point of view:

It has been pointed out to me, by people who I think should know, that in the near future there may be difficulty in selling these products [poultry and eggs] to Great Britain. They claim they have been told that the food ministry of Great Britain can procure these articles through the lend-lease law of the United States much more easily than they can get them in Canada.[22]

Apart from the problems of future developments in agriculture there were, in the summer of 1941, substantial North American surpluses of wheat, tobacco, and apples and there was some possibility that, by a judicious programme of agricultural planning in the United States and Canada, these surplus problems could be alleviated. There was even some discussion during the summer of 1941 of the possibility of co-operation in building up stocks of food to be shipped to Europe for relief in the post-war period. The initial, and optimistic, feeling was that the war and defence programmes would offer unprecedented opportunities for attaining a better balance of the agricultural sectors of the two countries and for securing some badly needed adjustment of wheat growing in the two countries.

During the war, annual conferences of Dominion and Provincial officials concerned with agriculture were held in Canada to develop and publicize production plans for the following year. Similar conferences were held in Washington. Observers from the two countries regularly attended these conferences which thus provided a useful means for the exchange of information on agricultural prospects. Despite the informality of these arrangements it is clear that they would be likely to have some influence on the plans of each country.

Agricultural planning problems fell naturally within the terms of reference of the Joint Economic Committees which devoted a good deal of attention to agricultural collaboration during the first year of their existence. The problem of securing any significant readjustments in agricultural production was so large and tangled that the Committes were content to confine their specific recommendations to relatively minor matters. After all, the Administration in the United States had been attempting since the advent of the New Deal to redirect agricultural production in the United States, a programme which had been consistently handicapped by the successful efforts of Congress to maintain or increase agricultural prices for quite different purposes. It was thus unlikely that any agreements or resolutions of the Joint Economic Committees could compete with the enormous power of vested interests in agriculture. Two interesting examples of a co-operative approach to common problems may be cited.

An incipient serious shortage of vegetable oils arose shortly after Pearl Harbor when supplies from the Far East were cut off, a shortage which was intensified by lack of shipping and the urgent needs of the United Kingdom and Soviet Russia for oils and fats. At the same time, as has already been mentioned, there was a prospective shortage of feed grains as a result of the increased livestock population in Canada and the United States. It was desirable, as a result, to expand the production of vegetable oils and feed grains, and it was the view of the Joint Economic Committees that there would be advantages if the two countries were to specialize. Accordingly, the Committees prepared a resolution dated February 27, 1942, that oil-producing crops, principally soybeans, should be increased in the United States, and that Canada should concentrate on a greater output of flaxseed, oats, and barley. In the United States, an increase in the output of soybeans would involve the diversion of land from corn, oats, and barley in the corn-growing area. In Canada, it was expected that some acreage could be shifted to oats and barley from wheat if prices were adjusted appropriately. The object of the resolution was to try to obtain an additional 100,000,000 bushels of oats and barley and some 200,000,000 pounds of vegetable oils. The second part of the resolution, the text of which is shown below, dealt exclusively with mutual commitments to forego special import and export restrictions on these products:

In order to encourage such a program, while at the same time providing necessary assurances in the matter of market outlets, the respective Governments agree, effective from next autumn, that:

(1) Canada shall facilitate the delivery in the United States, at the then current United States prices, of whatever quantity of flaxseed, oats, and barley Canada may be in a position to supply;

(2) The United States shall not impose additional restrictions on the importation of flaxseed, oats and barley moving from Canada to the United States;

(3) The United States shall facilitate the sale to Canada, at the then current United States prices, of whatever quantity of vegetable oils or vegetable oil seeds the United States may be in a position to supply;

(4) Canada shall not impose additional restrictions on the importation of vegetable oils or vegetable oil seeds moving from the United States to Canada.[23]

It was announced by the White House on April 10, 1942, that this resolution had been approved by both the President and the Prime Minister.[24]

The second proposal whose approval was announced at the same time was that the two governments should facilitate the movement of farm machinery and their crews across the border in the harvest season in order to promote the more economical use of machinery and manpower. Among other things, this would involve the suspension of the Canadian duty on farm machinery entering temporarily which amounted to one one-hundred and twentieth of the value of the machinery per month, the minimum levy being $25 per month,[25] and the relaxation of visa requirements by the United States. The resolution of the Joint Economic Committees, approved February 27, 1942, gives a clear exposition of the advantages of such trans-border movements. Its complete text is as follows:

The Joint Economic Committees of Canada and the United States recommend that the Governments of the two countries take suitable action:

(1) To permit used agricultural machines and their operators or normal crews, to move across the border without payment of duty, with a minimum of restrictions, and with such regulations as either country may consider necessary to insure that the machines or members of the crews return within a specified time to the country from which they came.

(2) To facilitate the seasonal movement of farm labor across the common boundary under such rules and regulations as will further the efficient distribution of labor for peak requirements.

The reasons for those recommendations are:

Shortages of agricultural machines and of farm labor skilled in their use impede the wartime agricultural programs both in Canada and in the United States; and scarcities of steel and other metals limit the current output of labor saving machinery. The movement of machines within each country has contributed to economies in the use of machines and labor and achieved greater efficiency of agricultural output. The removal of such regulations and restrictions as now impede the movements across the common boundary of both farm machines and the labor associated with them, would further increase their efficient use, thereby contributing to the common war effort.

Seasonal requirements for farm labor especially in adjacent areas of Canada and the United States ordinarily occur in a time sequence that gives opportunity for the movement of such labor, especially at planting and harvest time when labor shortage caused by the war might have serious effects on farm production in many localities on both sides of the border.[26]

The recommendations of the resolution were implemented by an exchange of notes between the two countries. The clearance problems involved were somewhat complex and in the United States the participation of the Department of State, Department of Agriculture, Treasury Department, and Department of Justice was required. The venture was so successful that the arrangements were continued in the years 1943-47 by the exchanges of further notes. This is an interesting example of an emergency wartime measure which has been perpetuated in the post-war period.

A number of other agricultural problems were considered by the Joint Economic Committees. One of these, the shortage of edible fats, was closely connected with the earlier efforts of the Committees to stimulate increased production of edible oils. While it was evident that the output of edible fat could be increased by encouraging the growing of heavier hogs, such a step conflicted with the Canadian policy, adopted earlier in the war, of concentrating on the production of bacon hogs. Canada was primarily interested in supplying bacon in the form of Wiltshire sides to the United Kingdom and for this reason the production of heavy hogs which yield more lard had been discouraged by appropriate price differentials between light and heavy hogs. The United States, in contrast, had been supplying to the United Kingdom pork products with a high lard content. There had been some modification of this policy, and a good deal of attention was being devoted in early 1942 in the United States to encouraging the production of bacon hogs, partly to retain some of the bacon market of the United Kingdom. The United States proposed that the two countries should adopt parallel policies with respect to hog weights. While the Canadian policy had been modified somewhat to lessen the discrimination against heavy hogs, the United States suggestion was not greeted enthusiastically by Canadian officials. Despite the lukewarm Canadian attitude, the Joint Economic Committees agreed, on May 2, 1942, that the two governments should agree, as follows:

(1) Canada and the United States to increase the average weight of hogs marketed, as follows:

(a) In Canada, by further raising minimum weight requirements and by maintenance of the policy already adopted of removing discounts on heavier weight hogs and of offering increased prices for heavier weight Wiltshires; and

(b) In the United States, by establishing a price for heavy hogs at or near the level established by the current ceilings on hog products and by establishing price discounts on light hogs.

(2) Canada and the United States to increase the number of hogs marketed by maintaining forward price assurances to producers at least as favourable as at present; and, by improving in Canada as far as possible the feed-hog price ratios to producers, and by maintaining in the United States the favourable feed-hog price ratios now prevailing by moving much more wheat into feeding channels, especially in areas which have expanded hog production sharply and which do not have enough feed.

(3) The United States to conserve corn supplies for hogs by encouraging cattle feeders to shorten the feeding period of beef cattle which are finished on corn; and, to facilitate the use of protein supplements by subsidizing the feeding of protein feeds.[27]

In another field altogether, the Joint Economic Committees attempted to promote increased exports of potatoes from Canada to the United States. In the spring of 1942, there were indications that the 1942 potato crop in the United States would be short, but this was by no means certain. The problem was to increase Canadian potato output and at the same time to protect Canadian growers, if, in fact, the output in the United States turned out to be sufficient. There was some discussion of the possibility of the authorities in the United States undertaking to guarantee a minimum price for a specified quantity (15,000,000 bushels) of table potatoes, a suggestion which did not merit much discussion in view of the risk of a fall in domestic potato prices below the guaranteed levels. However, the Committees did recommend that the United States agree to purchase up to 5,000,000 bushels of Canadian starch potatoes at prevailing prices in the United States with the understanding that some device would be worked out to avoid payment of duty. The starch was intended for shipment under lend-lease requisitions. The essential part of the Committees' recommendation of May 2, 1942, involved the following undertaking:

(1) Canada to take such steps as may be appropriate to increase the production of potatoes.

(2) The United States and Canada not to impose additional import restrictions on potatoes and products thereof.

(3) The United States to assure the purchase of Canadian potatoes offered for conversion to starch, up to 5,000,000 bushels, at the then prevailing United States prices for starch potatoes in the area of processing, and to facilitate the entry of such potatoes under applicable United States statutes relating to drawback of duty paid or to processing in bond, for meeting lend-lease commitments or for other exportation of starch and other potato products.[28]

Since the price of starch potatoes was one-half that of table potatoes, there was no particular reason to believe that the adoption of the recommendation would lead to much expansion of Canadian growers. In any case, Canadian growers might get a better price for their culls but the anticipated effects of the proposal would not revolutionize the Canadian potato industry.

The recommendations of the Joint Economic Committees on hog weights and potato exports were announced by the Canadian Department of Agriculture and a Canadian Press dispatch, dated June 1, 1942, started off:

Joint Canadian-United States action to increase the Canadian potato production for sale in the United States and to step up Canadian output of hog products was announced today by the Agriculture Department. The plans which have received formal approval of the Canadian government follow recommendations of the joint economic committees of Canada and the United States.[29]

The rest of the dispatch was entirely devoted to the potato problem. The Leader of the Opposition was enthusiastic about the potato agreement and stated, "I welcome this reported arrangement. It is a fine demonstration of how people can come together during war time."[30] The Minister of Agriculture was much more guarded in his comments, saying merely:

Honourable members have probably noticed that we have agreed with the United States Government—it was announced only this past week—that we are prepared to consider along with them certain arrangements with respect to the weight of hogs, and with regard to potatoes. These discussions will take place, although there are no commitments in connection with them.[31]

The Joint Economic Committees, which had been active, if rather ineffectual, in attempting to promote agricultural co-operation between Canada and the United States, became inactive in the late spring of 1942. At approximately the same time, a new instrument for international agricultural collaboration, the Combined Food Board, had been created and Canadian attention was turned increasingly to this new agency.

3. COMBINED PLANNING

After Pearl Harbor, and the loss of the rich food resources of the Far East, it became obvious that food would be one of the major wartime supply problems to be dealt with. Steps were taken in both Canada and the United States to institute more rigorous controls over domestic food supplies and plans were laid for the allocation of the food supplies of the Allied world. The issues involved in controlling the production and distribution of food and other raw materials were generically the same. Output had to be redirected and increased and allocated formally or informally to different claimant groups. In Canada, the needs of the United Kingdom were of dominant importance while in the United States wartime military demands, lend-lease requirements, and heavy civilian purchases combined to create serious shortages of food. The United Kingdom was not only an important consumer of imported foods but exercised a dominant influence over food production in the British Commonwealth.

The Combined Food Board was formed to cope with the serious dislocations of world food supply resulting from the Nazi conquest of major producing areas in Europe, not to mention the disastrous loss of sources of rice, oils and fats, sugar, and tea to the Japanese after Pearl Harbor. The food problem was a global one which necessitated international co-ordination. Following high-level discussions between the United Kingdom and the United States, the establishment of the Combined Food Board was formally announced by President Roosevelt and Prime Minister Churchill on June 9, 1942. The United States and the United Kingdom only were to be represented on this new Board. The Secretary of Agriculture and the Head of the British Food Mission in Washington were to be the two members. The object of the Combined

Food Board, as explained in the memorandum from President Roosevelt to the Secretary of Agriculture outlining the terms of reference of the Board, was to obtain a "planned and expeditious utilization of the food resources of the United Nations." It was also stated, more specifically:

The duties of the Board shall be:

To consider, investigate, enquire into, and formulate plans with regard to any question in respect of which the Governments of the U.S.A. and the U.K. have, or may have, a common concern, relating to the supply, production, transportation, disposal, allocation or distribution in or to any part of the world of foods, agricultural materials from which foods are derived, and equipment and non-food materials ancillary to the production of such foods and agricultural materials, and to make recommendations to the Governments of the U.S.A. and the U.K. in respect of any such question;

To work in collaboration with others of the United Nations toward the best utilization of their food resources, and, in collaboration with the interested nation or nations, to formulate plans and recommendations for the development, expansion, purchase or other effective use of their food resources.[32]

The creation of the Combined Food Board again aroused certain latent fears in Canada that the joint plans of the United States and the United Kingdom might lead to an unwelcome disruption of Canadian arrangements to supply food to the United Kingdom. Such forebodings were not new; they had been current when the passage of the Lend-Lease Act was assured early in 1941. Since the Canadian agricultural economy had become adapted to supplying staple foods to the United Kingdom, any significant shift of the United Kingdom orders to the United States would have upset the Canadian agricultural programme. Apart from this particular issue, Canada was vitally concerned with any international arrangements which might have repercussions for Canadian agriculture. For example, the whole question of food supplies for liberated areas was of considerable importance for Canada. In general, the agricultural sector of the Canadian economy is vulnerable to changes in the agricultural policies of other countries, and it was considered essential that there be representation of the Canadian point of view in any international planning. In addition, Canada was one of the major suppliers of food to the United Nations and felt entitled to a prominent voice in any combined agricultural planning that was contemplated.

Accordingly, the Canadian government made it known formally to both the United States and the United Kingdom in mid-July, 1942, after the Combined Food Board had been in existence for a little over a month, that Canada would like to belong to the Combined Food Board. The Canadian view that the actions of the Board would intimately affect Canada was made clear to the member countries. The Canadian action was confirmation of Harry Hopkins's opinion that one of the great difficulties of combined planning was that "everybody and his grandmother wants to be on the joint body."[33]   Hopkins's reference was to the Combined Chiefs of Staff where the issues were rather different. Nevertheless, the Canadian request was not looked on with favour, particularly by the United Kingdom, partly because it was likely to set a precedent and for other reasons. The United Kingdom was anxious to preserve the London Food Committee (later Council) intact and the admission of Canada might set a precedent which would lead some of the other Dominions, notably Australia, to switch from the London Food Council to the Combined Food Board. The London Food Council was an advisory body on which there were representatives of the United Kingdom, all the Dominions except Canada, the British Colonies, and several other countries, with the responsibility for collecting information on food production and requirements in the member countries. The British Food Mission in Washington acted as liaison between the Combined Food Board and the London Food Council, and the recommendations were passed on to the countries in this sphere of influence by the London Food Council. Canada was not a member, nor was the faintly colonial status which such membership implied very appealing.

It may be surmised that the United Kingdom was anxious to maintain the status and power of the London Food Council and to resist any moves which would enhance the importance of the food negotiations centered in Washington. The risk that Canadian membership on the Combined Food Board would set a precedent and eventually weaken the London Food Council therefore led to the initial rejection of Canada's request for full membership. Assurances were given, moreover, that the Canadians had gained an incorrect impression of the prospective operations of the Combined Food Board. Originally it was the intention that the Combined Food Board should confine its attention to foodstuffs which were critically scarce and that it would therefore not interfere with existing plans for producing and supplying such relatively plentiful foods as wheat, bacon, and cheese, in general, those foods being supplied to the United Kingdom by Canada under contract. The actions of the Combined Food Board were thus not apt to lead to any interference with Canada's main food exports. The view was also expressed that the Combined Food Board would not be concerned with the food requirements of liberated areas.

The unwillingness of the United States and the United Kingdom to grant Canada full membership on the Combined Food Board did not mean that the member countries would not recognize Canada's special position. Indeed it was suggested as an alternative that Canada should be free to appoint representatives on the commodity committees of the Board, and that Canada should be kept informed of the actions of the Board and could have a representative attend meetings where there was to be discussion of matters of concern to Canada. It was also proposed that there should be created a joint Canada-United States committee with the same status as the commodity committees of the Board to review the agricultural policy of the two countries.

In the period when these various proposals were under discussion, Canada had been invited informally to appoint members to the Combined Food Board committees dealing with agricultural seeds, oil and fats, meat and meat products, sugar, and fertilizer. As a result, Canadian observers were assigned to these committees although formal appointments were not made until some time later, partly so as not to prejudice Canada's request for full membership. There was, at first, some disappointment concerning the treatment of the Canadian request, but by the early fall of 1942, following assurances that the Canadian position would not be damaged by the lack of full membership, the decision was reached to participate at the level of the commodity committees. Accordingly, Canadian representatives, the majority of whom were Administrators of the Wartime Prices and Trade Board or officials of the Department of Agriculture, were formally appointed to the commodity committees of the Combined Food Board. The Washington representative of the Department of Trade and Commerce, who was the Commercial Attaché of the Canadian Legation at that time, was appointed to co-ordinate the work of the Canadian representatives.

By the fall of 1942, it was evident that the co-ordination of Canadian food policy was very desirable. A number of departments and agencies including the Department of Agriculture, the Wartime Prices and Trade Board, the Department of Fisheries, and the Department of External Affairs were concerned with some aspects of food but no provision had been made for the achievement of a common policy. To remedy this lack, a Food Requirements Committee was appointed in October, 1942.[34] It was established as an inter-departmental advisory committee to be primarily concerned with the division of Canadian food supplies between export and domestic demands. It was also empowered to make recommendations on food and agricultural policy to various government departments. Another important function of the Committee was to provide a focus for the submission of information about Canadian food supplies and needs to the Combined Food Board.

Around the end of 1942, some progress was made in carrying out the proposal that a joint agricultural committee be set up along the lines of the Joint War Production Committee. Early in January, 1943, there was a meeting between the Minister of Agriculture and the Secretary of Agriculture to consider North American agricultural production goals for 1943 and to make plans for the creation of the new standing committee. One of the main points dealt with in the conversations between the two officials concerned the expansion in the numbers of North American livestock. It was agreed that this was likely to lead to acute feed shortages, and that some provision should be made for building up stockpiles of feedstuffs and for the exchange of supplies if required. The conclusion was also reached that some shifts in production between the two countries would lead to the more efficient production of food for the United Kingdom. The general principle was accepted by the conferees that any restrictions on food consumption should be designed to impose substantially equal sacrifices on civilians in the two countries. The suggestion was made by the United States Department of Agriculture that Canadian production of flaxseed be reduced and it was intimated that additional Canadian production might not find a ready market in the United States. (There was some contrast between this view and that of the War Production Board which had suggested that Canada was jeopardizing the war effort by not increasing flaxseed production sufficiently.)

One of the results of the conference was indicated in the Speech from the Throne in January, 1943, when it was announced that a joint committee representing the Departments of Agriculture in the two countries would be formed to co-ordinate the efforts of the two countries in producing food for the United Nations.[35] Accordingly, a new and independent Joint Agricultural Committee of Canada and the United States was appointed on March 15, 1943. The Committee consisted of a Canadian Section and a United States Section, the Chairman of the Canadian Section being the Deputy Minister of Agriculture and the Chairman of the United States Section being the War Food Administrator. The order-in-council appointing the Canadian Section stated that the Committee's function was:

To keep agricultural and food production and distribution in Canada and the United States of America under continuing review, in order to further such developments as may be desirable in reference to those phases of wartime agricultural and food programmes that are of concern to both countries.[36]

The Joint Agricultural Committee was invited to submit recommendations to the Governor-in-Council through the Minister of Agriculture and to the appropriate United States authorities and report on the progress which had been made in achieving the aims it recommended.

The terms of reference of the Committee were distressingly vague and it is not surprising that the accomplishments of the Committee were correspondingly limited. The Committee met only a few times and did reach some conclusions concerning the desirability of increasing the production of feed grains in Canada for export to the United States and of using facilities in the United States for crushing Canadian flaxseed and other oilseeds. At the last meeting of the Committee held in mid-October, 1943, much of the discussion centered around the plan of the United States to increase wheat acreage from 54,000,000 acres in 1943 to 68,000,000 acres in 1944 to meet increased needs for feedstuffs and for the manufacture of industrial alcohol.[37] However, Canada was urged to reduce wheat production and to expand output of oilseeds and peas and beans.

These resembled similar recommendations embodied in resolutions of the Joint Economic Committees some time before, but progress under the new auspices was not very startling. One reason for the impotence of the Joint Agricultural Committee was the change in the status of the United States Member in March, 1943, when wartime food powers were switched from the Secretary of Agriculture to the War Food Administrator. Moreover, from the Canadian point of view there was no anxiety to strengthen the Committee since Canadian relations with the Combined Food Board were becoming increasingly close during this period. The Combined Food Board, in fact, afforded the first effective medium for agricultural co-operation between the two countries even though Canada continued to be represented on the commodity committees only.

During 1943, the course of development which had been predicted for the Combined Food Board when the Canadian request for full membership had been turned down had not come true. The Board was intimately concerned with almost all internationally traded foodstuffs and not merely those in critically short supply. Some experience had also accumulated to show that the lack of full membership was a disadvantage since policy decisions were often made at the top level which influenced the operations of the committees. It also appeared that the Board would be responsible for the food problems arising out of needs for relief and rehabilitation. The invasion of North Africa in November, 1942, had emphasized the immediacy of the problem. In this period, the world food situation was growing worse and rationing had become quite general in the United Kingdom, the United States, and Canada. In some cases, the maintenance of rationing was necessitated by the allocation recommended by the Combined Food Board, and it was the official feeling in Canada that a

country which voluntarily reduced consumption at the instance of the
Combined Food Board was entitled to representation at the highest level.
Accordingly, Canada again pressed for full representation on the Board.
This time the Canadian request was supported by the United Kingdom
which evidently felt that Canadian membership might strengthen the
position of the Combined Food Board. The fact that the Secretary of
Agriculture, although he was shorn of much of his authority, continued
as the United States Member had not strengthened the status of the Board.
Moreover, the United States had been entertaining a proposal to expand
the membership quite generally, a move which was opposed by the
United Kingdom, since it was felt this would weaken the bargaining
position of the United Kingdom and the Empire generally by centralizing
all international food allocations in Washington. As a result, Canada's
request for membership was acceded to by the United States and the
United Kingdom. On October 25, 1943, President Roosevelt sent the
following telegram to the Canadian Prime Minister:

Canada's contribution to the war effort in the whole field of production and the strength which she has thus lent to the cause of the United
Nations is a source of admiration to us all. The importance of Canadian
food supplies and the close interconnection of all North American food
problems make it appropriate and desirable that she should be directly
represented as a member of the Combined Food Board sitting in Washington. Mr. Churchill and I would accordingly be gratified if you would
name a representative to the Combined Food Board.[38]

Winston Churchill sent a message simultaneously which was identical
except that it referred to President Roosevelt in the last sentence. The
Canadian Prime Minister replied that "the Government of Canada is very
pleased to accept the invitation." The Minister of Agriculture became the
Canadian Member.

The announcement of Canadian membership on the Combined Food
Board released by President Roosevelt also contained news of a significant
change in the United States membership on the Combined Food Board.[39]
The Secretary of Agriculture was named neutral chairman and the War
Food Administrator became the United States Member. This centralized
responsibility for dealing with both domestic and foreign food allocations
from United States supplies in the hands of the War Food Administrator.
One of the changes put into effect was the establishment of a Food
Requirements and Allocations Committee with power to review all
domestic and foreign requirements for food. The Chairman of this
Committee was to be the Deputy War Food Administrator. Statements of
domestic requirements were to be prepared by the Food Requirements

Branch of the War Food Administration while the Foreign Economic Administration was to present export requirements.

With these major administrative changes, the Combined Food Board was in a better position to deal with the difficult problems involved in the international allocation of food. The Combined Food Board, like the Combined Raw Materials Board in another field, was concerned with the distribution of the global supplies under the control of the United Nations. Its principal concern was with food as such, but it was also interested in certain related items such as citric acid, tartrates, vitamins, essential oils, seeds, fertilizers, and agricultural and food processing machinery. Responsibility for agricultural and food processing machinery was shared with the Combined Production and Resources Board which took a somewhat more active interest in the problems in this particular field. Although the membership of the Board itself did not change after the admission of Canada, some of the commodity committees were expanded to provide representation of other countries. Thus, Newfoundland sat on the Committee on Fishery Products, Australia on the Cereals Committee, and France on the Committee on Fertilizers. Following the liberation of Europe, representatives of France, Belgium, and the Netherlands sat on the Committee on Fats and Oils and the Committee on Coffee, Cocoa and Spices. In addition, Norway was represented on the Committee on Fats and Oils.

A major part of the work of the Combined Food Board was to recommend the allocation of world supplies of critical food commodities. Its method of operation can be illustrated by reference to two commodities, tea and sugar.[40] Japanese military successes in the East Indies shortly after Pearl Harbor cut off important sources of tea, notably Java. The United Kingdom, as the most important consumer of tea, instituted bulk purchasing of the remaining tea supplies and undertook to allocate available quantities to the rest of the world. After the formation of the Combined Food Board, a Tea Committee was established in London and recommendations on international allocations were handled thereafter under the auspices of the Combined Food Board. Allocations were fixed at a uniform percentage of the pre-war level of imports of consuming countries with appropriate provision being made for the priority requirements of the armed services. The method of dealing with sugar was not substantially different, although the shortage of sugar was complicated by the lack of shipping space. The early success of German submarine warfare and the extension of Allied supply lines over the world meant that the quantity of sugar that could be imported from the Caribbean area was limited. Apart from this, sugar supplies from both the

Philippines and Java had been lost to the Japanese. Agreements were reached in the Combined Food Board to divide responsibility for off-shore purchases between government agencies of the United Kingdom and the United States. The Commodity Credit Corporation in the United States bought Caribbean sugar while other purchases were taken care of by the Ministry of Food. The major division of supplies was between the United Kingdom and the United States and responsibility for other areas was agreed on. Canada, for example, shared in the United Kingdom sugar pool. One important corollary of international allocations was the necessity for importing countries to restrict imports to the quotas which had been set. When private importation was prohibited this was a relatively simple undertaking but otherwise import permits and a complicated system of controlling individual importers was necessary.

In the case of tea and sugar, the function of international allocation was closely related to off-shore purchasing. It was abundantly clear in many cases that competitive purchasing of food in foreign markets would lead to a serious disruption of normal price relationships. A number of important agreements were reached by the Combined Food Board to assign procurement responsibility in particular areas to avoid the inflationary consequences of competitive buying. One instance of this arose in connection with purchases of canned meat in Latin America. The Ministry of Food assumed sole responsibility for buying Latin American supplies of canned meat, particularly corned beef, which was subject to allocation by the Combined Food Board. Since the United Kingdom had purchased the bulk of Latin American exports prior to the war, this was a natural and satisfactory arrangement. Another procurement agreement of this sort was reached in connection with fats and oils. In the fall of 1942, the United States and the United Kingdom each assumed responsibility for well-defined areas and concerted efforts were made by each country to stimulate the production of oilseeds, oils and fats in the countries within its sphere. Since about 50 per cent of Canadian needs were normally imported, these arrangements were of keen interest to Canada. The United States was responsible for most purchases of oils and fats in Latin America, procurement being handled by the United States Commercial Company. In turn, a Canadian Crown company, the Commodity Prices Stabilization Corporation, bought Latin American oils and fats from the United States Commercial Company. Open market purchases were also made by private Canadian individuals in the United States but such purchases were all subject to import control.

The Combined Food Board, in considering the most efficient disposition of world food supplies, was often faced with critical transportation difficulties, particularly in 1942 and 1943. This meant that it was some-times necessary to establish international allocations for food items, not because they were scarce, but because they required large quantities of shipping. Wheat is a case in point. Despite the existence of a world surplus in 1943, lack of shipping meant that Latin American and Australian supplies could be used only to a limited extent. North American sources had to be relied on at a time when transportation difficulties were acute. By early 1944, a serious shortage of feedstuffs was developing in the United States, and large quantities of Canadian wheat were being shipped to the United States for use as feed. At the same time, transportation on the Great Lakes was congested because of the late breakup and the necessity for transporting urgently needed quantities of iron ore. The Combined Food Board took an active interest in this situation and urged the transportation authorities to facilitate the movement of Canadian wheat to eastern ports. As a result, wheat was moved by direct rail from the Prairie Provinces to United States ports, loadings at Montreal were increased, and priorities were arranged for freight cars to handle wheat.

To a considerable extent, the Combined Food Board merely confirmed Canadian export patterns which had developed early in the war. Canada had undertaken to concentrate on supplying the United Kingdom and its dependencies from the beginning and despite the major shift in sources of food later on, this continued to be the main Canadian responsibility. Informal or tacit agreements on this point were later approved in general by the Combined Food Board. After Pearl Harbor, large Allied military forces congregated in the Southwest Pacific, which threw a heavy burden on the food supplies available in Australia and New Zealand. Food normally shipped to the United Kingdom was diverted and supplemented by additional shipments from the United States, while Canada stepped up exports to the United Kingdom to fill the gap. The same was true when supplies available from the Argentine were reduced. This kind of export specialization was obviously sensible in view of the increased efficiency in the use of shipping which resulted. Thus, despite the fact that United States and Canadian basic production plans were not greatly affected by informal and formal planning, there was a good deal of co-operation between the two countries.

Almost all aspects of the food problem were of intense public interest during the war, and there was always some danger that unilateral action by one country might have embarrassing consequences for the other. Primarily to eliminate the element of surprise, an agreement was reached by the member countries that no major revision of production or consumption plans would be adopted without prior consultation with the others.

One aim of this agreement was to provide for the exchange of information on prospective changes in food rationing, a matter that was of special importance for Canada and the United States. It cannot be said, however, that this channel of communication was very effective so far as rationing changes were concerned. Decisions in this field were sometimes made by national authorities in a way which did not facilitate the circulation of advance information.

At the time of the creation of the Combined Food Board in June, 1942, it was clear that the provision of food for liberated areas would be a major problem in the immediate post-war world. This responsibility was not specifically assigned to the Combined Food Board originally and it was not until the first meeting of the Council of the United Nations Relief and Rehabilitation Administration in November, 1943, that the rôle of the Combined Food Board, and the other Combined Boards, in the provision of relief supplies was clarified. In fact, the realization that the Combined Food Board would play an important part in determining the source of food exports for relief was one of the considerations which led Canada to press for membership on the Board.

In view of the importance of relief requirements and other food exports from the Canadian point of view, it became desirable to strengthen the domestic machinery which had been set up to review the availability of Canadian supplies. From the beginning of Canadian representation on the commodity committees of the Combined Food Board, the decisions on Canadian needs and available supplies were ultimately the responsibility of the Canadian Food Requirements Committee. This Committee provided a channel through which official Canadian views could be transmitted to the Combined Food Board and to which, in turn, the recommendations of the Combined Food Board could be forwarded. In July, 1944, the Food Requirements Committee was reconstituted and strengthened to enable it to deal more satisfactorily with the major policy problems which food exports involved.[41]

The mechanism for handling the food requirements of the United Nations Relief and Rehabilitation Administration and the food requirements for military relief was similar to that.existing in the Combined Production and Resources Board and the Combined Raw Materials Board for dealing with non-food relief. This meant that the commodity committees of the Board recommended different sources of supply for food requirements for relief. Comparatively speaking, Canada was not a major supplier of food for relief but continued to concentrate on the needs of the United Kingdom. In 1945 and 1946, the United States was faced with critical food shortages and the dislocation of supplies, and some efforts were made at this time to induce Canada to divert food from the United Kingdom to liberated areas. However, since the United Kingdom had been rationed at low levels since early in the war, the proposals were not greeted with enthusiasm by Canadian officials. The United Nations Relief and Rehabilitation Administration urged a modification of Canadian production policies and recommended the reduction of the livestock population and a substitution of grains which constitute a more efficient food, but this conflicted with the Canadian agricultural programme and did not find favour with the authorities. In 1946, Canada did make some shipments of wheat and coarse grains to a number of European countries, but it appears that there was a certain lack of co-ordination between Canada and the United States so far as shipments of food to liberated areas were concerned.

Finally, in June, 1946, the Combined Food Board was replaced by the International Emergency Food Council on which thirty countries were represented. Actually, even before this time, the country membership on the commodity committees of the Combined Food Board had increased markedly, and the tripartite control of much of the world's agricultural output was a thing of the past.

Co-operation between Canada and the United States in the field of agriculture was essentially different from co-operation in other fields. Their interdependence was, in general, unimportant. However, they were both dependent on the same external sources for large quantities of vitally-needed food commodities such as tea, sugar, and fats and oils. They were also both major suppliers of foodstuffs to other countries, such as the United Kingdom and the Union of Soviet Socialist Republics. As a result, the most important aspect of agricultural collaboration between the two countries was the process of formal or informal adjustment of shipments to other parts of the world. Attempts were made at different times and under various auspices to re-allocate production between the two countries in order to achieve a more efficient use of resources but the net result of such joint planning does not appear to have been very significant. The immobilities and rigidities of the agricultural economy of North America limited the possibilities of readjustments in either Canada or the United States. Within a world framework, the adjustment process was much simpler and the two countries were able to adapt their needs and supplies in a remarkable fashion.

REFERENCES FOR CHAPTER XII

1. Its name was changed to the Agricultural Supplies Board by P.C. 948, March 6, 1940. The members consisted of four heads of divisions in the Department of Agriculture, the Assistant Deputy Minister and the Executive Assistant to the Minister. See *Canada, House of Commons Debates,* June 2, 1942, p. 2970.

2. The Bacon Board was established by P.C. 4076, December 13, 1939. It was renamed the Meat Board by P.C. 4187, June 3, 1943, as its jurisdiction extended to other meats.

3. The Dairy Products Board was created by P.C. 2138, May 23, 1940.

4. The Special Products Board was set up by P.C. 2520, April 15, 1941.

5. The Agricultural Food Board was established by P.C. 1563, March 1, 1943.

6. *Canada Year Book,* 1946, p. 202.

7. *Ibid.,* p. 204.

8. *Canada, House of Commons Debates,* June 3, 1942, pp. 3022-3.

9. The Office of Agricultural Defense (later War) Relations was created by Memorandum No. 905 of the Secretary of Agriculture dated May 17, 1941, pursuant to a presidential directive to the Secretary of Agriculture dated May 5, 1941. See *United States at War,* Appendix 1, p. 528.

10. This Committee was established on June 4, 1942. WPB Press Release 1295, June 5, 1942.

11. Executive Order 9280, December 5, 1942, 7 *Federal Register* 10179.

12. Executive Order 9322, March 26, 1943, 8 *Federal Register* 3807. For about three weeks after its establishment the War Food Administration was known as the Food Production and Distribution Administration.

13. *Statutes of Canada,* 3 Geo. VI, c. 36.

14. *55 U.S. Statutes* 205, c. 133, Joint Resolution of May 26, 1941 (Bankhead-Fulmer Act). So far as wheat was concerned, the loan rate of 85 per cent was conditional on the reductions in acreage and the acceptance of marketing quotas.

15. *The United States at War,* pp. 352-3.

16. The Canadian price applies to No. 1 Northern at Fort William. See Harald S. Patton, "The War and North American Agriculture," *The Canadian Journal of Economics and Political Science,* August, 1941, p. 388.

17. Canada, Treaty Series, 1941, No. 6, *Exchange of Notes (May 28, 1941) Regarding Wheat Marketing between Canada and the United States of America* (Ottawa: King's Printer, 1943).

18. Harald S. Patton, *op. cit.,* p. 388.

19. Canada, Treaty Series, 1942, No. 11, *Exchange of Notes (April 24, May 20 and June 27, 1942) between the Governments of Argentina, Australia, Canada, the United Kingdom and the United States of America Bringing into Effect as from June 27, 1942, the Memorandum of Agreement Initialled at the Final Session of the Wheat Meeting Held at Washington from July 10, 1941, to April 22, 1942* (Ottawa: King's Printer, 1943).

20. *The Rôle of the Office of Civilian Requirements in the Office of Production Management and the War Production Board,* p. 235.

21. R. MacGregor Dawson, *Canada in World Affairs: Two Years of War, 1939-1941* (Toronto: Oxford for C.I.I.A., 1943), p. 222.

22. *Canada, House of Commons Debates,* June 2, 1942, p. 2969. The speaker was Mr. Ross of Souris.

23. U.S., Department of State, *Bulletin,* April 11, 1942, p. 314.

24. *Ibid.*, p. 313.

25. P.C. 86/7474, September 23, 1941.

26. U.S., Department of State, *Bulletin,* April 11, 1942, pp. 314-15.

27. Joint Economic Committees, Minutes of the eighth joint meeting, May 1 and 2, 1942.

28. *Ibid.*

29. Quoted in *Canada, House of Commons Debates,* June 2, 1942, p. 2973.

30. *Ibid.*, June 2, 1942, p. 2974.

31. *Ibid.*, June 3, 1942, p. 3025.

32. U.S., Department of State, *Bulletin,* June 13, 1942, p. 536.

33. Robert E. Sherwood, *Roosevelt and Hopkins,* p. 469.

34. P.C. 9692, October 22, 1942.

35. *Canada, House of Commons Debates,* January 28, 1943, p. 2.

36. P.C. 2044, March 15, 1943.

37. Canada, Department of Agriculture, Press Release, October 20, 1943.

38. Canada, Department of External Affairs, Press Release, October 28, 1943.

39. Executive Order 9392, October 28, 1943, 8 *Federal Register,* White House Press Release 2744, October 29, 1943.

40. The illustrative examples are taken principally from the *Report of the Combined Food Board,* issued by the War Food Administration in April, 1945 (Washington: U.S. Government Printing Office, 1945).

41. P.C. 4892, July 4, 1944.

CHAPTER XIII

RECONVERSION

AT INTERVALS throughout the wartime period the joint problems of demobilization and reconversion in Canada and the United States were the subject of planning and discussions. In the exchange of notes in early 1941 which presaged the creation of formal joint bodies to deal with the common economic problems of the two countries specific reference was made to the question of reconversion and to the probable post-war economic difficulties resulting from wartime changes in the two countries. From the Canadian point of view, there appeared to be some possibility that the reconversion period would be marked by economic dislocation. In the first place, Canada had constructed many large plants for the production of munitions, and it was felt that many of these could not easily be converted to civilian production. Second, approximately three-quarters of Canadian munition production was for the account of other countries which meant that Canadian orders might be cut back very rapidly and the economy disrupted. Of particular importance was the heavy dependence of Canada on the United States and, as a practical matter, it was not possible for Canada to pursue a reconversion policy widely different from the United States. Reconversion developments in the United States were thus of great importance for Canada.

1. RECONVERSION PLANNING

In Canada, the initial step in post-war planning was taken with the creation of a Cabinet Committee on Demobilization and Re-establishment in December, 1939. At first, the attention of this Committee was devoted solely to the problems of demobilizing the armed forces but, early in 1941, its scope was broadened to include all aspects of reconstruction or reconversion. Following this, an Advisory Committee on Reconstruction was established in September, 1941, to explore the field of reconstruction policies.[1] Finally, after it had been in existence about two years, this Committee submitted an overall report and supplementary reports on agricultural policy, natural resources, post-war construction, housing, post-war employment, and the post-war employment of women, and was disbanded. Its functions were absorbed by the Advisory Committee on Economic Policy at the beginning of 1944.[2] Apart from these Committees which were more or less directly associated with the Cabinet, both the

346

Senate and the House of Commons established separate committees on post-war problems. The House of Commons Committee on Reconstruction and Re-establishment was established on March 24, 1942, while the Senate Committee on Economic Re-establishment and Social Security was created on March 5, 1943. Both of these Committees were actively engaged in studying various measures of post-war reconstruction policy, but their interest did not normally extend to the detailed aspects of decontrol problems.

In the United States, the War Production Board was naturally most intimately concerned with reconversion problems. As early as April, 1943, the Chairman of the War Production Board requested Ernest Kanzler, the man who had directed the conversion of the automobile industry to war production, to study the problems which would arise in industry in the United States during the reverse process. A few months later, a report was submitted and, in the early fall, some of the research personnel of the War Production Board were directed to carry out a study of the reconversion problems that would be encountered after the defeat of Germany. At the end of November, the Chairman of the War Production Board summarized the policy to be followed in relaxing wartime restrictions in the following words:

Hereafter as manpower, facilities and materials become available in any given area, it shall be the policy of the War Production Board to authorize the production within that area of additional civilian goods, provided such production does not limit production for programs of higher urgency.[3]

In the meantime, Congress was displaying an active interest in reconversion and post-war problems. The National Resources Planning Board had early turned its attention to such matters, but there was a good deal of Congressional opposition to the continuation of this body and, as a result, the agency was dissolved in August, 1943. Two Senate committees were interested in reconversion problems, and both of them issued reports in November, 1943, outlining their views. The Senate Special Committee Investigating the National Defense Program urged early decisions by the government on various problems to be confronted by industry, particularly those relating to the termination of war contracts and the disposal of government-owned facilities.[4] The Senate Special Committee on Post-war Economic Policy and Planning had recommended immediate steps to meet issues arising out of contract cancellations, disposition of surplus property, industrial demobilization, post-war employment, and the co-ordination of reconversion activities.[5]

One of the important steps in working out a definite reconversion programme in the United States came early in November, 1943, with the establishment of a unit within the Office of War Mobilization under the direction of Bernard Baruch to analyse the problems of reconversion. In collaboration with John Hancock, Baruch undertook a detailed study which resulted in the so-called Baruch-Hancock report which recommended a set of basic policies to govern such matters as contract termination, the disposal of surplus property, and the administrative machinery needed in the period of reconversion.

The Baruch-Hancock report was released in mid-February, 1944, and about a week later the question of limited reconversion was raised in a meeting of the War Production Board by the Chairman. He had previously requested a study of existing limitation and conservation orders as an initial step in the development of specific plans for the relaxation of controls. Opposition to the proposals of the Chairman of the War Production Board to relax the restrictions on some metals and to institute a more liberal policy with respect to the maintenance of essential services was immediately voiced by the Under Secretary of War and the Under Secretary of the Navy, who were present at the meeting.[6] Not long after this, the Truman Committee noted some dissatisfaction with reconversion policies and commented as follows in its *Third Annual Report*:

The actual reconversion is now starting or about to start. At this stage, the materials have not yet been declared to be available, even when they are known to be in free supply.

However, increasing supplies of materials and a higher rate of cancellation of contracts make it evident that materials soon will have to be made available for further civilian production.[7]

It will be clear, even from this abbreviated account, that there were serious obstacles in the way of post-war planning from the beginning in both Canada and the United States. First, the magnitude and character of post-war problems could not be adequately assessed during the period when military requirements for munitions and manpower were growing rapidly. It was not until the level of war production and the size of the armed forces had become relatively stable that it was possible to make realistic plans. Second, responsibility for post-war planning was widely diffused, a factor which was of more importance in the United States than in Canada. Third, and this also was particularly true in the United States, post-war planning during the middle phase of the war was not looked on with favour in influential quarters. It was believed that industry and government officials, not to mention the civilian populace, would tend to be distracted at a time when attention should be completely centered on the goal of winning the war. This was an attitude particularly common among high military officials. An example of this, already briefly referred to, happened after some military cut-backs occurred late in 1943 and tentative plans were developed by the War Production Board for the relaxation of restrictions on construction and on the use of steel. The vigorous opposition of the War and Navy Departments to these proposals forced the War Production Board to shelve even these minor relaxations.

Despite such opposition, the advocates of planning for reconversion gained considerable ground in the early part of 1944. In part, this was a result of the wide publicity given to the Baruch-Hancock report on reconversion which recommended that the responsibility for the disposal of surplus property, the termination of contracts and re-employment be turned over to the Office of War Mobilization.[8] This was done in a series of executive orders issued by the President. The assignment of responsibility was confirmed by Congress when the Office of War Mobilization and Reconversion was created early in October, 1944. The new agency, which replaced the Office of War Mobilization, was to be responsible for the formulation of general plans for the transition to a peacetime economy. Within it were established the Office of Contract Settlement, the Surplus War Property Administration, and the Retraining and Reemployment Administration, whose functions had been assigned earlier to the Office of War Mobilization by the President.

In Canada, legislative action was also taken to create a new agency to deal with the economic problems of reconversion. It was forecast in the Speech from the Throne in January, 1944, that a new department would be established to be responsible for reconstruction. New legislation, which was passed in June, 1944, created the Department of Reconstruction.[9] It was merged with the Department of Munitions and Supply to form the Department of Reconstruction and Supply about the end of 1945.[10]

So far as relations between Canada and the United States were concerned, the major problem was the timing of reconversion and decontrol. This involved the consideration of the detailed provisions of restriction orders and it is therefore natural that the bulk of the negotiations between the two countries should be dealt with by the operating agencies concerned. In addition, however, the Combined Production and Resources Board and the Canadian Embassy played significant rôles in the co-ordination of the policies of the two countries.

2. THE RELAXATION OF CONTROLS

By late 1943, serious study was being given to methods of relaxing restrictions on the production of civilian goods, the significance of different methods depending to some extent on the existing structure of controls. The first and most obvious way of relaxation is simply to cancel any restricting or limiting order covering specified goods. This has the disadvantage of not assuring that essential goods will be produced or that readily available raw materials will be used. Another technique would be to issue permits or to grant appeals for the manufacture of restricted goods or the use of restricted materials. This has the same disadvantages as the first and suffers from the additional handicaps of being an administrative burden on officials and of placing officials in the position of having to determine the relative merits of different appeals. Another method is to release balanced amounts of materials for the production of specific quantities of essential goods. This involves the development of a programme of civilian requirements sufficient to meet essential needs. This method has distinct advantages although there are usually complex problems involved in determining minimum civilian needs. When a specific material is in free supply, the cancellation of all restrictions on the use of the material is a convenient device for eliminating unnecessary restrictions. In other cases, where the material is not abundant, specific relaxations of prohibitions on the use of the material can be introduced. All these methods are applicable under certain circumstances and the determination of the optimum method or methods to use in a period of decontrol is unlikely to be clear cut.

In Canada, the problems of decontrol were accentuated and complicated by the necessity of keeping in step with the United States. Canada is heavily dependent on the United States for components to be incorporated in civilian products. If, therefore, the United States did not favour Canadian policies, essential components might not be released. Possibly there would be a temptation for the United States to withhold all supplies of similar components and not merely those destined for civilian products. Such action might result from public criticism or Congressional pressure even though the administrators in the United States were sympathetic to Canadian actions. The precise methods of decontrol adopted in Canada were probably a matter of some indifference to the United States provided that Canada did not appear to be reconverting faster than the United States. There were then strong arguments for pursuing parallel decontrol policies from the point of view of Canadian self-interest. This in no sense implies that Canada was bound to secure the prior permission of the United States before introducing specific decontrol measures. It merely meant that any serious divergence in the Canadian policy might force the war agencies in the United States to adopt a less liberal attitude to the release of components or other materials for

Canada. It was thus agreed by the Canadian officials concerned that every effort should be made to keep United States officials, particularly those in the War Production Board, advised of Canadian plans in order to avoid misunderstanding and possibly worse. The goal of parallelism, unfortunately, proved to be very difficult to attain, primarily because of the erratic changes in reconversion policy in the United States in 1944.

In June, 1944, the Chairman of the War Production Board announced the tentative adoption of a plan for relaxing certain specific controls which would go far to facilitate reconversion.[11] First of all, he proposed to rescind the stringent restrictions on the use of aluminum and magnesium to permit the manufacture of essential products provided that labour was available. It was also a part of the plan that, under some circumstances, industry should be permitted to make experimental models and also to retool plants in anticipation of civilian products. He suggested, moreover, that firms not in tight labour areas should be allowed to resume civilian production on a limited scale subject to the permission of the manpower authorities and the War Production Board. Despite the vigorous opposition of the military authorities to the timing of the relaxations, some of the restrictions on the use of aluminum and magnesium were lifted[12] and three new priority regulations were later issued embodying the balance of the reconversion proposals. Priorities Regulation 23, issued July 22, 1944, permitted the manufacture of experimental models provided that no managerial, technical, scientific, or production workers would be diverted from war work.[13] Priorities Regulation 24, dated July 29, set down the circumstances under which a priority rating would be issued for the purchase of machine tools or manufacturing machinery for the resumption of civilian production.[14] In brief, the rules were that the requirements had to be small, the product essential and the equipment unavailable except with a rating. The most controversial of the relaxation orders, Priorities Regulation 25, issued on August 15, provided for the authorization by the War Production Board of the manufacture of certain items otherwise prohibited by limitation orders, on the condition that materials and manpower would not be diverted from war production.[15] However, no priority ratings would be issued to assist such production.

The most strongly criticized aspect of these plans was that authorizing the resumption of civilian production on the condition that manpower, materials or facilities would not be diverted from war production. This so-called "spot authorization program" was opposed by the War Manpower Commission and by the military authorities up to and including the Joint Chiefs of Staff. The appeals of military representatives to have the order reconsidered were ineffective, although its issuance was delayed from July 1 to August 15.

When the spot authorization plan became effective on August 15, it covered only about seventy-five classes of items, such as vacuum cleaners, lawn mowers, sewing machines, cutlery, flatware and hollow ware, electric fans, fountain pens and mechanical pencils, oil burners, typewriters, and miscellaneous kitchen utensils. There were a number of significant omissions from the list, including electric refrigerators and washing machines and automobiles. At this time, the War Production Board again warned that the issuance of the new regulation would not mean any large increase in civilian production, but was primarily a plan of decentralization whose importance would increase when men and materials were freed from war production.

It was suggested that the procedure to be followed by a manufacturer desiring to return to civilian production was made unnecessarily complex by the opponents of the plan. For example, material was to be obtained under the Controlled Materials Plan, but the application form required nineteen pages of explanation and instructions and four new forms and letters. In the early period of its operation, provision was made for the allotment of a very small volume of controlled materials for the spot authorization programme. However, the primary handicap to the effective working of the plan arose from the imposition of stricter manpower controls.

On August 5, the Director of War Mobilization issued a new directive placing employment ceilings on non-essential industries in labour shortage areas. The declared aim of this move was to transfer 200,000 workers to vital war production. While not a new idea, the directive emphasized that the employment ceilings authorized by the "priority referral system" which went into effect on July 1, were to be used to reduce non-essential employment. The plan was similar to a labour stabilization plan introduced on the West Coast by the Office of War Mobilization and announced on September 4, 1943. This scheme established Area Production Urgency Committees under the War Production Board and was later extended to all critical labour areas. These Committees were empowered to establish relative urgencies for manpower within the area, based on directives of the Production Executive Committee of the War Production Board. In addition, Manpower Priorities Committees were created under the War Manpower Commission to establish ceilings and control referrals in such a way as to meet the priorities established by the Area Production Urgency Committee and generally to ensure the proper use of manpower in the areas. The new directive of the Office of War Mobilization extended the coverage of both the Area Production Urgency Committees and Manpower Priorities Committees to relatively slack labour areas in addition to the tight labour areas previously included. The Area Production Urgency Committees were to authorize new civilian production in relatively slack labour areas only when manpower was certified available by the War Manpower Commission. Since the military services dominated the Area Production Urgency Committees, it was to be expected that the military representatives on these Committees would follow the policy of the Army Service Forces which was to oppose any reconversion at that time. The significance of the directive, apart from its geographical extension, was the fact that the manpower ceilings were to be used to decrease non-essential employment and not merely to stabilize it.

After the dispute with the Chairman of the War Production Board over the partial reconversion programme, the Army Service Forces gave considerable publicity to their military production problems. High ranking officers emphasized that despite the overall success of war production, specific programmes were lagging badly. The most difficult programmes in the fall of 1944 were rubber tires, heavy guns, artillery ammunition, explosives and fire control equipment, bombs, radar, trucks, tanks, construction equipment, and tentage fabrics. The main difficulty in most of these was the shortage of manpower, although in some instances it appears that the military requirements were unrealistic in view of the capacity available. There can be little doubt that the moves to tighten labour controls by the Office of War Mobilization were largely the result of pressure exerted by the armed services.

The erratic character of the reconversion programme in the United States has been commented on by Donald Nelson in terms which do not reflect favourably on military procurement policy. He states that the military authorities repeatedly misjudged requirements and goes on to say:

Most of the military programs which were behind schedule in the summer of 1944 were programs which the Army had cut back very sharply some months previously only to find that it had made miscalculations and would have to raise its sights again.[16]

Some of the difficulties of orderly reconversion planning are testified to by Nelson, who claims that "the Army was, quite openly, out to protect war production by the simple means of creating pools of unemployment."[17]

A series of warnings were issued during the latter part of November concerning the lags in critical munitions programmes and the seriousness of the manpower situation. Lieut. General Brehon Somervell, Commanding General of the Army Service Forces, stated publicly that 40 per cent of the munitions programmes was not on schedule and that about 27 per cent of the lagging programmes was classed as "critical." A good deal of publicity, including a radio appeal from General Eisenhower, emphasized the necessity for stepping up artillery ammunition output. The Chairman of the War Production Board announced that 200,000 workers were needed for urgent war programmes. In particular, he emphasized that the manpower shortage was hindering production in seven important lines: foundries and forge shops, ship-building, heavy artillery ammunition, radar, cotton duck and tent twill, heavy field artillery and gun carriages, and dry cell batteries. The seriousness of the situation had been emphasized about the middle of November by the Director of War Mobilization in a letter to the heads of five war agencies. In it he stated that unless manpower shortages in critical war production areas were remedied within a reasonably short time, he would order the suspension of authorizations for new civilian production. He said, "While a shortage of material and weapons exists in relatively few programs, it is sufficient, if not speedily overcome, to prolong the war."[18]

In the face of this situation, suddenly increased Army requirements for small arms ammunition had a severe impact. It was expected that 60,000 additional workers would be needed by June, 1945, bringing the total employment in small arms ammunition production to 115,600. An additional 50,000,000 pounds of brass strip per month would be needed for the revised programme. The immediate consequence of the change was a complete reversal of War Production Board policy on releasing additional amounts of copper for civilian production. All relaxation of Conservation Order M-9-c and any relevant limitation orders was halted. An earlier recommendation that high-cost copper mine production be discontinued was withdrawn, and it was urged that imports be stepped up to 250,000 tons in the second quarter of 1945. It was also recommended that recently authorized civilian programmes be re-examined, and that all releases of copper under the spot authorization plan be stopped.

Finally, on December 1, the Army, Navy, War Production Board and War Manpower Commission, recognizing the increasing seriousness of the manpower situation and lagging war production, directed that no new civilian production should be permitted under the spot authorization plan in areas of current acute labour shortage for a period of ninety days. Not long after, the suspension was also applied to other areas where the labour shortage was less acute.[19] Approvals under the spot authorization plan were to be given only in localities where war programmes were on schedule, where there was sufficient labour for military needs or where labour unqualified for war work was available.[20] The necessity for slowing down the pace of reconversion became clearer when an increased artillery ammunition programme was announced on December 4 by the Army Service Forces. The Chairman of the War Production Board, in announcing the increase, stated that 85,000 additional workers would be needed as well as about $500,000,000 in new facilities. This meant that the total labour deficit at that time appeared to be in excess of 300,000.

The War Production Board supplemented various other actions by issuing an internal order further limiting civilian production. The essential part of this order read:

It will be the policy of the War Production Board Requirements Committee and of the Division Requirements Committee not to approve increases in programs entitled to firm controlled materials allotments and base-ratings priority assistance in excess of the quantities necessary to fulfill essential requirements. It shall be generally presumed that the level of essential requirements does not exceed the fourth quarter 1944 production level authorized under approved programs, firm controlled materials allotments, or appeals. . . .[21]

Furthermore, the burden of proof rested with the claimant agency sponsoring a programme goal above the fourth quarter level to demonstrate positively that fourth quarter production level was clearly below essential requirements. In effect, this order froze most civilian programmes at existing levels.

The Canadian problem was to keep abreast of the gyrating policy in the United States. Canada dropped behind and drew ahead as the decontrol measures of the United States were successively relaxed and restricted. One fundamental difference in the two countries is noteworthy. In the latter part of 1944 and early 1945, the United States made extensive use of production controls to control the use of manpower. In Canada, manpower and production controls were independent, a fact which emphasized the difficulty of maintaining parallelism in decontrol measures. Nevertheless, surprising success was achieved in maintaining the satisfactory agreements on production controls and priorities which had been arrived at earlier in the war. Some of the problems involved in the reduction of war production in the two countries may be illustrated by referring again to the case of aluminum.

3. CUT-BACKS IN ALUMINUM PRODUCTION[22]

Quite early in 1943, evidence began to accumulate that aluminum was no longer scarce, indeed that there was a surplus available in the United States. In view of this, action was started by the War Production Board to permit the wider use of aluminum and plans for the expansion of facilities for fabricating and for making primary aluminum were cancelled during the last three months of 1943.

The change in the aluminum situation also had repercussions in Canada. As mentioned in an earlier chapter, the Metals Reserve Company re-negotiated its contracts with the Aluminum Company of Canada in September to provide a standard base price of 15 cents per pound for any deliveries after November 1, and modified some of the financial provisions of the contracts as well. The new contract was merely a symptom of the improved situation and considerable attention began to be devoted to the most satisfactory way of reducing the output of aluminum. Steps were taken by the War Production Board to close down a few potlines at the end of 1943 but, by early 1944, a reduction of 300,000,000 pounds a year was in prospect.

It was only natural that with the actual and prospective cut-backs in the United States, critical attention should be directed to the fact that the Aluminum Company of Canada was maintaining its rate of operations. The statement was made that the Canadian price was higher than the domestic price although this was denied by the War Production Board. It was also alleged by the New York State Power Authority in its 1943 annual report that the Aluminum Company of Canada would make a profit of $75,000,000 from the Shipshaw Project.[23] After a good deal of criticism of the Canadian contracts in the press and elsewhere, the War Production Board requested the Metals Reserve Company in April to postpone until 1945, 100,000,000 pounds of aluminum scheduled for delivery in 1944.

It was about this time that the War Production Board was under strong pressure from Congress to remove unnecessary controls and the liberalization of restrictions on the use of aluminum was a part of the four-point reconversion plan announced by the Chairman of the War Production Board in June. The aluminum order which was issued in mid-July expanded the list of permitted uses to include kitchenware and containers and provided also that aluminum could be substituted for any other metal in the production of civilian goods provided that the quarterly rate of production did not exceed that in effect in the second quarter of 1944. There were other modifications of the restrictions to permit the use of aluminum in connection with the spot authorization plan and for other purposes.

Despite these relaxations, aluminum continued to accumulate, and by midsummer, 1944, consideration was again given to revising the Canadian contracts. The Metals Reserve Company, acting on behalf of the War Production Board, reached an agreement with the Aluminum Company of Canada that 125,000,000 pounds would be delivered before the end of 1944, while the balance of the amount called for under the contract, 250,000,000 pounds, was to be delivered only if wanted. An advance of five cents a pound had already been made and this was to be forfeited on any amount ultimately cancelled.

During the fall of 1944, further substantial cut-backs in aluminum production in the United States were ordered. In some cases, there was strong local resistance to such action and there were instances where bitter references were made to the purchase of aluminum from Canada. The following paragraph in *Aluminum Policies of the War Production Board* illustrates the reaction which followed the closing down of an aluminum plant in California:

The Fresno Bee carried a denunciation of the action, apparently designed for local consumption, by Congressman Gearhart. "If the plant is closed," Gearhart declared, with pointed reference to Shipshaw, "it will be due directly to aluminum over production, the fruit of a boon-doggling project which, without the consent or knowledge of Congress, has set up competition for American business men outside American borders with the money of American taxpayers." He also asserted that $500,000,000 of American money had been spent on Shipshaw and that the Canadian metal was being purchased at 11 cents above the American market price.[24]

By November, 1944, there was a sudden and unexpected change in the aluminum supply situation because of the slowing down of the Allied offensive in Europe and the resultant increase in military orders. By this time, the domestic manpower situation in the United States had become stringent and there were prospective difficulties involved in increasing production sufficiently to meet the new requirements for aluminum ingot and fabricated items. It was decided in January, 1945, that purchases from Canada should be resumed and that Canadian potlines with a capacity of 10,000,000 pounds per month should be reopened. One consideration to be borne in mind was that the Metals Reserve Company stood to forfeit $11,500,000 in advances, if the Canadian contract was cancelled. Therefore, acting again at the request of the War Production Board, the Metals Reserve Company arranged for the delivery of 165,000,000 pounds of aluminum from Canada, the shipments to be made before July 10, 1945. About a month later, the Metals Reserve Company was requested to procure an additional 300,000,000 pounds. However, by this time there were certain legal restrictions on the payment of premium prices which were to be effective on June 1, 1945, and there was some hesitation on the part of the Metals Reserve Company to enter into negotiations. It was also anticipated that the resumption of Canadian purchases might be strongly criticized. Before the end of March, a new contract was announced after the War Production Board had urged the necessity of immediate action. The contract called for the delivery of 250,000,000 pounds at current market prices during 1945, but the Metals Reserve Company was firmly committed to take only 150,000,000 pounds since the balance could be cancelled without penalty on sixty-five days' notice.

The next major development can be summarized conveniently by quoting again from *Aluminum Policies of the War Production Board:*

On March 30 the Senate Small Business Committee, already studying the future of the light metals, opened an investigation of all Government contracts for Canadian aluminum. The hearings took somewhat the form of an inquisition, with War Production Board and RFC officials being required to justify the financing of Shipshaw in the first place and each of the contracts that followed. The attack came primarily from Secretary Ickes and his subordinates in charge of the Bonneville Power Authority, from Congressmen and others interested in the development of the Pacific Northwest, and from the Reynolds Metals Company. The contention was that the same money spent for Canadian aluminum would have produced more metal in Washington and Oregon, creating at the same time an American rather than a foreign postwar resource. . . . William L. Batt, who carried the load for WPB, succeeded reasonably well in establishing the pressing need for aluminum, and the prospect of speedier production in Canada, at the time the original contracts were made. The same arguments furnished the justification for the newest contract also, but the situation was changing rapidly, and by the date of Batt's appearance before the Senate Small Business Committee on April 10, the end of the European war again seemed in sight. The contract, however, had been written with this in view. On May 15, a week after the German surrender, the optional 150,000,000 pounds were cancelled, reducing the purchase to 100,000,000 pounds; and two months later a renegotiation of the contract was announced which cut the total to 75,000,000, all of which was to be shipped on or before August 18, 1945.[25]

Around the end of July, consideration was again being given to restoring part of the cut in the Canadian contract but further action was suspended as a result of the Japanese surrender. The obvious conclusion to be drawn from all this is that there were certain obstacles to the orderly reduction of aluminum capacity in Canada, the main one being the erratic character of the requirements of the United States. Under these circumstances, the co-ordination of reconversion in the aluminum industry in the two countries was difficult to achieve.

4. THE CO-ORDINATION OF RECONVERSION POLICY

In Canada and the United States, there had been a complete prohibition of the manufacture of a number of essential civilian items by the War Production Board in 1942. It later became clear that, in some cases, the manufacture of minimum essential quantities would be very desirable for civilian welfare and could be undertaken in a way that would not interfere with war production. The Office of Civilian Requirements was the principal sponsor of production programmes for a number of civilian goods, of which electric irons were a notable example. These civilian production programmes were approved by the Requirements Committee of the War Production Board and allocations and priority assistance were granted within the limits of the programme. In June, 1944, an agreement was reached between the Wartime Prices and Trade Board and the Canadian Division of the War Production Board covering comparable civilian programmes for Canada. The essence of the agreement was that if the Canadian programme permitted comparable levels of production in terms of base period output, the Canadian Division could issue priority ratings on Canadian imports of materials and components on its own authority. If, however, Canadian programmes were to exceed those contemplated in the United States, relative to base period production, prior approval of the War Production Board in Washington would be required before priority assistance could be granted. The Wartime Prices and Trade Board also undertook to keep the War Production Board fully informed of the details of Canadian plans for the resumption of production of specific civilian items. The agreement specifically referred to goods which contained an appreciable United States content in components or materials but there was to be a full exchange of information on any Canadian programmes not dependent on such imports.

This basic agreement was refined and extended as the pace of reconversion quickened in the summer and fall of 1944. Later agreements were reached that the benefits of Priorities Regulations 23, 24, and 25 would be extended to Canadian industry. This was consonant with the War Production Board policy of affording priority assistance to Canadian applicants as though they were domestic applicants. This had come to apply not only to military production but to essential civilian production as well. The original agreement on reconversion programmes was confirmed, which meant that the Canadian Division could authorize priority assistance for production schedules in Canada which were comparable to those approved for the United States.

If the Canadian programme contemplated production at levels

relatively higher than those authorized in the United States, the Wartime Prices and Trade Board would advise the Canadian Division of the details, and the contemplated plan would then be cleared by the Canadian Division with the Industry Divisions or the Program Adjustment Committee of the War Production Board. Should the War Production Board fail to concur in the Canadian programme, Canadian industry would have to rely on the spot authorization procedure outlined in Priorities Regulation 25. These arrangements applied only to official programmes. In cases where civilian production was being resumed without government sponsorship, the spot authorization procedure would be applicable to Canada, provided that the Priorities Officer certified that the production planned would relieve an existing or prospective pocket of unemployment.

Apart from civilian production programmes, it was agreed also that Canadian applicants would participate fully in the benefits of Priorities Regulation 23 and 24 which provided for the construction of experimental models and for the purchase of machine tools, manufacturing machinery, and allied equipment.

In addition to the operating agencies, it was natural that the Combined Production and Resources Board should be intimately concerned with the problems of reconversion. In particular, the United Kingdom was anxious to establish through the medium of the Combined Boards the principle that civilian production should be resumed more quickly in the United Kingdom than in the other two countries. This would have involved the detailed planning of military cut-backs in the three countries in such a way that war production in the United Kingdom would be cut relatively heavily in the transition period. Some system of clearances of military production plans would also be required, but this would not have been very practical in view of the inherent autonomy of the United States in such matters. The proposal was finally watered down and it was agreed merely that the three countries would formally exchange information on reconversion but that this would not imply any right of clearance or review by any of the member countries. The reports submitted under this scheme were to be made available to national agencies as a means of keeping them fully informed. While Canada welcomed the idea, the initial experience was not too successful. The submission of an outline of Canadian plans was regarded as an excuse for a rather critical but uninformed appraisal by officials in the War Production Board. In general, however, the exchange of information fostered by the Combined Production and Resources Board was an important contribution to the mutual understanding of reconversion problems. Particular attention was paid to this aspect of the Board's work in the revised terms of reference of the Board issued by the President and the two Prime Ministers in January, 1945. Their statement emphasized the importance of the Board's function as a "forum or focal point for consultation and interchange of information on mutual industrial and economic production problems."

Apart from the exchange of information, more substantive agreements were reached in the Combined Production and Resources Board on the treatment of war orders placed by the United Kingdom and the United States in Canada. It was clear that since only about 20 per cent of Canadian war production was to fill domestic requirements, Canada would be very vulnerable to rapid cut-backs in military orders by the United States and the United Kingdom, particularly in view of the temptation of a country to reduce its foreign orders first. Agreement was reached in the Combined Production and Resources Board that orders placed in Canada would not be cut more severely than domestic orders. This was clearly of great benefit to Canada in permitting a more orderly resumption of civilian production than might otherwise have been the case.

Military reverses in Europe around the end of 1944 led to a suspension of public discussion of reconversion by the War Production Board for several months. When victory in Europe appeared certain, additional plans were announced and, in particular, a few days after VE-Day, a substantial relaxation of controls was effected by the issuance of Priorities Regulation 27.[26] This new regulation applied only to manufacturers with output valued at less than $50,000 per quarter, and permitted them to obtain small amounts of production materials with automatic priority ratings of AA-4 and further permitted them to place orders for steel, copper, and aluminum under the Controlled Materials Plan. The regulation defined production materials as material or products including fabricated parts and sub-assemblies which were to be incorporated into the product.

With the end of the war in Europe, it became necessary to define the rôle which Canadian military forces would play in the war with Japan. There were undoubtedly many Canadians who felt that the important part of the war had ended with VE-Day, and it was recognized in the United States that Canada had been predominantly concerned with the European theatre. Some fears existed that the reconversion policies of the two countries might diverge and the United States might be forced to wage an undue share of the war against Japan. However, assurance was given by the President in a report to Congress dated May 22, 1945, that this was not the case. One part of the report stated:

There will be substantial reductions in the total volume of allied war production now that Germany has been defeated. Both in the United States and abroad, these reductions will permit some reconversion from war to civilian production and some increase in commercial exports. Plans for reconversion in the United States, Britain, and Canada are being co-ordinated on a broad front so that these nations will be devoting equitable shares of industrial capacity to the war against Japan.[27]

A similar assurance was given by the Acting Secretary of State for External Affairs in Canada, who released a statement on the same day to the effect that the relaxation of wartime controls in the two countries would be co-ordinated as closely as possible. He said in this statement that "both governments will consider and deal with the problems of the transition period from war to peace in the same spirit that was manifested in the Hyde Park Declaration."[28]

These public statements were based on an exchange of notes dated May 7 and May 15, 1945, the text of which was not publicly released until 1948. The desirability of continued economic co-ordination and co-operation during the balance of the war against Japan was emphasized by the United States in the originating note dated May 7, 1945. It took the form of a restatement of the general principles of the Hyde Park Declaration and went on to deal with a number of specific issues of reconversion policy. The exchange of notes contains such a detailed statement of the policies of the two governments that it is worthwhile to reproduce the text in full. The first note, signed by Mr. Ray Atherton, the United States Ambassador to Canada, read as follows:

Under the Hyde Park Declaration of April 20, 1941, measures were taken to make the most prompt and effective utilization of the productive facilities of the United States and Canada for wartime purposes. As the period of reconversion approaches, the Government of the United States has given consideration to the continuance of co-operative measures. It believes that these measures apply as a matter of course to the Pacific War and it has noted that the Declaration itself contains no termination date, specific or implied. Accordingly, under the instructions of my Government, I have the honor to propose that the general principles of the Hyde Park Declaration be continued on a fully reciprocal basis for the remainder of the war and that the same spirit of co-operation between the two countries should characterize their treatment of reconversion and other problems of mutual concern as the transition to peacetime economy progresses.

Consequent upon the degree of integration resulting from our wartime measures of co-operation in the economic field, numerous specific problems will arise from time to time. One such problem to which urgent attention is being given is the reconversion of industry to the maximum extent compatible with vigorous prosecution of the war against Japan. The problem is particularly urgent from the viewpoint of the United States because the Hyde Park Declaration was implemented in large part by the equal application to Canada of domestic procedures in respect of priorities and allocations.

It is evident that during this initial phase of reconversion, priorities administered by the respective control agencies of the two governments are of the utmost importance to industries seeking to prepare for normal trading conditions. In response to informal inquiries received from Canadian officials in Washington and on condition of reciprocity, particularly where Canada is a principal supplier of materials needed for reconversion and civilian production, the Government of the United States would be prepared to implement the following principles as regards requirements which Canadian industry may desire to fulfil in this country for reconversion purposes:

1. The application of the priorities powers towards Canadian requirements should be as closely parallel to the application of the same powers toward domestic requirements as is practicable.

2. Canada should, in general, be given priorities assistance only of a character and to an extent parallel to priorities assistance given similar requirements in the United States, including any machinery needed for immediate reconversion. To the extent, however, that components could be obtained by Canada without benefit of priorities assistance, no objection could be made to more rapid reconversion activities in Canada.

3. Assistance should be given to Canadian companies through their priorities officer to grant automatic AA-4 priorities and firm CMP allotments to manufacturing concerns producing less than $50,000 of product per quarter, similar to such assistance granted domestic small firms. Similarly, the rating privileges of Pri. Reg. 24 and L-41, as they may be amended, should be available to Canadian applicants.

4. It is recognized that complete parallelism of revocation and relaxation of orders between the United States and Canada is not possible because of the differences in the situations in the two nations. However, an effort should be made, in conjunction with the Canadian authorities, to reach the greatest parallelism possible. If it should become necessary for Canada to relax their orders more rapidly than the United States, in no case should priorities assistance be given to a Canadian manufacturer to make civilian goods which are prohibited in this country by War Production Board order.

While the problem of reconversion of industry is the first of the problems which my Government believes it mutually desirable to consider under the principles of the Hyde Park Declaration, other problems will shortly arise. The Canadian Ambassador's note, No. 156 of April 30 to the Secretary of State regarding the disposal of surplus war-like stores arising from orders placed by either government in the other country may, when the dimensions of the subject become more clearly defined, provide an instance in which my Government will seek the favorable consideration of your Government under the Hyde Park principles. Other questions will inevitably arise in connection with the relaxation of wartime controls affecting trade, such as the War Exchange Tax and procedures applicable to exports to the other American republics.

In his statement on the initial period of reconstruction presented to Parliament by the Minister of Reconstruction last month, the Minister referred to the great wartime increase in the output and exchange of goods which was dependent on close collaboration among the Governments of the British Commonwealth and of the United States. He stated that postwar collaboration along equally bold and imaginative lines was essential in the interest of expanded world trade. At Washington on March 13, 1945, a similar statement was made by Prime Minister King and by the late President Roosevelt in regard to the problems of international economic and trading policy.

In view of the high degree of economic interdependence of the Canadian and American economies, the Government of the United States desired to assure the Government of Canada that it will consider and deal with the problems of the transition from war to peace in the spirit of the Hyde Park Declaration which gave rise to such successful co-operation for war purposes. My Government would greatly appreciate a similar assurance on the part of the Canadian Government, together with an expression of its views on the principles which the United States Government would be willing to apply in the initial problem of the reconversion of industry.[29]

The text of the Canadian note in reply dated May 15, 1945, and signed by Mr. Brooke Claxton, Acting Secretary of State for External Affairs, was as follows:

The Government of Canada welcomes the assurance of the Government of the United States, contained in your note No. 320 of May 7, that it will consider and deal with the problems of the transition from war to peace in the spirit of the Hyde Park Declaration which gave rise to such successful co-operation for war purposes.

The Canadian Government agrees that post-war collaboration along bold and imaginative lines is essential in the interests of expanded world trade.

The Government of Canada on its part desires to assure the Government of the United States that the same spirit of co-operation, which was manifested in the Hyde Park Declaration, will characterize the Canadian Government's consideration and treatment of the problems of the period of transition which are of mutual concern.

The principles which the Government of the United States would be willing to apply on condition of reciprocity in the initial problem of the reconversion of industry are acceptable to the Canadian Government. The Canadian Government believes indeed that the principles proposed will minimize for both Governments the difficulties of reconversion.

The Canadian Government assumes that "the condition of reciprocity" implies a continued adherence to the principle of reciprocity followed throughout the war when both Governments have made allowance for the difference in the conditions existing and in the methods of control adopted in the two countries.[30]

One significant virtue of the restatement of principles contained in these notes was that they provided for the continuity of policy even if sudden changes in the war agencies in Washington occurred. A detailed set of understandings had been worked out with the War Production Board over a period of years, and it was clearly desirable to have the general principles of parity and co-operation a matter of permanent record. Should the War Production Board be dissolved and its personnel disbanded, this understanding would make it unnecessary to re-argue all the old issues and re-establish the policy of co-operation with a new agency.

The modification of the priorities system which would become necessary with the end of hostilities was the subject of intensive planning from the summer of 1944 on. The War Production Board constituted a Committee on Demobilization of Controls after VE-Day (CODCAVE) which drew up a detailed blueprint of a simplified priorities system. Its plans were approved by the War Production Board early in October, 1944, and were later kept under review by the Committee on Period One (the interval between the defeat of Germany and the defeat of Japan), which had been established in February, 1945. In accordance with these plans, the Controlled Materials Plan was liberalized shortly after the defeat of Germany and a greatly simplified priorities system was adopted. The new system provided for an MM preference rating which would be applicable to military production and a CC rating which could be used to break bottlenecks in civilian production or to encourage certain civilian production programmes.

Again, early in July, 1945, the War Production Board affirmed its policy of providing priority assistance to Canadian civilian production programmes. At this time, it was agreed that priority assistance would be afforded to Canadian programmes up to 8 per cent of the corresponding programmes being sponsored by the War Production Board. This assistance was to be provided without regard to the retention of controls in Canada, but only so long as similar assistance was being given to producers in the United States.

With the sudden defeat of Japan, there was a general revocation of control orders in both the United States and Canada. This was done in a wholesale fashion and no attempt was made to co-ordinate relaxations in the two countries during the hectic few weeks that followed VJ-Day.

Despite the difficulties of pursuing precisely parallel reconversion policies in the two countries, Canada was able to maintain the general principles of parity unimpaired throughout the reconversion period. The principle was also accepted that, in special circumstances, priority assistance would be forthcoming to permit Canadian civilian production at levels which were comparatively higher than in the United States. In part, this was a result of the care and patience expended in explaining and justifying Canadian policies and plans to the War Production Board. This episode provides a clear demonstration of the beneficial effects of mutual consultation and explanation. At times, the situation was ripe for misunderstanding and recrimination. The harmonious relations which existed in fact were the fruits of the previous years of intensive educational and missionary effort, dating from the Hyde Park Declaration.

REFERENCES FOR CHAPTER XIII

1. P.C. 6874, September 2, 1941.

2. P.C. 9946, December 31, 1943.

3. *Minutes of the War Production Board,* November 30, 1943, p. 293.

4. U.S., Senate Special Committee Investigating the National Defense Program, *Outlines of Problems of Conversion from War Production,* (78th Cong., 1st. sess.), Senate Report 10, part 12, November 5, 1943, p. 3.

5. U.S., Senate Special Committee on Post-War Economic Policy and Planning, (78th Cong., 1st sess.), Report No. 539, p. 2.

6. *Minutes of the War Production Board,* February 22, 1944, pp. 312-13.

7. U.S., Senate Special Committee Investigating the National Defense Program, *Third Annual Report,* pp. 9-10.

8. U.S., Congress, Senate, Document No. 154, (78th Cong., 2nd. sess.), *Report on War and Post-War Adjustment Policy* by Bernard M. Baruch and John M. Hancock (Washington: U.S. Government Printing Office, 1944).

9. *Statutes of Canada,* 8 Geo. VI, c. 18, June 30, 1944.

10. *Ibid.,* 9-10 Geo. VI, c. 16, December 18, 1945.

11. *Minutes of the War Production Board,* June 13, 1944, pp. 339-40.

12. Supplementary Conservation Order M-1-i as amended July 15, 1944 (aluminum), 9 *Federal Register* 8014; Supplementary Conservation Order M-2-b as amended July 15, 1944 (magnesium), 9 *Federal Register* 8016.

13. Priorities Regulation 23, July 22, 1944, 9 *Federal Register* 8781.

14. Priorities Regulation 24, July 25, 1944, 9 *Federal Register* 9202.

15. Priorities Regulation 25, August 15, 1944, 9 *Federal Register* 9945.

16. Donald Nelson, *Arsenal of Democracy: The Story of American War Production* (New York: Harcourt, Brace, 1946), p. 403.

17. *Ibid.,* p. 402.

18. *New York Times,* November 17, 1944, p. 1.

19. *Ibid.,* December 2, 1944, p. 1.

20. The original suspension applied to so-called Group I areas, in which there was a current acute labour shortage, while the next suspension applied to Group II areas, i.e., areas where there was a labour stringency or where a labour shortage was anticipated within six months.

21. War Production Board, General Program Order 5-10, effective December 7, 1944.

22. This section is mainly based on the account in *Aluminum Policies of the War Production Board.*

23. Quoted in *ibid.*, p. 275.

24. The quotations from the *Fresno Bee* of August 3, 1944, are cited in *Aluminum Policies of the War Production Board*, p. 293.

25. *Ibid.*, pp. 311-12.

26. Priorities Regulation 27, May 10, 1945, 10 *Federal Register* 5450.

27. *Nineteenth Report on Lend-Lease Operations for the Period Ended March 31, 1945* (Washington: U.S. Government Printing Office, 1945), p. 9.

28. *New York Times,* May 22, 1945, p. 10.

29. Canada, Treaty Series, 1948, No. 1, *Exchange of Notes (May 7 and 15, 1945) between Canada and the United States of America Providing for the Continuation of the Principles of the Hyde Park Declaration into the Post-war Transitional Period with Special Reference to the Problem of Reconversion of Industry* (Ottawa: King's Printer, 1948).

30. *Ibid.*

CHAPTER XIV

COMPARISONS OF CONSUMPTION LEVELS

By 1942, civilians in Canada and the United States began to suffer inconveniences because of the lack of certain consumers' goods. Initially, governmental restrictions on the output of civilian commodities applied mainly to durable goods such as automobiles and washing machines, which were large users of scarce metals, facilities, and skilled labour. Sufficiently large inventories of consumers' durable goods remained to satisfy many essential needs. Moreover, the purchase of many of the items which were restricted earliest could be postponed without seriously damaging either the economy or civilian morale. As military demands grew and as inventories were depleted, definite shortages of essential goods such as food, textiles, and footwear developed. Public interest in consumer problems was high, and it was natural that the question of the welfare of civilians became a political issue of some significance. In the United States, in particular, some sections of the press were eager to find examples of "bureaucratic inefficiency" in the administration of restrictions, especially consumer rationing. Invidious comparisons between Canada and the United States became common and sometimes rather curious. For example, newspapers hostile to the Administration would periodically contain reports to the effect that Canada was a land flowing with milk and honey compared to the United States. The press contained lush descriptions of the flitches of bacon, the thick steaks, and the rich cream alleged to abound in Canadian cities. The stories were primarily designed to impress upon the reader in the United States the conclusion that governmental fumbling was the cause of the new and unwelcome austerity. Such flattering, if inaccurate, descriptions of Canadian food supplies were recognized by Canadian officials as a source of discord. Quite apart from such inspired publicity, there were widespread misconceptions in each country concerning consumption levels in the other. Some specific examples of the issues which arose in comparisons of civilian consumption levels will throw some light on an important aspect of the wartime relations between Canada and the United States.

1. Consumers' Durable Goods

In the fall of 1941, a series of governmental restrictions were issued in both countries limiting the output of most consumers' durable goods.

These actions were taken as a result of existing and prospective shortages of metals which threatened to slow down war production. In the United States, the Civilian Supply Division of the Office of Production Management was the main proponent of rapid conversion at that time and was responsible for the initial curtailment. In Canada, the Controller of Supplies had jurisdiction over commodities such as domestic refrigerators, stoves, electric irons and toasters, fans and phonographs, which were obvious targets for restriction. The imposition of restrictions in the two countries were carefully synchronized, a highly desirable move since there was a good deal of opposition to the conversion of civilian industry in the United States at that time. The restriction on the manufacture of domestic refrigerators in both countries is an interesting case in point. In the United States, output restrictions were imposed by the Office of Production Management in Limitation Order L-5 dated September 30, 1941.[1] The initial order divided producers into three classes depending on monthly sales in the twelve months ending June 30, 1941. Class A producers were those who had sold a monthly average of 16,000 or more. Class B producers were those selling between 5,000 and 16,000, while Class C producers sold less than 5,000 per month. The limitation order restricted the output of Class A producers in the five months from August 1 to December 31, 1941, to 50,400 or five times 55 per cent of the monthly average in the base period. Class B producers were restricted to 17,750 or five times 63 per cent of the monthly base period average. Class C producers were limited to five times 71 per cent of monthly average output in the base period. In the case of Class A and B producers, whichever of the options was higher was allowed. It was calculated that this scheme of restriction involved a reduction of 43.2 per cent below production in the twelve months ending June 30, 1941. In Canada, the restriction order was simpler. On October 1, 1941, the day after the issuance of Limitation Order L-5, the Controller of Supplies put out an order limiting the monthly output of domestic refrigerators in Canada to 75 per cent of the monthly average in the calendar year 1940.[2] It appeared superficially that output in Canada was being cut 25 per cent compared to 43.2 per cent in the United States. The unfairness of this appealed to certain sections of the press in the United States, and there was a good deal of unfavourable comment on the disparity of the restrictions. For example, the *Chicago Daily Tribune* carried the following Associated Press story, datelined Ottawa, October 1, on the front page and added some parenthetical and italicized comments:

Canadian domestic production of radios, refrigerators, stoves, vacuum cleaners and electric washing machines has been reduced to 75 per cent of 1940 output, the Department of Munitions and Supply announced tonight.

[*The Canadian slash of 25 per cent in consumers' goods production is far less than the reductions ordered or planned in the United States. The Office of Production Management has ordered cuts of 48.4 per cent and 43.2 per cent, respectively, in United States production of automobiles and refrigerators. OPM officials said similar cuts were pending in output of household washing and ironing machines, vacuum cleaners and other electrical appliances.*][3]

Closer investigation showed that the restrictions in the two countries were almost precisely the same. All Canadian producers would have fallen in the Class C category and would therefore have been allowed 71 per cent of their base period monthly output in the United States. It is probable that the monthly average output in the first six months of 1941 was sufficiently higher than in the first six months of 1940 to more than compensate for the difference between 75 and 71 per cent. The similarity of the restrictions was by no means evident to the uninitiated although some relatively simple explanation might have avoided the misunderstanding. About ten days after the orders were issued the Joint Economic Committees noted the situation and did issue an explanatory press release in which they commented favourably on "the high degree of similarity and simultaneity already achieved in the imposition of limitations on output in civilian industry."[4] By this time, the damage had been done and it is doubtful if the initial inaccurate impression conveyed by the Associated Press story could be corrected. This was the first of many similar episodes, and stories about the relative laxity of Canadian controls continued to crop up in the press in the United States. Sometimes, there were basic differences in the problems of the two countries and the unavoidable variations in the way in which restriction orders were phrased tended to stimulate invidious comparisons. In other cases, there were real differences, or at least, differences in the timing of restrictions, which provoked a good deal of comment unflattering to Canadian controls. Much of the hostile criticism related to a wide variety of metal-using goods whose production was completely banned in the United States in the spring of 1942 by Conservation Order M-126.[5] A similar order was issued by the Wartime Prices and Trade Board shortly after this,[6] and there was almost continuous consultation between the administrators concerned with these restrictions in the two countries in an effort to achieve uniformity of practice. The orders were revised frequently with the result that relatively minor differences existed for short periods, although they were usually not minor enough to escape attention in the press. As might be expected, comparisons were most frequent in the case of consumer goods in general use, of which footwear may serve as an example.

2. The Case of Footwear

The high level of demand for footwear in the United States, in conjunction with a serious shortage of leather occasioned by heavy military requirements, led the Office of Price Administration to introduce consumer rationing of leather footwear in early 1943.[7] The initial ration was fixed at three pairs of shoes per person per year. Despite this, it was decided that footwear would not be rationed in Canada. The fact that Canadian civilians were thus presumably better off immediately provoked a good deal of unfavourable comment in the United States. The Canadian argument was that the annual consumption of leather footwear in Canada was somewhere between two and two and one-half pairs of shoes per capita and that the imposition of consumer rationing at the level permitted in the United States would probably make no significant difference in the volume of Canadian consumption. For example, in 1943, the per capita consumption of men's leather shoes in the United States was estimated to be 2.10 pairs compared to 1.62 pairs in Canada while the per capita consumption of women's leather shoes was 3.39 and 2.94 pairs respectively.[8] It was also believed that footwear made of leather substitutes, which was unrationed, was more readily available in the United States than in Canada. The absence of consumer rationing of footwear in Canada certainly did not mean that Canadian civilians could purchase all the leather footwear they wanted, although this impression was fairly common in the United States.

The disparity of controls in the two countries was complicated by the fact that Canada continued to import footwear from the United States. The quantities involved were minute in terms of total production in the United States and, except for special shoes for crippled feet, were not regarded as important by the Wartime Prices and Trade Board. In fact, prior to July 1, 1943, Canada had not submitted statements of requirements for footwear to the War Production Board. At that time, in order to assist the War Production Board in controlling its allocations, an arbitrary Canadian quota of 500,000 pairs was established for the twelve months ending June 30, 1944. Later, the quota was reduced to 400,000 pairs for the year ending December 31, 1944.

Sales to Canada created one problem which was the concern of the Office of Price Administration, the agency responsible for shoe rationing.

In the rationing system, ration coupons turned in by consumers flowed back through the different distributive levels to the manufacturer. A retailer, for example, had to furnish ration currency to his suppliers to replenish his inventory. However, when a sale was made to Canada, the Canadian purchaser was obviously unable to provide the exporter in the United States with ration coupons. In consequence, an arrangement was made with the Office of Price Administration that orders properly certified by the Wartime Prices and Trade Board could be used by exporters in the United States as ration currency for the replacement of shipments to Canada. At the same time, this order-approval system was designed to provide the Canadian authorities with a method of limiting imports to the quota which had been agreed on. The scheme had certain unsatisfactory features. In particular, there appeared to be some uncertainty in the United States whether approval of exports to Canada was mandatory, and as a result there were an appreciable number of shipments outside the quota.

Early in 1945, the Office of Civilian Requirements began to press for the elimination of the Canadian quota. Up to this time, the Canadians concerned had not attached much importance to imports from the United States. This is indicated by the fact that requirements had not been formally submitted to the War Production Board prior to the middle of 1943. Nor was any vigorous objection raised to the decision of the War Production Board to cut the Canadian quota from 100,000 in the first quarter of 1945, to 75,000 in the second quarter, to zero in the third quarter. Special arrangements were made for a quarterly quota of 10,000 pairs of shoes for crippled feet. The elimination of the Canadian allocation was not taken very seriously and the Wartime Prices and Trade Board was even asked whether it would prohibit the import of shoes from the United States. The reply was that any action taken primarily to protect United States supplies would have to be taken by the United States government.

It later appeared that this casual attitude was a mistake, for the elimination of the quota caused a good deal of difficulty in Canada. Certain stores and certain areas had specialized in imported shoes, with the result that there occurred a geographical maldistribution of shoes as well as hardship to individual retailers.

The irritating features of the leather footwear situation were aggravated by the anomalous regulations governing exports and imports in the United States. Up to about the end of 1943, the ration orders of the Office of Price Administration required the surrender of ration coupons for casual imports of such rationed commodities as footwear, sugar, processed foods, and meats, fats and oils. There were naturally instances in which persons in the United States had used all their coupons and were unable to pay ration coupons for gifts of rationed commodities sent from other countries. One particular case attracted some attention in the press. Evidently a United States soldier in Brazil had sent his mother a pair of shoes. Because she did not have a ration coupon she was unable to obtain her gift. This was cited by the press as a horrible example of the activities of the Office of Price Administration. Apart from this, anyone returning to the United States from Canada with rationed goods which were impounded was apt to be irritated. Nor were the post offices in the United States well equipped to handle the rotting meat and malodorous cheese which sometimes accumulated. Partly as a public relations measure, the Office of Price Administration relaxed its regulations in December, 1943, to permit ration-free entry of casual imports of footwear.[9] Canadians were never required to pay ration currency to the Canadian authorities for imported shoes. Moreover, during all of 1944 and the first half of 1945, shoes worth less than $25 could be exported by the retailer in the United States to Canadian purchasers who were not required to surrender ration coupons to the United States authorities either. In line with the policy of the Office of Civilian Requirements, pressure was exerted on the Office of Price Administration around the middle of 1945 to close this particular loophole, which was done by an amendment to the footwear rationing order issued in July.[10] According to the new regulation, shoes having a declared value of $25 or more could be exported to Canada under a purchase order approved by the Canadian Administrator of Wholesale Trade, but for shoes valued at less than $25, either a ration coupon had to be turned in or an export permit obtained. This was clearly designed to cut off casual imports by private Canadian individuals. At the same time, the Office of Price Administration undertook to make special arrangements if the new regulations should cause any hardships to Canadians seeking to buy special shoes for crippled feet in the United States.

Despite critical murmurings in the United States, there is no clear evidence that, compared to normal consumption levels, Canadian civilians were better shod than civilians in the United States during the war. In the United States, reliance was placed on formal consumer rationing, while Canada used somewhat looser but nevertheless effective controls over retail distribution.

3. FOOD

Food rationing was probably the most politically explosive of all the wartime controls. The introduction of a rationing scheme, or any changes in it, were certain to affect more people than any other government edict. The officials concerned with rationing were harassed at once by the general public, the press, particular business groups, and other government agencies. Usually, the pressure was for the relaxation of restrictions on the grounds that they were either unnecessary or too severe. It is natural also under the circumstances that the welfare of civilians in one country should be compared with that in other countries. At different times, the opinion was widely held in both Canada and the United States that domestic rationing restrictions were more rigorous than in the other country.

It was perhaps fortunate that clear-cut comparisons of consumer rationing in Canada and the United States could not often be made because of essential differences in the rationing programmes. This was particularly true of food rationing. It continues to be difficult to assess the relative position of consumers over the whole wartime period because of continual and differential changes in the rationing schemes. It may, nevertheless, be useful to review the rations of certain major food groups in late 1944 and early 1945 when the rationing programmes in the two countries had reached a phase of maturity.

The parallel attempt to adopt rationing controls got off to a bad start with the introduction of sugar rationing in 1942. In January, 1942, the Wartime Prices and Trade Board was notified by the Office of Price Administration that sugar rationing would be introduced in the United States in about two months and that this would be announced publicly in a few days. In the opinion of Canadian officials, this was a precipitate and possibly unnecessary move which should, in any case, be postponed. Although these views were conveyed to the appropriate officials in the United States, the machinery was in motion and could not be stopped. It was quite clear that Canada would have to follow suit mainly because the suspicion that rationing was to be introduced was sufficient to ensure the necessity of rationing. However, it was decided in Canada that there was not time to set up the complex administrative machinery necessary to handle consumer rationing to meet the deadline established by the United States. As a result, the Wartime Prices and Trade Board decided to introduce a voluntary system of rationing immediately. At about the same time that the prospective introduction of sugar rationing was announced in the United States, the Wartime Prices and Trade Board made a strong plea to individuals to limit their purchases of sugar to three-quarters of a pound a week.[11] This has been described as the "honour system" of rationing, although there were certain sanctions which could be applied to persons who were found to have not enough honour and too much sugar. As a make-shift arrangement, the scheme was fairly satisfactory and did provide a breathing space for the organization of a system of coupon rationing.

Coupon rationing for sugar was introduced in the United States on May 11, 1942,[12] and shortly after this, the voluntary limit on sugar consumption in Canada was reduced to one-half pound per person per week.[13] Finally, about a month later, it was announced that coupon rationing of sugar would be introduced in Canada on July 1, 1942.[14] The Canadian restrictions were not appreciably different from those which had been adopted earlier in the United States; individuals were allowed to purchase one-half pound of sugar a week upon the surrender of ration coupons.

Because sugar rationing had been introduced early and was felt almost universally, it is natural that it should have been the subject of many informed and ill-informed comparisons. In January, 1945, the consumer ration for an individual in Canada was twenty-four pounds a year or slightly less than one-half pound per week. In the United States, the ration had been twenty-four pounds a year until about a month previous, when it was reduced by the postponement of one sugar coupon. The effect of this was to reduce the ration of consumers in the United States to about twenty pounds per annum. Account must also be taken of sugar consumed in manufactured form, in soft drinks, cakes and candies, for example. When the industrial consumption is added in, actual per capita consumption of all sugars and syrups in 1944 was as follows: United States, 94.9 pounds; Canada, 89.6 pounds. There was, in other words, substantial equivalence in the treatment of civilians as far as sugar rationing was concerned. It might be noted that the United States military rations for sugar were very much higher than in either the British or Canadian armies.

The standard consumer ration of sugar in the two countries was relatively stable and not sufficiently different to excite much comment. In contrast, the sugar quotas of industrial users fluctuated a good deal. Any sustained divergence of the levels of industrial consumption of sugar was avoided by the continual consultation of the rationing authorities in the two countries and the adoption of uniform percentage quotas. Any significant differences in the treatment of manufacturers in the two countries would have provoked serious dissatisfaction.

The issuance of home canning sugar was not only a source of considerable administrative difficulty, but a matter which stimulated unfortunate comparisons and claims and counter-claims concerning the relative position of consumers in the two countries.[15] The allowance of sugar for home canning in the United States in 1944 and 1945 was twenty-five and twenty pounds respectively, whereas it was widely believed in Canada that the comparable allowance was ten pounds. This was, however, a most misleading conclusion.

The confusion arose out of the fact that the Canadian home canning sugar programme in both years was merged with the preserves rationing scheme. Under this programme, ration coupons required for the purchase of preserves were normally validated at the rate of one every two weeks or twenty-six a year. These coupons could be used to purchase specified quantities of jams, jellies, preserves, canned fruits, etc., or one-half pound of sugar. In 1944, in addition to this sugar alternative, ten pounds of sugar per person were made available for home canning by the validation of special stamps. In 1945, home canning sugar was distributed by the validation of twenty extra preserves coupons. This meant that if all preserves coupons were used to purchase sugar, a maximum of twenty-three pounds per head was allowed for home canning. No other items included in the preserves rationing scheme could be legally purchased under these circumstances. Since approximately one-half of the preserves coupons were used for the purchase of sugar, this meant that the Canadian ration was roughly equivalent to that allowed in the United States. Precise comparisons could not be made easily because of the essential differences in the two rationing schemes, but over-simplified statements that twice as much sugar was allowed for home canning in the United States as in Canada were unjustified.

There was a great deal of comment in the press and elsewhere on the amount of butter consumed in the two countries. In January, 1945, the Canadian ration was six ounces per week or 19.5 pounds per annum. It is difficult to compare butter rationing since in Canada the value of the weekly coupons was expressed in pounds or ounces while in the United States the ration value of butter was expressed in points per pound. Each consumer was entitled to spend a fixed number of points per month for purchases of meats and edible fats, the point values of individual items being adjusted periodically to influence the quantities bought. At the high level of twenty-four points per pound then current, butter was rapidly becoming a substitute for margarine. In 1944, per capita consumption of butter in the United States was twelve pounds and in addition, margarine was consumed to the extent of four pounds per capita. In Canada, the 1944 per capita consumption of butter was twenty-seven pounds, substantially higher than in the United States. No margarine was, of course, consumed in Canada. However, per capita butter consumption is traditionally higher in Canada than in the United States. The average consumption per capita in the years 1935-39 was 30.8 pounds in Canada compared to 16.7 pounds in the United States.

Although it had a rather fantastic quality, one canard about Canadian butter was circulated widely in the United States, and continued to appear despite forceful denials. On November 3, 1944, a story appeared in a newspaper in Binghampton, New York, relating to two tourists who had just returned from a hunting trip to Canada and had brought with them six pounds of butter. It is claimed that these tourists were offered the butter ration-free in a Canadian store and were charged thirty-eight cents per pound. When these tourists examined the wrappers of the butter closely, presumably after having smuggled it into the United States, it is alleged that they were considerably surprised to discover on them the legend "Lend-lease, Waverley, N.Y." The implication of the story was that butter was being shipped to Canada under lend-lease and being sold in a free and easy fashion at a price appreciably below that current in the black market. Apparently, the article was syndicated and released to the rural press in the United States, for it reappeared on numerous occasions during the next few months. Despite its incredibility, the Office of Price Administration and the Foreign Economic Administration had to deny the story repeatedly, an indication that it was apparently widely believed.[16] The comments on butter were relatively innocuous compared to the flood of invidious comparisons which arose as a result of meat rationing or the absence of it. The introduction of meat rationing in the two countries was preceded by the close consultation of rationing officials in the two countries. In the United States, meat rationing was introduced on March 20, 1943.[17] This was followed by an announcement by the Minister of Finance at the end of March, that meat rationing would also be introduced in Canada.[18] It was actually introduced on May 27, 1943.[19] By around the end of February, 1944, the decision was reached in Canada that the retention of meat rationing was no longer justifiable and it was decided to suspend meat rationing, effective March 1, for an indefinite period. The Canadian action caused rationing officials in the United States a good deal of concern since it was anticipated that this unilateral relaxation would stimulate dissatisfaction with the rationing policies of the Office of Price Administration and with the foreign aid programme of the Administration, in general. In order to minimize public criticism, the Office of Price Administration announced simultaneously a substantial liberalization of meat rationing which diverted public attention from the Canadian action. The respite was temporary, however, and a spate of criticism developed over the ensuing year. Sometimes Canada was cited as a shining example to administrators in the United States. The following comments of a member of Congress may serve as an illustration:

Mr. Speaker, I have here an advertisement which says, "Buy All You Want. Rationing Suspended. No Coupons. Buy Your Favourite Roasts, Steaks, Cuts, Prime Commercial Beef, Sirloin Steaks, 39 Cents a Pound. Round Steak, 35 Cents a Pound. Short Rib Roast, 29 Cents a Pound." In addition, there is listed almost every kind of meat. No points are necessary. No black market prevails.

Do not become jubilant about this, however, because it does not come from a paper in the United States. It is from a Canadian paper. I rise to ask the question; If Canada, under efficient management, can do this with meat and shoes, and can give their motorists a better break in gasoline allowances than we get in the United States, and when we further consider that much of these products come from the United States; when are we going to see an end to administrative muscle-dancing on rationing in the United States, and some common sense put into the program?[20]

There were a number of reasons for the temporary suspension of meat rationing in Canada in the spring of 1944. In the first place, the increase in livestock production in Canada had been so great since the outbreak of the war, that after export commitments to the United Kingdom had been met, there was still sufficient meat available in Canada to satisfy the unrestricted demands of consumers. There were, moreover, difficulties in the way of expanding Canadian exports as a result of shortages of labour, packing house facilities, and transportation, especially ocean shipping. Because of the heavy rate of slaughterings, there was continual congestion in Canadian stockyards and considerable agitation for the lifting of the embargo on the shipment of live cattle to the United States. This proposal was supported by unofficial views expressed in the United States that it would be a generous gesture if Canada were to ship some excess meat to the United States. The Minister of Agriculture took note of this situation and stated that he had discussed the possibility with the United States authorities. According to his statement, these officials were opposed to the suggestion that Canadian cattle be exported because of difficulties being experienced in handling the volume of slaughtering in processing plants in the United States.[21] In addition, it was felt that it would not be politically advisable to import meat or cattle from Canada to be paid for in cash while, at the same time, the United Kingdom was receiving meat under lend-lease from the United States. Once the notion that the United States was, in effect, lend-leasing Canadian meat gained currency, it would probably be a difficult one to explain convincingly, to judge from some of the other misconceptions which evidently were common. In the *Nineteenth Report to Congress on Lend-Lease Operations,* a chapter devoted to "Lend-Lease fact and fiction" contains the following comment:

4. Fiction
Britain is not getting any meat from Canada because she can get it from the United States under lend-lease.

Fact
During 1944 Canada shipped to Britain approximately one-third of her total production of meat, including 700,000,000 pounds of bacon and the beef from 325,000 head of cattle. These shipments were made largely without payment by Britain under Canadian mutual aid, which is similar to our lend-lease program.[22]

Despite the possibility of misunderstanding, a fairly large shipment of Canadian lambs to the United States was permitted at one time in 1944. This action led to bitter complaints by producers in the United States who claimed that the influx of Canadian supplies had added to the already serious congestion in packing houses.

In contrast to the United States, where the maintenance of meat rationing was dictated largely by maldistribution of supplies, distribution difficulties in Canada were not sufficiently important to justify the retention of rationing throughout 1944. Any local shortages which arose in Canada after the suspension of meat rationing were unimportant and temporary. The contrast between the situation in Canada and the United States is mainly a result of geographical differences. In Canada, with a few exceptions, local supplies of meat are available for the large cities, while in the United States, the heavy concentrations of population on the East and West Coasts are far distant from the producing areas. Moreover, in the United States the population in and near the producing areas is sufficiently great to absorb a disparate proportion of the meat supply. Thus, the more even distribution in Canada was largely a result of physical and transportation consideration and not of any superiority in Canadian control measures.

Despite all the critical comparisons, Canadian per capita consumption of meat in 1944 was only 157.7 pounds compared to 155.4 pounds in the United States. There was, therefore, little justification for the view that the Canadian level of consumption was appreciably higher than in the United States. It was also worthy of note that military consumption of meat by the United States was in excess of 500 pounds per soldier per annum, a level much higher than in the armies of Canada or the United Kingdom. By the spring of 1945, the Canadian supply situation had altered and it was necessary to reimpose meat rationing effective September 10, 1945. Shortly after VJ-Day, meat rationing was abolished in the United States, although it was continued in Canada until early in 1947.

The major rationing technique in the United States involved the allocation of a fixed number of points to consumers and the corresponding establishment of point values for rationed goods. The point-price of rationed commodities was varied in accordance with changing demand and supply conditions. The essence of this scheme was that the individual was allowed a good deal of freedom in choosing rationed commodities. In Canada, on the other hand, the point system was never adopted but instead the value of a coupon was fixed in terms of a rationed commodity or commodity group. This meant that precise comparisons of the levels of consumption of most rationed commodities were impossible. There were some advantages in this, particularly since it eliminated the pressure for conformity which would have otherwise been present, and enabled the rationing authorities in the two countries to meet their special problems in the way that seemed to be most suitable.

One aspect of food rationing caused a good deal of difficulty and irritation to the rationing officials in Canada and the United States. This was the question of keeping officials in the other country advised of any major changes in rationing plans. The problem arose with special acuteness when the rationing of some commodity was being introduced for the first time. It was apt to be embarrassing, and this was borne out in practice several times, when rationing was inaugurated in one country without the knowledge of officials in the other. Continuous efforts were made to maintain contact between the operating officials of both countries and to exchange information on current rationing plans. The Combined Food Board took note of the problem and, at one time, passed a formal resolution that the officers of the Board should be notified in advance of any prospective changes. Unfortunately, and this is particularly true in the United States, rationing was politically important and sometimes decisions were made at the highest political levels. This meant that rationing officials were sometimes incompletely informed until after a decision had been made and announced. Once the rationing programme of the two countries had become stabilized, the importance of this problem tended to diminish. Moreover, the improved channels of communication between the Wartime Prices and Trade Board and the Office of Price Administration lessened the possibility of surprise actions by either country.

4. Official Studies of Consumption Levels

At the time of the formation of the Combined Food Board, it had been agreed that the food supplies of the United Kingdom and the United States would be treated as a common pool. This implied that there would be some effort to even out the disparities in the diets of the two countries which would involve, among other things, large lend-lease shipments of food from the United States to the United Kingdom. The growing shortage of food in the United States naturally stimulated comparisons of nutrition levels in the two countries. A good deal of misinformation on the subject was available and there was some difference of official opinion on food consumption levels in the United Kingdom. The Combined Food Board saw the necessity for a comprehensive and unbiased study of food consumption. In May, 1943, the Board recommended that a committee of experts be appointed "for the purpose of providing a working basis for the guidance of the Combined Food Board and of the appropriate Governmental agencies of the two Governments in the allocation of foods in short supply." The terms of reference also outlined the duties of the committee of experts, which were:

to consider and compare the pre-war and present and prospective food consumption of the civilian populations of the United States and the United Kingdom;
to formulate an agreed basis for the measurement, and appraisal of the relative effects of changes in the consumption of particular foods in the two countries;
to give due regard to differences, both permanent and temporary, in the habits and conditions of life and feeding of the populations concerned, and other relative circumstances.[23]

An invitation extended to Canada to participate in the work of the committee was accepted, although Canada was not at the time a full member of the Combined Food Board.

An interim report on food consumption levels was submitted in the summer of 1943 and a more detailed report was completed in November. The main purpose of the report was to compare food consumption in 1943 with pre-war levels, 1934-38 in the United Kingdom and 1935-39 in the United States and Canada. The general conclusion of the report was that with minor exceptions sufficient food supplies were available in all three countries to meet requirements. In the United States and Canada consumption of most food groups had increased or remained substantially unchanged while there had been many decreases in the United Kingdom. It was also pointed out that there had been a marked increase in the monotony of the United Kingdom diet and a sharp drop in the availability of foods suitable for main courses. The only significant lack in the Canadian diet appeared to be ascorbic acid.

The original study was supplemented by an analysis of food consumption in 1944. The main conclusions of the 1944 report were:

The 1944 level of civilian consumption in the United States and Canada is much higher than that of the United Kingdom in respect to dairy products (except cheese), meat, eggs, sugars, and fruit. In contrast, to compensate for the shortage of other foods, the consumption of potatoes and flour has increased appreciably in the United Kingdom during the war period, and considerably greater quantities of these foods are now eaten in Britain than in either the United States or Canada. Despite some improvement in 1944, therefore, the range of foods which can be bought in the United Kingdom is still much more restricted than in the other two countries, and the diet continues to suffer from a lack of palatability compared to the pre-war diet.[24]

These studies provided a factual background against which rational decisions concerning the international allocation of food could be made. Admittedly, the statistical data on which the reports were based were sometimes inadequate but they were preferable to the kind of confused comparisons which had threatened to engender serious misunderstanding of the relative well-being of civilians in the United Kingdom and in the United States and Canada.

Despite the estimation difficulties involved in dealing with a relatively simple group of commodities such as food, there were other fields where comparisons were even more elusive. It was sometimes tempting to make comparisons of the relative contributions of Canada and the United States in the form of mutual aid or lend-lease. Any such comparisons must be based on some measure of the burden of international aid, a concept which involves a number of serious difficulties. A comparison of net outlays relative to population or national income was not very useful since international aid constituted a relatively small fraction of the burden of the war. Other aspects of the burden of the war would have to be taken into account and international comparisons of this sort were beset with difficulties, not the least of which was the inadequacy of statistical information on national wealth.

The analysis of food consumption levels was supplemented by broader studies of consumption levels also prepared under the auspices of the Combined Boards. Towards the end of 1942, elaborate studies of the civilian sectors of the economies of the United Kingdom, the United States, and Canada were undertaken at the request of the Combined Production and Resources Board. There were substantial differences in the method of presentation for each country as a result of the fact that the reports were compiled at different times by groups working independently. The attempt to prepare a single collated report was a failure. This was partly because the report was inadequate on technical grounds. The draft report also showed that consumption levels in the United States were very much higher than in the United Kingdom, and primarily on these grounds, it was decided to suppress it. Most of the Canadian study was carried out by the Wartime Prices and Trade Board which submitted a massive "Report on the Non-military Sector of the Canadian Economy." The abortive end of the project was quite disappointing to those who had been responsible for the preparation of the Canadian report. Despite the unsatisfactory results of this initial effort, the Combined Production and Resources Board later expressed the wish to have the comparative analysis of the civilian economies of the three countries kept up to date.

Late in 1943, the Executive Director of the Combined Production and Resources Board appointed a working group composed of representatives of the United States, United Kingdom, and Canada, to plan a study of levels of civilian consumption in the three countries. The Canadian representative offered a number of objections to the proposed study mainly on the grounds that the need for it had been inadequately shown. The British, who were the prime sponsors of the project, pointed out that it would serve as a guide to demobilization and production planning in the future. Since the Combined Production and Resources Board would have to make decisions concerning the resumption of civilian production and the distribution of military cut-backs, it was believed that such a detailed statistical analysis was essential. Closely allied to this, the study was intended to be useful as a quasi-political document which would throw some light on the distribution of the burden of the war among the member countries.

Although continued Canadian co-operation remained in doubt, the working group reached substantial agreement on the methods to be followed in January, 1944, but no further action was taken until the United Kingdom submitted a revised proposal to the Executive Committee of the Combined Production and Resources Board. The members of the original working group were asked to meet to reconsider this proposal and submit recommendations concerning it. This group recommended that a formal committee be appointed to undertake a combined study of consumption levels with the following terms of reference:

To assemble on a comparable basis, data showing changes since pre-war in non-food consumption levels and civilian economic developments in the United States, United Kingdom, Canada and to make periodic reports to the Board on this subject.

It was noted by the United Kingdom representative that the Lord President's Committee of the War Cabinet in the United Kingdom had recently set up a committee of statistical experts to collect and analyse material on non-food consumption in the United Kingdom. This Committee would be able to co-operate in a combined study of non-food consumption levels with corresponding experts in Canada and the United States. The approach suggested by the United Kingdom was that the study should consist of two main parts. The first part would be an analysis of the changes in consumption levels since before the war in the three countries separately. A limited number of main categories of consumption would be defined and, for each category, total and per capita consumption would be shown for the years 1938 to 1943. These data would be supported, as far as possible, by quantitative figures of actual consumption of important individual items within each category of consumption; for example, purchases of footwear would be shown in numbers of pairs within the main category of clothing. The second part would be devoted to a comparison of the level of civilian consumption of particular items in the three countries in 1943, the items being carefully selected to ensure complete comparability between the three countries.

In the meantime, the Canadian authorities in Ottawa who would be responsible for the major portion of the statistical and analytical work continued to express their opposition to Canadian participation. While recognizing the statistical difficulties of the project the Canadian representatives attached to the Combined Production and Resources Board pressed for Canadian co-operation. They emphasized the importance of providing the Combined Production and Resources Board and other persons concerned with a factual analysis of the burden of the war on the civilian populations in the member countries. It was a foregone conclusion that levels of civilian consumption in the United Kingdom would be substantially below those in either the United States or Canada. However, a clear and careful demonstration of this fact was essential if the problems anticipated in the reconversion period following the defeat of Germany were to be solved in an orderly manner. In particular, the question was closely related to the future of lend-lease, the lend-lease settlement, and the distribution of war production between the United Kingdom and North America in the period between the defeat of Germany and Japan. If the Combined Production and Resources Board was to exercise any intelligent influence in the latter field, a clear and unassailable picture of the civilian economies in the member countries would be necessary.

Apart from these policy considerations, there was no doubt that the United Kingdom was anxious to undertake a comparative analysis of consumption levels to counteract the misinformation which had circulated in the United States concerning the effect of the war on the British people. While this was recognized primarily as a problem between the United States and the United Kingdom, the natural tendency of the Canadians would be to support the position of the United Kingdom.

Even if Canada refused to participate, both the United Kingdom and the United States would proceed with the projected study. Under these circumstances, Canada, as a full member, would be in a somewhat curious position. The upshot of the discussions was that Canada agreed to participate on the condition that the research and statistical labour would be restricted as much as possible.

Finally, after an extended series of meetings in London, Washington, and Ottawa, the Special Committee assigned by the Combined Production and Resources Board to conduct the study completed a detailed report which was approved by the Board and published in September, 1945, under the title, *The Impact of the War on Civilian Consumption in the United Kingdom, the United States and Canada.* Some of the main conclusions of this report, which are listed below, throw interesting light on the relations of the three countries:

(1) In the United Kingdom aggregate per capita purchases of consumer goods and services valued at prewar prices decreased between 15 and 20 percent from 1938 to 1941, and during the following 3 years remained slightly below the 1941 level.

(2) In Canada and the United States aggregate per capita consumer purchases measured on an approximately comparable basis were, in 1943 and 1944, 10 to 15 percent higher than in 1939. Such purchases were at about the same level in 1943 and 1944 as in 1941. In respect to the level of employment, 1941 for Canada and the United States is a base year more closely comparable to 1938 in the United Kingdom than is 1939 for these two countries.

(3) In 1938 and 1939 the physical volume per capita of consumer purchases was probably between 10 and 20 percent lower in the United Kingdom than it was in the United States; with the wartime rise in the United States and fall in the United Kingdom the difference between levels in the two countries materially widened.

(4) The war's impact on consumption in the United States and Canada came later and its effects on consumption were both more gradual and less severe than was the case in the United Kingdom. The war effort absorbed a major fraction of national resources first in the United Kingdom, nearly a year later in Canada, and a year and a half later in the United States. The differences in the war's repercussions on consumption were due in part also to the fact that Canada and the United States were geographically more remote from the war.

(5) In 1943 and 1944 war product represented something like half the value of total gross national product both for the United Kingdom and for Canada and between 40 and 45 percent in the United States.

(6) The war products of the three countries were to some extent complementary. Thus the United States was able to contribute munitions somewhat more than in proportion to the size of its population; the United Kingdom had a considerably higher proportion of its manpower in the armed forces than either of the other countries and was enabled to do so partly because of contributions of food, raw materials, and munitions from Canada and the United States.

(7) In all three countries additions to the stock of nonwar buildings and capital equipment ceased, many capital goods were not replaced as they wore out, and business inventories of civilian goods were run down. When peacetime uses of war surplus property (munitions plants, army trucks, merchant ships, etc.) are taken into account, however, only in the case of the United Kingdom was there a net reduction in national wealth, i.e., in productive capacity and command over foreign resources, and there the reduction was a material one.

(8) Per capita consumer purchases were able to increase in Canada and the United States while the level of consumption was decreased appreciably in the United Kingdom for three main reasons:

(a) Total national product could not be expanded as much in the United Kingdom as in the other two countries. In spite of the fact that, as in the United States, many housewives, youths, and older persons were drawn into the labor force after 1942, the total supply of labor imposed an over-all limit on United Kingdom production. Restrictions on the use of labor for nonwar output were developed to an extent not attempted in the United States and Canada even in 1944.

(b) The United Kingdom was very dependent on imports of food and basic materials. The shortage of shipping limited the amounts of such imports.

(c) Because the war's impact on civilian production came earlier and so was longer continued in the United Kingdom, business inventories of consumer goods were earlier depleted there; in Canada and the United States they were still helping to keep consumer purchases above production in 1944.

(9) The experience of the United Kingdom was markedly less favorable than that of the United States and Canada in almost every category of consumption.[25]

The short interval between the defeat of Germany and the defeat of Japan meant that the usefulness of the report on consumption levels in planning the gradual reconversion of military production on a combined basis was limited. Nevertheless, it seems probable that the report was of some value in the negotiations between the United States and the United Kingdom immediately after the war on the financial settlement of lend-lease and related matters.

REFERENCES FOR CHAPTER XIV

1. Office of Production Management, Limitation Order L-5, September 30, 1941, 6 *Federal Register* 5008.
2. Department of Munitions and Supply, Controller of Supplies Order No. C.S. 8, October 1, 1941.
3. *Chicago Daily Tribune,* October 1, 1941, p. 1.
4. Joint Economic Committees, Press Release, October 11, 1941.
5. Conservation Order M-126, May 5, 1942, 7 *Federal Register* 3364.
6. Wartime Prices and Trade Board, Administrator's Order, A-224, June 13, 1942.
7. Office of Price Administration, Ration Order No. 17, February 7, 1943, 8 *Federal Register* 1749.
8. Report of a Special Combined Committee set up by the Combined Production and Resources Board, *The Impact of the War on Civilian Consumption in the United Kingdom, the United States and Canada* (Washington: U.S. Government Printing Office, 1945), pp. 96-9.
9. Office of Price Administration, Ration Order 17, Amendment 47, December 8, 1943, 8 *Federal Register* 16605. This amendment applied only to imports not intended for resale and permitted the ration-free entry of two pairs of shoes only.
10. Office of Price Administration, Ration Order 17, Amendment 106, July 31, 1945, 10 *Federal Register* 9539.
11. Wartime Prices and Trade Board Order No. 93, Respecting sugar rationing, January 24, 1942.
12. Office of Price Administration, Rationing Order No. 3, April 21, 1942, 7 *Federal Register* 2966, 3242.
13. Wartime Prices and Trade Board Order No. 136, Respecting domestic sugar rationing, May 19, 1942.
14. Wartime Prices and Trade Board Order No. 150, Respecting sugar rationing, June 16, 1942.
15. *Canada, House of Commons Debates,* April 28, 1944, p. 2429.
16. *Nineteenth Report to Congress on Lend-Lease Operations for the Period Ended March 31, 1945* (Washington: U.S. Government Printing Office, 1945), p. 45. It is noted here that all lend-lease butter exports by the United States had been shipped to the Union of Soviet Socialist Republics.
17. Office of Price Administration, Rationing Order No. 16, March 20, 1943, 8 *Federal Register* 3591.
18. *Canada, House of Commons Debates,* March 31, 1943, pp. 1715-17.
19. Wartime Prices and Trade Board Order No. 276, Respecting the rationing of meat, May 17, 1943.
20. *Congressional Record,* March 28, 1944, p. 3197.
21. *Canada, House of Commons Debates,* December 5, 1944, p. 6971.
22. *Nineteenth Report to Congress on Lend-Lease Operations for the Period Ended March 31, 1945,* p. 42.
23. Report of a Special Joint Committee set up by the Combined Food Board, *Food Consumption Levels in Canada, the United Kingdom and the United States* (Ottawa: King's Printer, 1944), p. 7.
24. Second Report of a Special Joint Committee set up by the Combined Food Board, *Food Consumption Levels in the United States, Canada and the United Kingdom* (Washington: U.S. Government Printing Office, 1944), p. 2.
25. Report of a Special Combined Committee set up by the Combined Production and Resources Board, *The Impact of the War on Civilian Consumption in the United Kingdom, the United States and Canada,* pp. 1-2.

CHAPTER XV

CONCLUSION

IN AUGUST, 1940, Mr. Winston Churchill, in referring to the willingness of His Majesty's Government to lease certain Atlantic bases to the United States, noted that "these two great organizations of the English-speaking democracies, the British Empire and the United States will have to be somewhat mixed up together in some of their affairs for mutual and general advantage."[1] Subsequent events were to confirm Mr. Churchill's perceptive forecast, particularly so far as the United States and Canada were concerned.

Even in peacetime, there is an enormous amount of business to be transacted by representatives of the governments of the two countries. The laws of one country sometimes affect the nationals of the other and the existence of a common frontier engenders administrative and jurisdictional issues. These matters and others of a similar sort normally constitute the bulk of the diplomatic business conducted by Canada and the United States. Many of the matters dealt with through such channels bear directly or indirectly on economic relations between the two countries, but they have been regarded as outside the scope of this book. One practical reason for the omission is that detailed records of ordinary inter-governmental negotiations are not usually published.

Instead, attention has been concentrated on the special economic problems which developed during the war and which were often dealt with outside ordinary diplomatic channels. One of the early problems of economic adjustment arose in the latter half of 1940 and early 1941, when the predominant aim of both Canada and the United States was to bolster the position of the United Kingdom. To supply the needs of the United Kingdom, Canadian capacity for the production of munitions had to be increased rapidly, a fact which intensified Canada's dependence on the United States for capital equipment and other essential imports. In view of the weakened external financial position of the United Kingdom, Canada was no longer able to offset the resultant adverse balance of payments with the United States in the traditional way. Thus, Canada's reserves of gold and United States dollars were becoming seriously depleted by early 1941 and threatened to impair Canada's ability to continue making cash purchases in the United States. The device of lend-lease was developed in the United States to circumvent this difficulty, but this particular solution was not applied to Canada for several important reasons. For one thing, it was the Canadian view that lend-lease was intended essentially for beleaguered countries and that, under the circumstances, Canada was under some sort of obligation not to accept such aid. Morever, the acceptance of lend-lease aid would scarcely be consonant with Canada's traditional desire to avoid any sense of dependence on the United States. To cite these reasons is not to suggest that the advantages and disadvantages of lend-lease aid were deliberated at length by the Canadian authorities. It appears rather that serious consideration was not given to the possibility of obtaining lend-lease aid.

An alternative, and obviously rational, solution of Canada's dollar shortage was to effect a geographic redistribution of war production in North America in such a way as to permit Canada to concentrate on the production of munitions and other goods which could be produced relatively more efficiently in Canada. This would presumably lead to an increase in Canadian exports to the United States and would thus alleviate the Canadian dollar shortage.

It was agreed in the Hyde Park Declaration that steps should be taken to provide for the more effective use of North American resources by co-ordinating the war production plans of the two countries. It was also agreed that governmental purchases by the United States in Canada would be increased to stimulate this adjustment. This policy of economic co-ordination was both bold and imaginative and visualized the dissolution of barriers and rigidities which had been developing for many years.

A number of special difficulties were encountered in achieving the specific aims of the Hyde Park Declaration immediately. By late 1941, it was clear that the goal of economic co-ordination or integration was still to be attained. Purchases by the United States in Canada were hindered by tariffs, by special legislative restrictions on foreign procurement, and by the initial reluctance of the armed services to place orders in Canada. Administrative barriers were also hampering Canadian buying in the United States. Some industries in Canada were unable to achieve comparable treatment in the priorities system in the United States and supplementary export controls over some commodities imposed additional obstacles. There had, moreover, been little check on the tendency of each country to produce all kinds of munitions without much regard to the advantages of international specialization.

After Pearl Harbor, the military needs of the United States suddenly became so urgent that most of the administrative barriers to procurement by the United States in Canada were quickly eliminated. Provision was also made for the more complete participation of Canada in the priorities system of the United States. Considerable success was thus achieved in removing a number of the special restrictions on purchases by the United States in Canada. Munitions could be imported duty-free and without regard to the special restrictions limiting government procurement to domestically produced goods. Except in minor instances, these restrictions were lifted for all other countries as well as Canada.

The policy enunciated in the Hyde Park Declaration was clear enough and did not necessitate the creation of any complex administrative machinery to implement it although a Crown company, War Supplies Limited, was set up to facilitate purchases by the United States in Canada. However, partly as a result of the intensified demands for raw materials stemming from lend-lease requirements, and partly because of the multiplication of common economic problems arising from increased war production, two international agencies, the Materials Co-ordinating Committee and the Joint Economic Committees were formed in May and June of 1941. Later in the year, in order to reaffirm the object of economic co-ordination enunciated in the Hyde Park Declaration, the Joint Economic Committees sponsored the formation of the Joint War Production Committee which, with its technical sub-committees, was to deal with the detailed aspects of co-ordinating war production in the two countries. The activities of these Committees pointed up some of the administrative problems involved in the establishment of machinery to deal with wartime economic problems.

It was apparently believed in 1941 that special wartime economic problems could not be handled adequately through the traditional channels of communication of the Department of External Affairs and the Department of State. One of the main reasons for this was the shortage of people equipped to deal with the technical problems which were of dominant importance. Instead, two types of international committees were created in the early stages. The first type was composed of co-ordinate operating officials, the members of which were separately responsible for domestic controls or production and jointly for the co-ordination of operations in the two countries. The Materials Co-ordinating Committee and the sub-committees of the Joint War Production Committee are examples of committees whose members were the ranking officials in each country responsible for the domestic aspects of most of the problems dealt with by the committees. On the other hand, there were interagency and inter-departmental joint committees, such as the Joint Economic Committees and the Joint War Production Committee, with broad terms of reference, whose members were senior administrative officials not necessarily with any specific responsibility for items on the agenda of the committees. In the latter case, the decisions of the committees were embodied in policy recommendations to the two governments, but detailed ways of implementing the proposals were not usually dealt with. This contrasts with the former type of committee where the decisions of the operating officials concerned could usually be translated into action without formal government approval. A committee which could make decisions and act on them was a more functional administrative body under the circumstances than a committee, no matter how senior, which was restricted to broad policy questions. For example, a formal recommendation that the two countries should pursue "a more coordinate export control policy" was not likely to provide useful guidance to the administrators concerned unless this provided a basis for action in particular cases. It was more useful when a committee could decide whether 1,000 tons of copper scrap should be shipped to some third country destination.

Outside the more or less formal committee structure, there was a great deal of communication between individual administrative officials. Officials of the war agencies of the two countries continually visited Washington and Ottawa or met on neutral ground in Montreal or New York. These personal contacts were very conducive to mutual understanding and improved co-ordination. Inter-governmental policy agreements are not apt to be very effective unless the administrators responsible for putting them into effect are themselves convinced of the desirability of the policy and are willing to exert themselves to achieve the desired ends. The establishment of special Canadian missions in Washington and of an office of the War Production Board in Ottawa was invaluable in improving the liaison between the two countries and in providing focal points for the discussion of day-to-day operating problems as well as issues involved in the inter-relations of controls in the two countries.

Joint planning through formal committees may well become ineffectual unless some technique for implementing joint agreements is available. Conversely, agreements between individuals may be easy to implement, but may involve the assumption of unwarranted authority by one or both parties to the agreement. For example, an agreement which will affect the amounts of a commodity available for consumption in a country may involve policy considerations on which a general or specific ruling by the government is desirable. From this point of view, the evolution of combined planning as a technique of inter-governmental negotiation was a forward step in both theory and practice. The essence of combined planning was that the decision of the Combined Boards reflected the commitments of the responsible authorities in the member countries. Agreements reached through the Combined Boards were something more than recommendations to the member governments; they formally recorded the fact that the governments had agreed to pursue a certain course of action. While technically, combined planning was based on ministerial decisions, the delegations of authority to the ministerial representatives on the Combined Boards were broad, a fact which permitted decisions to be reached quickly. Perhaps the outstanding feature of the Combined Boards from the Canadian point of view was the informal and friendly relations between the senior representatives of the three countries. Tacit standards of reasonableness were established which were of great benefit in resolving issues as they arose. Without a spirit of mutual trust, it becomes necessary to rely on documentary agreements and the letter and not the spirit of understandings. A great deal has been said and written about the warm personal relationships which existed between officials of Canada and the United States during the war. The value of the Combined Production and Resources Board as a medium of co-operation was greatly increased by the spirit of friendliness and understanding which existed among the people who worked together.

Nevertheless, it is easy to place too much reliance on informal understandings and on the ability of officials to resolve their problems by discussion. It must be recalled that the policy of co-operation which guided relations between Canada and the United States during the war developed in a very favourable milieu. The general level of consumption was going up in both countries. Canada's needs from the United States were usually relatively small and did not materially influence levels of consumption in the United States. The fact that Canada was treated generously is at least partly attributable to this. Suppose, on the other hand, that the military course of the war had been different and that it had become necessary to restrict civilian consumption to austerity levels. It is not too difficult to imagine circumstances under which North American consumption might have had to be reduced to levels similar to those reached in the United Kingdom. If this had occurred, there is no question that the relations between Canada and the United States would have been different. For one thing, the policy of the United States with respect to exports to Canada would undoubtedly have been modified. As it was, there was never any very serious controversy over exports to Canada, but, under less favourable conditions, it is probable that public pressures would have forced a much more rigorous scrutiny of the free-hand extension of the principles of economic co-operation laid down in the Hyde Park Declaration. Most of the administrative agreements, such as that concerning Canadian participation in the United States priorities system, were based on a careful consideration of what could easily be defended in public. However, public opinion and the attitude of Congress are liable to be revised in the face of a changing domestic or international situation. Therefore, it seems unwise to depend too heavily on the assessment of public and Congressional opinion by officials who may not be particularly skilled in such matters. Fortunately, during the war, most people in the United States were usually either favourably disposed to or indifferent to the programme of economic co-operation with Canada. Reliance on agreements with the wartime agencies was subject to another disability arising out of the unstable character of many of the wartime agencies. Powers and responsibilities were shifted freely from one agency to another, personnel changed, and new agencies were created. From the Canadian point of view, it was fortunate that the War Production Board changed as little as it did. There was no guarantee that the policy agreements reached with the War Production Board would be automatically accepted by a successor agency.

Under these circumstances, it might have been desirable to record agreements on policy in a somewhat more formal manner through the diplomatic machinery of the Department of External Affairs and the Department of State. This does not imply that negotiations between operating agencies should be conducted through diplomatic channels, merely that agreements whose importance seems to warrant it be later confirmed in precise language. The Hyde Park Declaration, which embodied a diplomatic agreement, was clearly more useful than if it had been an inter-agency or inter-departmental agreement. Similarly, the reaffirmation of the principles of the Hyde Park Declaration contained in the exchange of notes of May, 1945, was valuable in the reconversion period. Apart from the other matters dealt with, this exchange of notes laid down the conditions under which priority assistance would be given to Canadian civilian production programmes and stated explicitly that new priority regulations would be applicable to Canada. This minimized the possibility of a sudden or erratic change in United States policy towards Canada during the transition period. It might well have been desirable to have confirmed many other operating agreements in this way.

These considerations raise the general question of the relation between the Canadian Legation or Embassy and the non-diplomatic Canadian missions in Washington during the war. The non-diplomatic missions were continually conducting negotiations of a quasi-diplomatic character, and there was always some risk that some informal agreement would be reached which would be in conflict with established Canadian policy, although it was more often the case that the agreement in fact established Canadian policy. It was sometimes suggested, as an alternative, that all negotiations with United States agencies should be handled through diplomatic channels. This was a quite impracticable suggestion, since from the Canadian side at least, the Department of External Affairs had neither the staff nor the facilities to deal with the enormous number of detailed technical questions involved in negotiations with war agencies in the United States. Nevertheless, a greater measure of co-ordination of Canadian activities in the United States might have been attained by attaching non-diplomatic missions to the Canadian Legation or Embassy. This would not necessarily involve any loss of independence by operating missions in conducting their day-to-day operations. However, if general policy questions were to be cleared through the Embassy, there would be greater opportunity for the establishment of consistent policies which could, if necessary, be confirmed with the Department of State.

One virtue of dealing through diplomatic channels is that more attention is apt to be paid to the delicate questions of sovereignty and autonomy. This was particularly important in the case of Canada and the United States during the war, when there was some risk that Canadian independence of action might be jeopardized because of commitments to the United States. In fact, any tendency to subservience was fiercely resisted by Canadian officials. Sometimes, of course, the dividing line between subservience and co-operation was thin and it must be admitted that there were groups in Ottawa who were suspicious of the blandishments of Washington.

Canada did not, of course, expect to receive concessions from the United States as a matter of right. The Canadian attitude was that the policy of economic co-operation was a good thing because it promoted a common endeavour. Parity of treatment so far as war production is concerned was sought after, not because Canada, as a sovereign nation, had a vested right to insist on it, but because this was a way of furthering the war effort. Canadian officials were both willing and able to show that the policy of co-operation as applied in specific instances would lead to greater war output. They were willing to rely on this criterion completely. The comparable treatment of civilians in the two countries was another goal which was justifiable on less specific grounds. It was an eminently sensible goal not only because it lessened the discontent stimulated by invidious international comparisons but because it probably led to a more efficient use of resources in general.

The goal of economic integration enunciated in several policy declarations was an elusive one. There were obvious gains to be achieved by a policy of economic co-operation, but there were a number of limitations on the extent to which the policy could be applied. The impression which is sometimes given that trade barriers between the two countries were practically eliminated during the war does not appear to be supported by the evidence available. For example, there seems to be an element of exaggeration in the following quotation from an official United States government publication:

> The implementation of the Hyde Park agreement during the war resulted in an unprecedented co-ordination of the economies of the United States and Canada—in the pooling of supplies, in the development of complementary industrial plants and agricultural programs, and in the almost complete erasure of national boundaries for certain purposes. This extraordinary cooperative effort in the economic field contributed materially to the successful conclusion of the war.[2]

It might even be wondered whether the achievement of complete international specialization or integration was practical. This state of affairs implies that all government controls over the international movement of goods have been abandoned and that there is an appropriate international division of labour. The conclusions which have emerged from the foregoing examination of the wartime relations of the two countries might stimulate some doubt on this score, at least as far as private trade is concerned.

In the operation of the priorities system, for example, Canadians were not at a disadvantage compared to residents of the United States. The mere existence of the priorities system, however, meant that there was a substantial barrier to trade which had not existed before the war. From the point of view of one aspect of economic co-operation, i.e., freedom of trade accompanied by international specialization, it is doubtful if the degree of co-operation achieved during the war represented any significant advance over the pre-war period. The large volume of business conducted by government agencies was, however, usually free from restrictive regulations of a traditional type. It was the new brand of restrictions, typified by priority and allocation controls and export controls, that constituted the really formidable trade barriers. The imposition of such controls led to an enormous increase in inter-governmental consultation, but many of the discussions revolved around the channelling of applications and the principles which would govern the application of the rules of one country to the nationals of the other. The complete abrogation of the restrictions was usually not practical except in a few instances. In some cases, it was possible to eliminate or substantially reduce the special wartime restrictions which were imposed. This itself was a remarkable achievement in view of the strong autarchic tendencies which naturally developed during the war.

One complex problem which arose continually during the wartime period centered around the control over Canadian exports to the United States. The problem stemmed mainly from the disparity in the price levels of the two countries which in turn reflected a major difference in the administrative controls in the two countries during the war. In Canada, executive powers under the War Measures Act were virtually unlimited with the result that the imposition of rigid price control was a relatively simple administrative step. In the United States, on the other hand, it was necessary to appeal to Congress for legislative authority, the authority being given on the condition that some protection be given to special interests. This meant that price stabilization was inherently more difficult in the United States, and that prices tended to be stabilized at higher levels than in Canada. Higher prices in the United States tended to drain off excessive quantities of Canadian goods, to disrupt domestic distribution and to make it difficult to fill high priority needs of other export markets such as the United Kingdom. It therefore became generally necessary to introduce government controls over exports to the United States. In some cases, these controls amounted to embargoes and their existence led to a good deal of misunderstanding between the two countries. Although there was superficially some conflict between the retention of these controls and the goal of integration, it was evident that this depended on the administration of the controls. Canadian policy was to provide for equitable sharing of supplies although instances arose, notably in forest products, where there was some doubt that this was achieved.

There was a great deal of negotiation between the United States and Canada concerning exports to third countries. Early in the war, Canada's external trade policy was influenced by the necessity of counterbalancing the consistently adverse balance of payments with the United States. Later, after the need for United States dollars had abated, Canada sought to maintain customary markets in Latin America. This necessitated detailed, if uneasy, arrangements with the United States concerning the sharing of Latin American markets and the provision of shipping space for imports and exports. Canadian insistence on the maintenance of export outlets was a clear recognition of the almost inevitable trade problems which could be forecast for the post-war world.

The protection of Canada's reserves of United States dollars was an important aim of the agreements on economic co-operation which were reached by the two countries in 1941. The lifting of trade barriers, the elimination of restrictions on procurement, and the co-ordination of war production programmes did ultimately contribute to the alleviation of Canada's shortage of United States dollars. At the same time, the various measures undertaken by the United States to alleviate Canada's adverse balance of payments undoubtedly led to a more efficient use of North American resources. This is the most important single aspect of economic co-operation between the two countries during the war. A number of specific examples have been described earlier to show that firmly rooted immobilities and rigidities in several important sectors of the North American economy, notably in agricultural and in forest products, limited the extent to whch integration was possible. Perhaps more important is the fact that people are accustomed to think and plan in national rather than international terms. This does not imply the absence of goodwill or a co-operative attitude but merely that the co-ordination of activities which are primarily of concern to one country with activities in another country is apt to be an afterthought. So far as the United States and Canada are concerned, it was difficult to achieve much more than marginal adjustments, although the importance of these was often substantial. Sometimes, there is a tendency to believe that the economic integration of the United States and Canada during the war progressed further than it actually did. To echo the White Knight: "I don't believe that pudding ever *was* cooked! In fact, I don't believe that pudding ever *will* be cooked! And yet it was a very clever pudding to invent."

REFERENCES FOR CHAPTER XV

1. Hansard, *Parliamentary Debates,* 5th series, vol. 364, August 20, 1940, p. 1171.

2. Richardson Dougall, "Economic Cooperation with Canada, 1941-1947," U.S., Department of State, *Bulletin,* June 22, 1947, p. 1185.

INDEX

Act of Chapultepec, 183
Administrator of Farm Machinery and Equipment, 105
Administrator of Publishing, Printing and Allied Industries, 284
Administrator of Wholesale Trade, 373
Advisory Commission to the Council of National Defense: administrative arrangements, 53; Agricultural Adviser, 320; Agriculture Division, 320; appointment, 51; Commissioners, 53; Consumer Protection Division, 55; distribution of machine tools, 70; first important wartime agency, 51; imports of aluminum from Canada, 141; members, 52; orders for airplanes, 72; Price Stabilization Division, 55; Priorities Board, 72; shortage of woodpulp, 269; *see also* machine tools, priorities
Advisory Committee on Economic Policy, 152, 163, 346
Advisory Committee on Export Control, 152, 154, 185 *n.*
Advisory Committee on Reconstruction, 346
Agricultural Adjustment Act, 324
Agricultural exports: bacon, 318, 319, 324; butter, 324; cheese, 318, 324, 326; dehydrated foods, 318; dominant rôle, 323; eggs, 319, 326; evaporated milk, 318; export contracts, 320; exports of potatoes, 330-1; exports to the United Kingdom, 324; flax, 318; food contracts, 326; Food Requirements Committee (Canada), 335; hogs, 326; meat, 324; milk, 324; Ministry of Food, 318-19; pork products, 330; poultry, 326; wheat, 325-6; Wiltshire sides, 329; *see also* agricultural planning, Combined Food Board, price control, United Kingdom
Agricultural Food Board, 319
Agricultural planning: exports of potatoes, 330-1; feed grains, 337; flaxseed, 336-7; hog weights, 330-1; import and export restrictions, 328; Joint Agricultural Committee of Canada and the United States, 336-7; Joint Economic Committees, 327-32; production of edible oils, 329; trans-border movement of farm machinery and crews, 328; United Nations Relief and Rehabilitation Administration, 343; vegetable oils and feed grains, 327; wheat acreage reduction, 323; *see also* agricultural exports, Combined Food Board, Joint Economic Committees
Agricultural Supplies Board, 151, 318, 344 *n.*

Agricultural Supplies Committee (*see* Agricultural Supplies Board), 318
Alaska, 35, 196
Alaska Highway, 35, 196, 209 *n.*
Albania, 166
Alexander, Ben, 277
Allocations: adding machines, 128; basis of control, 68, 128; calculating machines, 128; cotton textiles, 136-9; dictating equipment, 128; farm machinery, 105; hides, 238; Latin American requirements, 123; Manila hemp, 238; mica, 238; nickel, 238; non-ferrous metals, 238; nylon, 238; office machinery, 128-9; parity of treatment, 146; "parity" principle, 123; procurement quotas, 129; punch card machinery, 128; Requirements Committee, 120, 123; rubber, 238; shellac, 238; silk, 238; sisal, 238; steel plate, 118-19; tin, 238; trade barriers, 395; tungsten, 238; *see also* Combined Raw Materials Board, Controlled Materials Plan, Department of Munitions and Supply, Joint Economic Committees, Office of Production Management, Requirements Committee, Supply Priorities and Allocations Board, War Production Board, Wartime Prices and Trade Board
Aluminum: Aluminum Company of America, 141-2; Aluminum Company of Canada Limited, 142-5, 356-7; Aluminium Limited, 142; Canadian contracts renegotiated, 145; Canadian purchases, 358; change in supply situation, 357; contractual arrangements, 144; Controlled Materials Plan, 135; co-ordinated planning, 141; co-ordination of reconversion, 358; criticism of purchases from Canada, 145; cut-backs, 355-8; expansion of facilities, 118; expansion programme in the United States, 143; exports, 182; Materials Co-ordinating Committee, 25; relaxation of restrictions, 351; requirements of the United States, 204; shortage, 142; *see also* Conservation orders, export control, Materials Co-ordinating Committee, Office of Price Administration, priorities, Priorities and Allocations Board
Amtorg Trading Corporation, 205
Apportionment, 68
ARCADIA Conference, 68
Argentine, 171, 178, 181, 183, 221-2, 325, 341
Army, United States (*see* War Department)

399

situation, 285; system of allocating, 280; thirty-pound newsprint, 198, 295, 300-2; *see also* committees of the Combined Boards, export control, Office of Price Administration, price control, shipping controls, Wartime Prices and Trade Board

Newsprint Administrator, 281, 285-6, 299, 301

Nicaragua, 222

Nigeria, 239

North Africa, 231

North West Purchasing Limited, 209 *n*.

Northern Rhodesia, 249

Norway, 166, 269, 339

Office for Emergency Management, 51

Office of Agricultural Defense Relations, 320

Office of Contract Settlement, 349

Office of Defense Transportation, 220

Office of Economic Stabilization, 58, 62

Office of Economic Warfare, 159

Office of Export Control, 157-8, 199

Office of Foreign Economic Co-ordination of the Department of State, 159

Office of Foreign Relief and Rehabilitation Operations, 159, 256

Office of Government Reports, 51

Office of Lend-Lease Administration, 33, 75, 116, 122, 124, 125, 133, 159, 205, 253, 321

Office of Price Administration: Administrator, 56, 61; Canadian butter, 377; Combined Export Markets Committee, 253; export premiums, 136, 138-9; export prices, 63; food prices, 322; Food Requirements Committee (U.S.), 321; General Maximum Prices Regulation, 62; inadequate authority to control prices, 60; legislative exemption of agricultural products, 62; lumber price ceilings, 308; Maximum Export Price Regulation, 63; maximum prices on pulpwood, 292; newsprint prices, 296-8; obstacles to establishing effective price control in the United States, 62; pressure from farm groups, 61; prices of agricultural products, 61, 321; rationing programme, 380; shoe rationing, 371-3; sugar rationing, 374; *see also* Congress, lumber, newsprint, price controls, rationing, Wartime Prices and Trade Board, woodpulp

Office of Price Administration and Civilian Supply, 55, 56, 57, 116, 270

Office of Procurement and Materials of the United States Navy, 214

Office of Production Management: allocation of steel plate, 118, 119; aluminum capacity, 142; aluminum from Canada, 143; assigned widened priority powers, 56; Associate Director-General, 54, 56; Canadian construction projects, 81;

cargo space applications, 217; Civilian Supply Division, 369; conversion, 369; Council, 24; created, 53; curtailment of paper products, 274; cuts in consumers' goods, 370; Deputy Director of the Production Division, 25; Director-General, 24, 54, 56, 72, 75; Director of Priorities, 24-5, 72-3, 84, 85, 89; Division of Civilian Supply, 57, 58; Division of Priorities, 54; Division of Production, 54; Division of Purchases, 54; export priority ratings, 158; exports of aluminum, 141; import priorities, 214; imports into the United States, 217; imports of essential materials, 213; Interdepartmental Shipping Priorities Advisory Committee, 216; issuance of serial numbers to Canadian mines, 110; Latin American requirements, 175; machine tools, 200; materials control, 67; policy respecting exports of mining machinery, 108; priorities, 68; priority assistance from, 80, 97; priority powers delegated, 54; priority ratings for shipping, 212; priority regulations covering mine machinery, 110; Regulation No. 3, 73; request to machine tool manufacturers, 71; Shipping Liaison Section, 214; Shipping Priorities Advisory Committee, 214; Tools Section, 76, 84; woodpulp, 270; *see also* allocations, aluminum, Army and Navy Munitions Board, civilian requirements, Department of Munitions and Supply, machine tools, Materials Co-ordinating Committee, preference ratings, priorities, shipping controls

Office of the United States Rubber Director, 238

Office of War Mobilization, 349, 352-3

Office of War Mobilization and Reconversion, 58, 349

Ogdensburg Agreement: mutual aid, 37; new phase of relations between Canada and the United States, 15; text, 7; *see also* conferences between Franklin Delano Roosevelt and W. L. M. King, Permanent Joint Board on Defence

Oil Controller, 46

Order Board (Delivery) Control, 68

Ottawa Agreements, 1, 190

Overriding directives, 68

Panama, 222

Paper: Combined Pulp and Paper Committee, 293-4; compulsory reduction of consumption, 280; speculative purchasing, 280; standardization and simplification, 279; supply situation, 285; *see also* newsprint, Office of Production Management, Wartime Prices and Trade Board

Paraguay, 222